American Law
and
Legal Systems

American Law and Legal Systems

Third Edition

James V. Calvi

West Texas A&M University
A Member of the Texas A&M University System

Susan Coleman

West Texas A&M University
A Member of the Texas A&M University System

 Prentice Hall, Upper Saddle River, New Jersey 07458

Library of Congress Cataloging-in-Publication Data

CALVI, JAMES V., (date)
    American law and legal systems / James V. Calvi, Susan Coleman.—3rd ed.
       p.   cm.
    Includes bibliographical references and index.
    ISBN 0–13–565490–4
    1. Law—United States. I. Coleman, Susan L. II. Title.
KF387.C28 1997
349.73—dc20
[347.3]   96-12288
                                                         CIP

Acquisitions editor: *Michael Bickerstaff*
Editorial/production supervision: *Kim Gueterman*
Cover designer: *Wendy Alling-Judy*
Buyer: *Bob Anderson*

This book was set in 10/12 Palatino by NK Graphics and was printed and bound by Courier Companies, Inc. The cover was printed by Phoenix Color Corp.

Printed in the United States of America
10 9 8 7 6 5 4 3 2 1

ISBN 0-13-565490-4

Prentice-Hall International (UK) Limited, *London*
Prentice-Hall of Australia Pty. Limited, *Sydney*
Prentice-Hall of Canada Inc., *Toronto*
Prentice-Hall Hispanoamericana, S.A., *Mexico*
Prentice-Hall of India Private Limited, *New Delhi*
Prentice-Hall of Japan, Inc., *Tokyo*
Simon & Schuster Asia Pte. Ltd., *Singapore*
Editora Prentice-Hall do Brasil, Ltda., *Rio de Janeiro*

With love and gratitude

To my wife Leesa and my daughters
Jennifer and Jessica

and

In loving remembrance of

my dear friend and cousin,
Norma Sue Mayben
(1956–1995)

and
my father,
John Buchanan Coleman
(1922–1993)

Contents

11 *PROPERTY* 262

12 *FAMILY LAW* 286

13 *CONCLUSION* 310

APPENDIX: LEGAL RESEARCH 318

GLOSSARY 329

TABLE OF CASES 344

INDEX 351

Preface
to Third Edition

One of the themes of *American Law and Legal Systems* is change. In looking back since the first edition appeared in 1989, it is apparent that the law has changed even in so short a period of time. One of the luxuries of having a third edition of a book is the ability to reflect on the changes that have occurred since the book was first written. Another is to clarify points which were not as lucid as they seemed at the time. At the same time, we hope that we have retained some of the down-to-earth language we thought essential to the understanding of law for introductory students. As always, it is for the reader to decide such questions.

The third edition of *American Law and Legal Systems* contains the usual attempt to update material to make it as current as possible. In addition, significant additions have been made. Chapter 2 (History of Law) has been expanded to include a section on Chinese socialist law. Chapter 6 (Constitutional Law) now includes a section on civil liberties. The topic of civil liberties had been prominently covered in the first edition but eliminated in the second. It is our hope that the inclusion of a brief civil liberties section will serve as a happy compromise.

Chapter 7 (Criminal Law) includes a new section on a neglected area of the law—juvenile justice. Chapter 9 (Torts) contains new material on the battle over tort reform in the United States. A section on intellectual property now appears in Chapter 11 (Property). Intellectual property is a rapidly changing area of the law especially in an era of international markets, trade treaties, computer software, and worldwide webs. Finally, Chapter 12 (Family Law) raises new questions about the concept of family and its changing nature in American society.

We would like also to thank those people who have provided their continued support throughout the revision process. First, our families for being there with love and understanding. Next, our colleagues and friends in the Department of History and Political Science of West Texas A&M University. A special note of thanks to Marilyn Smith who proofread the final copy and provided her usual cheerful help when things came unglued. Our thanks to Sandra L. Quinn-Musgrove, Our Lady of the Lake University; Ronald D. Server, Prairie View A&M University; and James Marshall, Michigan State University who gave of their time by reviewing the manuscript.

As we have done in the two previous editions, we would like to conclude by thanking the wonderful people at Prentice Hall. Some of them are new and some have become like old friends, but all of them have been extraordinarily helpful over the years. First, we would like to thank Mike Bickerstaff, Political Science editor, for his support and encouragement. We also want to thank Kim Gueterman, production editor, and Donna Mulder, copy editor, for all the help they provided.

Preface
to Second Edition

When we wrote the first edition of *American Law and Legal Systems*, we did so because of our dissatisfaction with the textbooks then available for introduction to law courses. After reading the critiques of the first edition, we now understand more fully how difficult it is to write a book that fits the needs of everyone who teaches this course. That is one reason it is so nice to have a second edition. We were able to think about the comments of the book's reviewers and incorporate their suggestions and ideas. Naturally, we believe this will constitute a major improvement over the first edition.

In addition to the usual updating of material, we have added several new topics in the second edition. Included are sections on the punishment phase of the criminal justice system (Chapter 7) and on alternate dispute resolution (Chapter 4). We expanded the coverage of appellate courts to include additional discussion of the appellate process and the functions of appellate courts in the judicial system (Chapter 4). The chapter on constitutional law (Chapter 6) now includes a much broader range of constitutional issues and concepts. We feel the revision better reflects the field of constitutional law than did the more narrow First Amendment focus of the first edition. Finally, an appendix on legal research will benefit students whether the text is used for introductory law, criminal justice, business law, or legal assistant courses.

As with the first edition, there are many people to thank for their support. We would like to thank our families for their loving support. We would also like to thank the members of the History and Political Science Department at West Texas State University for their personal and institutional backing, especially Marilyn Smith, our departmental secretary. We want to thank our students who had to endure our occasional inaccessibility while we hid in the library. We wish to thank the following professors who graciously reviewed the manuscript and provided invaluable suggestions for the second edition: Michael Johnson, Iowa Lakes Community College, and Joseph F. Schuster, Eastern Washington University.

Finally, we wish to express our appreciation to the people of Prentice Hall for the second chance this book represents. We would especially like to thank Karen Horton, Political Science editor. Karen was an absolute joy to work with and was always available to answer questions. A mere phone call to Karen never failed to generate added enthusiasm, energy, and determination for our task. We also thank Dolores Mars, Karen's assistant, Rob DeGeorge, production editor, and Diane Lange, copy editor, for all their good work on our behalf.

Preface
to First Edition

We decided to write an introductory law book for a simple reason: We were dissatisfied with the existing choices. We felt that some introductory law books—often the ones written by lawyers—were too legalistic in their approach. These books often contained excerpts from Supreme Court cases and basically taught law the same way as their lawyer-authors had been taught law. Other introductory law books leaned too much toward social science in their orientation. We decided a more balanced approach was needed. We also wanted to write a book that could be easily understood by a layperson, but which had enough technical information to introduce the beginner to the intricacies of the law. To that end, we have included chapters that deal with what is commonly known as "everyday law": contracts, wills, family law, and torts. We have included a glossary to call special attention to important legal terms and doctrines. We divided the chapters so that each of us could write in his or her own area of expertise. Consequently, the chapters dealing with the more technical aspects of the law were written by Susan Coleman, a licensed attorney; the chapters dealing with the social and political aspects of the law were written by Jim Calvi, an unlicensed political scientist. We reviewed each other's chapters as they were written in order to achieve the necessary balance. We are happy to report that the incidents of bruised egos were minimal.

It is with heartfelt gratitude that we thank those people who helped us in this endeavor. Naturally, we want to thank our families, who put up with us through endless rewrites and self-imposed deadlines—especially Sue Coleman, who helped compile the Index and Table of Cases. We would also like to thank our colleagues at West Texas State University for the personal and institutional support provided. We would especially like to thank Dr. Jim Woodyard of the Killgore Research Center, who displayed untiring effort and unending patience as we learned (and relearned) the deep, dark secrets of word processing and computer usage. It is no exaggeration to say that we could not have done it without him. We wish to thank the following professors who graciously reviewed the manuscript: Karl Andresen, University of Wisconsin-Eau Claire; Robert L. Bock, Western New England College; James Magee, University of Delaware; and Lee S. Weinberg, University of Pittsburgh.

We want to thank the people of Prentice Hall for their patience and understanding in leading two relative novices through the intricacies of book publishing. First, Karen Horton, Political Science editor, who gave us the opportunity to bring this idea to fruition. Second, Marjorie Shustak, who served as production editor and answered our numerous inquiries about the process. Third and finally, Nancy Morgan Andreola, copy editor, who showed us that we don't write nearly as well as we thought.

American Law
and
Legal Systems

Introduction

In order to understand the American legal system, one must first come to terms with the question, What is law? Americans have always had ambivalent feelings about law. Our rhetoric is full of noble ideals such as "equal justice under law" and the "rule of law." We pride ourselves on having a "government of laws, not men," and on the assertion that "no one is above the law." At the same time, disregard for the rule of law has been part of our political tradition. We are a nation born of violent revolution, and during our frontier period, vigilante groups often took the law into their own hands. Even in our own time we debate the role of civil disobedience in the civil rights, animal rights, abortion, and antinuclear movements. *Civil disobedience* is the belief that a person has a moral right to disregard an unjust law. In our own time the debate over the role of civil disobedience continues. In the 1960s the radical left believed ending the war in Vietnam or achieving civil rights for African-Americans justified the use of violence. In the 1990s the radical right uses similar arguments to justify violence against abortion clinics. Some paramilitary militia groups have even challenged the legitimacy of the government itself.

In many ways the questions we ask ourselves about the nature of law are the same ones we ask about our political system and about society at large. How do we account for the conflicting attitudes Americans have toward law? How can persons who are law abiding one minute turn into a lynch mob the next? How can a nation founded on the basis of its citizens' "inalienable rights" systematically deny those rights to African-Americans and other minorities? How can we explain these contradictions? The answers to these questions are not easy, but we can begin to understand the paradox by understanding the nature of law both in general terms and in American society specifically.

In this chapter we will focus on several aspects of law in America. First, we will examine the functions of law in society. Second, we will discuss the source of law in society in order to help us understand why people do or do not obey the law. Next we will define the different kinds of law in our legal system, with examples of the various forms the law takes. Finally, we will conclude with a case study of *Bob Jones University* v. *United States,* which illustrates a number of the chapter's major points.

FUNCTIONS OF LAW IN SOCIETY

Society tends to place far too much emphasis on the negative aspects of law. Many view the law as a list of things they are forbidden to do. Perhaps this attitude is only natural, given our socialization. As children we were continually told, "Don't do this" and "Don't touch that," so it is understandable that our first contact with authority has negative connotations. Law, like the restrictions placed on us by our parents, defines the boundaries of acceptable and unacceptable behavior. But law is more than just a list of forbidden activities; it touches every aspect of our lives and should be viewed as a positive force. Following are some of the functions of law in our society.

Law bestows benefits on people. One of the positive aspects of law that perhaps we seldom consider is that it bestows benefits upon people. Government, no matter what its form, uses its law-making power to determine who receives certain benefits and who does not. Laws deciding eligibility for programs like Social Security, food stamps, unemployment compensation, and veterans' benefits are just a few examples; laws determining who may operate an automobile, practice law, sell real estate, or receive tax deductions are some others. Law is thus closely connected to the political system since it is government that determines "who gets what, when, and how."[1] The law becomes a major concern of interest groups who try to secure the passage of laws beneficial to them while blocking the passage of those that harm their interests. Finally, it is the government's ability to meet the demands of interest groups and its fairness in allocating benefits that provide an important measure of governmental effectiveness.

Law reflects society's values. Interest groups do not use the law just to promote their selfish economic interests. Law has important symbolic value in our society. Interest groups, like pro-life and pro-choice groups, want the law to promote certain values that they cherish in society. This is why some people and groups are willing to work to promote school prayer, ban flag desecration, and punish homosexuality. It is why others are equally willing to push for separation of church and state, freedom of expression, and tolerance of individual lifestyles. People on both sides of a controversial issue believe it is important for the law to reflect the correct view which, of course, means their personal view of public policy. It is the eagerness of groups to see their views reflected in the nation's laws that occupies the major portion of political debate in a country.

Law creates new programs. The next function of law is closely related to a previous one. Government, by passing laws that bestow benefits, must create both new programs and the bureaucracies to administer them. Programs such as flood control, crop insurance, welfare benefits, and highway construction by their very nature benefit people in varying degrees. Some programs, like highway construction and flood control, are seemingly for the general welfare but also bestow benefits (like big profits) on highway contractors and insurance companies. Battles between the president and Congress over the nation's budget are actually struggles over the funding levels of new and existing programs that have been created by the government.

Law proscribes certain activities. As we have noted, most of our thinking about law centers around what we may *not* do. Law forbids behavior that causes harm to other people or to their property. Some behavior is termed ***malum in se***, or "wrong in itself." Consequently, the law forbids murder, rape, arson, theft, and other forms of antisocial behavior. There are also laws banning activities that, while not harmful in themselves, are forbidden simply because society disapproves of them. Neither parking in a "no parking" zone nor letting the meter expire is really wrong in itself, but both are against the law. These are examples of ***malum prohibitum***—acts that are wrong merely because they have been prohibited by government. Finally, some forms of behavior—such as gambling, prostitution, or homosexual activities—are debatable as to whether they are wrong in themselves or simply wrong because a majority in society thinks they should be prohibited. In any case, it is only by banning and punishing certain activities that people can live together in society in relative harmony.

Law provides predictability. One final function of law is to provide a measure of predictability so that we can conduct our affairs with some certainty. Contract law is a good example of law fulfilling the need for predictability; without contracts enforceable in courts, businesspersons could not conduct their affairs. We also seek predictability because we want some assurance that those in power will not act arbitrarily. One element of due process is the requirement that a law forbidding an activity cannot be "void for vagueness."[2] Some Supreme Court justices, for example, have expressed concern over upholding pornography laws when the Court itself has such difficulty defining pornography.[3] Lawyers want some assurance that the law governing the outcome of yesterday's cases will serve as guideposts for today's decisions and tomorrow's cases. That assurance is why lawyers so eagerly look for *precedents* when presenting cases. Lawyers hope that such precedents will help guide the judge's decision and make the outcome more predictable.

Despite the comforting assurances of predictability that we seek in the law, there is, paradoxically, unpredictability as well. Professor Lief Carter reminds us that if law always predicted the outcome of disputes, people would never go to court. When the law fails to predict the outcome of a dispute and both sides believe they have a chance to win, lawsuits follow.[4] Carter notes that the use of ambiguous wording in statutes and court opinions is one reason for the unpredictability of law. Phrases such as "due process of law" and "beyond a reasonable doubt" illustrate the ambiguity of the language of law.[5]

These functions of law give us some clues as to the nature of law by making us aware of its purpose for a society. Law can be seen as a battle for scarce resources, as a way of organizing society, or as a source of predictability and stability. But understanding the functions of law in society is not enough. Another important aspect of law is the *source* of law in a society. We now turn our attention toward understanding why people obey the law.

SOURCES OF LAW IN SOCIETY

It is because law performs such important functions that it becomes necessary to examine the source of law in society. The source of law concerns not only the legitimacy of the law in the eyes of the people, but also the legitimacy of the lawmaker. In an absolute monarchy, the will of a single individual and the law are one and the same. In the film *The Ten Commandments*, the Pharaoh had only to say, "So let it be written, so let it be done," and his word became law. How can the will of a single person be so readily accepted by others as binding? In other words, from where did the Pharaoh derive his power, and why did his people obey him?

The answer to why humans obey can be as varied as humans themselves, but generally the reasons can be reduced to two: People obey either because they believe that they should or because they are afraid not to. Compliance with the law is much easier to effect if the lawmaker can convince the people that he or she has the right to make the law. In some societies—ancient Egypt and pre–World War II Japan, for example—the lawmaker was seen as a god. Thus, people obeyed the Pharaoh and the Japanese emperor out of both religious respect and fear. During the Age of Absolutism in Europe, the theory of the *divine right of kings* governed people's thinking about the source of the king's power. In Roman Catholic theology, the Pope was chosen by God to be the "Vicar of Christ" on earth and was considered to be infallible in matters of Church doctrine. Similarly, people believed that the king was chosen by God to rule over them in secular matters. Just as the Pope was infallible in Church matters, the belief that "the king can do no wrong" was based upon the belief that God had chosen the king and guided him. But what if the king should suffer the misfortune of being dethroned? Did this disprove the theory that the king was king "by the grace of God"? No, because in the Bible, as everyone knew, God had replaced Saul as king of Israel with David when Saul displeased Him. As a result, all law, spiritual and temporal, was inspired by God, and to disobey God's earthly representative was to disobey God Himself; the punishment was eternal damnation, a powerful penalty in the minds of medieval people.

Law, as understood by medieval thinkers, came from God and was considered to be eternal and immutable. During the Age of the Enlightenment, however, both religious and political thinkers began to challenge the absolutism of popes and kings. The idea developed that the lawmaker received his authority, not from God by virtue of his fortunate birth, but from the consent of the governed. Thomas Jefferson incorporated the concept of natural law into the Declaration of Independence when he invoked the notion that persons are endowed by their Creator with certain "inalienable rights." But he also emphatically stated that governments are instituted among men to protect those natural rights and that when a government no longer does so, it is the right of the people to alter or abolish it. Jefferson then chronicled a long list of abuses of power by George III to justify the drastic step the Colonies were about to take.

The Declaration of Independence and the philosophy behind it added a new wrinkle to the relationship between the people and their government. Government derived its power from the consent of the governed, not by some accident of royal birth. Implicit in the concept of government by consent is the idea of majority rule. American democracy, of course, links majority rule with representative government, wherein elected representatives of the people make the laws that bind all members of society. The legitimacy of both the law and the lawmaker rests on what we refer to simply as the democratic process. As long as laws are passed in accordance with the democratic "rules of the game," people are likely to obey them willingly.

The Declaration of Independence also speaks of persons possessing "inalienable rights." Law recognizes that individuals possess rights that are not subject to the whim of the majority. Therefore, in a democratic society law reflects two important values. First, laws must be passed by acceptable procedures such as adherence to majority rule. It is extremely important that these procedures be viewed as fair by all, especially political or other minorities. Second, laws must be viewed as fundamentally fair. An unfair law even if enacted by a majority vote is unfair nevertheless. Again, it is very important that individuals and minorities perceive a law as inherently fair. African-Americans could not be expected to view segregation laws passed by white Southern legislatures as inherently fair even if they were passed by a majority following accepted procedures for enacting legislation.

Why have we discussed the question of legitimacy at such length? At the beginning of this chapter, we stated a paradox of law in America: We are a nation born of revolution, and yet we strongly believe in the rule of law. How do we reconcile these two apparently contradictory ideas? In order to do so, we must look at three approaches to the nature of law.[6]

The natural-law approach. *Natural-law* theorists believe that the laws that govern relationships among people, like the laws that govern the physical universe, are sown in nature. These laws are eternal and immutable, just as God, the source of all law, is eternal. Natural law is often referred to as a form of "higher law," in order to distinguish it from lesser—that is, man-made—law. Natural law has moral overtones, and those who invoke it often call it "God's law." Ascertaining just what is and is not God's law can be risky business, but its advocates echo the belief of Justice Potter Stewart that they "know it when they see it."

Appeal to natural, or higher, law provides a justification for *civil disobedience.* For example, if one's conscience tells one that war is morally wrong, then one has a moral obligation not only to resist induction into the military, but also to commit overt acts of civil disobedience in order to raise the consciousness of the community about the evils of war. It was by appealing to the conscience of society that Mahatma Gandhi and Martin Luther King, Jr., were able to make both those in authority and the general public see the immorality of colonialism and segregation.[7] Opponents of nuclear war have tried to make the question of nuclear disarmament into a moral issue which justifies admittedly illegal behavior such as sit-ins and trespassing on nuclear facilities. Invoking this higher law is one way in which a minority can hope to convince the majority to change its mind by appealing to the majority's sense of morality.

A discussion of natural law inevitably leads to the question of whether it is possible to "legislate morality." If by legislating morality it is meant that law can change a person's *values,* then law obviously cannot legislate morality. A law prohibiting gambling is unlikely to prevent someone who sees nothing wrong with it from betting on the Super Bowl. In such a case the law has altered neither the person's values nor his or her behavior. Among those persons who choose not to gamble are those who refrain from doing so out of fear of punishment rather than a conviction that gambling is "immoral."

It would be wrong, however, to conclude that law has no impact on morality. A generation or two ago many Americans thought it was perfectly acceptable to use the law to force African-Americans to attend separate public schools, drink at separate water fountains, and eat at separate restaurants. But most younger Americans today are surprised to learn that such laws ever even existed. Undoubtedly, 30 years of civil rights and antidiscrimination laws have changed the views of many Americans about the morality of racial segregation. It is in this sense that law can indeed legislate morality.

Positive-law approach. A second approach, *positive law,* is the belief that law should simply reflect the will of the majority. Law is stripped of any moral overtones and boils down to the old adage "Might makes right." Despite the immorality of segregation or colonialism, if a majority wishes to have a segregated society or a colonial policy, then they may have it. Those who disagree with the law can certainly work within the democratic process to change it (albeit an unlikely occurrence), but they must accept it as the legitimate reflection of the will of the majority. Under no circumstances may the minority resort to unlawful methods to effect change. The law, then, becomes whatever a majority wants at a particular point in time.

Sociological approach. The *sociological theory of law* holds that law represents a reflection of the values, mores, and culture of the society that produces it, and that as the society changes, the law will also change. For example, we have seen tremendous change in our own society as a result of the women's movement. As traditional views of the role of women have changed, laws dealing with the rights of women in employment, pension plans, credit, and child support have changed to keep pace. Although the law may lag behind a bit, it eventually catches up and reflects society's prevalent views.

The sociological approach is even more evident in our view of criminal behavior. Criminal law, you will recall, defines what type of behavior is antisocial and therefore proscribed. Some behavior is wrong in itself and is almost universally condemned. Other acts are wrong merely because they have been prohibited. At one time the manufacture and sale of alcoholic beverages were against the law, but after some experience with Prohibition, the measure was finally repealed. Today the use of marijuana is against the law in most states, but as society's views change, we may expect some change in marijuana laws as well. Many states have already reduced the crime of possession of marijuana from a felony offense to a misdemeanor.

How would each of the three approaches just described deal with an issue such as homosexual marriages? The natural-law theorist might argue that such marriages are a sin against God, violate natural law, and should not be legalized. The positive-law theorist would argue that the morality of homosexual marriages is irrelevant; a majority of people are still opposed to them (assuming this to be true), and they should therefore remain illegal. The advocate of the sociological approach would argue that while our society is not yet ready to accept such marriages, a more tolerant atmosphere may prevail at some future time.

In a sense, American law encompasses all three of these approaches. The resulting paradox is the same one that is inherent in our political system and in society in general. On one hand, we believe that law should reflect the will of the majority; on the other hand, we accept the notion that minorities also have rights under the law. It is a source of frustration to many who wonder why we permit flag burning if a majority of Americans oppose it, and why we do not have prayer in the schools when a majority favor it. Is the law a manifestation of the majority's will or isn't it? Reconciling this paradox is never easy and seldom satisfying.

KINDS OF LAW

It should be clear by now that one's feelings about the origins of law and the functions it performs in society are crucial to understanding the legal system itself. One final obstacle remains: understanding the kinds of law that exist in the legal environment. This section will introduce the various kinds of law, and the final section will use a case study of *Bob Jones University* v. *United States* to illustrate them. We will begin by distinguishing substantive law from procedural law.

Substantive versus procedural law.   It is important at the outset to differentiate between the substance of the law and the process or procedures of the law. The former—that is, **substantive law**—is concerned with the content, or substance, of the law. In criminal law, for example, the substantive law will define what kind of behavior is considered to be antisocial and prescribe the kind of punishment that will be imposed for engaging in it. The substantive law will clearly define the elements of the crime (for example, the necessary evil intent) and the range of punishment (5 to 10 years' imprisonment) that may be handed out upon conviction. As previously discussed, the determination of what behavior is forbidden and what punishment is appropriate is made by elected representative bodies such as the Congress and the state legislatures. Likewise, in civil law, the legislature of each state is free to specify the legal grounds for a civil action, such as a divorce proceeding. Mental cruelty, adultery, irreconcilable differences, and incompatibility are common substantive grounds for a divorce.

Procedural law governs the *process* of the law. In a political system such as ours, we are as much concerned about *how* the law is applied as about the substance of the law itself. Terms like "kangaroo court" and "railroading a defendant" indicate that our system of law is also concerned about fundamental fairness. Consequently, we guarantee everyone, especially those charged with criminal offenses, *due process of law.* We make this guarantee because our system of constitutional government is based upon the idea that there are limits to governmental power and that even those in authority must adhere to the rule of law. We wish to prevent government from acting toward us in an arbitrary fashion, and so we believe that even a person charged with the most heinous crime is entitled to "have his or her day in court" governed by a set of preordained rules of fairness. Thus, we guarantee the accused the right to remain silent before his or her accusers, the right to a trial by jury, and the right to counsel. Even after a conviction, the Constitution protects the condemned person from cruel and unusual punishment.

Of the two types, substantive and procedural, the latter tends to generate more controversy. Although debate rages over questions like whether marijuana use should be a crime or whether the punishment for using it is too severe, people generally defer to their elected representatives on these issues. However, procedural due process comes under attack because it provides the "loopholes" through which criminals are sometimes allowed to slip. All of us are aware of cases in which a criminal has been set free because the police failed to comply with certain "technicalities" in the law. Astounded citizens want to know the justice in letting a factually guilty person go free because "the constable blunders."[8]

There is no satisfactory answer to the question, What about the rights of the victim? But we should understand that the framers of our Constitution had firsthand experience with a tyrannical government and believed that in the long run it was better to risk letting the guilty go free than to risk creating an arbitrary and tyrannical government. Even though most citizens will never need the protection of the Bill of Rights, it is also true that it is better to have them and not need them than to need them and not have them. Understanding this fact does not necessarily make it acceptable to many people, however, and so the debate over how much "process" is due to those accused of crime will undoubtedly continue.

In the discussion of the other types of law that follows, it is important to keep in mind that each type has both substantive and procedural aspects. For example, in administrative law, the Social Security Administration has regulations (laws) that determine who is *eligible* for Social Security benefits. However, it has separate regulations that set forth the *procedures* that must be followed when applying for benefits. It should also be noted that substantive rules and procedural rules influence each other. For example, a person who is denied benefits may be turned down because he or she failed to follow the proper application procedures, not because of ineligibility.

Criminal and civil law. Several references have already been made to criminal and civil law, but now we want to define them more clearly. *Criminal law,* as we have indicated, deals with activities that have been formally forbidden by a society's government. The range of crimes extends from parking violations to murder. As we have seen, some crimes are "wrong in themselves," and some merely wrong because society has seen fit to prohibit them. We have also seen that the Constitution provides a number of procedural safeguards for those accused of crime.

The importance of the role of government in criminal law cannot be overestimated. Of course, government is responsible for detecting and preventing crime, as well as for seeing that criminals are caught and punished. But more important, government prosecutes criminals. This statement, while hardly revealing, is significant because of its implications. At one time, perhaps in philosopher John Locke's "state of nature," each person was individually responsible for his or her own protection, or else relied upon a family or clan for protection. When someone was injured, it was the duty of the individual to seek revenge; if the victim was unable to do so, the responsibility fell upon the family or clan. In our civilized society, we consider a crime to be an injury not only to a particular individual, but also to society as a whole, and it is society's responsibility to seek retribution on behalf of the victim. Instead of permitting blood feuds and vendettas to disrupt society, the government assumes the responsibility for prosecuting and punishing persons charged with crimes. Thus, criminal cases are typically entitled *People* v. *Jones, State* v. *Jones,* or *The State of Texas* v. *Jones* to indicate the state's active role as prosecutor. It was a significant step in the advancement of law in society when people began to permit government to seek retribution on their behalf. It is because of this awesome power that government has over our lives and liberties that we impose the procedural safeguards discussed in the previous section. Without significant checks on the power of government, our freedom would soon be lost.

Civil law governs the relationships between individuals in the course of their private affairs. It deals with such matters as contracts, property, wills, and torts. When two or more persons have a dispute, it is in the best interests of society as a whole to ensure that the dispute is resolved peacefully. Unlike criminal prosecutions, in which the government is an active participant, the government's main interest in civil cases is to provide a forum, a court of law, in which to resolve the dispute. The government itself does not care who wins the dispute as long as it is settled peacefully. Although the cost of providing courts to resolve these essentially private disputes is considerable, it is justified on the grounds of maintaining harmony in society. The fact that citizens are willing to submit their disputes to the courts and abide by the court's decision is in itself a tribute to the legitimacy of a society's judicial system.

One final point about criminal and civil law should be made. It is possible for both a criminal *and* a civil action to arise out of the same set of facts or the same incident. Two examples should clarify this point. Suppose Wilson runs a red light and collides with Johnson's car, causing considerable damage to it. The police will issue a traffic ticket to Wilson for running the light and he will be punished, probably by having to pay a fine. The state's interest is limited to punishing Wilson for disregarding one of its traffic laws. There is still the matter of Johnson's car, however. Wilson has damaged her property—which, in legal terminology, is called a *tort*. A tort is a legal injury one person has caused another. Let's further suppose that Wilson has no liability insurance (itself a crime in many states) to cover the damages, so Johnson decides to sue him in order to force him to pay for the damage he has caused. This suit is a *civil action*, and if Wilson loses the suit, he will be made to pay the cost of repairing the car. Thus, two legal actions, one criminal and one civil, arose from a single automobile accident.

Our second example is similar but a bit more complicated. Anderson starts a fight with Cooper. Anderson hits Cooper, breaking the latter's jaw. Anderson is arrested for assault, convicted, and given a year in prison as his punishment. Cooper has suffered a broken jaw, however, and has had to pay his own medical expenses. He decides to sue Anderson in order to force him to pay his medical bills. Again, the latter suit is civil in nature, and if Cooper wins, Anderson can be forced to pay. Someone might suggest that Anderson is being subjected to "double jeopardy" since he is being hauled into court twice for the same offense. But the prohibition against double jeopardy limits the number of times the *government* can prosecute a person for a *criminal offense* and does not protect Anderson from a civil action started by the person he has injured.

Constitutional law. In the United States and in each of the 50 states, the most basic fundamental law is a constitution. The national Constitution declares that "This Constitution, and the Laws of the United States which shall be made in Pursuance thereof; and all Treaties made, or which shall be made, under the Authority of the United States, shall be the supreme Law of the Land."[9] The Constitution adds that state judges must take an oath to uphold it and that state constitutions and state laws may not conflict with the national Constitution.[10]

Noted constitutional scholar C. Herman Pritchett has asserted that a good constitution should do four things: It should provide for the structure of government, place limitations on government, list the powers of government, and provide for an amending process.[11] The U.S. Constitution does all four, but with one small problem: The Framers had a tendency to write as if everyone understood exactly what they meant. The Eighth Amendment, for example, prohibits "cruel and unusual punishment" for criminal offenses, but we are given no clue as to just what is to be considered cruel or unusual. The executive power is vested in the president, but no attempt is made to define the scope of the executive power. The Framers probably figured that they had done the hard part, and it was up to future generations to do the rest.

Because the Constitution is so ambiguous and because it serves as our fundamental law, courts—especially the U.S. Supreme Court—have played an important role in our political, as well as legal, system. The Supreme Court has an opportunity to expand the meaning of the Constitution each time it interprets it. With its power of judicial review—the power to invalidate laws or actions contrary to the Constitution—the Supreme Court effects changes never dreamed of by the Framers. Whether the Court is settling an ordinary dispute or the flag-burning case, defining the meaning of "interstate commerce" or the Establishment Clause, the Court breathes life into the words of the Constitution. *Constitutional law, then, represents the sum of thousands of Supreme Court and lower-court decisions which have been settled in over 200 years of constitutional development.* We will say more about the role of the Supreme Court in subsequent chapters.

Statutory law. We have already noted that one of the major sources of positive law is statutes passed by elected representative bodies. Congress and state legislatures pass statutes on the national and state levels, while city and county governments pass ordinances on the local level. In most cases, statutes are passed by a simple majority vote of the legislative body, subject to a veto by the chief executive. The content of *statutory law* may serve any number of purposes. Statutes may be passed to create or abolish government programs, increase the penalty for a crime, make an appropriation from the treasury, or raise the salaries of government workers. Statutes can regulate business activities, create new judgeships, impose a new tax, or proclaim a new holiday. In short, statutes can do anything that does not conflict with the Constitution—including making everyone rise an hour earlier each morning during the summer months.

You will recall from our earlier discussion of natural law and positive law that there is an inherent conflict between constitutional and statutory law. Constitutional law deals with fundamental rights of citizens, such as freedom of speech and press. These are "natural rights" upon which no government, not even one based on the principle of majority rule, may infringe. Statutory law, on the other hand, reflects the collective will of the majority (at least insofar as we have faith in representative government). In exercising its power of *judicial review,* the Supreme Court must decide whether to adhere to the fundamental law or to a law that reflects current opinion on a particular subject. By their very nature, the kinds of issues the Court is asked to resolve (abortion, capital punishment, and so on) are ones that require tough choices to be made between two or more conflicting sets of values. We will have more to say about judicial review in Chapter 6 because understanding this inherent conflict is crucial to understanding not only our legal system, but our political system as well.

Administrative law. Under the U.S. Constitution, it is the Congress which has the power to regulate various activities that affect our lives on a daily basis. Thus, it is within congressional power to regulate railroads, telecommunications, labor activities, airlines, and many other aspects of business and industry. Given the structure and makeup of Congress, it is impossible for it to have the expertise needed to regulate highly technical industries like broadcasting or nuclear energy. Consequently, Congress has seen fit to delegate its authority to regulate business and industry to more specialized bodies it has created within the executive branch of government. Over the years it has created numerous executive departments (such as the Department of Transportation) and so-called independent regulatory agencies (such as the Federal Trade Commission) to perform the tasks Congress is incapable of doing itself. These executive agencies have been empowered to promulgate rules and regulations which have the force of law. For example, the Federal Aviation Administration (FAA) may promulgate a rule requiring commercial airlines to prohibit smoking on most domestic flights or to require children to wear seatbelts on airplanes. The Food and Drug Administration (FDA) may specify the procedures with which drug manufacturers must comply before they may market a new drug. Failure to comply with an agency's regulations may lead to a heavy fine or other penalty.

Lief Carter, a noted expert on administrative law, has pointed out that administrative law is often confused with regulatory law. What we have discussed thus far is technically *regulatory law*. Administrative law, by contrast, is the law that controls those whom Congress has empowered to regulate on its behalf. As Carter has noted, "Administrative law . . . governs the bureaucrats themselves."[12] Administrative agencies are not directly accountable to the people, and yet, as we have seen, the rules they promulgate are just as binding as any statute passed by a legislative body. We have also seen that our political system seeks to reduce the potential for official abuse of power. Administrative law governs the bureaucrats to ensure that they will not act in an arbitrary manner or abuse their power. Although this area of law is of increasing importance, it still receives relatively little attention from scholars.

Case law. There is an old maxim that says, "I will let you write the law if you will let me interpret it." The implication of this statement, of course, is that while a law may appear to be clear and unequivocal when written, it can be subjected to many different interpretations. In Mosaic law, the command "Thou shalt not kill" is precise and to the point. Yet questions about its meaning still arise. What about killing in self-defense? What about an accidental killing? Shouldn't the word "kill" actually be interpreted as "murder"? *Case law* develops when judges interpret the meaning of constitutions, statutes, or other forms of written law. It may also include interpretations of other cases that have previously been decided under the law. Instead of trying to write laws that attempt to cover every conceivable contingency, lawmakers prefer to write general laws subject to judicial interpretation. Then, as circumstances and real cases or controversies arise, the judge may interpret the law to resolve the conflict in question.

Whenever judges interpret a law in a particular way, they create a precedent, or rule of law. As we have seen with constitutional law, each time the Supreme Court interprets the Constitution, it breathes new meaning into it and may create a new precedent. In the classic case *Miranda* v. *Arizona*,[13] the Supreme Court ruled that persons accused of a crime must be given information about their constitutional rights to remain silent and to consult with an attorney. This case created a precedent that in future cases, not just in Miranda's case, any person subject to a custodial arrest must be given these same "*Miranda* warnings." The Court, in effect, created a new rule of law where one previously had not existed. Although the justices claim only to "find" law, it is decisions like *Miranda* that leave the Court open to charges that the justices are really "making law." We will have more to say about judicial lawmaking in Chapter 6.

Common law.   It is customary to save the best for last. Anglo-American law is rooted in the tradition of the common law. In 1881, Justice Oliver Wendell Holmes, Jr., wrote, "The life of the law has not been logic: It has been experience."[14] What Holmes meant is that law is not so much a function of our ability to logically deduce solutions to every conceivable conflict as it is a response to what he called "the felt necessities of the time."[15] Common law developed as a response to the need to find solutions to the pressing issues of the time.

Common law originated during the period of English history when there were very few written laws. Beginning about the time of Henry II, English kings sent their judges throughout the country to dispense the king's justice with little or no statutory law to guide their decisions. When conflicts arose and no statute applied, judges still had to resolve them somehow. As a result, decisions were based on rules of law, which in turn were based on an individual judge's sense of equity or fairness. Like King Solomon, who had to decide which of the two women should be given the baby, English judges had to make on-the-spot decisions to resolve pressing disputes. Once a rule of law thus formulated was recognized as just and reasonable, other judges in other jurisdictions would adopt it and apply it in their own, similar cases. Eventually the rule would be written down and used by all judges in the realm. A rule of law became "common," not in the sense of being ordinary, but in the sense of being common to all parts of England.

The reader should note the close relationship between common law and case law. Both rely heavily on the rule of precedence and both allow the judge discretion in interpreting the law. Common law, like case law, is often described as "judge-made." One important difference exists: Unlike case law, which is a court's interpretation of an existing constitution or statute, common-law rules developed in the absence of any positive law. In addition, a common-law rule can be set aside by the enactment of a statute. For example, under the common-law doctrine of *caveat emptor* ("let the buyer beware"), the purchaser of an item was expected to examine the merchandise before buying it in order to avoid being cheated by the merchant. If the purchaser failed to do so, he was partly to blame for not being careful; that is, he should have taken care so that he would not be cheated. Today, most states have laws to protect consumers from fraudulent business practices, and the common-law doctrine of *caveat emptor* is no longer applicable. Thus, the common-law doctrine may be superseded by the enactment of positive law.

BOB JONES UNIVERSITY V. UNITED STATES

Our approach to the discussion of the functions, sources, and kinds of law might lead one to believe that law can be neatly categorized. In reality, it is a bit more complicated. The following Supreme Court decision, *Bob Jones University v. United States,* illustrates how a single case may involve several kinds of law and incorporates a number of the points made in this chapter.

Background of the case.[16]   Section 501 (C) (3) of the Internal Revenue Code contains a description of organizations that are granted tax-exempt status by the national government. Section 170 of the Code specifies that individual contributions to these organizations may qualify as charitable deductions on individual tax returns. Until 1970, Bob Jones University was granted tax-exempt status under Section 501 (C) (3) by the Internal Revenue Service (IRS). Due to its interpretation of a lower federal court ruling,[17] however, the IRS notified the University in November 1970 that it could no longer grant tax-exempt status to "private schools which practice racial discrimination," nor could contributions made to them be charitable deductions under Section 170. The IRS formalized this policy by promulgating Revenue Ruling 71–447.

Bob Jones University is an institution dedicated to teaching fundamentalist Christian beliefs. Until 1971, it had completely excluded African-Americans. From 1971 to 1975 it accepted applications from African-Americans who were married within their own race. The university permitted the enrollment of unmarried blacks in 1975 but also enforced a strict policy banning interracial dating and marriage and expelling any student who espoused the idea. According to the IRS interpretation, an organization qualifies for tax-exempt status only if it is a "charitable" institution within the common-law meaning of that term. Under the common law, an institution that pursues activities contrary to public policy is not charitable. The IRS ruled that by practicing racial discrimination, Bob Jones University was acting against a clear "national policy to discourage racial discrimination in education."[18]

Ruling in the case.   Bob Jones University challenged the revocation of its tax-exempt status on three grounds. First, it asserted that the IRS had no authority to promulgate Revenue Ruling 71–447. Second, the University challenged the IRS's interpretation of Section 501 (C) (3). According to the University's interpretation, the section grants tax-exempt status to organizations that operate exclusively for ". . . religious, charitable, scientific, . . . *or* educational purposes."[19] Because the word "or" separates "charitable" from "educational" purposes, the IRS's application of the common-law definition of "charitable" was inappropriate. Since the University clearly is organized for educational purposes, it should have qualified for the exemption. Finally, the University argued that the IRS's construction of Section 501 (C) (3) and Section 170 violated the Free Exercise Clause of the First Amendment because the University's racial policy was based upon sincerely held religious beliefs.

In an 8–1 decision, the Supreme Court rejected all three of the University's challenges in an opinion written by Chief Justice Warren E. Burger. The Court rejected the University's contention that the IRS had no authority to promulgate Revenue Ruling 71–447 without specific congressional authorization. Chief Justice Burger noted that since the inception of the tax code, Congress had granted broad authority to the IRS to interpret the tax laws. He wrote, "In an area as complex as the tax system, the agency Congress vests with administrative responsibility must be able to exercise its authority to meet changing conditions and new problems."[20] The Chief Justice then proceeded to note that any time after the promulgation of Revenue Ruling 71–447, Congress could have modified it; Congress had chosen not to do so, however, indicating tacit approval of the policy. Thus, if Congress felt that the IRS's ruling was arbitrary or constituted an abuse of its authority, Congress could have done something about it during the ensuing 10 years and did not.

The Court also rejected the University's contention that the IRS misapplied the term "charitable" and that it should qualify for tax-exempt status solely because of its educational purposes. The Chief Justice stated that it was clearly the intent of Congress to exempt "charitable" organizations—that is, organizations that serve a public purpose, and not purposes contrary to established public policy. In a footnote to the opinion,[21] Chief Justice Burger pointed out that if the University's interpretation was accepted, then a school for training terrorists (clearly "educational" in purpose) would qualify for an exemption. He concluded that Congress surely did not intend for that to happen.

Finally, the Court rejected the University's First Amendment claim that the revocation of the tax exemption constituted a violation of the Free Exercise Clause. In previous cases[22] interpreting that clause, the Court has ruled that the government may justify a limitation on religious liberty by demonstrating "an overriding governmental interest." Chief Justice Burger concluded that the government's interest in eradicating racial discrimination in education was "compelling" and that it justified the burden on religious liberty. He noted that although the denial of tax benefits would have an impact on the University, it would not prevent the University from observing the tenets of its religion.[23]

Analysis of the case. The *Bob Jones University* case illustrates several of the points previously made in this chapter. First, it involves several kinds of law: constitutional, statutory, regulatory, administrative, case law, and common law. The constitutional question raised was the free exercise claim made by the University. Statutory law was involved when the Court was called upon to interpret Section 501 (C) (3) and Section 170. The common law definition of "charitable" adopted by the IRS was a major issue in the case. The question of whether or not the IRS had the authority to promulgate Revenue Ruling 71–447 was one of the administrative law, while the IRS's use of "charitable" in promulgating the Ruling was one of regulatory law. Finally, the Court cited numerous precedents, not included in our analysis, to substantiate its decision, thus illustrating the use of case law.

Second, *Bob Jones University* demonstrates the conflict between minority rights and majority rule. There is no reason to doubt that the officials of the University were sincere in their racial viewpoint or that their views were grounded in their religious beliefs. In following the course they chose, these officials undoubtedly believed that they were obeying a higher law, superior to the laws of the IRS or even the United States government. But the Supreme Court's opinion made it clear that the racial views of Bob Jones University were incompatible with a public policy endorsed by all three branches of the national government. The conflict was between the University's right to act upon its sincerely held religious beliefs and the majority's right to eradicate racial discrimination in the field of education.

Third, the case demonstrates the role of courts in supervising the government bureaucracy. The Supreme Court had to decide whether the IRS's application of the term "charitable" to the University was reasonable and within IRS's power. A ruling either that the IRS's application was unwarranted or that it had exceeded its authority would have resulted in a victory for the University.

Finally, the case illustrates how judges make decisions. Attorneys for the University offered some sound arguments that Congress intended to exempt organizations that are "charitable *or* educational" rather than "charitable *and* educational." Courts must often ascertain the intent of Congress when interpreting an ambiguous statute. Even when one or more interpretations are reasonable, courts must choose one over the other. In cases of far-reaching importance, such as *Bob Jones University*, the interpretation chosen will have a broad impact as a precedent in future cases. It is in this manner that law is an evolving concept that appears to be static but is actually constantly changing.

CONCLUSION

We began this chapter by asserting that there is a paradox of law in the United States. Americans possess ambivalent feelings about law. These feelings result from the fact that people disagree over what law is, where it comes from, and what it should do. We said that our ambivalence about law is related to the ambivalence we have about our society in general. We might all believe in "equality of opportunity" in principle, but disagree over the propriety of affirmative action programs. Likewise, we can agree with the ideal of the rule of law without agreeing on just what that means. There is no right or wrong, or even single, answer to the question, What is law? Our view of the law depends on what we consider to be the functions of law and the source of law. In the final analysis, we must decide for ourselves what law really is.

Understanding the major ideas in this chapter is important to understanding what will follow. Without a firm grasp of these basic concepts, it will be more difficult to fully appreciate much of the discussion of the material covered in the remaining chapters.

NOTES

1. Harold Lasswell, *Politics: Who Gets What, When, How?* (New York: McGraw-Hill, 1936).

2. Anthony G. Amsterdam, "The Void-for-Vagueness Doctrine in the Supreme Court," *Univ. of Pennsylvania Law Review,* Vol. 109 (1960), p. 67.

3. *Ginzburg* v. *United States,* 383 U.S. 463 (1966) (Black, J., dissenting).

4. Lief Carter, *Reason in Law,* 4th ed. (New York: HarperCollins, Inc., 1994), pp. 30–32.

5. Ibid.

6. cf. David Eliot Brody, *The American Legal System: Concepts and Principles* (Lexington, Mass.: Heath, 1978), pp. 4–7.

7. Martin Luther King, Jr., "Letter from Birmingham Jail," in Fred R. Harris, *America's Democracy,* 2nd ed. (Glenview, Ill.: Scott, Foresman, 1983), pp. 117–118.

8. *People* v. *DeFore,* 242 N.Y. 13, 150 N.E. 585 (1926) (Cardozo, J.).

9. U.S. Constitution, Art. VI, sec. 1, para. 2.

10. Ibid.

11. C. Herman Pritchett, *The American Constitutional System,* 5th ed. (New York: McGraw-Hill, 1981), p. 2.

12. Lief H. Carter, *Administrative Law and Politics: Cases and Comments* (Boston: Little, Brown, 1983), p. 38.

13. *Miranda* v. *Arizona,* 384 U.S. 436 (1966).

14. Oliver Wendell Holmes, Jr., *The Common Law* (Boston: Little, Brown, 1881), pp. 1–2.

15. Ibid.

16. The facts of this case are summarized from the majority opinion of Chief Justice Warren E. Burger, *Bob Jones University* v. *United States*, 461 U.S. 574 (1983).

17. *Green* v. *Kennedy*, 309 F.Supp. 1127 (D.D.C., 1970).

18. *Bob Jones University* v. *United States*, 461 U.S. 574 (1983), at 579.

19. Ibid., p. 585.

20. Ibid., p. 596.

21. Ibid., footnote 18, pp. 591–592.

22. *Prince* v. *Massachusetts*, 321 U.S. 158 (1944); *United States* v. *O'Brien*, 391 U.S. 367 (1968); *Goldman* v. *Weinberger*, 475 U.S. 503 (1986).

23. *Bob Jones University* v. *United States*, 461 U.S. 574 (1983), at 603–604.

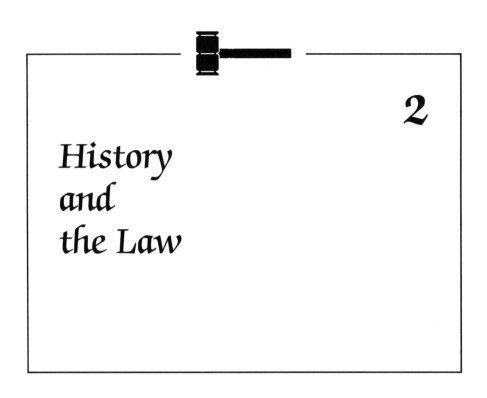

History and the Law

2

The life of the law has not been logic; it has been experience. . . . The law embodies the story of a nation's development through many centuries and it cannot be dealt with as if it contained only the axioms and corollaries of a book of mathematics. In order to know what it is, we must know what it has been, and what it tends to become.[1]

All societies develop methods of resolving conflicts among their members. Some are formally organized, such as the U.S. court system, while others are much more primitive; but it is imperative that the rules governing a society be enforced if chaos is to be prevented.

The need to maintain order in society is not recent. Ancient civilizations created laws and legal systems to control their members and to resolve conflicts. Remnants of these legal systems linger, and many of today's theories and practices may be traced to them. Cases such as *Roe* v. *Wade,* the abortion case, are replete with historical references to other, older systems of legal doctrine.

LAW THROUGH THE AGES

One of the earliest extant sets of laws is the Code of Hammurabi, developed by King Hammurabi of Babylon in about 2000 B.C. It set forth the rules of human behavior demanded by the gods as supplemented by the ruler's edicts.[2] The code was frequently harsh; for example, adulterers and a person accusing another of murder but who could not prove it were punished by death. A wife who "has not been careful but has gadded about, neglecting her house and belittling her husband" shall be thrown into the water but, on the other hand, if the husband is found to have wrongfully belittled her, she could take her dowry and return to her father's home. A wife could be set aside for not providing her husband with children but the husband had to give her the marriage price and give to her the dowry her father had provided.[3] In addition, the wife's property rights were protected from her children. Thus, women were at least partially protected and were not treated solely as the property of the husband. Hammurabi's Code of nearly 300 laws covered such diverse topics as administration of justice, property, irrigation, loans and interest, regulation of trade, slavery, marriage and the family, adoption, personal injury, and building and wage regulations.[4]

In addition to a well-developed system of criminal law, ancient Mesopotamians developed strict patterns in drafting contracts which are still employed today. First, the object of the transaction—for example, a marriage contract or lease of real property—was clearly indicated. Second, all parties to the transaction were listed with a clear identification of their roles in relation to each other, for example, seller and buyer. Third, other clauses delineating details such as price or the obligations undertaken were added. Fourth, the witnesses present at the time of transaction were identified in the document. To prevent fraudulent alteration, the actual documents were sealed in clay cases which were inscribed with the same information. In case of a dispute, the judge would compare the writings of the two to see if they matched.[5]

Egyptian law, like the civilization itself, was highly developed. From the time of the Old Empire (3000–2500 B.C.), the administration of justice was centralized with judges being chosen from the aristocrats and from one of six great law courts, and later judges were also priests.[6] Some records of criminal trials still exist. For example, in 1100 B.C., during the reign of Ramses IX, bands of thieves were charged with robbing the tombs of the Pharaohs as well as those of private individuals for the gold and other valuables.[7] Although the death penalty existed, it was often commuted to penal servitude or slavery.[8]

In civil matters, the plaintiff proceeded first and presented his case while standing in front of a seated court (the practice followed today in federal courts). The defendant was then summoned to present an answer. After the court rendered its decision, both parties orally accepted the judgment of the tribunal.[9] The right of inheritance was primarily through maternal, rather than paternal, lines.[10] Egyptologists have located written contracts setting obligations of the parties.[11]

Hebrew law blended characteristics of both systems. It was based on the premise that law is of divine origin (the Ten Commandments, for example)—that is, that God is the source of all law. It advanced the legal theory of revenge—"an eye for an eye"—a theory later mitigated by the idea of forgiveness, which was advanced in the New Testament. Early Hebrew law was based on the Pentateuch (the first five books of the Old Testament, or the Mosaic Code) and the Talmud (a legal encyclopedia and collection of traditions which governs many aspects of Jewish life). Ancient Hebrew law provided for some 36 capital crimes, which were punished by beheading, strangling, burning, and stoning, depending on the nature of the crime. Imprisonment was not initially used as a form of punishment; instead, the usual corporal punishment was flagellation, or whipping. Slavery was the punishment for theft. The Hebrew system had two striking features: (1) There were no advocates or lawyers involved, and the witnesses were the accusers and prosecutors; and (2) all courts had more than one judge—3 at the lowest level, 23 at the next, and 71 at the highest court in Jerusalem.[12]

The Greeks also made major contributions to legal philosophy. The laws of Greece in the fourth and fifth centuries B.C. were flexible and could be tailored to fit the dispute when it was brought before the king, who relied on the gods for help in making his decisions. This individualization probably stemmed from the fact that Greek citizens could participate in government and were therefore influential.

Several prominent philosophers considered the role of law in society. For example, Draco felt that all crimes were equal and should be punished alike; it was the violation of the law, the act against society, that was critical, and not the harm to the individual. Plato and Aristotle struggled with the question of whether the required conduct was fair and just by nature or merely required by convention or legislative enactment. For them, law was primarily a method of maintaining the status quo and the social order.[13]

Following the Greeks, the Romans became the dominant force in the development of law. Cicero, noted Roman lawyer, furthered the idea of natural law, a single law or scheme of laws that governs the entire universe and to which all natural things conform. Inanimate objects were bound to such laws by natural necessity but people discerned the law of nature through reason, and all people were equal in their capacity to discern the natural law. Natural law was the foundation for all actual laws and customs; it was the supreme and permanent law to which all human order must conform if it was to have any truth or validity. The Church Fathers, early Christian writers from the first through seventh centuries, viewed this supreme law as the universal and eternal law of God, and St. Augustine, by criticizing the emperors who persecuted early Christians, indicated that states, not just individuals, could commit injustices when they transgressed against God's law. The idea that breaking a secular law was the same as sinning against God dominated European thinking in the Dark Ages and into the Middle Ages, times when the Catholic Church was the predominant unifying social institution.[14] However, by the thirteenth century, religion and morality were viewed as separate and apart from civil order and law. Secular law was given an autonomous role of its own, although canon law or church law continued to develop.[15]

Cicero also defined three elements of law: legislation, administrative edicts, and judicial reasoning on the basis of legal tradition. Today, these same three dominate U.S. law. *Roman law* was highly developed, and it had spread throughout the far reaches of present-day Europe under the empire's superb administrative system. Even after the fall of the western empire in 476, the eastern empire, led by the emperor at Constantinople, continued to develop the concepts of Roman law. In A.D. 528, the emperor Justinian collected the laws of the vast empire and published them as the Code of Justinian, or *Corpus Juris Civilis.* The authority and power of this collection are immense. Justinian's Code is a cornerstone of today's so-called *civil-law* systems. Much of the *canon law* developed by the Catholic Church reflects Justinian's Codes, and its precepts can be found in common-law countries as well. Although the Code essentially disappeared during the Middle Ages, it was revived during the twelfth century by professors at the Italian universities, especially at Bologna. This initiated the growth of new law and the system of legal science; however, the process was a long and complex one, spurred on by changes in both the political and commercial spheres that accompanied the revitalization of trade and the emergence of Europe from the Dark Ages.[16]

René David and John E. C. Brierley in their comparative study of legal systems and jurisprudence describe Romano-Germanic law or civil law as "a rule of conduct intimately linked to ideas of justice and morality."[17] Ascertaining and formulating these rules are primarily done by legal scholars in university settings rather than by courts and practitioners. In describing the civil law as the predominant legal system in the world, we are not speaking of a particular set of laws or statutes but instead of the methodology and philosophy used to resolve various legal issues. It is distinct from any set of local laws or the study of the actual laws governing property, venue, or inheritance. Although Swedish universities began teaching national law as early as 1620 at Uppsala, most European universities did not initiate national law courses until the eighteenth century: 1707 at Wittenberg, 1741 in Spain, 1758 at Oxford, and 1800 at Cambridge. Before that time, only Romano-Germanic and canon law were taught at the universities.[18] Law was studied not to provide the solution in a particular trial or to give students mastery of legal technique but rather to tell "judges how they should decide in justice."[19] The universities were not entrusted with application of the law but instead stated how the law was to be viewed and how knowledge of law might be attained.[20] The rules themselves were "woven from many strands: existing customs and practices, the customs of merchants, canon law, the revived Roman law, and, at a later stage, natural-law philosophies."[21]

Historically, Romano-Germanic law governs relationships among individuals rather than the relationship between individuals and government.[22] However, during the seventeenth and eighteenth centuries, the natural-law school, or movement, became the dominant paradigm at the universities. This school blended the idea of a universal, unchanging law, common for all time and for all nations, with the approach to legal reasoning establishing by the civil law. The two were not contradictory in the area of private law. The natural-law movement is noted for two major changes in the civil-law system. First, accompanied by transformations in the political and religious systems of the time, law too was modified to reflect the natural rights of persons and to guarantee the liberties of the individual.[23] Under traditional Roman law, the public law dealing with the relations between those who govern and those who are governed was left to persons other than jurists, but this was forever changed by the natural-law movement and the public law is now an integral part of the civil-law system.

Second, the natural-law school spurred extensive codifications, which led to the fusion of theoretical and practical law.[24] Justinian had not been the only ruler to order compilations of the laws. Various Germanic leaders also initiated written collections of various legal customs including the Salic Law, which was compiled under Clovis toward the end of the fifth century. These codes primarily concerned the amount of fines for various offenses and contained relatively few civil provisions, although the Salic Law did provide that no woman could inherit property. Women were not left without other protections, however; there were heavy fines for insulting women and the killing of a woman resulted in the most extreme penalties.[25]

From the fifth century forward, Europe depended increasingly on codes but it was not until the natural-law school that national codes achieved their preeminent status. In civil-law countries, the law is extensively codified, and decisions are based on the code as designed by the legislature, rather than on binding judicial precedent. The premise is that each case should be decided on its own merits within the parameters prescribed by the codes. "From the Anglo-American point of view, French legal reasoning appears to start with a highly generalized proposition of law to which the facts are then fitted, rather than to begin with a detailed examination of the facts followed by application of a narrowly formulated rule."[26] These systems employ an inquisitorial process of trial. The judge, rather than being a passive party, is an active participant in the trial. The judge's assigned task is to ascertain the truth, and the entire process revolves around him or her. The judge investigates the fact-gathering process. There are fewer technical rules of evidence and procedure, and trials are often rather informal, more closely resembling an administrative hearing than a full-blown trial. Judges, however, are rigidly bound by the Code and the description of their judicial duties, and conformity is required.[27] The same transactions and activities are governed or barred by the civil codes as by common-law jurisdictions; it is the approach taken in legal reasoning and methodology which distinguishes them. Generally, judges in these systems are specially trained for their role; they are not elevated from among practicing lawyers. In France, virtually anyone can give legal advice or prepare legal documents, but specialists must be hired for litigation and presentation of oral argument.[28]

Today, the civil-law tradition dominates in Europe, South America, Scotland, Quebec, and Louisiana. Many of the former French colonies of Northern Africa adapted much of the Napoleonic Code and grafted it onto tribal and customary law. The Napoleonic Code, adopted in 1804, provided a unified system of law for the country as a whole, replacing a system of localized laws. The 1896 Germanic Code was later adopted by Japan and by precommunist China. Thus, the widespread use of the civil system has extended far beyond the boundaries of Europe.[29]

Nearly 100 years after Justinian codified the Roman law, a new religion developed in the Middle East, the teachings of which have expanded into a major legal system with worldwide influence. "The sacred law of Islam is an all-embracing body of religious duties, the totality of Allah's commands that regulate the life of every Muslim in all its aspects. . . . Islamic law is the epitome of Islamic thought."[30] Before Islam, the law in the area for both the Bedouins and the sedentary populations was the law of the ancient Arabian tribal systems, and the pattern of adhering to tradition and precedent continues. Islam supplied a uniform system of laws, a system that was not limited by national boundaries but encompassed all of the followers of Allah. The schism among Muslim sects (which continues to this day) affected the interpretation of the law, but many of the basic precepts are adopted by all.[31] Modern nations in the Middle East often seek to synthesize Islamic laws and western legal systems. The religious law prevails with regard to family, inheritance, and criminal matters, while the western influence is frequently stronger in the area of commercial matters. The "most potent" western source is the Napoleonic Code, which is modified to meet the unique requirements of Islam.[32] One of the most obvious influences of Islamic law in the United States is the prisoners' rights cases in which incarcerated Black Muslims claimed the protection of the First Amendment's Free Exercise Clause.

Americans are known for their insular approach to many things, not the least of which is law. The English common law has so dominated our jurisprudence that we tend to overlook other systems; but that system was not created in a vacuum, nor was it the only highly developed one. For example, treatises describing the Chinese codes, which were developed as early as 220 B.C., are extant. In his work *Law and Society in Traditional China*, T'ung-Tsu Ch'u argues that Chinese society remained essentially static until the twentieth century, and that the prominent elements of the system—status by kinship and by social stratification—and the laws remained remarkably unaltered from the law codes of the Ch'in (221–207 B.C.) until this century.[33]

Today there are four dominant legal systems: the common-law systems (which will be discussed in the next section), the Romano-Germanic (civil) law systems, the socialist systems, and the religious systems such as Islamic,

Hindu, and Jewish.[34] The religious systems primarily emphasize the religious duties of the person regardless of nationality. However, they are nonetheless important because these religious precepts frequently supplement the national laws in regulating certain types of relationships, especially family and inheritance matters in the Far and Middle East.[35]

Socialist systems of law have three purposes: (1) to provide for national security; (2) to regulate economics on the basis of socialist principles; and (3) to educate the general population as well as any lawbreaker about the law.[36] The legal system of China exhibits the typical characteristics of the socialist systems. The Constitution establishes the People's Republic of China as a "socialist country under the people's democratic dictatorship and led by the proletariat on the basis of a worker-peasant alliance. Socialism is the political system of the country where all power belongs to the people."[37] Furthermore, the Constitution provides that the state's economic system is one of "socialist public ownership," that is, one of collective and national ownership of the means of production, although private enterprise is now an important component of the economic reforms.[38]

The basis of the law is legislation as in the Romano-Germanic system.[39] The National People's Congress (NPC) is the sole authority for the creation of laws and regulations as well as the enforcement and adjudication of such; there is no doctrine of separation of powers.[40] The NPC and its Standing Committee alone have the right to enact and revise basic statutes and laws, although local ordinances may be created within the provinces, municipalities, and autonomous regions. However, all power and authority stem from the NPC.[41] The primary purpose of the judiciary is to maintain social order and to reduce criminality through the principle of prevention first. The goal is to "mobilize all citizens in an effort to eliminate the root causes of the crime and eliminate the social and economic causes within the environment which creates it."[42] Criminal penalties stress ideological reform through education and productive labor.[43] One interesting aspect of Chinese criminal law is that confessions are to be discounted. It is the role of the court to investigate, to seek the truth from the facts, and to apply the law.[44]

To maintain social order, the Chinese rely very heavily on programs disseminating basic legal knowledge to the public at all levels of the educational system from elementary schools through universities and through a variety of other programs such as those at workplaces and at various locations. Because China was a feudal state for thousands of years, many citizens lack basic familiarity with the law and a legal system; therefore, intensive efforts by the state have been mounted to overcome this unfamiliarity.[45] However, one aspect of prior Chinese jurisprudence that has been maintained and incorporated into the socialist system is mediation. "From the time of antiquity, the common people have formed the habit of asking prestigious persons to mediate settlements in clans, villages, and neighborhoods."[46] This tradition has been systematized with local mediation committees elected by the people with the goal of allowing the "quarreling parties to treat each other in a spirit of mutual understanding and accommodation, so as to solve misunderstanding."[47] This tradition of mediation is becoming more important in the West with courts in the United States following the pattern of requiring mediation between litigants before conducting full-blown court proceedings.

The dramatic change of the last few years with the dissolution of the Union of Soviet Socialist Republics and the changing political and economic realms of the former Eastern Bloc countries is requiring the transformation of the legal systems within each of these states.[48] Basic notions of authority, legitimacy, property, individual and commercial relationships, and procedures must be rethought and reconceptualized. Many elements of the Romano-Germanic civil-law system are already embedded in the jurisprudence of the former communist countries, and most legal commentators expect the emerging systems to encompass even more of the traditions of these systems.[49]

Each of these systems or branches of law derives from common origins, and each system serves the same purposes. They cannot be wholly separated from one another in tracing the sources and effects, nor should they be, especially in today's global community and economy.

THE ENGLISH HERITAGE

Development of the common law.   During the Dark Ages following the collapse of the Roman Empire, anarchy and confusion predominated. No one source of authority had the might to enforce order. Any restraints on antisocial behavior developed within tribes or within local areas, and most conflicts were resolved by violence. As society emerged from that period, the demand for order increased, and the primary source was the Roman civil law, especially Justinian's Code. In England, however, the pattern was broken. The earliest extant code of that country was a succinct collection of laws created by Æthelbert, Christian King of Kentings, about A.D. 600. These laws essentially set the fines for injury to the person or property of another. For example, if an ear was cut off, the fine was 12 shillings; if the ear was pierced, the fine was 3 shillings; and if hearing was lost, the fine was 25 shillings. There was no provision relating to commercial transactions and very little relating to other relationships; however, a widow who had borne a living child was entitled to receive one-half of her husband's estate. A woman who left her husband with her children could have half the goods, while if the husband kept the children, she was entitled to a share of the goods equal to a child's share.[50]

This Code was expanded by Canute, who ruled England, Norway, and Denmark, from 1017 to 1035, and whose laws were written in English.[51] The Danes had conquered not only England but also northern France (which came to be known as Normandy), sections of Ireland and Scotland, and the Orkney, Shetland, and Hebrides islands. Their legacy included a type of grand-jury proceeding, property transactions in which land could freely be bought and sold, and flourishing borough institutions.[52] The word *law* itself is Norse, not English.[53]

By the early twelfth century, Anglo-Saxon England differed from other European realms in that there was an organized system of justice. The country was divided into vills, or townships, a number of which composed the hundred, while several hundreds formed the shire. The administration of justice was primarily local. There were public courts at both the hundred and shire levels, and there were courts headed by the lord of the manor, who resolved disputes among his own tenants.

Court procedure was fairly uniform. Each party appeared in court. The plaintiff would allege the improper activity in the form of an oath, and the defendant would enter a denial in the form of an oath. Generally, the defendant would then present a requisite number of character witnesses (frequently 12) who would swear that the defendant was telling the truth; these witnesses did not testify as to the facts of the case, but merely as to the veracity of the defendant. The communities were small, and all the trial participants were known to each other. Those who swore falsely were subject not only to distrust from their peers, but also to punishment imposed by God.

In criminal cases, 12 freemen served as the accusers before the court and presented the names of those they believed to have committed crimes. Guilt or innocence would then be proven either by compurgation (the process, just described, of clearing a person by oaths of others as to his veracity) or by ordeal. Trial by ordeal frequently involved burning a person's hand or arm, binding the wound, and examining it after a short period. If the wound was clean, the accused was cleared of the crime. Another creative method of trial was to toss a bound person into a stream. If he sank, he was innocent; if he floated, he was guilty. Either result was quite unfortunate. The Anglo-Saxons also employed fines or a system of reparation for those found guilty. They used the system even for homicides; each person's life had a value, set according to his or her station, with the king's being the most valuable. The *wergild*, the fine, was divided among the king for the loss of a subject, the lord for the loss of a vassal, and the deceased's family. The Normans added the possibility of trial by combat, wherein one could either compete for oneself or hire a champion to engage in battle. Although the methods were crude, these courts provided a forum for grievances to be heard.

The Normans greatly strengthened the administrative organization of the country and tightened the control of the government in the hands of the monarch. In addition, feudalism, which had just begun to flourish in England, became the dominant social order. William the Conqueror assumed ownership of land for himself as monarch, but he allowed his followers dominion over great tracts of it in exchange for certain services and goods, including military service or agricultural products. In turn, William's tenants subdivided the land and responsibilities until they had established an entire chain of reciprocal duties, reaching from the monarch to the lowliest serf.

William also maintained his own tribunal, the King's Court, both for the protection of royal interests and as an appellate court for those litigants who could travel to the royal court; however, the vast majority of cases were resolved in the hundred or shire courts or in the seignorial courts of the barons. It was a time of establishing new patterns in resolving conflicts, of turning from self-help methods of revenge to a quasi-formal means of adjudication; nevertheless, much of Anglo-Saxon law and customs continued relatively unchanged. William and his successors did not overturn the laws that they found, but instead supplemented them with a strong centralized judiciary and uniformity of decisions.

Henry II, the first Plantagenet, who ruled from 1154 until 1189, had a major influence on the development of English law and the centralization of the judicial system. His goals were two: The first was to ensure that the fees paid by litigants flowed into the royal coffers and not to the barons, and the second was to consolidate royal control. Crimes became wrongs against the king as well as against the individual, and more serious criminal matters came before the Curia Regis, an advisory body of the king's counselors who carried out judicial, executive, and administrative functions. Juries were employed in trial, supplanting the older systems of trial by compurgation, ordeal, and combat.

Henry II bolstered his control over local courts by vigorously applying the royal executive writ, which directed his subjects to perform or to refrain from certain actions; failure to obey the writ could result in punishment. A writ might very well order judges of the shire, hundred, or seignorial courts to find for a particular plaintiff, a usurpation of authority which contributed to the demise of the local courts. In addition, Henry II revived the practice, instituted by Henry I, of sending judges from the Curia Regis into the countryside to settle disputes, although their primary task was revenue collection. It was Edward I who, by the Statute of Westminster in 1285, institutionalized the practice of sending itinerant judges on circuits to render justice.

As these changes were occurring, other developments were also taking place. By the end of the thirteenth century, there were three law courts in the secular realm and a firmly entrenched system of ecclesiastical courts. The latter enforced canon law as handed down by the Catholic Church and had sole jurisdiction over matters of marital relationships and inheritance. The canon law was composed of papal decrees, writings of church scholars, and Scripture; it was heavily influenced by Italian law and by the training that the priests received in the traditions of Roman law. The domination of the ecclesiastical courts over marriages lasted until the mid-nineteenth century, although the Catholic Church was supplanted by the Church of England.

The three law courts were distinguished by function, although their jurisdictions often overlapped. The Court of Common Pleas, located in London, dealt with disputes that were essentially civil in nature. The Court of the King's Bench was mobile; it initially followed the king on his journeys across the countryside. It exercised appellate jurisdiction over the Court of Common Pleas and over matters, including criminal matters, involving the king. The third court, the Exchequer, dealt primarily with matters of revenue and taxation.

The outcome of the monarchs' centralization of the judicial system is the rejection of the civil-law tradition in England and the substitution of the common law. Strong kings who consolidated judicial power in their own hands, and who imposed a uniform system of tribunals over the entire country rather than allowing the local courts to remain viable, contributed mightily to the development of the common law, often termed *judge-made law*. Due to the paucity of statutes, the judges formalized the customs and mores of the times into court decisions and applied the same rules in whatever corner of the realm they happened to be. Consistency was facilitated by written reports of judicial decisions kept by the king's courts, collected by such authors as Henry of Bracton, and used as authority or precedent by subsequent judges.[54] Common law "describes that part of the law that is enacted, non-statutory, that is common to the whole land and to all Englishmen."[55] It became the basis for the legal systems of the English-speaking nations of the world.

Development of equity. The business of government in England during the thirteenth century was carried out by two governmental departments: the Exchequer, which handled fiscal matters, and the Chancery, which was the secretarial department. The Chancery was headed by an official called a chancellor, usually a cleric, who was responsible for handling the government's paperwork, including the writs for courts. The writs served three purposes: (1) as the document giving the plaintiff access to the courts in exchange for the payment of a fee; (2) as a method of designating which court would decide the case; and (3) as a tool for directing the sheriff to summon the defendant for the court appearance. The Chancery eventually developed standard writs for various legal wrongs, but by statute (the second Statute of Westminster in 1285) the Chancery was empowered to "let a writ be made by those learned in the law so that for the future it shall not befall that the court shall delay over-long in doing justice to complaints."[56]

Although the common-law courts were initially creative and flexible, they soon petrified, adopting rigid, harsh procedures. In addition, the courts could provide only one remedy—damages. The reservoir of justice remained the king, who was God's secular representative on earth. In those situations in which the remedy provided by the common-law courts was inadequate, or when the plaintiffs were impoverished and could not afford the court fees (or their opponents were influential and wealthy), the complainants petitioned the king to consider their causes. The king, in turn, transferred to the chancellor the laborious task of reading the numerous petitions, and soon the petitions were filed directly with the Chancery rather than with the monarch. But the plea remained the same: "to do what is right for the love of God and in the way of charity."[57] Remember that the chancellors were ecclesiastics who were trained in Roman and canon law, with its foundation of natural law. The appeal was to the conscience of the chancellor and a higher system of justice.[58] If the chancellor agreed with the petition, the defendant would be ordered to appear before the chancellor to respond to the allegations. At that time, the defendant would be placed under oath and questioned by the chancellor, who determined questions of both law and fact and then shaped a remedy.

It is for the formation of extraordinary relief that the Chancery achieved its greatest fame in jurisprudence. As pointed out earlier, the sole remedy in common-law courts was monetary damages; however, that is not always an adequate solution. Suppose that there is a building of substantial historic significance in your community, but over the years it has deteriorated; now the new owner of the property is determined to tear it down. The payment of monetary damages will neither reconstruct the building nor pay the community for the loss of a symbol of its past. Preservationists would seek an injunction to prevent the destruction of the building. The *injunction,* a court order directing a person to refrain from carrying out certain acts, could halt demolition of the building. If the property owner defied the injunction, he or she would be subject to certain legal penalties, such as fines and possibly even a jail sentence. The injunction is an example of the remedies created by the courts of *equity;* the common-law courts, on the other hand, as originally structured, would not intervene and would wait until the injury had occurred to award damages—a patent absurdity. Other equitable remedies included specific performance and trusts, both of which will be discussed in later chapters. The result of the chancellor's activities was to forge parallel court systems, each with different remedies.

Thus, for some 400 years, England had two types of courts—the historic common-law courts and the more flexible courts of equity; in the late nineteenth century, the two were merged, and all courts were to apply the rules of both, with equity being dominant in case of conflict. The remedies fashioned by the English jurists during these centuries are basically the same as those used by courts today. The remedies provided for particular types of legal wrongs are discussed in connection with particular theories, but it is appropriate to describe the traditional forms of redress here also. Judges, whether in common-law or equity courts, adhered to the principle that "for every wrong there is a remedy," and they struggled to create the forms of judicial relief available today.

One approach to the study of remedies is to examine them from the perspective of both the plaintiff and the defendant. A court may award specific relief and substitutionary relief to a successful plaintiff. *Specific relief*, such as an injunction or an order for the defendant to perform his or her portion of a contract, is an equitable remedy and is directed to individuals and their activities. It has limited application and is not always the most appropriate nor the most desirable remedy. *Substitutionary relief*, the basic common-law remedy, generally refers to the award of money as compensation for a loss. The losing defendant may be imprisoned (for contempt of court, as an example), required to pay either compensatory or punitive damages or to transfer property to the plaintiff, or required to perform or to refrain from some act.

A second approach is to identify the type of legal wrong and the related remedial goals. Tort law deals with injuries sustained by individuals and with their lawsuits against those who injure them. There are three general remedial goals in tort law: restoration to the status quo, compensation or indemnification, and punishment. For example, assume that there has been an automobile accident with injuries sustained by the drivers and property damage to the cars. The repair work done to the vehicles to remove the dents and replace the headlights is an example of restoration to the status quo, or to the preaccident condition. The money paid to the injured party for his or her hospital bills and lost wages illustrates the principle of compensation or indemnification, whereby the party is reimbursed for pecuniary losses stemming from the accident. A money award may be assessed by the jury to punish the wrongdoer for egregious acts, such as driving while intoxicated and injuring a child. In contrast, the goals of contract remedies include the following: (1) putting the party in the position he or she would have been in if the contract had been fulfilled; (2) restoring the parties to their original positions; (3) compensating the plaintiff for any detriment incurred in reliance on the contract (such as a painter purchasing paint in expectation of the homeowner fulfilling his portion of the contract); and (4) punishing the party breaching the contract. Obviously, some of the goals are similar in both areas (restoration of the plaintiff to his or her original position and punishment of the wrongdoer), but other remedies are tailored to rectify specific legal wrongs.[59]

Equity provided the flexibility to tailor remedies to situations in which the legal remedies were not adequate. It added a sense of a fairness, of an appeal to the conscience of the purveyors of justice, which greatly strengthened the system. Frederick Maitland, one of the greatest English legal scholars and a noted expert on equity, described its place in jurisprudence:

> [W]e ought to think of equity as supplementary law, a sort of appendix added on to our code, or a sort of gloss written round our code, an appendix, a gloss. . . . The language which equity held to law, if we may personify the two, was not "No, that is not so, you make a mistake, your rule is an absurd, an obsolete one"; but "Yes, of course that is so, but it is not the whole truth." . . . We ought not to think of common law and equity as of two rival systems. Equity

was not a self-sufficient system, at every point it presupposed the existence of common law. Common law was a self-sufficient system. . . .

[I] do not think that any one has expounded or ever will expound equity as a single, consistent system, an articulate body of law. It is a collection of appendixes between which there is no very close connexion. If we suppose all our law put into a systematic order, we shall find that some chapters of it have been copiously glossed by equity, while others are quite free from equitable glosses.[60]

THE AMERICAN EXPERIENCE

The colonists who moved to the New World brought with them the legal traditions of their homelands. Vestiges of each system—Dutch, English, French, and Spanish—can be found in the laws of the various states.

History of a system of law is largely a history of borrowings of legal materials from other legal systems and of assimilation of materials from outside the law. In the history of Anglo-American law there are successive borrowings and adaptations from Roman law (e.g. the rules as to title by occupation), from the canon law (e.g., our law and practice as to marriage and divorce and probate and administration), from the modern Roman law and Continental codes (e.g., in our law of riparian rights), and from the commercial law of Continental Europe . . . [61]

The dominant scheme was the common-law system of England. Formalistic in tenor and designed to deal with a highly structured society, it was inadequate for the demands of the colonists. They tempered the system and forged new precepts that more accurately reflected the social and economic realities of the New World. One hallmark of the new system was the merger of law and equity, and the power of a single judge to render both types of remedies in the appropriate cases (as opposed to the English scheme of parallel court systems). A second characteristic of the new system was the abolition of the common-law power of judges to define crimes, and the substitution of the legislature as the body to identify criminal activity and to determine the appropriate range of punishment. In the new land, there was increased emphasis on the individual, because of both the religious beliefs and the need to be self-sufficient in opening up new territory. The colonists adopted those portions of the common law that were appropriate and modified others, and each colony developed innovative approaches to conflict resolution. In sum, there was no abandonment of important principles or abrupt break with the English system, although adjustments were made to suit the new environment.

Those who formed the Constitution struck out anew free of previous shackles in an effort to obtain a better order of government more congenial to human liberty and welfare. It cannot be seriously claimed that they intended to adopt the common law wholesale. They accepted those portions of it which were adapted to this country and conformed to the ideals of its citizens and rejected the remainder. In truth there was widespread hostility to the common law in general and profound opposition to its adoption into our jurisprudence from the commencement of the Revolutionary War until long after the Constitution was ratified.[62]

To illustrate the adaptation process, consider the incorporation of established elements of citizens' rights against government into the fundamental laws of the United States. The Magna Carta, signed by King John in 1215 and regarded as one of the most important documents in the history of the English-speaking world, constituted formal recognition by the monarch of certain rights held by citizens. It contains several provisions that were adopted into the U.S. Constitution. For example, the section of the Magna Carta that stated that there should be no criminal "trial upon . . . simple accusation without producing credible witnesses to the truth therein" was the foundation of the rights guaranteed to criminal defendants in the Fifth and Sixth Amendments. Similarly, Section 39, which provided that "no freeman shall be taken, imprisoned or disseised, or outlawed, or banished, or in any other way destroyed, nor will we go upon him, nor send upon him, except by legal judgment of his peers or the law of the land," was the basis of the constitutional provisions preventing deprivation of life, liberty, or property without due process of law. Other basic guarantees found in the English Bill of Rights of 1689, such as the ones preventing the suspension of laws without the consent of Parliament and protecting the freedom of speech which "ought not to be impeached or questioned," were wholly adopted by the writers of the U.S. Constitution. Fundamental liberties available to the English were identified and guaranteed to the former colonists, but the influence of the English pattern extends to both substantive and procedural laws as well.

Following the Revolution, legislatures representing the will of the sovereign people came to supplant judges as the primary lawmakers. This was due, in part, to several factors. First, the absolute governments in Europe had been successfully challenged by legislative bodies, as indicated by the victory of Parliament and Oliver Cromwell over the absolute monarchs in the English Revolution of 1688. Second, these entities represented the will of the sovereign people to have a democratic and representative government. Third, the Founding Fathers were familiar with the law on the Continent, with its strong tradition of the legislature as absolute lawgiver; in addition, English law and the king's judges were in some disrepute in this nation following the Revolution. Fourth, the legislature was the dominant branch of government during these formative days. Fifth, the Constitution of the United States, unlike that of Great Britain, carefully prescribes the responsibilities of each governmental branch; however, judges retain the option to approve new theories of recovery and to demand new procedures in accordance with their assigned constitutional duties.[63]

In addition, the legislatures began in the early 1800s to codify the various statutes within the states. Unfortunately, legislatures pass laws in a haphazard order and amend them at later dates, again with no particular attention paid to organization. The purpose of the codification movement in the United States was to collect the related statutes and arrange them coherently in order to facilitate their use. Although some advocates anticipated that these codes would be used as the continental codes were, that has not been the result; instead, courts retained much of their power to determine the constitutionality of the codes, and judges still rely more on precedent than on the code provisions. Today's practitioners, laypersons, and judges routinely use codes, such as the Internal Revenue Code or the Penal Code, but they use them primarily as references or collections of statutes; the interpretation of the statutes is left to the judicial and administrative branches. Some of the codes are merely reenactments of judicially established rules, such as the various codes of criminal or civil procedures and the Uniform Commerical Code. Both the uniform laws that are adopted by individual states and the Restatements (standard compilations of laws in various substantive areas) have contributed to the consistency of laws within a nation composed of 51 sovereign entities invested with the power to make law.

Nevertheless, judges remain the most potent and powerful component of the American legal systems. It is they who work daily with the law and who give it a unique twist to fit the situations confronting the courts. The reliance of judges on precedent and the doctrine of *stare decisis* remains as strong and viable as it was in the day of Henry II. **Stare decisis** refers to the policy of courts to follow the rules laid down in previous judicial decisions and to refrain from disturbing established points of law. The purpose is to ensure stability and certainty in the legal system. Litigants are aware of the results in similar prior cases and make their decisions in regard to the lawsuit accordingly; *stare decisis* enhances predictability. Judges are entrusted with great power and authority, not only in deciding specific cases but also as lawgivers.

THE AMERICAN LEGAL PROFESSION

As will be discussed in Chapter 3 on court organization, most American judges—although not all—are practicing attorneys at the time they assume the bench. Americans have a love–hate relationship with lawyers. On the one hand, lawyers are highly regarded and respected; on the other, many citizens share the feelings of Plato, Shakespeare, and others who have launched scathing attacks on the legal profession and its practitioners. For instance,

King Ferdinand of Spain commented that, on the colonization of the West Indies, "no lawyers should be carried along, lest lawsuits should become ordinary occurrences in the New World."[64] Americans both appreciate and resent lawyers' specialized knowledge and the power that information carries.

Most lawyers in the United States today have at least a baccalaureate degree in addition to three years of law school. They must also be licensed by the state in which they practice and by the federal courts in which they try cases. This was not historically true. Attorneys lacked formal legal education; instead, they trained as apprentices by "reading" law with established practitioners. In fact, reading the learned treatises about the law, especially William Blackstone's *Commentaries on the Laws of England*, was the major method of legal education. Few reports of court cases were available, and Blackstone's comprehensive restatement of the law served as the principal collection for students for many years. His work was eventually supplemented by American scholarly writings, published reports of court cases, and formal legal training.

Modern legal education centers around universities, as has always been the case in civil-law countries. The usual educational model is for students to read cases, extract the general principles, and then submit to classroom interrogation by professors. Law classes rarely involve lectures; instead, they are conducted along the lines recommended by Socrates—that is, a continuous series of challenging questions to be answered by the students. The students are to apply to hypothetical situations the reasoning and rules of law they have abstracted from assigned cases. The procedure resembles that used by a judge in examining the pertinent precedent and applying it to the case at bar.

This format enables students to think in terms of plaintiffs and defendants and to consider only those facts relevant to the guiding principle of the case. It is an impersonal analysis. It obscures the reality that the cases involve real people with real injuries, a fact which has been frequently criticized. In his book *Persons and Masks of the Law,* John T. Noonan examines the treatment of one of the most famous of all tort cases, *Palsgraf* v. *Long Island Railroad Company.* In part, his purpose is to challenge impersonal, detached treatment and to advance the argument that scholars and lawyers "should be concerned with law not as a set of technical skills which may be put to any use but as a human activity affecting both those acting and those enduring their action."[65] The facts of the *Palsgraf* case, as described in the opinion, were that a railroad passenger carrying some fireworks was jostled by railroad employees who were trying to assist him. The passenger dropped the fireworks, which exploded, and the shock of the explosion knocked down some scales, which struck and injured the plaintiff. She sued the railroad company.

For law students, this meager description raises the question of whether the railroad should be held liable for damages since neither it nor its employees directly caused the injury. For Noonan, the description of the facts obscures as much as it reveals. The opinion does reveal that the plaintiff is a woman, but it says nothing about "her age, marital status, maternal responsibilities, employment or income. What injuries she had suffered, whether she had been almost decapitated or whether she had been mildly bruised . . . What compensation she had sought or what compensation she had been awarded."[66] (As an aside, Mrs. Palsgraf, age 43, had three children, two of whom were with her at the time of the accident. She was a janitor in the apartment building in which she lived and earned about $8 a week. She was struck on the arm, hip, and thigh, but the lingering effect was a stammer, which her physicians attributed to the trauma of the accident. She was awarded $6,000 from a company with assets valued at $1,700,000 in 1924, the year in which the accident occurred. In addition, the railroad industry had a dismal safety record, with 6,617 people killed and 143,739 injured that year.[67])

Interesting though these parenthetical facts might be, they are irrelevant to the law student because they do not add to the understanding of the legal principles of the case. Both the ability to sort through the various accounts in order to reduce the event to its barest legal bones and the resulting detachment are valued skills for most lawyers. They actively pursue detachment from the parties and their misery. The reason advanced is that the advocate must be able to accurately assess the situation and choose the appropriate legal tactics, a task hampered by the involvement of emotions. Yet Noonan challenges the accuracy of that premise:

> Focusing on the rules, [the professors] instilled in students a sense that the legal system was not the creature of individual caprice or the expression of raw power, but tradition constantly refined by reason. . . . Their purpose, as is mine, was to increase the sense of responsibility of those who by their thought and action make the system exist. But, for me, the responsibility comes in the response to other persons.[68]

Litigants, who are emotionally involved with their lawsuits and usually care passionately about the outcomes, often have difficulty dealing with the impersonality of their attorneys and of the legal system, and might very well agree with Noonan. They seek revenge or justification and are frustrated with their advocates' lack of involvement. Watching the opposing lawyers talking and laughing together in the halls during breaks, they suspect collusion. Laypersons not familiar with courthouse proceedings fail to recognize the norms that bind the court personnel. "Courts are not an occasional assemblage of strangers who resolve a particular conflict and then dissolve, never to work together again. Courts are permanent organizations."[69] The judge, clerk, court reporter, and bailiff are a fairly static group. Attorneys work together and oppose each other on a fairly regular basis. Thus, group norms promote the establishment of friendly relations among the work-group participants.

These same norms characterize every legal system. In the United States, the bench and bar are closely connected, not only as officers of the court but also by training. In the United States, as contrasted with continental nations, there is no specialized track for those who aspire to judicial positions; nor are there formal divisions between those who argue cases in court and those who do not, such as is found in France and Great Britain. The English distinguish between barristers, who are courtroom advocates, and solicitors, who are general practitioners who do not appear in higher courts. Barristers are specialists who seldom have the right of direct access to the lay client and whose referrals come from solicitors. Each of the branches is governed by professional organizations—the Law Society for solicitors and the four Inns of Court for barristers—which control membership and the discipline of its members. Again, the group is essentially closed, tied together by professional norms and education.

Bar associations at the local, state, and national levels help unify the legal profession in the United States. The American Bar Association (ABA), a voluntary organization, is generally dominated by the more conservative elements of the bar and plays an active role in the selection of federal judges, especially Supreme Court justices. State bar associations may be integrated; that is, all practitioners of law within the state must belong to the association. Integrated bars often govern the conduct of the lawyers within the state; otherwise, a state commission or court will consider grievances against lawyers. The Code of Professional Responsibility, a code of ethics, governs the professional behavior of attorneys. Violation of the Code may lead to reprimands, temporary suspensions, or permanent disbarment of erring lawyers, depending on the severity of the breach.

Lawyers are both cursed and praised. They are criticized for their detachment and applauded for their honed analytical skills. They are reviled for feeding upon the sorrows of others and acclaimed for representing the downtrodden of our society. They are denounced as too powerful and too influential in government, but they are frequently elected to office. The bar is not a monolithic group, however. The members represent a wide spectrum of political philosophies and interests, as indicated by the varying approaches to their profession and its practice.

CONCLUSION

The American legal system is a hodgepodge of borrowed principles and homegrown theories. An adaptable system, it changes to meet the needs of the times. Its origins can be traced through 4,000 tumultuous years, and it owes an indelible debt of gratitude to the lawmakers (and lawbreakers) who have gone before. It represents the sometimes controversial efforts of society to provide justice and fair treatment in the resolution of conflicts and in the prescription of appropriate behavior.

NOTES

1. Oliver Wendell Holmes, Jr., *The Common Law* (Boston: Little, Brown, 1881), p. 1.

2. Robert W. Ferguson and Allen N. Stokke, *Concepts of Criminal Law* (Boston: Holbrook Press, 1976), p. 26.

3. Nels M. Bailkey, ed., *Readings in Ancient History,* 2nd ed. (Lexington, MA: D. C. Heath and Co., 1976), p. 32.

4. Ibid., pp. 28–35.

5. A. Leo Oppenheim, *Ancient Mesopotamia* (Chicago: University of Chicago Press, 1964), pp. 280–282.

6. Adolf Erman, *Life in Ancient Egypt,* trans. H. M. Tirard (reprint, New York: Benjamin Blom, 1969), p. 87.

7. Ibid., pp. 130–137.

8. Ferguson and Stokke, p. 29.

9. Erman, pp. 140–141.

10. Ibid., p. 156.

11. Ibid., pp. 145–147.

12. Walter M. Chandler, *The Trial of Jesus From a Lawyer's Standpoint* (Norcross, GA.: The Harrison Co., 1976), pp. 35–87.

13. Ferguson and Stokke, p. 29.

14. William Seal Carpenter, *Foundations of Modern Jurisprudence* (New York: Appleton-Century-Crofts, Inc., 1958), pp. 29–35.

15. René David and John E. C. Brierley, *Major Legal Systems in the World Today* (London: Free Press, 1968), p. 27.

16. Arthur T. von Mehren, "The Civil Law System: An Historical Introduction," in John Honnold, ed., *The Life of the Law* (London: Free Press, 1964), pp. 486–493.

17. David and Brierley, *Major Legal Systems,* p. 14.

18. Ibid., p. 30.

19. Ibid., p. 29.

20. Ibid., p. 39.

21. von Mehren, "The Civil Law System," p. 489.

22. David and Brierley, *Major Legal Systems,* p. 14.

23. Ibid., p. 35.

24. Ibid., p. 48.

25. Carpenter, *Modern Jurisprudence,* pp. 91–98.

26. René David and Henry D. deVries, "French Legal Tradition," in John Honnold, ed., *The Life of the Law* (London: Free Press, 1964), p. 520.

27. Stephen Landsman, *Readings in Adversarial Justice: The American Approach to Adjudication* (St. Paul, Minn.: West Publishing Co., 1988), pp. 38–39.

28. David and deVries, pp. 519–525.

29. Rudolf B. Schlesinger, "The Code Systems," in John Honnold, ed., *The Life of the Law* (London: Free Press, 1964), pp. 494–509.

30. Joseph Schacht, *An Introduction to Islamic Law* (Oxford: Clarendon Press, 1964), p. 1.

31. Ibid., pp. 1–99.

32. Schlesinger, pp. 506–507.

33. T'ung-Tsu Ch'u, *Law and Society in Traditional China* (Paris: Mouton & Co., 1965).

34. David and Brierley, *Major Legal Systems*, pp. 14–20.

35. Ibid., p. 19.

36. Stephen Vago, *Law and Society*, 4th ed. (Englewood Cliffs, NJ: Prentice Hall, 1994), p. 11.

37. Du Xichuan and Zhang Lingyuan, *China's Legal System* (Beijing, China: New World Press, 1990), p. 214.

38. Ibid., p. 216.

39. David and Brierley, *Major Legal Systems*, p. 18.

40. Xichuan and Lingyuan, *China's Legal System*, p. 30.

41. Ibid., p. 32.

42. Ibid., p. 81.

43. Ibid., p. 105.

44. Ibid., p. 107.

45. Ibid., p. 146.

46. Ibid., p. 200.

47. Ibid.

48. Ruby Kless Sondock and J. W. Looney, "Change in the Soviet Legal System: A Nation of Laws?" *Texas Bar Journal*, 52, no. 6 (June 1989), pp. 650–653.

49. Vago, *Law and Society*, pp. 11–12.

50. F. L. Attenborough, ed., *The Laws of the Earliest English Kings* (New York: Russell & Russell, Inc. 1963), pp. 2–17.

51. F. W. Maitland, "History of English Law," in Helen M. Cam, comp., *Selected Historical Essays of F. W. Maitland* (Cambridge: Cambridge University Press, 1957), pp. 97–98.

52. Theodore F. T. Plunkett, *A Concise History of the Common Law*, 5th ed. (Boston: Little, Brown, and Co., 1956), pp. 9–10.

53. *Webster's New International Dictionary of the English Language*, 2nd ed. (Springfield, MA: G. & C. Merriam, 1937), p. 1401.

54. C. Gordon Post, *An Introduction to the Law* (Englewood Cliffs, N.J.: Prentice-Hall, 1963), pp. 18–61.

55. F. W. Maitland, *Equity: A Course in Lectures*, rev. by John Brunyate, (Cambridge: The University Press, 1969), p. 2.

56. Post, p. 40.

57. Maitland, *Equity*, p. 5.

58. S. F. C. Milsom, *Historical Foundations of the Common Law* (London: Butterworths, 1969), pp. 74–87.

59. Kenneth H. York and John A. Bauman, *Cases and Materials on Remedies*, 2nd ed. (St. Paul, Minn.: West Publishing Company, 1973), pp. 1–10.

60. Maitland, *Equity*, pp. 18–19.

61. Roscoe Pound, *The Formative Era of American Law* (Boston: Little, Brown, 1938), pp. 94–95.

62. *Green v. United States*, 356 U.S. 165 (1958) at 212.

63. Pound, pp. 52–79.

64. Chandler, p. 62.

65. John T. Noonan, *Persons and Masks of the Law* (New York: Farrar, Straus & Giroux, 1976), p. xi.

66. Ibid., p. 113.

67. Ibid., pp. 113–139.

68. Ibid., p. xi.

69. James Eisenstein and Herbert Jacob, *Felony Justice: An Organizational Analysis of Criminal Courts* (Boston: Little, Brown, 1977), p. 20.

3

Court
Organization

Court organization in the United States is complicated by our federal form of government. Instead of a single, unified court system such as exists in Great Britain or France, the United States actually has 51 court systems—the federal courts and the courts of the 50 individual states. This situation results in two very different consequences for the American legal system. First, Congress and the state legislatures are free to organize their respective court systems to meet their own needs. The results are that not only is the federal court structure different from those in the states, but there is also tremendous diversity among the individual states. A trial court might be called a district court in one state, a superior court in another, and a supreme court in yet another. Most states have a single supreme court; two states, Oklahoma and Texas, have two courts of last resort—one for civil appeals and one for criminal appeals. Such diversity makes it difficult to generalize about the "typical" state court system.

A second consequence of our federal form of government is its impact on substantive and procedural law. As will be noted in Chapter 7, each state is free to determine for itself what behavior is forbidden, and each is free to establish reasonable punishment for defined crimes. Consequently, two states may have entirely different definitions of the same criminal act and two entirely different penalties for it. Likewise, in the case of civil law, different states may have different grounds for divorce. For example, for many years Nevada had a liberal divorce law, which prompted many people from outside the state to establish residency in Nevada so that they could obtain a "quickie" divorce. When other states began to liberalize their own divorce laws, it became unnecessary for people to travel to Nevada. Federalism also impacts the role of precedent in the law. Since each state's substantive law is unique to that state, it follows that interpretations of state laws by state judges will also be unique. What is true for substantive law is also true for procedural law. Although rulings of the U.S. Supreme Court have tended to make criminal procedural law more uniform throughout the country, rules of civil procedure may vary slightly from state to state. As a result, a lawyer trained in the law of one state sometimes finds it necessary, upon moving to another state, to seek additional training in the substantive and procedural law of the new state. Indeed, many states require lawyers from other states to pass their own bar exams even though they were licensed to practice in their home states.

Such problems notwithstanding, this chapter will try to describe court organization in the United States. Since any attempt to describe all 50 state systems would be tedious and repetitious, no such attempt will be made. Although there are enough similarities among state court systems to allow some generalization, the reader should keep in mind that each state's system is truly unique. Since the federal court system offers a relatively simple introduction to court structure, we will begin with it and will return to state systems later in the chapter.

THE FEDERAL COURT SYSTEM

The federal court system is characterized by two types of courts: constitutional and legislative. *Constitutional courts* are sometimes referred to as *Article III courts* because they are created under Article III of the Constitution, which authorizes Congress to "ordain and establish" courts inferior to the Supreme Court.[1] The Constitution also states that judges of both the supreme and inferior courts "shall hold their Offices during good Behaviour,"[2] which is tantamount to a lifetime appointment, subject to removal only through the impeachment process. Finally, Congress may not reduce the salaries of constitutional court judges "during their Continuance in Office."[3] U.S. district courts, U.S. courts of appeal, and the U.S. Supreme Court are examples of constitutional courts.

Legislative courts are also created by Congress, pursuant to one of its other legislative powers. For example, Article I empowers Congress to make all laws ". . . for organizing, arming, and disciplining the Militia."[4] Under that authority, Congress may establish military tribunals for the purpose of disciplining soldiers. Similarly, Article IV empowers Congress to make rules and regulations for U.S. territories.[5] The judges who serve in the legislative courts do not have lifetime appointments, nor are their salaries protected as are those of Article III judges. However, all federal judges are appointed by the president, subject to confirmation by the Senate. While it should be noted that these and other differences[6] between constitutional and legislative courts exist, the line is not always a clear one. For example, in 1956 Congress changed the status of the U.S. Customs Court from a legislative to a constitutional court.[7] Ultimately, Congress determines the status of federal courts. Let us now proceed to discuss each of the two types of federal courts separately.

Constitutional courts.   Constitutional courts may be classified as either courts of general or specialized *jurisdiction*. Article III of the Constitution establishes federal jurisdiction over certain parties to a case and over certain subjects. For example, the federal judicial power extends "to all Cases affecting Ambassadors, other public Ministers and Consuls" and "to Controversies between two or more States."[8] Thus, if a foreign ambassador is a party to a case, federal courts have jurisdiction regardless of the subject matter of the case. Similarly, Article III gives federal courts jurisdiction over "Cases of admiralty and maritime Jurisdiction."[9] Consequently, if the subject matter of the case is admiralty or maritime, the federal courts have jurisdiction regardless of who the parties are. Finally, Article III states that "The judicial Power shall extend to all Cases, in Law and Equity, arising under this Constitution, the Laws of the United States, and Treaties made, or which shall be made, under their Authority."[10] This means that if a case raises what is called a federal question—an interpretation of the Constitution, a federal statute, or a U.S. treaty—federal courts may hear the case. Generally speaking, it is a constitutional court of general jurisdiction that will hear these kinds of cases.

As previously noted, under its delegated powers Congress may make uniform laws on the subject of bankruptcies,[11] may lay and collect taxes, and may impose duties on goods coming into the United States.[12] Because of the specialized subject matter of some areas of the law, Congress has created specialized courts with jurisdiction limited to specialized subject matter; these are the constitutional courts of specialized jurisdiction. Since most readers will be more familiar with the courts of general jurisdiction, we will begin our discussion of constitutional courts with them.

The federal courts of general jurisdiction are organized in three tiers, or levels. The first tier consists of the U.S. district courts. When Congress first created the lower federal courts in 1789, it merely created one for each state, or 13 federal district courts. As the nation grew, it became apparent that some states needed more than one federal court, so Congress created new ones while maintaining the tradition that district courts should not cross state lines.[13] Today there are 89 federal district courts in the 50 states and one each in the District of Columbia, Guam, the Virgin Islands, the Northern Mariana Islands, and Puerto Rico for a total of 94 federal district courts. States that have more than one federal district court use geographical designations to distinguish among them. For example, a court may be named the U.S. District Court for Eastern Kentucky to distinguish it from the U.S. District Court for Western Kentucky. The number of federal judges assigned to each federal district varies. The U.S. District Court for Eastern Oklahoma has 1.33 judgeships[14] assigned to it, while the Southern District of New York has 28 judgeships authorized. It is common for each major city within the federal district to have at least one judge assigned to it. In all, Congress has authorized 649 permanent federal district court judges in the United States,[15] although in recent years there has been an unusually large number of vacancies in the federal courts. For example, there were 118 vacancies on all federal courts as of January 1, 1994.[16]

In addition to federal judges, each district has a number of retired judges, called senior judges, who hear cases on a part-time basis. As of 1993 there were 242 senior judges at the district court level and 326 bankruptcy judges.[17] Finally, there were 389 full-time and 110 part-time magistrate judges as of 1994.[18] Magistrate judges issue search and arrest warrants and handle arraignments and preliminary hearings for the federal courts.

The U.S. district courts, which are the main trial courts for the United States, have both criminal and civil jurisdiction. When our Constitution came into existence, the states already had fully functioning state court systems, and opponents of the Constitution feared that the newly created federal courts would supplant state courts. To alleviate this concern, the judicial power of the federal courts was limited so that most legal controversies would continue to be settled by state courts. In 1993, for example, only 276,636 civil and criminal cases were filed in U.S. district courts,[19] compared with over 100 million cases filed in state courts in 1990.[20] Nearly 17 percent of the federal cases filed in 1993 were criminal cases, while the remaining cases were civil rights, labor, Social Security, tort, or contract cases. About 23 percent of the federal civil cases filed in 1993 were *diversity of citizenship suits.*[21] Because the Framers of the Constitution believed that state courts would favor their own citizens over citizens of another state, federal courts were given jurisdiction over cases involving citizens of different states. In 1995, legislation entitled the Federal Courts Improvement Act was introduced which, if passed, will raise from $50,000 to $75,000 the amount needed for the diversity suit and will index the amount to the rate of inflation.[22]

U.S. district courts function like other trial courts in the country: A single judge presides, and a jury hears the evidence. Federal courts have their own unique rules of evidence, but evidence is submitted and a verdict is reached in the same manner as in state trial courts. Federal courts are no better or worse than state courts in many ways; they are just different because of the different jurisdiction, organization, and procedures. Nor are state courts necessarily inferior to federal courts. Unless a case raises a federal question or otherwise falls within the jurisdiction of the federal courts, the decisions of state courts are not reviewable by federal courts. Indeed, federal judges are required to respect the interpretations of state laws by state courts if there is not a federal question raised.

The second tier of federal courts with general appellate jurisdiction consists of the U.S. courts of appeals. There are currently 13 permanent U.S. courts of appeals. Eleven of the courts of appeals are designated by number. For example, the U.S. Court of Appeals for the Fifth Circuit includes Texas, Louisiana, and Mississippi, and any appeal from one of the nine district courts of those states is heard by it. The twelfth court of appeals, the U.S. Court of Appeals for the District of Columbia, mainly hears appeals from federal regulatory agencies such as the Federal Trade Commission (FTC). The thirteenth court of appeals is the U.S. Court of Appeals for the Federal Circuit, which hears cases from the Merit Systems Protection Board and Patent and Trademark Office and similar federal agencies. Finally, in 1971 Congress created the Temporary Emergency Court of Appeals. This "temporary" court of appeals heard all appeals from district courts arising under Section 4(e) of the Economic Stabilization Act of 1971, the Emergency Petroleum Allocation Act of 1973, the Energy Policy and Conservation Act of 1975, and the Emergency Natural Gas Act of 1977. In April 1993 Congress finally abolished the Temporary Emergency Court of Appeals and transferred its few remaining cases to the U.S. Court of Appeals for the Federal Circuit.[23]

Since U.S. courts of appeals hear only cases on appeal from U.S. district courts or federal regulatory agencies, they naturally have the same substantive jurisdiction. In 1993 a total of 50,244 cases was filed in the federal courts of appeal, of which nearly 24 percent were criminal cases and another 25 percent were prisoner petitions from persons already incarcerated.[24]

The number of appeals court judges total 168, with the number of judges assigned to individual circuits varying from 6 for the First Circuit to 28 for the Ninth Circuit.[25] Normally appeals are heard by groups of three judges, called *panels.* When an appeal reaches the court, three judges are assigned to hear it, and the decision of a majority decides the case. Occasionally, the court of appeals will decide to hear a case *en banc,* which simply means that all of the judges assigned to that circuit will hear the case.[26] In a majority of federal cases, the court of appeals is the last stop. For a variety of reasons, including time, money, and the unlikely chance of Supreme Court review, the parties will abandon their fight, resulting in the decision of the court of appeals being the final one.

The third and highest tier is, of course, the U.S. Supreme Court, consisting of the Chief Justice of the United States and eight associate justices. Unlike the other federal courts discussed in this chapter, the Supreme Court was created by the Constitution. However, the Constitution is silent about the number of justices and other aspects of the Court's organization. For example, the first Supreme Court had only six members, and right after the Civil War it had ten members. In 1869 Congress set the number at nine, where it remains today. President Franklin D. Roosevelt's famous courtpacking attempt in 1937 has been the only really serious attempt to alter the Court's membership since 1869. Roosevelt tried to expand the number of justices to as many as fifteen, but the attempt failed. It appears that the number will remain at nine for some time to come.

As previously noted, Congress has created some constitutional courts that have specialized jurisdiction. Among these are the U.S. Court of International Trade and the Court of Appeals for the Federal Circuit. The Court of International Trade was created by Congress in 1980 to be the successor of the old U.S. Customs Court. Its jurisdiction covers disputes over goods imported into and exported out of the United States. Such disputes include controversies over the admissibility of goods and the duties owed on them.[27] A second specialized constitutional court is the U.S. Court of Appeals for the Federal Circuit, created in 1981. This court was given jurisdiction which formerly belonged to the U.S. Court of Custom and Patent Appeals. It also hears appeals from the Court of International Trade, the Patent and Trademark Office, the Merit System Protection Board, and the U.S. Claims Court.[28] Other courts of questionable constitutional status are the Rail Reorganization Court, the Foreign Intelligence Surveillance Court, and the Foreign Surveillance Court of Review. These last three courts use federal judges borrowed from other federal courts.[29]

It should be apparent by now that the federal court system is a hodgepodge of courts created by Congress in a piecemeal fashion to deal with cases arising under federal jurisdiction. As two noted experts on the federal court system have observed, ". . . the distinction between a constitutional and a legislative court is of the type that would have delighted those meticulous medieval scholastics who argued about how many angels would fit on the head of a pin."[30] With that caveat in mind, we now turn our attention to the legislative, or Article I, courts.

Legislative courts. As discussed earlier, Article I courts are created by Congress to implement one of its legislative powers. Although confusion exists about the exact status of some federal courts, two major distinctions generally differentiate legislative courts from constitutional courts. First, judges of legislative courts do not have lifetime appointments, but instead serve fixed terms of office. The length of the term designated by Congress is often a long one in order to ensure judicial independence, but it is a fixed term nonetheless. The second distinction is that a legislative court judge's salary is not protected, as in the case of constitutional court judges. The Constitution stipulates that the compensation of Article III judges "shall not be diminished during their Continuance in Office."[31] Congress has recently tried to clarify the status of individual federal courts by designating whether they are to be legislative or constitutional, but, as we have seen, it has not been entirely successful.

Three courts that bridge the legislative–constitutional court gap are the U.S. District Courts in three American territories: Guam, the Virgin Islands, and the Northern Marianas.[32] These three courts hear the same kinds of cases heard in regular federal district courts, but they also hear cases involving local laws.[33] This would be analogous to a single court being authorized to hear cases involving both state and federal law. Congress governs the territories of the United States under Article IV of the Constitution and may make laws for them much the same as a state legislature does for a state. The judges on these courts do not enjoy life tenure, but serve four- to eight-year terms.[34]

Another example of a legislative court is the U.S. Claims Court (formerly the U.S. Court of Claims), which has jurisdiction over claims against the U.S. government involving alleged violations of public contracts.[35] These claims arise because the federal government does business with thousands of private businesses and contractors. Any dispute over the terms of government contracts is handled by this court. The U.S. Tax Court, created by Congress in 1924, is also a legislative court. It consists of 19 judges who serve 15-year terms. Although the U.S. Claims Court and the regular district courts also have jurisdiction over tax cases, the Tax Court is the only court the taxpayer can appeal to before the payment of the disputed tax. In the Claims Court and in district courts, the taxpayer must first pay the tax and then try to recover it later.[36] Finally, bankruptcy-court judges serve as adjuncts to the district courts. Until 1978, bankruptcy-court judges served six-year terms and were appointed by the district court judge. In 1978 Congress lengthened their terms to 14 years and made them presidential appointees. When the Bankruptcy Reform Act of 1978 was declared unconstitutional by the Supreme Court,[37] Congress passed new legislation retaining the 14-year term but leaving the selection of bankruptcy judges to the courts of appeals.[38]

The newest legislative court is the Court of Veteran Appeals signed into law by President Ronald Reagan in November 1988. This seven-judge court hears appeals from the Board of Veterans Appeals. An appeal from the Court of Veteran Appeals may be taken to the Court of Appeals for the Federal Circuit.[39]

The final legislative court is the U.S. Court of Military Appeals. This court consists of three civilian judges who are appointed for 15-year, staggered terms. As its name implies, the Court of Military Appeals reviews the decisions of courts martial. Its caseload consists mainly of cases involving military personnel discharged for bad conduct or sentenced to prison under the Uniform Code of Military Justice. In most instances the decisions of the Court of Military Appeals are not reviewable by the Supreme Court. The exceptions are cases in which there is a question about the jurisdiction of the military court over the defendant and cases involving military personnel in non–service-related offenses.[40]

In conclusion, the federal court system is composed of courts created by

Congress under either its Article I or Article III powers. The federal courts are not "superior" to state courts; rather, they exist alongside state courts. The vast majority of cases are tried in state courts, and it follows that they will resolve many important cases. Nevertheless, the federal courts remain an alternative forum that citizens can turn to for relief if state courts prove unresponsive. It is no surprise to discover that southern African-Americans preferred to file their civil rights cases in federal rather than state courts, since southern judges were notoriously unsympathetic to African-American claims. It is quite possible that, with the appointment of conservatives to the federal bench by Presidents Reagan and Bush, African-Americans may begin to press their claims in state courts. Despite the confusion caused by federalism, a dual court system provides additional guarantees that justice will eventually prevail.

STATE COURT SYSTEMS

As we have noted, there is no "typical" state court system because federalism allows each state to adopt a court system fitted to its individual needs. Consequently, the most that can be done is to describe state courts in general, without being too specific about any particular state's courts. The following section describes the structure and jurisdiction of courts that are found in some form or fashion in each of the 50 states.

Courts of limited jurisdiction. All state courts have had their jurisdiction limited in some way. The jurisdiction of any court comes from the state constitution or from statutes passed by the state legislature, or both. Some state constitutions spell out the jurisdiction of the courts in great detail, while others leave the details of court jurisdiction to the discretion of the legislature. In either case, courts are dependent upon others for the source of their jurisdiction. Similarly, the organization and number of state courts will also be determined by the constitution or by state statutes. Courts of limited jurisdiction, as their name implies, are created to handle cases of a limited or specialized nature. In this section we will examine some of the more common courts of limited jurisdiction found in the states.

One of the most common courts of limited jurisdiction is the municipal court. Municipal courts are often, although not always, limited to minor offenses or misdemeanors. Municipal courts are often referred to as "traffic courts" because their main function is to hear cases involving traffic violations within the city limits. Municipal courts frequently have jurisdiction over cases involving violations of city ordinances. Cities possess *ordinance power*—that is, the power to enact laws enforceable within the city limits. Such laws include prohibitions against discharging firearms, burning trash, and letting animals run loose within the city limits. Persons who receive traffic citations or citations for other offenses may have their cases heard in municipal court.

The phrase "You can't fight city hall" must have been coined by someone after an experience in municipal court. Typically, the defendant's cause is a lost one. That is because it is usually the defendant's word against the word of the arresting officer, and judges tend to believe the latter. That is also why most people simply pay the fine and save themselves the trouble of going to court even if they believe themselves to be innocent. Those who do choose to fight a ticket often discover that municipal court is not what they expected. First, attorneys are infrequently used in municipal court because their fees often exceed the fine. The defendant normally opts to "tell it to the judge" in his or her own words without benefit of counsel. A second difference is that there is often no jury. Although some states give the defendant the right to a jury trial, most of the matters that come before a municipal court are relatively trivial, and most defendants prefer a bench trial, in which the judge decides the outcome. A third, and somewhat surprising, difference is that in some cases the judge may not even be a lawyer. Although many municipal court judges are lawyers, some states allow city officials, such as the mayor, to double as municipal court judge, especially in small towns. Finally, although appeals are allowed, like jury trials, they do not occur very often. Again, considering the fine involved, the time and trouble associated with an appeal are seldom worth the effort. If the average citizen ever encounters a courtroom situation as a party to a case, however, it is quite likely to be in a municipal court.

A second common type of court of limited jurisdiction is the justice of the peace court. JP courts, as they are commonly called, have a variety of functions, not all of which are judicial in nature. Justices of the peace in some states are still permitted to perform marriages, and in some states they serve as coroner in cases in which foul play is suspected in someone's death. Most justices of the peace also have minor administrative duties, such as preparing the court's yearly budget and hiring court personnel.

JP courts usually have both criminal and civil jurisdiction. Their criminal jurisdiction extends to misdemeanor offenses that occur within the limits of their geographic boundaries. Crimes such as petty larceny and simple battery are the kinds that are most likely to be tried in JP court. Most states limit the amount of punishment a JP court can hand out. For example, a JP court's criminal jurisdiction may be limited to offenses in which the maximum penalty is six months in the county jail or a $500 fine. In addition to hearing trials, justices of the peace often conduct arraignments for persons accused of more serious crimes.

The civil jurisdiction of a JP court is limited to small monetary amounts—$2,000, for example. That is, the amount involved in the lawsuit cannot exceed $2,000 if the JP court is to have jurisdiction. This is why JP courts are frequently called *small claims courts.* Although lawyers are allowed to appear in JP courts in most states, the litigants often just represent themselves and let the judge decide the case without a jury. The popular television show "The People's Court" did much to familiarize the general public with the operation of small claims court.

As can be seen, the kinds of cases handled by the typical JP court are more varied than those of a municipal court. However, many states still do not require justices of the peace to be licensed attorneys, a common criticism of the JP system. The JP system is a holdover from an era when people believed that anyone with a little common sense could fairly apply the law in simple cases. Whether that remains true today is debatable. However, justices of the peace, through strong and effective lobbying of state legislatures, have retained their essential functions and character despite repeated attempts to reorganize them out of existence. It appears that the office, though accused of being antiquated, will be with us for some time to come.

A third category of courts of limited jurisdiction includes county courts. Like municipal courts, which are limited to exercising their jurisdiction within city limits, county courts' jurisdiction is limited to county lines. County courts typically have a greater expanse of jurisdiction than either municipal or JP courts. In criminal cases, for example, county courts may have jurisdiction over offenses with penalties as great as one year in prison and relatively high fines. For civil cases, the amount in controversy may be as high as several thousand dollars. County courts may also function as courts of appeal for lower courts of limited jurisdiction. County courts are frequently *courts of record* (which means that a transcript is made of the proceedings), whereas municipal and JP courts usually are not. When an appeal is made to a county court from a lower court, it is not an "appeal" in the usual sense of the word. In actuality, since no record exists in the lower court, the county court conducts a *trial de novo*. A *trial de novo* is, in effect, an entirely new trial, or a trial from the beginning.

Like other judges in courts of limited jurisdiction, the judges of county courts are not required to be licensed attorneys in some states. However, states that have attempted to modernize their judicial systems are requiring judges at all levels to have law degrees. Many states retain the tradition of the county judge as the political leader of the county. In such states, county judges are as much administrative officials as judicial ones. A county judge may be responsible for duties such as budget preparation and the county welfare system. County judges probate wills, take responsibility for wards of the county, commit persons to mental institutions, and serve as juvenile court judges in some states. It is at this level that we see a fusion of judicial, executive, and legislative functions that is not as evident at the national level, with its stricter adherence to the system of separation of powers. For this reason, characterizing the office of county judge as a purely judicial one is misleading.

Courts of general jurisdiction. A second level of courts in most state judicial systems consists of courts of general jurisdiction. A court of general jurisdiction has the power to hear any case that falls within the general judicial power of the state. That is, a court of general jurisdiction has the authority to render a verdict in any case capable of judicial resolution under the constitution and laws of the state. Cases involving the state's criminal laws, civil code, or state constitution fall within the judicial power of the state. Laws regulating marriage, corporations, real estate, insurance, and education are just a few of the categories of law within the state's authority. It will be recalled that the Framers of the Constitution intended that most lawsuits would fall within the judicial power of the states, thus ensuring the continued importance of state courts.

Courts of general jurisdiction are the major trial courts of the state. As noted in the chapter's introduction, they may be called superior courts, district courts, circuit courts, or, as in the case of New York, supreme courts. For the sake of simplicity, we will refer to this type of court as a district court. Despite the general nature of the district court's jurisdiction, they too are limited by geography. The state legislature typically divides the state into well-defined and numbered judicial districts that have definite boundaries. These boundaries may coincide with county lines, consist of several counties, or even overlap and disregard county lines. Although most judicial districts will have only a single judge assigned to each, others will be multijudge districts. Finally, the boundaries of the districts may overlap, in which case two or more judges will exercise concurrent jurisdiction over suits. In these instances, the judges may agree to specialize by allowing one judge to hear exclusively criminal cases while the other hears only civil cases. Such informal specialization is common in large metropolitan areas because of the workload faced by urban courts.

Courts of general jurisdiction have both criminal and civil jurisdiction but may, as just noted, specialize out of necessity. Some judges may prefer to handle divorces, while others concentrate on juvenile cases. The criminal jurisdiction of these courts includes felony offenses. Most states adhere to the definition of a felony as any offense for which the penalty exceeds one year of imprisonment or imprisonment at the state penitentiary as opposed to a county jail. Felony cases, then, include more serious crimes, such as burglary and murder. The civil jurisdiction of district courts has no upper limit as to the amount in controversy. Lawsuits may run into the millions or hundreds of millions of dollars. The kinds of cases range from the typical divorce case to multimillion dollar tort or breach of contract cases. This point illustrates again the importance of state courts: When the stakes are high, state courts do not play second fiddle to federal courts. The operation of trial courts will be examined more closely in Chapter 4.

Appellate courts.   All states have some kind of appeals mechanism available for litigants who were unsuccessful at the trial-court level. Most states have created an intermediate appeals court between the trial courts and the state's highest court of appeal. Like the U.S. courts of appeals, the purpose of intermediate appeals courts is to guarantee the litigants the right to at least one appeal while preventing the state's highest court from having to hear "routine" appeals. The intermediate appellate courts screen out the routine cases so that only the most important cases reach the state's highest court. However, this screening process does not mean that intermediate appellate courts are totally lacking in discretion in selecting cases. Like all appellate courts, intermediate courts of appeals are limited to deciding questions of laws raised during the trial, decide cases in panels or *en banc*, and rely upon written decisions in making their rulings.

Every state has a ***court of last resort,*** usually called the state supreme court.[41] As the name implies, a court of last resort is a litigant's last chance to have his or her case decided favorably once the case has exhausted all other appellate avenues. Most states have a single court of last resort which handles both civil and criminal appeals, but two states, Oklahoma and Texas, have two courts of last resort. In Texas, for example, the state supreme court hears only civil cases, while criminal cases are handled by the Court of Criminal Appeals. Many states have chosen to pattern their state's highest court after the U.S. Supreme Court in the number of justices, procedures, and so forth. But, as we have seen, states have shown considerable independence in creating their court systems, and state supreme courts should not be viewed as merely "little Supreme Courts."

The duties of state supreme courts are identical to those of other appellate courts except that their decisions are final unless an appeal is made to the U.S. Supreme Court. As previously noted, when a state's highest court makes a ruling involving the interpretation of the state constitution, a state statute, or a precedent in an earlier state case, that ruling is final. The exception is when the case raises a federal question; such a matter may be taken to the U.S. Supreme Court. Another duty of state supreme courts includes ruling on opinions of the state's attorney general. Some states permit the attorney general to make preliminary interpretations of state laws, which are binding unless overturned by a state court. Finally, state supreme court justices, especially the chief justice, are often given additional duties by the state. For example, the state's chief justice is usually given the task of presiding over impeachment trials. In addition, other justices may have to serve on various state boards or commissions dealing with the judiciary. A common practice is to have several supreme court justices serve on the state's judicial conduct board.

The coexistence of state and federal court systems adds an element of complexity not present in nations without federalism. Nevertheless, it is the possibility that each state may approach court organization in its own unique fashion that makes federalism an attractive form of government. There is much to criticize about state courts. There are too many judges and courts, delays in coming to trial are too long, the procedures are antiquated and overly complex, and so forth. Lawyers, like most of us, are loath to change a system with which they have become familiar, and judges see plans to unify, modernize, or reorganize the court structure as threats to their power and prestige. But change does come, albeit slowly, to court systems, just as it does to all areas of the law. As in most cases, those with patience will eventually prevail.

JUDICIAL SELECTION

Once when New York Yankee manager Casey Stengel was reminiscing about his own career as a major league ballplayer, Mickey Mantle expressed surprise that Stengel had once been a major leaguer. Stengel reportedly replied, "Do you think I was born 60 years old and manager of the New York Yankees?" Although this story may be apocryphal, it does serve to remind us that judges are not born judges at any age. The selection of judges at both the state and federal level is a complex and political process. The selection method as well as the criteria for selection will have much to do with the kinds of persons chosen for the bench. The selection process is not only political, but also highly partisan and heavily influenced by the organized bar. In this section we will examine in detail the selection of federal judges of the three major constitutional courts and then describe the process used to select judges in the states.

Selection of federal judges.   The selection of federal judges is a deceptively simple process: The Constitution authorizes the president to nominate Supreme Court justices with the consent of the Senate, and Congress has extended the practice by statute to other federal judges. Surprisingly, there are no constitutional or legal qualifications for appointment to the federal bench. Theoretically, the president could appoint anyone reading this book to a federal judgeship as long as the Senate concurs. In reality, of course, there are informal qualifications to be met, and each president may add to or subtract from the list of qualifications. A general qualification is that the nominee be a lawyer, preferably a graduate of one of the nation's prestigious law schools. The nominee need not have previous judicial experience, but some presidents prefer that their nominees do have prior experience on a state court. Some presidents require a certain number of years of legal experience, a minimum or maximum age limit, and even a clean bill of health before they will consider a person for nomination.

Although most presidents are loath to admit it, they also consider such factors as sex, race, religion, ethnicity, and even geography when choosing nominees. Despite protests that he was seeking the most qualified person for the job, President Richard Nixon in 1970 consciously tried to place a southerner on the Supreme Court. When his two southern nominees, Clement Haynesworth and G. Harrold Carswell, were rejected by the Senate, Nixon nominated Harry Blackmun of Minnesota to fill the vacancy. President Jimmy Carter promised to and did nominate qualified African-Americans and women to the federal bench. Even partisan politics come into play, as evidenced by the fact that approximately 90 percent of all federal judges belong to the same political party as the president who appointed them.

Finally, a president may require some general ideological qualifications of his nominees. For example, it is no secret that President Ronald Reagan chose to appoint only persons of conservative ideology to the federal bench.[42] The extent to which a president weighs professional competence, past judicial experience, age, ideology, and partisanship will vary with each president. A president normally determines the general criteria for his nominees and then allows the other significant actors in the process, such as the attorney general and the deputy attorney general, to recruit candidates who conform to his standards. Just how the process of choosing particular individuals occurs will be discussed later in this chapter. At this point it is preferable to have a general overview of the entire selection process.

Once a nominee for the federal bench has been determined, the Federal Bureau of Investigation (FBI) is called upon to do a background check. In the past, FBI background investigations were conducted only on the nominee actually selected. Since the Nixon administration, however, background checks have been run on all serious contenders.[43] The purpose of the background check is to ensure that there is nothing in the candidate's background that might prove embarrassing to the president. It would not do if the president's nominee turned out to be a spouse abuser or to have a history of drunken driving. Even past and present political and social affiliations are checked out; membership in a racially segregated club, a restrictive covenant in a property deed, or some ill-considered remarks in a speech may come back to haunt a candidate for the federal bench. Even thorough investigations can fall short of the mark, as evidenced by President Ronald Reagan's withdrawal of the nomination of Douglas H. Ginsburg to the Supreme Court. Ginsburg's admission that he used illegal drugs in his younger days embarrassed Reagan, who was known for his antidrug stance.

The next step, the rating of the nominee's qualifications by the ABA, is not a part of the formal selection process. The ABA has created the Committee on the Federal Judiciary to serve as a kind of watchdog over the federal judiciary. The Committee is composed of prominent attorneys from each of the federal circuits. Their job is to review the qualifications of the president's nominee according to "judicial temperament, age, trial experience, character, and intelligence."[44] Once evaluated, the nominee is rated "exceptionally well-qualified," "well-qualified," "qualified," or "not qualified." Although every president would like all of his nominees to receive the highest rating, the weight given to the ABA rating will depend on the individual president. During the Eisenhower administration, for example, the president refused to appoint anyone rated "not qualified." This, in effect, gave the ABA a virtual veto over nominations to the federal bench. President Nixon followed a similar policy early in his administration, but later began to submit his nominees' names to the ABA only after he had announced them publicly.[45] Other presidents, notably Kennedy and Johnson, have given less weight to ABA ratings by proceeding with the nominations of persons even rated "not qualified." The influence of the ABA seems to have waned in recent years, as evidenced by the fact that President Reagan failed to consult with the Committee when he nominated Sandra Day O'Connor to the Supreme Court.[46]

After the various clearances have taken place, the nominee's name is formally submitted to the Senate Judiciary Committee for confirmation hearings. The Judiciary Committee handles judicial nominations in much the same way as it handles regular legislation within its jurisdiction. That is, formal hearings are held on the nomination and testimony is taken. The nominee is "invited" to testify, of course, but it is really a command performance. In general, the Committee hearings are fairly routine. If a nominee for district judge who has the blessing of his home state's senators is being considered, most of the members of the Judiciary Committee are not interested in the nomination. After all, if the nominee is incompetent, the damage will be confined to a single federal district court in someone else's home state. As we shall see, however, nominees for the courts of appeals and the Supreme Court are subject to much greater scrutiny.

If the nominee, regardless of the court level, is noncontroversial, the witnesses before the Committee are usually a parade of supporters who have come to sing the praises of the nominee. On the other hand, a nominee who is controversial because of past judicial decisions, public statements, or political philosophy may come under fire from interest groups. Interest-group opposition, especially when the Supreme Court is involved, can be intense. Civil rights groups, women's groups, labor organizations, pro- and antiabortion groups all may wish to testify for or against the nominee. Coalitions of interest groups did successfully defeat the Carswell and Haynesworth nominations of President Nixon in the early 1970s and President Reagan's nomination of Robert Bork in 1987. Interest groups may uncover information about the nominee's background that was overlooked or ignored by the FBI and the ABA. Interest-group activity, even if ineffective, serves to remind us of the political nature of the judicial selection process.

In recent years, there has been growing concern about the role of the Senate Judiciary Committee in the selection process especially at the Supreme Court level. As mentioned, interest groups opposed to Robert Bork successfully defeated his nomination, although by all accounts he was well qualified to serve on the Supreme Court. Critics allege that Bork was subjected to stricter and harsher scrutiny regarding his views of the Constitution than had previous nominees appearing before the Senate Judiciary Committee. However, one study of 23 Supreme Court nomination hearings indicates that Bork's experience was not unique.[47] The researchers classified questions of the Senate Judiciary Committee members as either "character," "competence," or "constitutional philosophy" questions. The study discovered that in 15 of the 23 hearings, questions concerning the constitutional views of the nominee exceeded 75 percent of the questions asked and in eight hearings the percentage exceeded 80 percent. The researchers also found that in the three nomination hearings immediately following Bork's (Anthony Kennedy, David Souter, and Clarence Thomas) the percentage of constitutional philosophy questions exceeded 75 percent of the questions asked.[48] Paul A. Freund and Stephen Carter argue in separate articles that nominees to the Court historically have been required to defend their constitutional views before the Senate.[49]

Finally, after all the testimony has been given and all the witnesses heard, the Judiciary Committee votes to recommend approval or rejection of the nomination to the full Senate. If the nomination is approved by the Committee, approval by the Senate is almost assured. Very little, if any, debate takes place unless the nominee is controversial. A vote is taken, and if it is approved by a simple majority, the nominee is confirmed. Upon being sworn in, the president's nominee is a federal judge for life.

Although the process of FBI investigation, ABA scrutiny, Judiciary Committee hearings, and Senate confirmation is the same for the appointment of all federal judges, the process by which the selection is narrowed from a large pool of candidates to a single individual differs according to the level of federal court involved. Selection of district court judges is heavily influenced by state politics and the state's U.S. senators. Selection of court of appeals and Supreme Court judges tends to be influenced more by the president and national politics. We shall examine the selection process at each level and compare all three.

There is an old saying that a federal judge is just a lawyer who knows a president. At the district-court level, however, it is more accurate to say that a federal judge is a lawyer who knows a U.S. senator. That is because at the district-court level, the selection process is heavily influenced by the state's senators. It will be recalled that the boundaries of U.S. district courts are entirely within the boundaries of a single state. U.S. senators have traditionally felt that the appointment of federal officials within their states should be their prerogative; that is, the president should clear any federal appointment in a state with the senators of the president's party. This tradition is known as *senatorial courtesy.* Should a president attempt to nominate someone to the federal bench without the senator's blessing, the senator in question would merely ask his or her colleagues in the Senate to defeat the nomination and, except under unusual circumstances, the Senate would reject the president's nominee. In the past, a senator merely had to state that the president's nominee was "personally obnoxious" to him, and that was sufficient justification. Today, senators are expected to provide more substantive grounds for invoking senatorial courtesy.[50]

Because of senatorial courtesy, the actual selection process works like this: Let us assume that there is a Republican president in the White House. When a vacancy occurs on the federal bench, the attorney general will contact the Republican senators concerned for input into the selection. If there is only one Republican senator, the choice of a nominee is essentially made by him or her. In some cases the senator may have in mind a specific candidate who generally meets the president's criteria for nomination. In such a case, if the person is not totally objectionable to the president (and in some cases even if he is), the president will nominate the senator's candidate. Senators often use federal judgeships to reward political supporters in their home states for past political support. Another possibility is that the senator may have several qualified candidates for the position but is reluctant to alienate the others by actively promoting one over the others. In that case the senator may merely send a list of acceptable candidates to the attorney general and let the president make the final choice. This removes the onus from the senator of offending the persons not selected. A variation of this approach is for the senator to establish his own merit-selection process. The senator may ask a committee of judges, lawyers, law professors, and the like to screen the applicants and select the person best qualified. This approach also takes the pressure off the senator who does not want to offend his or her supporters. Finally, a senator may choose to stay out of the process by allowing the president to make the choice. The senator would merely retain the option of exercising a veto over the final choice in the event that the president selects a Democrat or someone from a rival faction of the party. This latter strategy keeps the senator from being obligated to the president.

If there are two Republican senators in the state, both might be consulted and asked to agree on a single candidate. What is more likely to happen, however, is that one senator will fill the current vacancy and the other senator will get to fill the next one, alternating the choice between the two senators. If the state has no Republican senators, the attorney general may consult with state Republican officials, party leaders, or Republican members of the House of Representatives. Under these circumstances, the president is freer to choose whomever he pleases for the judgeship. Finally, in some unusual circumstances, a strong Democratic supporter of the president might be consulted as a courtesy, especially if that senator's vote may be needed on a crucial upcoming vote in the Senate. Generally speaking, however, the selection of district court judges is a partisan process left to the party faithful.

The selection of persons to fill vacancies on the courts of appeals is less sensitive to the pressures of senatorial courtesy than is selection at the district court level for two reasons. First, the federal circuits consist of several states, unlike district courts, which are located entirely within a single state. Since, by tradition, the president is free to nominate anyone from the circuit, no single senator can claim the appointment as a personal prerogative. Custom dictates that court of appeals judgeships be fairly evenly divided among the states within the circuit so that all of the judges do not come from the same state. For example, if a judge from Texas retires from the Fifth U.S. Court of Appeals, the expectation is that another Texan will be named to the bench and that the state's senators will be consulted if they belong to the president's party. However, the senators from Texas are not in a position to force a particular candidate on the president, as they are at the district-court level. If they try to "muscle" the president with the threat of senatorial courtesy, he can merely nominate a candidate from either Louisiana or Mississippi, the two other states in the Fifth Circuit. Still, the president may need the support of the senators from Texas and may therefore allow them considerable influence over the nomination.

A second reason for the decreased influence of senatorial courtesy at the court-of-appeals level is the perception that these positions are more important than district-court judgeships. A district-court judge's influence is confined to a single state or part of a state. If a district-court judge is lazy, incompetent, or corrupt, the damage is limited to one court. However, the decisions of appeals-court judges serve as precedents for every district court in the circuit. Because only a small fraction of federal cases move on to the Supreme Court, the decisions of the courts of appeals are often final. The decisions of a court of appeals may never be reviewed or overturned by the Supreme Court, so the precedents set by them are the law within that circuit. Consequently, more emphasis is placed on the professional competence of candidates for the courts of appeals. For these reasons, politics is not allowed to play as great a role as in the selection of federal district judges.

Senatorial courtesy is virtually nonexistent where the nomination of a Supreme Court justice is involved. This does not mean, of course, that a president may totally disregard the Senate when making a nomination. Historically, around 20 percent of the presidents' nominees have been rejected by the Senate, which indicates that its members do not take their obligation to give "advice and consent" lightly. A Supreme Court justice is in a position to influence public policy in America for many years; the nominee must therefore be chosen carefully. Justice William O. Douglas, appointed by Franklin D. Roosevelt in 1939, served until 1975, some 30 years after Roosevelt's death. Every president knows that the person he names may have an impact on constitutional law in the United States long after he has left the White House. For this reason, presidents are keenly aware of the importance of each nomination to the Court.

Despite the importance of nominations of the Supreme Court, it does not necessarily follow that politics plays no role in the selection process. Indeed, it is because the stakes are so high that we might guess that politics plays an even greater role in the selection of Supreme Court justices. Generally speaking, nominees are chosen for their ideology, their representational qualities, and their professional competence, in roughly that order of importance. Let us examine all three areas in order to ascertain how each influences the president's decision to select a particular individual to serve on the Supreme Court.

As will be discussed in Chapter 6, the Constitution, like the Bible, is open to a variety of interpretations. This means that two individuals can read the same section of the Constitution and arrive at two totally different interpretations. And since judges, like major-league managers, are not born 60-year-old judges, each person who comes to the Supreme Court arrives with his or her "bags packed." That is, each justice comes to the Court with preconceived ideas about such issues as abortion, the death penalty, law and order, affirmative action, and civil liberties. Although it is not uncommon for a justice to change views once on the Court, a majority come with their views set. In making his nomination to the Supreme Court, a president seeks to nominate a person whose views are similar to his own. Whether he is a liberal or a conservative, a loose or strict constructionist, pro- or antiabortion, the president wants a nominee who will decide constitutional issues as he would if he were on the Court. Presidents have had their share of disappointments: Theodore Roosevelt was disappointed with Oliver Wendell Holmes, Jr., and Dwight D. Eisenhower regretted his nomination of Earl Warren as Chief Justice. Consequently, the better informed he is about the political and judicial philosophies of his nominee, the less likely it is that a president will be stuck with a justice he does not like.

Even more revealing of the political nature of the Supreme Court selection process are the representational qualities that presidents seek in their nominees. Presidents are reluctant to admit that politics influences their choices for the Court, but that is indeed the case. That is because the judiciary is supposed to be "above" politics. In a nation that stresses equality before the law, it is incongruent to admit that political considerations influence the selection process. But just as the nominee's political philosophy is taken into consideration, so are the nominee's representational qualities. The Supreme Court is a very important political symbol in our system of government. Because of the significance of the Court's symbolism, it is important to certain groups in our society that they be represented on the Supreme Court. As a result, there has developed the tradition of reserving certain "seats" on the Supreme Court for representatives of prominent groups. For example, early in our nation's history many Catholics believed that as a significant religious minority, they were entitled to have at least one Catholic on the Court. Chief Justice Roger B. Taney became the Court's first Catholic justice, thus creating the "Catholic seat" on the Court. President Woodrow Wilson named the first Jewish justice, Louis Brandeis, in 1916, and President Lyndon Johnson made Thurgood Marshall the first African-American to sit on the Court in 1967. President Ronald Reagan broke the gender barrier with the nomination of Sandra Day O'Connor to the Court in 1981. President Bill Clinton created a second woman's seat with the appointment of Ruth Bader Ginzburg in 1993.

Some Court watchers believe that the next significant barrier to be broken will come with the nomination of a Hispanic justice to the Court. Although presidents profess to seek the best-qualified person regardless of race, religion, or gender, the reality of the process is that these political factors cannot be ignored.

The influence of representational qualities on a Supreme Court nomination can be illustrated with a few examples. In one situation a president might wish to use a Supreme Court nomination to reward a group that has helped him politically. When President Johnson nominated Thurgood Marshall, he did so in part to show his appreciation for the support of African-American voters in the 1964 election and in anticipation of their continued support in 1968 (although Johnson ultimately did not seek reelection). Another group important to Democratic presidential candidates is Jewish voters. Only two Jews have been nominated to the Supreme Court by Republican presidents and one, the nomination of Douglas H. Ginsburg by President Reagan, was unsuccessful. Every other Jewish Supreme Court justice has been nominated by a Democratic president. This is because Jewish voters constitute a consistently loyal part of the Democratic coalition. Therefore, when Jewish justice Abe Fortas resigned from the Court in 1969, President Richard Nixon felt no obligation to nominate a Jewish replacement. As a result, the "Jewish seat" remained vacant until the nomination of Ruth Bader Ginsburg by President Clinton in 1993. As of early 1996, there were two Jewish justices on the Supreme Court.

A second instance in which the president might use a nomination to the Supreme Court for political purposes is when he is trying to curry the favor of an important political group. We have already mentioned the nominations and Senate rejections of Clement Haynesworth and G. Harrold Carswell. In 1968, Richard Nixon had devised his so-called Southern Strategy for winning the presidency. The Southern Strategy called on Republicans to appeal to disgruntled conservative Democrats in the South who were opposed to the liberal policies of the national Democratic party. Nixon hoped to establish a Republican base in the South from which to launch his 1972 reelection bid. As part of the Southern Strategy, Nixon promised to nominate a southerner to the Supreme Court. (President Nixon apparently did not consider Justice Hugo Black of Alabama a southerner.) Thus, when Justice Abe Fortas resigned, Nixon chose to nominate not a Jew but a southerner, Clement Haynesworth. When the Senate rejected the Haynesworth nomination, Nixon nominated another southerner, G. Harrold Carswell. After the Senate rejected Carswell, Nixon accused the Senate of prejudice against southerners. Even in defeat Nixon won: He could point out to southerners that he had twice tried to place one of their own on the High Court but had been thwarted in his attempts by the northern liberal Democrats in the Senate.

Finally, a president might nominate a particular person to the Supreme Court as a means of bolstering his support among a key political group. Voting studies indicated that in the election of 1980, President Reagan had not done as well among women voters as men voters. This was probably due in part to Reagan's opposition to the Equal Rights Amendment (ERA). When Justice Potter Stewart announced his resignation in 1981, it gave Reagan an opportunity to mend his fences with an important bloc of voters. Reagan's nomination of Sandra Day O'Connor helped put to rest criticisms that he was "anti-women."

The last area of qualifications presidents consider in their choice of Supreme Court nominees is professional competence. As previously noted, presidents would like their nominees to receive the highest possible ABA approval rating and overwhelming Senate approval. Naturally, the president seeks persons of high intellect, character, and integrity for the Court. The public expects and the Senate demands that Supreme Court justices be of the highest caliber. What, then, does the president seek by way of professional competence? Some presidents want their nominees to have previous judicial experience on either a lower federal court or a prominent state court. Judicial experience does not guarantee that a person will be a great, or even good, Supreme Court justice. There are some indications that political experience is more important than judicial experience. Chief Justice John Marshall was Secretary of State when he was nominated to the Court by President John Adams. Chief Justice Earl Warren was a former governor of California, Hugo Black was a senator from Alabama, and William O. Douglas was chairman of the Securities and Exchange Commission when nominated. With the exception of Black, who had only minor judicial experience, none had been a judge prior to his appointment. Yet each, in his own way, left an indelible mark on our constitutional law. The common thread seems to be a history of public service in often highly political positions. That is not to say that justices with judicial experience have all been failures; it simply means that judicial experience does not ensure judicial greatness.

Some presidents consider prominence in the legal profession an important qualification for a Supreme Court nomination. Lewis Powell was a former president of the ABA when named to the Court by President Nixon. Overall, judicial experience and professional competence, although important, take a back seat to ideological and representational qualifications. That is because there are enough outstanding judges and lawyers in the country to give the president the luxury of basing his choice on nonprofessional criteria.

Selection of state judges.   The selection of judges for state courts varies according to several factors. First, due to federalism, states may vary the selection method according to their individual wishes and needs. Basically, there are three selection methods from which to choose: election, appointment, and merit selection. States may use a combination of selection methods; they may choose, for example, to elect lower-court judges and to appoint appellate and supreme-court judges. Another factor is the influence of the state bar association. State bars have promoted merit selection in the past because it is believed to increase their influence in the selection of judges. Still another factor is the political environment of the state. Some states look upon judgeships as just another political office, to be controlled by election or patronage. Other "reform" states have tried to remove the judiciary from politics as much as possible. In this section we will examine each of the three methods of judicial selection used by the states, indicating the strengths and weaknesses of each.

One method, used in approximately half the states, is to elect judges by a popular vote of the people. Candidates for judgeships run on either a partisan or a nonpartisan basis. If the state has partisan elections, the judicial candidate vies for the nomination in the primary, campaigns just as any other candidate would, and wins if he or she receives a majority (or plurality) of the vote. The election method became popular in the states during the period known as Jacksonian Democracy. Jacksonian Democracy held that if it was a good idea to elect some officials to government office, it was a good idea to elect all of them, including judges. Judges, after all, make political decisions (abortion, busing, prayer in schools, for example), so the people should be able to hold them accountable for those decisions. The election of judges would guarantee that judges would not become judicial tyrants. The fact that a judge must periodically face the voters and run on his or her record ensures that the judge will not stray too far from local community standards when applying the law. It also guarantees that judges will not abuse their power, as federal judges are often accused of doing.

Those who oppose the election method do so for several reasons. First, elections undermine judicial independence. If we are to have a nation of laws, not men, we must allow judges to apply the law as they see it without fear of political reprisals at the next election. Subjecting them to election tempts judges to make rulings that are popular but not necessarily legally or even morally correct. Second, the election method does not guarantee that the most qualified person will be elected to the bench. Studies indicate that elections favor white, male, middle-class, and professional candidates. The possibility of qualified minorities becoming judges is reduced with the election method. A third criticism is that most voters are not qualified to evaluate candidates for judicial office. The average voter is simply not equipped to assess the professional competence or judicial temperament of candidates for the bench.[51] Even if there is an incumbent who has a record on which to run, the average voter is unfamiliar with the decisions a judge has made. The exception, of course, is when the judge has made a controversial ruling resulting in a move to unseat the judge at the next election. The voters may never hear of the many good rulings the judge has made, but may hear of only the controversial one. Finally, critics of judicial elections argue that the election method demeans the judicial system by forcing candidates for the bench to campaign for office. Candidates often must solicit campaign contributions from the same lawyers who will later come before them in court. It is unreasonable, critics argue, to assume that a judge will be able to treat impartially the lawyer who gave him $5,000 during the last campaign. Similarly, a judge might be biased against a lawyer who supported the judge's opponent in the last election. For these reasons, critics argue that election injects politics into the judicial system in ways that undermine the integrity of the process.

Regardless of the relative merits of electing judges, a little-known phenomenon occurs in some states that use elections, and that is the practice of appointing persons to fill the unexpired term of retiring or resigning judges. The process works like this: An incumbent judge who is ready to resign or retire announces his intentions a year or so before his term expires. This allows the governor to name a replacement to serve out the rest of the unexpired term. The newly appointed judge now has the advantage of seeking reelection as the incumbent. In most cases, any other lawyer who was considering making a bid for the judgeship will back off for fear of offending the new judge, whom he may later have to face in court. Since most incumbents are reelected, challengers are difficult to find and the incumbent usually runs unopposed. The voters, instead of choosing among several qualified candidates, find that they have little choice but to ratify the governor's preselected candidate. In Texas, for example, a survey revealed that nearly two-thirds of the judges had initially reached the bench by appointment and not by winning an election.[52] In such cases, judges are lawyers who know a governor.

The second method of judicial selection used in the states is the appointment method. The appointment of state judges often parallels that of federal judges. candidates are nominated by the governor with the consent of the state senate, or perhaps with the consent of both the senate and the house of representatives. Confirmation by one or more chambers of the state legislature prevents the governor from merely appointing his friends to office.

Its supporters argue that the appointment method allows the governor to choose judges on the basis of their qualifications. As previously noted, the average voter is unqualified to evaluate the qualifications of judges. The governor and his advisers, on the other hand, are in a better position to make such evaluations. The governor, with the advice of the state bar association and other judges, is better able to ensure that the most qualified persons are chosen. Another argument is that well-qualified persons are more willing to serve if appointed rather than elected. This argument asserts that the onerous task of running a political campaign for election discourages otherwise qualified applicants from seeking judicial office. A third argument is that the appointment process allows a governor to name well-qualified minority group members to the bench. Proponents of the appointment method argue that minority representation on the bench influences how other minority members perceive the judicial system. Finally, supporters of the appointment method point to the high caliber of federal judges who were selected by appointment.

Opponents of the appointment method make an equally strong case against it. They argue that lifetime appointments encourage arbitrariness in the courts. Judges should be held accountable for their decisions to the people. Second, the appointment process leads to cronyism. The governor is inclined to use judicial appointments to reward his friends with public office, regardless of their qualifications; this injects an element of partisan politics into the selection process as well. Finally, while it is true that the quality of federal judges is high, it is not the appointment method that has produced that quality. Federal judgeships pay more and are more prestigious than many state judgeships; hence, the federal bench attracts a higher quality of applicants from the outset.[53]

The third method of judicial selection is merit selection, often called the **Missouri Plan** because the state of Missouri pioneered its use. Merit selection is an attempt to combine the best features of the election and appointment methods. One of the key features of merit selection is the presence of a judicial nominating committee. The judicial nominating committee is usually composed of a combination of lawyers, laypersons, and incumbent judges. When a vacancy occurs in a judicial post, it is the job of the judicial nominating committee to serve as a screening committee. Persons wishing to be considered for the judgeship may submit their own credentials or they may be nominated by someone else. The judicial nominating committee screens the applications and reduces the choices to three candidates. The names of the three candidates are then submitted to the governor, who must appoint one of the three to the judgeship. The person appointed then begins his or her tenure on the court.

A second key feature of the Missouri Plan is the use of a retention election. After the newly appointed judge has served a probationary period of at least one year, he or she must go before the voters for their approval. The judge has no opponents, however. The voters are simply asked, "Shall Judge X of the state [Supreme Court] court be retained in office?" The voter votes either yes or no. If the voters approve, the judge begins a full term of office. Terms of office for judges under the Missouri Plan are generally long—from 8 to 12 years—in order to ensure judicial independence. At the end of the term, a judge must stand for retention again, with the voters being asked the same question. If the voters approve once again, the judge serves another full term. A judge may continue to serve as long as he or she wishes and as long as the people vote to keep the judge in office. If a judge loses the retention election, the position is declared vacant and the judicial nominating committee must begin the process of filling it.

Supporters of merit selection are generally enthusiastic about the method. The Missouri Plan, like the appointment method, gives a greater role to those most knowledgeable about judicial qualifications. As is the case with the election method, judges are periodically held accountable to the voters; judicial tyranny is thereby discouraged. At the same time, lengthy terms of office offer the judge a certain amount of judicial independence. A judge may make a controversial ruling with less fear that the voters will punish him or her for it at the next election, especially if the ruling is made early in the judge's term. Supporters argue that merit selection combines the positive features of the election and appointment methods with few, if any, of their drawbacks.

Critics of merit selection are not convinced that the method is as effective as its supporters claim. First, they point out that merit selection gives inordinate influence to the organized bar. The lawyer-members of the judicial nominating committee are usually chosen by the state bar, and the judge-members are also lawyers. This means that even if there are nonlawyers on the committee, they are outnumbered by the lawyers. Another problem is that the lay members are at a disadvantage in evaluating judicial qualifications. They may allow the lawyers on the committee to unduly influence them in the screening process. Another criticism is that merit selection does not eliminate politics from judicial selection as its supporters claim. The political struggle shifts from partisan politics to the politics of the state bar. State bars usually have factions which try to control the selection of lawyer-members to the judicial nominating committee. Partisan politics may also enter the picture: A Republican governor who is given the choice of two Democrats and one Republican by the judicial nominating committee may conclude that the lone Republican is the "best" candidate. Even after a judge has reached the bench, partisan politics may enter into the retention election. For example, Chief Justice Rose Bird of the California Supreme Court was a frequent target of conservative Republicans, who disapproved of her liberal judicial philosophy. Finally, critics of merit selection argue that there is simply no conclusive evidence that merit selection actually produces a higher caliber of judges than either election or appointment. Given the subjective nature of evaluating judicial qualifications, it is unlikely to be proven that merit selection provides better judges.

REMOVAL OF JUDGES

The office of judge is one of the most prestigious in American society; yet judges, like other humans, are susceptible to the vices of corruption, abuse of power, alcoholism, and so on. Consequently, we hear every year of cases of judges being removed from the bench for various offenses. Judicial removal involves three very different kinds of situations. The first is the case of the judge who has committed an illegal act either before or after taking office. Judges have been accused of soliciting murder, accepting bribes, and committing perjury, among other crimes. In a sense, the case of a judge who commits a crime is the easiest to deal with because the judge is treated like any other criminal defendant and is therefore entitled to due process of law.

The second kind of situation occurs when a judge has abused his or her power but has not necessarily committed a crime or an impeachable offense. For example, William Perry, a Long Island traffic court judge, had a coffee vendor brought before him in handcuffs so that he could berate the vendor for selling him a bad cup of coffee.[54]

The third situation occurs when a judge is either incompetent or senile. In some ways, this is the most difficult of the three situations to deal with. For example, a judge who may have served with distinction for many years may simply have stayed too long on the bench. Most states have mandatory retirement for judges at age 70, but senility does not always wait until then to strike. A judge, regardless of age, may simply be incompetent. Since there is no formal training for judges in the United States, virtually every lawyer is a potential judge. Yet lawyers have different talents and temperaments, so it is possible that a well-meaning judge may just be in over his or her head. Removal of the senile or incompetent judge must be handled carefully. Friends of the judge will usually suggest privately that it is time to resign or retire, but if the judge refuses, forced removal may be necessary.

Removal of federal judges.   There is only one formal method of removing Article III judges and that, of course, is impeachment. The Constitution specifies that impeachment is by a majority vote of the House of Representatives, followed by a trial in the Senate. Conviction is by a two-thirds vote of the Senate, and the penalty may not extend beyond removal from office and disqualification from holding further offices under the authority of the United States. There have been 13 impeachment proceedings against federal judges: Five were acquitted by the Senate, seven were convicted, and one resigned from the bench before articles of impeachment could pass the House. The seven who were convicted by the Senate were John Pickering of New Hampshire, West H. Humphreys of Tennessee, Robert W. Archbald of the United States Commerce Court, Halsted L. Ritter of Florida, Harry E. Claiborne of Nevada, Alcee L. Hastings of Florida, and Walter L. Nixon of Mississippi. Pickering was removed in 1804 because of insanity and chronic alcoholism; Humphreys was removed in 1862 for supporting the Confederacy. Archbald, in 1913, and Ritter, in 1936, were convicted of various types of misconduct in office. Of the seven, Humphreys and Archbald were barred from holding further office under the authority of the United States.[55]

There have been three federal judges impeached since 1986. Judge Harry E. Claiborne of Nevada was convicted of tax evasion on August 10, 1984, and sentenced to two years in federal prison. But Claiborne refused to resign from the bench following his conviction and continued to draw his (then) yearly salary of $78,800 while in prison. The House of Representatives finally voted to impeach Claiborne on July 22, 1986, by a vote of 406–0.[56] On October 9, 1986, Claiborne was found guilty on three of the four articles of impeachment by the Senate.[57] Judge Alcee L. Hastings of the Southern District of Florida was accused of bribery in 1983 but acquitted. Nevertheless, the Judicial Conference of the United States recommended impeachment and the House did so by a 413–3 vote in August 1988. The Senate convicted and removed Hastings by a 69–27 margin on October 20, 1989.[58] Finally, Judge Walter L. Nixon, Jr., was convicted of perjury in February 1986. He, like Claiborne, refused to resign and collected his $89,500 salary while in prison. The House impeached Judge Nixon in May 1989 by a vote of 417–0, and the Senate convicted him on November 3, 1989, by a vote of 89–8.[59]

The federal removal process illustrates the problem with impeachment as the only means of removing federal judges. First, the impeachment process is cumbersome, especially the trial stage in the Senate. The Senate, in effect, may be forced to delay other legislative matters pending the outcome of the impeachment trial. A second problem is that impeachment must cover a variety of judicial removal situations. John Pickering, the judge impeached for insanity and alcoholism, undoubtedly deserved to be removed from the bench, but he probably did not deserve the ignominious distinction of being the first federal judge to be removed from office. George W. English was impeached by the House in 1926 for "partiality, tyranny, and oppression."[60] The question raised by English's impeachment (he resigned before conviction by the Senate) was whether "partiality, tyranny, and oppression" constitute "Treason, Bribery, or other high crimes and misdemeanors," the grounds for impeachment specified by the Constitution. In other words, the impeachment process must cover activities ranging from "partiality" to murder, with the same punishment for both. Finally, as the Claiborne case illustrates, even a judge who has been convicted of a felony may continue to draw his or her salary until the long impeachment process has run its course. In recognition of this problem, Congress passed the Judicial Councils and Reform and Judicial Conduct and Disability Act in 1980. The act establishes a procedure for investigating complaints against federal judges. If the allegations merit action, a committee composed of federal judges may investigate. Possible disciplinary actions include "private or public reprimand or censure, certification of disability, request for voluntary resignation, or prohibition against further case assignments."[61]

Removal of state judges.   Just as in other areas of court organization, the states have addressed the problems of judicial removal in a variety of ways. Forty-five states allow their state legislatures to impeach state judges.[62] The impeachment process in the states parallels the federal model with some modifications, such as the size of the majority needed to impeach in the house or to convict in the senate.

Another method of removal is *legislative address.* Legislative address, unlike impeachment, is not reserved for high crimes and misdemeanors but may be used in cases of incompetency, senility, or partiality. The judge in question does not have to commit an indictable offense to warrant removal. Under legislative address, the unfortunate Pickering could have been spared the indignity of impeachment.

A third method of removal that is popular in some states is the *recall.* Recall is a method of removing officials, not only judges, from public office before the expiration of the official's term. Recall begins with the circulation of a recall petition. Suppose a judge was deemed deserving of removal from office. A group of citizens could start a recall campaign by securing a specified number of signatures on a recall petition. In some states the petition must be signed by a specified percentage—for example, 5 or 10 percent—of the voters. If enough valid signatures are collected, the judge in question must face a retention election similar to that used under the Missouri Plan. However, the question before the voters would be, "Shall Judge X of the [state supreme] court be removed from office?" The voters answer either yes or no. Other states allow alternative candidates to run against the incumbent judge in the recall election. This permits the voters to show their discontent with the incumbent by electing someone else to the position. In 1977, a Wisconsin judge named Archie Simonson made some inappropriate remarks about the "provocative clothing" worn by the young victim during a rape trial he was conducting. The remarks so angered women's groups in Madison that they mounted a successful recall campaign against Simonson.[63]

Finally, a fourth device used by some states to discipline judges is the *judicial conduct board/commission.* As we have seen, the severity of alleged offenses against judges ranges from the trivial to the very serious. Some allegations made against judges prove to be no more than the unfounded complaints of disgruntled litigants who lost a case over which the judge presided. Still other complaints are more serious and deserve some disciplinary action. Similarly, the punishment should fit the offense. For this reason, some states have created judicial conduct boards to investigate allegations made against judges to determine whether disciplinary action is warranted. If a judge is found guilty of misconduct, the board is empowered to discipline the offender. Such discipline could be a private or public reprimand, censure, suspension, or a recommendation of removal from office by impeachment or legislative address. State judicial conduct boards thus possess a variety of punishments that are appropriate to the seriousness of the offense.

CONCLUSION

In this chapter we have examined court organization in the United States. Because of our federal form of government, we have a federal court system superimposed on the 50 state court systems. In addition, federalism results in considerable variation among the states in the organization of their courts as well as in their substantive and procedural law. Federalism has resulted in different approaches to the selection and removal of judges. In short, our federal form of government adds complexity to our courts, but it also adds an element of diversity so that each state may deal with judicial organization, selection, and removal in its own way. For better or worse, federalism has had a remarkable impact on our judicial system.

NOTES

1. U.S. Constitution, Art. III, sec. 1.

2. Ibid.

3. Ibid.

4. Ibid., Art. I, sec. 8, clause 16.

5. Ibid., Art. IV, sec. 3, clause 2.

6. See Henry J. Abraham, *The Judiciary: The Supreme Court in the Governmental Process*, 4th ed. (Boston: Allyn & Bacon, 1977), pp. 8–9.

7. Ibid., p. 12.

8. U.S. Constitution, Art. III, sec. 2.

9. Ibid.

10. Ibid.

11. Ibid., Art. I, sec. 8, clause 4.

12. Ibid., Art. I, sec. 8, clause 1.

13. The one exception to this rule today is the District Court for Wyoming, which covers the Montana and Idaho parts of Yellowstone National Park. See Stephen L. Wasby, *The Supreme Court in the Federal Judicial System*, 2nd ed. (New York: Holt, Rinehart and Winston, 1984), p. 33.

14. One judge is assigned one-third time to the Eastern district and two-thirds time to the Western district of Oklahoma.

15. Administrative Office of the United States Courts, *Annual Report of the Director of the Administrative Office of the United States Courts: Judicial Business of the United States Courts, 1993* (Washington, D.C.: Government Printing Office, 1993), p. 7.

16. Ibid., p. 22.

17. Ibid., p. 35.

18. Administrative Office of the United States Courts, *Directory of Public Access Services*, http://www.uscourts.gov/.

19. Administrative Office of the United States Courts, *Annual Report, 1993*, p. 1.

20. Kenneth G. Pankey Jr., "The State of the Judiciary," *The Book of the States, 1992–93* (Lexington, Ky.: The Council of State Governments), note 2, p. 219.

21. Administrative Office of the United States Courts, *Annual Report, 1993*, p. 1.

22. Administrative Office of the United States Courts, "Courts Improvement Bill Transmitted to Congress," *The Third Branch*, Vol. 27, No. 5 (May 1995), p. 6.

23. Administrative Office of the United States Courts, *Annual Report, 1993*, p. 6.

24. Ibid., p. 4.

25. Administrative Office of the United States Courts, *Report of the Proceedings of the Judicial Conference of the United States, 1989* (Washington D.C.: Government Printing

Office, 1989), p. 5; and Sheldon Goldman and Thomas P. Jahnige, *The Federal Courts as a Political System,* 3rd ed. (New York: Harper & Row, 1985), pp. 21–23.

26. Because of its size (28 judgeships), not all of the judges of the Ninth Circuit sit *en banc.* See Wasby, pp. 42–43.

27. Wasby, p. 41.

28. Ibid., pp. 45–46.

29. Lawrence Baum, *American Courts: Process and Policy,* 2nd ed. (Boston: Houghton Mifflin Co., 1990), p. 37.

30. Goldman and Jahnige, p. 18.

31. U.S. Constitution, Art. III, sec. 1.

32. Until 1982, the federal district court for the Canal Zone was included in this group, but that court was abolished after the ratification of the Panama Canal Treaty.

33. Wasby, p. 36.

34. Ibid.

35. Howard Ball, *Courts and Politics: The Federal Judicial System* (Englewood Cliffs, N.J.: Prentice-Hall, 1980), pp. 73–74.

36. Wasby, p. 40.

37. *Northern Pipeline Construction Co.* v. *Marathon Pipe Line Co.,* 102 S. Ct. 2858 (1982).

38. Robert A. Carp and Ronald Stidham, *The Federal Courts* (Washington, D.C.: Congressional Quarterly Press, 1985), p. 30.

39. Administrative Office of the United States Courts, *Annual Report 1989,* p. 50.

40. Wasby, pp. 46–47.

41. In New York, trial courts are called *supreme courts;* therefore, the highest appellate court is simply called the *Court of Appeals.* See Baum, p. 47.

42. David M. O'Brien, "The Reagan Judges: His Most Enduring Legacy?" in *The Reagan Legacy: Promise and Performance,* ed. by Charles O. Jones (Chatham, N.J.: Chatham House Publishers, Inc., 1988), pp. 60–101.

43. Wasby, p. 75.

44. Carp and Stidham, p. 107.

45. Ibid., pp. 107–108.

46. Ibid., p. 108.

47. Frank Guiliuzza III, Daniel J. Reagan, and David M. Barrett, "The Senate Judiciary Committee and Supreme Court Nominees: Measuring the Dynamics of Confirmation Criteria," *Journal of Politics,* Vol. 56 (August 1994), p. 776.

48. Ibid., pp. 776–777.

49. Paul A. Freund, "Appointment of Justices: Some Historical Perspectives," *Harvard Law Review,* Vol. 101 (April 1988), pp. 1146–1163; Stephen Carter, "The Confirmation Mess," *Harvard Law Review,* Vol. 101 (April 1988), pp. 1185–1201.

50. Wasby, p. 77.

51. In 1976, Texas voters elected Don Yarbrough, who was later accused of soliciting to commit murder and convicted of aggravated perjury, to the state supreme court.

52. Richard H. Kraemer and Charldean Newell, *Texas Politics,* 2nd ed. (St. Paul, Minn.: West Publishing Company, 1984), p. 243.

53. Robert S. Lorch, *State and Local Politics: The Great Entanglement* (Englewood Cliffs, N.J.: Prentice-Hall, 1983), p. 220.

54. Nicholas Henry, *Governing at the Grassroots: State and Local Politics,* 2nd ed. (Englewood Cliffs, N.J.: Prentice-Hall, 1984), p. 208.

55. Henry J. Abraham, *The Judicial Process,* 3rd ed. (New York: Oxford University Press, 1975), pp. 43–44.

56. "House Votes 406–0 to Impeach Federal Judge," *Congressional Quarterly,* Vol. 44, No. 30, July 26, 1986, pp. 1683–1684.

57. Senate Finds Claiborne Guilty, Strips Him of Federal Judgeship," *Congressional Quarterly,* Vol. 44, No. 41, October 11, 1986, pp. 2569–2570.

58. Hastings Removed from Bench After Conviction by Senate," *Congressional Quarterly,* Vol. 47, No. 42, October 21, 1989, p. 2800.

59. Senate Convicts Judge Nixon, Removes Him from Bench," *Congressional Quarterly,* Vol. 47, No. 44, November 4, 1989, p. 2955.

60. Abraham, p. 43.

61. Carp and Stidham, p. 127.

62. Richard D. Bingham, *State and Local Government in an Urban Society* (New York: Random House, 1986), p. 223.

63. Henry, p. 209.

4

Procedure
and
Evidence

The difference between substantive and procedural law was first introduced in Chapter 1. Substantive law was defined as that which is concerned with the content or substance of the law. Legal definitions of crimes are examples of the law's substantive content. Procedural law was defined as governing the *process* of the law. Later chapters will deal with civil and criminal substantive law in greater detail. In this chapter we will elaborate on procedural law by examining it in both civil and criminal contexts. Before we begin the discussion of the actual civil procedure, it is important to review the reasons for our insistence upon strict rules of procedure. In Chapter 1 we stated that most Americans want to prevent government from acting toward them in an arbitrary manner. We are so concerned with the problem of arbitrary government that we have adopted an elaborate system of criminal procedural safeguards to ensure that the innocent person is not wrongfully convicted of a crime. We even accept the inevitability that some guilty persons will go free if "the constable blunders." That is the price we pay to protect our civil liberties.

Our desire to check government capriciousness in criminal cases does not tell us why we also have such elaborate procedural requirements in civil cases, in which, by definition, the government is unconcerned about the outcome. The answer lies in the fact that government, by passing laws, sets up the "rules of the game." No one would even begin to play a board game without some prior knowledge of its rules; likewise, before a person will risk his time, energy, and money in a lawsuit, he wants to know the rules that govern the process. Common sense, therefore, dictates that the rules of civil procedure be known beforehand.

There is, however, another important reason for studying the rules of procedure in civil cases that does directly involve the government. It was an extremely important step in the advancement of civilization when people began relying on government or some other societal institution to resolve disputes. In prehistoric times it may have been a clan or tribal leader who was responsible for settling disputes among people. In later times it may have been a king or a council. Regardless of who the dispute settler was, the willingness of individuals to submit their disputes to some neutral third party was a vital characteristic of an advanced society. One important aspect of the willingness to submit disputes for peaceful resolution is the perception by all parties that the dispute-settler is fair. Two teams willingly allow a neutral umpire to apply neutral rules of play to their game of baseball if both teams perceive the umpire and the rules to be fair. Then, if a call should go against them, they accept it even if they do not agree with it. Similarly, if courts of law designated to settle disputes among citizens are perceived by all to apply neutral rules of procedure fairly, the losing party will more readily accept the bitter pill he must swallow. In societies in which courts are not perceived as fair and just, people will often resort to illegal or extralegal means to ensure that they receive justice.[1] Consequently, the government has a tremendous stake in maintaining the appearance (and the reality) of its system of justice even though it seldom cares about the outcome of a particular case. Its main interest is in ensuring that the appearance of justice is preserved.

With this background in mind, we turn our attention to the discussion of the rules of civil procedure. In order to avoid confusion and for the purposes of instruction, we have simplified the process as much as possible. In addition, since there are several types of civil actions, we have chosen to use a tort case to illustrate the civil legal process. We hope that this will help the reader to become generally familiar with civil procedure.

CIVIL PROCEDURE

Every tort case begins with a dispute or controversy that cannot be resolved in a less formal manner. A person who feels that he has been injured by another may begin a civil action against him. The person filing the suit is called the *plaintiff,* and the person against whom the suit has been filed is called the *defendant.* Prior to actually filing a suit, the plaintiff will usually consult a lawyer, who will advise him about the soundness of his case. If the lawyer feels her prospective client has a good case, she may either agree to handle it personally or refer him to someone else who specializes in the kind of case in question. Lawyers often agree to work on the basis of a *contingency fee*, which means the lawyer is paid only if the client's claim is successful. The contingency fee is typically from 30 to 40 percent of the award. Should he lose, the client pays only for court fees and other expenses involved in pursuing the case.

Often the plaintiff's lawyer will initially suggest an informal resolution of the conflict. She may call or write to the defendant to convey her client's intent to sue, in the hope that the defendant will see that the plaintiff "means business" and will thus be persuaded to settle out of court. The defendant, in turn, may have retained his own lawyer in anticipation of the plaintiff's action. It is quite possible that after the lawyers for both sides confer, an informal agreement can be worked out, thus avoiding the formal legal process. A majority of cases are resolved after some informal negotiating by the lawyers involved or after referral to some alternative dispute resolution program.

When informal methods fail, the next step is the filing of the *complaint.* In the complaint, the plaintiff relates the injury he has received at the hands of the defendant, alleges negligence and liability on the defendant's part, and states what remedy he seeks from the court. In the case of a tort, for example, the complaint will describe the injury; allege that the defendant's negligence caused the injury, thus making him liable; and seek relief, usually in the form of a monetary award for damages. The plaintiff may seek *general damages* to cover items like hospital bills, lost income, and damage to his property. The purpose of general damages is to compensate the plaintiff and to return him, as nearly as possible, to his condition prior to the alleged injury. In addition, if the defendant's behavior has been especially wanton, reckless, or reprehensible, the plaintiff may seek *punitive damages.* Punitive damages are designed to impose monetary punishment upon persons who act in a reckless manner toward fellow human beings. Its purpose is to make an example of the defendant and warn others that society will not tolerate that type of behavior. Movie stars frequently ask for punitive damages against newspaper tabloids that exhibit "reckless disregard for the truth" when publishing stories about the private lives of celebrities.

After the complaint has been filed in the court with the appropriate jurisdiction, the next step is to notify the defendant formally that a legal action has been brought against him by the plaintiff. This is called the *service.* The defendant is served a copy of the complaint listing the allegations made against him by the plaintiff. Along with the copy of the complaint, the court clerk also issues a *summons* to the defendant. The summons directs the defendant to submit what is called an *answer* within a certain number of days. The answer is the defendant's written account of what happened. The defendant's answer, prepared by his attorney, will deny the facts as alleged in the complaint or deny liability or both. Often the defendant will file a *demurrer,* or motion to dismiss the complaint; however, the motion is infrequently granted. It is extremely important that the defendant respond to the summons because failure to do so could result in a *default judgment* being given to the plaintiff. Failure to respond is tantamount to an admission of liability, and the plaintiff would become entitled to the damages sought in his complaint.

After the pleadings have been completed, the process known as *discovery* begins. Despite the tendency of movie and television scriptwriters to create situations in which a surprise witness drops a bombshell, real-life court cases seldom happen that way. In fact, the general tendency is for both sides to lay all their cards out on the table. This is done for a number of reasons. First, going through the formal trial process is expensive and time-consuming. Second, putting the decision in the hands of a jury may be risky. A case may seem airtight to everyone but the jurors, and strange verdicts and awards are possible. A third reason for laying the cards on the table is to determine if some facts of the dispute can be agreed upon beforehand, thus saving the need to establish them at the trial. Fourth, once the cards are on the table, one side or the other may decide it cannot win, and serious negotiations about a settlement may begin. Lawyers often find that their clients have not been totally candid with them. As a result, certain facts left out of the client's version of the events may come to the lawyer's attention during discovery. Either lawyer may then advise the client to settle the case out of court. Finally, both sides will know exactly what they are up against and can plan their courtroom strategies accordingly.

Discovery can take a number of forms. One of the more common ones is a *deposition,* which can be taken in either of two ways. One way is to have a *witness* and/or one or more of the *parties* appear at the office of one of the lawyers in the case and answer questions put to him by the lawyer. The witness is under oath, and a stenographer either records the questions and responses verbatim, or it is videotaped or otherwise electronically recorded. Or a witness may be questioned in the presence of both lawyers and subjected to direct questioning by one and cross-examination by the other. As in the first instance, everything said is recorded. Like all forms of discovery, a witness's testimony may be so devastating to one party's case that the lawyer may urge him to reach a settlement with the other party.

An *interrogatory* is a second form of discovery. An interrogatory is a written question directed to one of the parties to the case by the other party. Unless questions are answered, the person may be cited for contempt. For example, if the case involved an automobile accident, a lawyer might ask, "Were you drinking?" "Had you been drinking?" "How much?" "How fast were you driving?" Truthful answers must be given because the same questions may be asked at the trial while the party is under oath.

The last form of discovery involves the production of physical evidence in the possession of one of the parties. The judge may issue a *subpoena duces tecum,* which is a court order requiring a person to appear in court or at deposition and to produce specified documents pertinent to the case. In a debt-collection case, for example, the defendant might be required to produce a receipt or a canceled check as proof of payment of the debt. In a personal-injury case, the plaintiff might have to produce copies of a medical exam and of hospital and doctor bills to establish the extent of the injury.

Discovery is designed to expedite the legal process. If certain facts can be agreed upon by both parties before the trial, these facts will only need to be recorded as having been stipulated as true by both sides. In a personal-injury case, for example, the extent of the plaintiff's injury might be agreed upon by both sides because the real issue is not whether the plaintiff was injured, but whether the defendant was liable for the injury. This simplifies the case for the jury, thus enabling them to concentrate solely on the issue of liability.

Remainder of the pretrial process.

After the discovery process has been completed, the parties can make a pretrial motion requesting a *summary judgment.* In a personal-injury suit, for example, if there is no dispute over the facts but only over the legal question of liability, the plaintiff may request that the judge grant a summary judgment in his favor. That is, the plaintiff is asking the judge to settle the legal question of the defendant's liability in favor of the plaintiff. If it is clear that the defendant's negligence caused the injury, the judge will grant the plaintiff's motion. In most cases, however, the defendant's negligence is not clear-cut, and the plaintiff's motion is denied. The defendant may also request a summary judgment. According to the rules of civil procedure, the plaintiff must make what is called a *prima facie case.* This term means that at first glance, or "first face," the plaintiff's version of the facts is credible. If the plaintiff has failed to make a prima facie case, the defendant may ask the judge to rule that he was not negligent and to dismiss the plaintiff's case. As already noted, most cases are not easily settled if they have gone this far, and the motion is usually denied.

Selection of the jury.

Once the preliminary maneuvering is over, the focus turns to the actual resolution of the conflict at trial. The first order of business is the selection of the jury, if a jury is to be used. The parties to the case, if both are agreeable, may choose to have a *bench trial,* in which the judge becomes the *trier of fact* while simultaneously acting as the interpreter of the law. After submission of the evidence, the judge alone will decide the outcome of the case. In highly complex or technical cases, the parties often prefer to let the judge decide the case since laypersons who compose juries, frequently lack the expertise to make a learned decision. In other instances—personal-injury cases, for example—the parties prefer to let the judge decide simply because juries are unpredictable, sometimes allowing irrelevant factors, such as the wealth of the defendant, to be considered in awarding damages.

If a jury is used, its members are selected from a pool of prospective persons, called a *venire*. Although we generally think of juries as comprising 12 persons, the number can be less than 12, even as few as 5, in civil cases. Each prospective juror, or *venireman*, takes the stand to be asked a few questions by each attorney and perhaps the judge. The initial questions are generally simple ones, designed more to put the person at ease than to elicit information. Lawyers want to know if the prospective juror has any prejudices concerning the client's case. For example, a lawyer representing an insurance company will try to ascertain the venireman's attitude toward insurance companies. If the venireman appears hostile to insurance companies, the lawyer will try to prevent his selection.

A venireman may be struck from a jury in two ways: challenge for cause and peremptory challenge. If, as we have seen, the lawyer's questioning reveals prejudice on the part of the venireman, the lawyer may cite that as a reason for excluding the person. This is known as a *challenge for cause*, and the judge must agree that the reason given is sufficient to exclude the person. The use of challenge for cause is unlimited. The second type of challenge is called a *peremptory challenge;* if a lawyer feels that a venireman's presence on the jury would harm her client's chances of winning but she cannot specify a cause sufficient to satisfy the judge, the lawyer may strike the person without giving any reason. The rules of civil procedure limit the number of peremptory challenges for each side to a specified number, usually around six. This process of questioning prospective jurors and striking some from the jury is called *voir dire,* which means "to speak truth."

After the jury has been selected, they are sworn in and said to be *impanelled.* The jury's major function is to serve as the trier of fact. They are to listen to the evidence presented in the case and decide who is telling the truth and which party deserves to win. In a sense, the jury serves as the conscience of the community. Although the jurors are not personally concerned with the outcome of the case, they are interested in seeing that the case is resolved in a peaceful, fair manner. For that reason, it is important that the jury be selected from a representative cross section of the community. The parties to the case are more inclined to accept the final verdict if they perceive the jury to be fair and impartial. As we have noted, this acceptance by the parties is crucial to the acceptance of the legitimacy of the entire judicial system.

Submission of evidence.   After the jury has been impanelled, the trial begins. Each lawyer is allowed to make an *opening statement* to the jury, in which he or she outlines his or her case. Generally speaking, the opening statement will inform the jury as to exactly what the lawyer intends to prove and how he or she plans to prove it. After both lawyers have made their opening statements, the plaintiff's lawyer calls her first witness. In civil law, since the plaintiff is the complaining party—that is, the one who initiated the lawsuit—he bears the burden of proof. The standard of proof in civil law is the *preponderance of the evidence* standard; that is, a preponderance, or a majority, of the evidence must support the plaintiff's allegations against the defendant. If the plaintiff fails to meet this standard, the defendant will win the case. Therefore, the plaintiff begins the trial by presenting his case to the jury.

The plaintiff's lawyer calls her first witness and proceeds to question him. This is known as *direct examination.* When the plaintiff's lawyer has finished, the defendant's lawyer may *cross-examine* the plaintiff's witness. On cross-examination, the defendant's lawyer is free either to limit his questions to topics raised by the plaintiff's lawyer or to open a new line of questioning. When the defendant's lawyer has finished, the plaintiff's lawyer may *redirect,* or ask additional questions of the same witness. On redirect examination, however, the plaintiff's lawyer may ask only questions raised by the defendant's lawyer on cross-examination; she may not open a new line of questioning. Upon completion of redirect, the defendant's lawyer may *re-cross-examine* but also is limited to questions raised on redirect. When both lawyers have asked all of their questions, the witness is excused.

Strict rules of procedure govern the questioning of witnesses and the admission of evidence. The hearsay rule, for example, forbids witnesses from testifying about facts of which they have no direct knowledge or information. Lawyers are forbidden to ask *leading questions* of their own witness. A question such as "Did you see the defendant strike the plaintiff on the evening of May 1?" would be improper. However, the question "What did you see on or about 6:00 PM on the evening of May 1?" would be acceptable. During the questioning of a witness, a lawyer may note his objection to either the other lawyer's question or the witness's response. The judge must make a ruling to either sustain the objection as valid or overrule it as invalid. These objections, and the judge's subsequent rulings, may provide the losing party with the legal grounds on which to base a future appeal. Objections to a judge's ruling must be "timely"; after-the-fact objections when the trial is over usually do not provide grounds for an appeal.

During the examination of witnesses, the lawyers will submit physical evidence to substantiate their cases. For example, while questioning the attending physician in a personal-injury suit, the lawyer may introduce into evidence a copy of the written medical report on the plaintiff's injury. As with testimony, the defendant's lawyer may object to the introduction of the medical report, forcing the judge to make a ruling on its admissibility. The judge's ruling may also serve as grounds for an appeal if the ruling is incorrect. Any incorrect ruling may be considered a reversible error by an appeals court at some later date. Reversible error results in a new trial for the losing party.

As we can easily see, the presentation of evidence is the heart of the trial. Because the evidentiary stage of the trial proceeding is so important, we will return to it later in this chapter in order to examine in greater depth the rules of evidence as they apply to both civil and criminal cases. For now, let us continue with our overview of civil procedure.

After the plaintiff's lawyer has called all of her witnesses and submitted all of her physical evidence, the defense may present its side of the case. The defense calls its rebuttal witnesses and the same procedure of questioning is followed, except this time it is the defendant's lawyer who conducts direct examination and the plaintiff's lawyer who cross-examines. The main strategy of the defense is to rebut as much of the plaintiff's damaging evidence as possible. One way to rebut a plaintiff's tort case is to show *contributory negligence* on the part of the plaintiff. If the defendant's lawyer can show that the plaintiff was wholly responsible for his own injuries, the defendant is not liable. The theory is that the plaintiff should come before the court with "clean hands"; that is, he should be able to show that he did not contribute to his own injury through his own negligence. Another defense strategy is to show *comparative negligence* on the part of the plaintiff. Unlike contributory negligence, which removes the defendant's liability, comparative negligence assumes that both parties are partially to blame for the plaintiff's injury. The plaintiff will not be allowed to recover for that portion of his injury for which he himself was responsible. A showing of even partial negligence on the plaintiff's part will at least reduce the amount of damages the defendant will have to pay. Thus, a good offense is also a good defense. We should emphasize, however, that these defense strategies are limited to tort cases and are not used for other civil actions.

Following the submission of all the oral and physical evidence, the two lawyers will address the jury a final time in their *closing statements.* The plaintiff's lawyer will summarize her case to the jury with the assertion that a preponderance of the evidence supports her client's claims against the defendant. The defendant's lawyer will summarize his own rebuttal evidence and ask the jury to rule in favor of his client.

Final actions.   Once the evidentiary stage of the trial is complete, some additional legal maneuvering is possible before the case is actually submitted to the jury. Either side may request a *directed verdict.* A motion for a directed verdict is a lawyer's request that the judge direct the jury to bring in a verdict favorable to his client. If, for example, the plaintiff has failed to carry the burden of proof in the case, the judge might well grant the defense lawyer's motion for a directed verdict. Similarly, if the defendant has failed to rebut successfully the plaintiff's allegations and evidence, the judge might grant the plaintiff's motion. Generally, however, few judges are willing to take the decision out of the hands of the jury, and so these motions are routinely denied. Like all denied motions, the judge's refusal to order a directed verdict can be appealed.

Once all the formal pleadings have ceased, the judge charges the jury. In his *charge to the jury,* the judge explains the applicable law as it relates to the case and describes what the jury must decide if they are to rule in favor of the plaintiff. The judge also explains what the jury must find if they are to rule for the defendant. After the charge has been completed, the case is formally submitted to the jury.

Jury deliberation and verdict. Once the jurors have the case, the fate of both parties is in their hands.[2] In a tort case, such as the one we have been discussing, the jury is called upon to render one of two types of verdicts. The first type is called a *general verdict.* Under a general verdict, the jury could find the defendant liable and award the plaintiff the monetary damages he sought, less than what he sought, or more than what he sought. The jury could also find that the defendant was not liable; the plaintiff would then not be entitled to damages. A second type of verdict, called a *special-issues verdict,* presents the jury with a series of questions that it must answer. For example, in a comparative-negligence case, the first question might be, "Do you find the defendant not liable for plaintiff's injury?" If the answer is No, the next question might be, "Do you find the defendant 10 percent liable?" The percentage—20 percent, 30 percent, and so forth—is increased incrementally until the jury reaches the appropriate degree of comparative liability for each party. Damages would then be awarded to the plaintiff on the basis of the percentage of comparative liability. If, for example, the total amount of damages sought by the plaintiff was $50,000 but the jury found the defendant only 60 percent liable, then the defendant would pay the plaintiff only $30,000 in damages. Of course, should the jury rule that the defendant was not liable for the plaintiff's injuries, there is no other decision to be made and the jury's job is over.

After the jury has reached its verdict, the foreman informs the bailiff, who in turn notifies the judge. Court is reconvened and the jury's verdict is formally read. Verdicts in civil cases, unlike many criminal cases, need not be unanimous. The judge may poll each individual juror to make sure there is no mistake about the decision. The judge then thanks the jurors for their service and dismisses them. The trial stage of this particular civil case is now over.

Appellate procedure. The person who loses the case at trial has the right to appeal the decision. The grounds for the appeal may vary but generally fall into two categories. The first alleges that the judge made an error or errors regarding questions of law. Recall our previous discussion of the need for attorneys to make timely objections to the judge's rulings on points of law. When an attorney makes such an objection and the judge overrules it, there is a disagreement over a point of law. That disagreement provides the legal grounds upon which the appeal may be based. The appellate court must first decide whether the trial judge was correct in his ruling. If the trial judge is ruled to have been incorrect, the appellate court must next determine whether the error was serious enough to warrant a new trial. In the case of a reversible error, the appellate court concludes that the error was so serious that it might have adversely affected the outcome of the trial. In that instance, a new trial will be ordered. If the error is found to be a harmless error, however, the judgment of the trial court will be affirmed. An appellate court will frequently refuse to overrule the trial judge if the alleged error falls into an area committed to the trial judge's discretion. In such an instance, the trial judge is presumed to be correct and the appellate court is precluded from overruling him.

The second category of appeals, known as *remittitur,* occurs in cases in which money damages have been awarded. Such appeals are often based on the grounds that the award was excessive. Juries find it difficult to determine the proper monetary damages to be awarded. In a libel suit, for example, how much is a person's reputation worth, and how can money compensate the victim for damage to his reputation? These are difficult questions to answer, and juries sometimes get carried away and award more in damages than is warranted. An appellate court may reduce the award if, in its judgment, the award was excessive.

As a general rule, litigants have the "right" to one appeal of a trial court decision. The right to an appeal must be based on a statute or it may be granted with the permission of the court. The person requesting the appeal is called the *appellant* and the person against whom an appeal is made is called the *appellee.* Since state appellate procedures vary, the following discussion summarizes the federal appellate process for a civil case as outlined in *The Federal Rules of Appellate Procedure.*[3]

The first step in the appeals process is for the appellant to file a notice of appeal. The appellant (normally the losing party at trial) must file a notice of appeal with the clerk of the U.S. district court within 30 days of the date of the district court's judgment. If the United States, one of its officials, or one of its agencies is a party to the case, 60 days are allowed to file a notice of appeal. The district court may, for good cause, extend the time allowed for filing an appeal. The notice of appeal must specify the party making the appeal, and designate the judgment appealed from and the court to which the appeal is made. The district court clerk must mail a copy of the notice of appeal to the counsel of record for the appellee and another copy to the clerk of the court of appeals. The appellant must also pay the appropriate fees to the district court clerk, who also receives the docket fee on behalf of the court of appeals.

Within 10 days of filing his notice of appeal, the appellant must order a copy of the transcript of the lower-court proceeding from the court reporter. Transcripts need cover only those parts of the trial actually under appeal. Ten days after the transcript is ordered, the appellant must file a statement of the issues to be appealed. The appellant must send the appellee a copy of the statement of the issues and a copy of appellant's transcript order. Within ten days of receiving the copy, the appellee may request a copy of appellant's transcript and any additional pages of transcript the appellee may need.

Each party pays the cost of transcript requests. Alternatively, at this point the two parties may agree to a statement on how the issues under appeal arose.

Whenever either party takes certain actions concerning the appeal, it is required to notify the other party of the action taken by the process called *service*. For example, the appellant is required to serve the statement of issues to the appellee. Service may be either *personal service* or service by mail. Personal service would include delivery of the notice to the appellee's attorney, his or her secretary, or any other responsible person representing appellee. Whether service is personal or by mail, proof of service is required.

Once the notice of appeal, transcripts, and other forms have been properly filed, the clerk of the court of appeals enters the appeal upon the court of appeals court docket. The clerk also notifies the parties of the date on which the record was filed. Within 40 days after the date on which the record is filed, the appellant must file a written brief called the *principal brief.* The appellant's principal brief must contain a table of contents, a statement of the subject matter and appellate jurisdiction, a statement of the issues being appealed, a statement of the facts of the case, the appellant's legal arguments with citations, and a short conclusion stating the precise relief sought. The appellant's principal brief may not exceed 50 pages. The appellant must provide 25 copies of the principal brief to the court and 2 copies to the appellee. If the appellant fails to file a brief, the appellee may move for a dismissal of the appeal.

The appellee has 30 days after receiving the appellant's principal brief to submit a brief. The appellee's brief must generally follow the same format as the appellant's and may not exceed 50 pages in length. The appellee must also submit 25 copies of the brief to the court and 2 copies to the appellant. If the appellee fails to file a brief, the court may deny him the right to be heard at oral argument. Fourteen days after receiving the appellee's brief, the appellant may file a *reply brief.* The reply brief may not exceed 25 pages, and the same requirements about the number of copies apply.

The next stage of the appellate process is an optional step called a prehearing conference. The prehearing conference is an attempt to simplify the issues being appealed and any other matters under dispute. The prehearing conference tries to win a consensus on possible areas of agreement in order to expedite the proceedings.

The court of appeals is finally ready to hear the case. The clerk schedules *oral argument* and notifies the parties of the date, time, place, and amount of time allotted for the hearing. Oral argument is the part of the procedure where the lawyers for the parties appear before the judges to argue their sides of the case. The appellant's lawyer is permitted to open and conclude oral argument. Lawyers are not permitted to read extensively from their briefs and are expected to be prepared to answer questions the judges might ask. If either side should fail to appear at oral argument, the court will hear the arguments of the side that is represented. If neither side appears, the court will decide the case on the basis of the written briefs. The court may, however, decide that no useful purpose will be served by oral argument and not schedule it at all.

Occasionally, a court of appeals will be asked to hear a case *en banc.* This means that the entire court, not just a panel of three judges, will hear the case. Generally, the court will agree to an *en banc* hearing if the case raises a question of exceptional importance or when an *en banc* hearing is necessary to ensure uniformity of the court's decisions. For example, two separate panels could rule differently on essentially the same point of law. An *en banc* hearing can provide a definitive ruling binding on all members of the court.

Decisions of the court of appeals are by majority vote. Upon receipt of the court's judgment, the clerk makes a notation in the court docket which constitutes the entry of judgment. Written opinions are frequent, but not required. Dissenting and concurring opinions may also be filed by the judges. The clerk then mails copies of the judgment and any opinions to all parties. Within 14 days after the entry of judgment, unless the United States is a party in which case the time is extended to 45 days, the losing party may file a petition for rehearing. The petition for rehearing may not exceed 15 pages and is filed and served just like the briefs. There is no oral argument about the petition for rehearing. If the petition for rehearing is granted, the court may make final disposition of the case without reargument or it may restore the case to the calendar for reargument. However, in most cases, petitions for rehearing are denied and the judgment of the court of appeals is final.

If the appellant wins his appeal, the trial court's judgment is usually altered in some fashion. The court of appeals may order a new trial to be held or simply remand the case with orders to correct the lower court's judgment. If the appellant wins, the appellee must bear the cost of the appeal unless the court orders otherwise. The appellee, however, may choose to appeal the appellate court's ruling to the Supreme Court. If that is done, the appellee is now the appellant. If the appellant loses the appeal, the judgment of the trial court is affirmed and he pays the cost of the appeal. The appellant may also choose to appeal to the Supreme Court; however, as noted in Chapter 3, access to the Supreme Court is limited, and for most litigants, the decision of the court of appeals ends the case.

The Supreme Court has both original and appellate jurisdiction, but as a practical matter it functions almost entirely as an appellate court. For example, in 1992 there were 7,245 cases on the Court's dockets, of which only 12 were cases coming to it under its original jurisdiction.[4] There are three ways in which a case may reach the Supreme Court under its appellate jurisdiction. The first is an appeal as a matter of right. Congress has stipulated that under certain conditions a party has an absolute right to have a case heard by the Court. For example, if a state law has been declared unconstitutional because it conflicts with a U.S. statute or treaty, or with the Constitution itself, the state may appeal to the Supreme Court. In reality, however, the Court may refuse further considerations of the merits of the case by dismissing it for "lack of a substantial federal question." Just what constitutes a "substantial" federal question is simply left to the discretion of the judges.

The second avenue of appeal is through the ***writ of certiorari.*** A *writ of certiorari* is an order from a higher court to a lower court to send up the record of a case so that the higher court may review it. Since 1925 the Supreme Court has had complete discretion in deciding whether or not to issue *certiorari* in specific cases. The Court operates under the ***rule of four,*** which states that at least four of the nine justices must agree that a case merits the Court's attention before it will issue the writ.

The final way in which a case may reach the Supreme Court is through ***certification.*** Certification is used when a lower court seeks clarification on a question of law before it can make a ruling in a case. For example, President Franklin D. Roosevelt once dismissed a man named Humphrey from the FTC. Humphrey sued the government for lost wages. The lower court, before it could decide if Humphrey was entitled to his lost wages, first had to decide if his dismissal had been legal. In *Humphrey's Executor* v. *United States*,[5] the Supreme Court ruled that the dismissal was not legal. Cases that reach the Court through certification are relatively rare since the Court seems to prefer that the lower court make a ruling, which it may then later review if it chooses to do so.

Once the Supreme Court has agreed to hear a case, both parties are required to submit written briefs stating the exact nature of the controversy, their side's position, the legal precedents upon which they are relying, and arguments justifying why the Court should rule in their favor. In addition, all transcripts and other court papers from the proceedings of the lower courts are submitted to the Court. ***Oral argument*** is next; here the attorneys for both parties appear in person before the justices to argue the case. Each side is given 30 minutes to present its case, with the understanding that any justice may interrupt to question the lawyers. Oral argument is not just a rehash of the written briefs; it is designed to allow the justices to clarify issues presented by the case before the Court.

The actual outcome of the case is decided during the Supreme Court's conference. By tradition, each justice shakes the hand of the other eight justices upon entering the conference room. This is to ensure that the conference begins on a friendly note. The Chief Justice presides over the discussion of the case, and then a tentative vote is taken. At least six of the nine justices must participate in order to decide a case, and a simple majority determines the outcome. If, for example, one justice fails to participate in a case and the others are deadlocked 4–4, the decision of the highest court below the Supreme Court will stand. In such instances, a similar case that raises the same issue will have to come before the Court before there will be resolution.

After the case has been discussed and voted upon in conference, the next stage is the opinion writing. If the Chief Justice is in the majority, he assigns the task of writing the ***majority opinion*** to one of the justices in the majority, which includes, of course, himself. If the Chief Justice is not in the majority, the job of assigning the majority opinion goes to the senior associate justice in the majority. The majority opinion is important for several reasons. First, it explains to the parties directly involved in the case why each side won or lost. Second, it establishes a precedent for future cases that raise the same substantive issue. Third, it provides cues for court-watchers as to how the Court might decide similar issues in future cases.

Although there is no official "minority opinion," the justices in the minority may informally decide that one of them should write the main *dissenting opinion* setting forth the reasons for the minority's disagreement with the majority. However, any of the justices in the minority is free to write a separate dissent or to join another's dissent, or both. In addition to being critical of the majority's legal reasoning or analysis of a case, dissenting opinions can provide the opponents of a particular decision with powerful arguments for opposing that decision. Also, a well-argued dissent may even convince enough members of the majority to change their minds, turning a minority into a majority; a justice may change his or her mind at any time prior to the actual announcement of the decision in the case.

There are instances in which a majority of the Court may agree on the outcome of a case—that is, on who should win the case—but cannot agree on the reasons why the party should win. For example, a justice may agree that one side should prevail but cannot agree with the legal reasoning given in the majority opinion. In such instances a justice may choose to write a separate *concurring opinion.* A concurring opinion is one in which the justice agrees with the outcome of the case but not with the legal grounds relied upon by the majority. In a concurring opinion, a justice sets forth his or her own rationale for reaching the same result as the majority. Concurring opinions often do little more than provide additional grounds for reaching the Court's decision. However, there are situations in which the consequences of a concurrence could be significant. Suppose, for example, the Court were divided 5–4 in a particular case and one of the justices in the majority refused to sign the majority opinion, preferring to write a separate concurring opinion. In this case there would be no majority opinion. Instead, the opinion of the four remaining justices in the majority becomes what is known as a *plurality opinion.* The outcome of the case would not be changed in this situation, but the case would have no value as a precedent because a majority of the Court could not agree on the legal grounds for the case. This is another situation in which the issue will probably have to come before the Court again for final resolution.

Written opinions of the Court are products of much compromise. The justice assigned to write the majority opinion drafts a copy of the opinion and circulates it among the other eight justices for comments and criticisms. At the same time, any justice writing a separate dissenting or concurring opinion does the same. In this manner, each justice knows exactly what arguments the others plan to use in their opinions and may use that information in writing subsequent drafts of his or her own opinion. A justice may incorporate any comments suggested by another justice in the final draft of the opinion. The author of the majority opinion must be especially careful in drafting that opinion, since failure to take into account the suggestions of the other justices in the majority could lead to one or more concurring opinions—a situation that should be avoided if possible. Obviously, authors of dissenting and concurring opinions, while sensitive to the criticisms of the other justices, do not have to worry about keeping a majority together. Consequently, they are freer to express their own views in their opinions.

When all of the opinions have been written and rewritten, the Court is ready to announce its decision. The justices assemble in the courtroom, and the Chief Justice announces that the Court's decision has been made. The author of the majority opinion summarizes the Court's decision, and any other justices who have written separately may summarize their opinions. The process of Supreme Court decision making is now complete.

Once all appeals have been exhausted and a final judgment entered, the civil case is over except for the execution of the trial court's decision. In a negligence case such as we have been using to illustrate the civil process, the defendant will have to pay the damages awarded at the trial. This may require the defendant to sell his property or to borrow the needed money, but it usually means the defendant's insurance company will pay off. Should a defendant refuse to pay the damages, the plaintiff may resort to two alternatives to get what is due to him. First, the plaintiff may ask the court for a *writ of execution.* This writ authorizes a sheriff or other law enforcement officer to seize the property or bank accounts of the defendant. If property is seized, the sheriff may sell it at auction. The plaintiff's award plus any additional expenses are deducted from the proceeds, and the remainder is returned to the defendant. The second course of action is *garnishment.* In some states the defendant's salary may be garnished to pay the plaintiff. This means that a certain percentage of defendant's salary is withheld from his paycheck until the plaintiff's award is paid in full. The drastic measures described here are necessary to enforce the court's authority. The victorious party, in this case the plaintiff, must be able to rely upon the power of government to enforce the judgment. Otherwise, as suggested at the beginning of this chapter, few persons would be willing to go to the trouble of bringing a lawsuit, and many would resort to extralegal or illegal methods to resolve conflicts.

CRIMINAL PROCEDURE

Criminal and civil processes are similar enough that it is unnecessary to repeat every step of the procedure in detail. However, the reader should keep in mind the major difference between the two procedures. The defendant who loses a civil suit may be forced, as we have just seen, to pay damages to the plaintiff and perhaps even have his property confiscated in the process. As serious as that penalty may be, it hardly compares to the loss of life or liberty that the criminal defendant faces upon conviction for a crime. It is because the consequences of a criminal conviction are so serious that the U.S. system of justice goes to great (some say excessive) lengths to ensure that the innocent go free and only the guilty are punished.

Another important distinction about the criminal justice system also must be understood. A person who is *factually* guilty—that is, one who really committed the crime of which he or she is accused—must be found to be *legally* guilty as well.[6] Unless the determination of legal guilt is accompanied by strict adherence to the rules of criminal procedure, there is denial of due process of law. No matter how firmly convinced we may be that the accused actually committed the crime, the full coercive power of the State cannot be imposed until legal guilt has been proven "beyond a reasonable doubt." Our belief that a person is innocent until proven guilty reflects the difference between factual and legal guilt. With these two distinctions in mind, we begin our discussion of criminal procedure.

Pretrial procedures. The process of criminal justice begins with the arrest of the defendant. The defendant's arrest may result from a complaint sworn out by the victim of the crime, who is called the **complaining witness.** The complaint is sworn out before a magistrate, who then issues an **arrest warrant.** If the crime was committed in the presence of a police officer, the officer is the complaining witness and will secure the arrest warrant from the magistrate if the defendant is not already in custody. The arrest warrant authorizes the police to take the accused into custody and to bring the accused before the magistrate.

When the accused is taken into custody, he is brought before the magistrate "without undue delay" for what is termed the **initial appearance.** Prior to the famous *Miranda* v. *Arizona*[7] decision, the major purpose of the initial appearance was to allow the magistrate to inform the accused of his constitutional rights to remain silent and to have the assistance of counsel. At one time, the police, in their eagerness to secure confessions, unfortunately often delayed presenting the accused before a magistrate until after he had been subjected to the lengthy periods of questioning. In *Mallory* v. *United States*,[8] the accused, Andrew Mallory, was arrested in the early afternoon and was questioned throughout the day until he confessed. Mallory was not brought before a magistrate and informed of his constitutional right to remain silent until the next day. The Supreme Court overturned Mallory's conviction on the grounds that the police had acted improperly in delaying Mallory's initial appearance. In addition, according to the Court, the fact that Mallory was of fairly low intelligence made it even more imperative that he have the assistance of counsel.

As a result of the *Mallory* and *Miranda* decisions, the police are obliged to inform the accused of his constitutional rights whenever a custodial arrest is made, thus lessening the importance of the initial appearance. The initial appearance remains significant, however, because the magistrate will inform the accused of his right to a *preliminary hearing* and will set *bond* for him. Bond is money or property left as security to ensure that the accused will not flee from the jurisdiction of the court. If the magistrate feels that the accused is reliable, has ties to the community, or is unlikely to flee, he may release the accused on his own *recognizance.*

Unless the accused waives it, the next step may be the preliminary hearing. The purpose of the preliminary hearing is to determine whether there is *probable cause* to believe a crime has been committed and whether there exists sufficient evidence that the accused committed it. The preliminary hearing is largely one-sided, with the prosecutor offering enough evidence to convince the judge that there is sufficient probable cause to continue proceedings against the accused. Should the judge decide that sufficient probable cause exists, the accused is *bound over.* If probable cause is insufficient, the accused is released but may be rearrested and recharged at some future time. As indicated, accused persons often waive their right to a preliminary hearing on the advice of counsel since in most cases the police will have enough evidence to have the accused bound over.

The next stage of the criminal justice process is the formal accusation, called the *indictment.* About half the states and the federal government have indictment by *grand jury.* A grand jury is a body of from 12 to 23 persons who decide whether the accused should be tried for a crime. The grand jury passes a *true bill,* which declares that there is sufficient evidence to require the accused to stand trial. The passage of the true bill by a majority of the grand jury constitutes the indictment. If the grand jurors decide that there is insufficient evidence, they return a *no bill.* Critics of the grand jury maintain that it is little more than a rubber stamp for the prosecutor since a grand jury rarely fails to follow the prosecutor's recommendation in a case.[9] Defenders of the grand-jury system maintain that it serves to protect accused persons from malicious prosecution and harassment by unscrupulous prosecutors. As is often the case, one's perspective is based on one's view of the criminal justice system.

The remaining states have chosen to use what is called indictment by *information.* Under this method, the indictment is made at the discretion of the prosecuting attorney. Indictment by information is preferred by those who seek greater efficiency in criminal justice since it is less troublesome than the grand-jury system. Although subject to possible abuse by overzealous prosecutors, the states that use indictment by information seem to be satisfied with it.

Following the indictment, the accused is brought before a judge for *arraignment.* At the arraignment, the accused is formally notified of the charges and is asked to enter a plea. The accused may plead not guilty, in which case a trial will be scheduled. A second option is for the accused to plead guilty. If the defendant's lawyer and the prosecutor have worked out a *plea bargain,* the defendant may agree to plead guilty in exchange for leniency or some other consideration on the part of the judge. Plea bargains, therefore, are arrangements by which the defendant exchanges a guilty plea for a reduced sentence, a lesser offense, or dismissal of other charges.[10]

Finally, the defendant may choose to plead **nolo contendere** to the charges, which literally means "no contest." A *nolo contendere* plea is tantamount to a plea of guilty, and the judge is free to impose any sentence allowable after either a guilty plea or a conviction at trial. The major difference is that a *nolo* plea is a denial of culpability on the part of the defendant. In effect, the defendant denies any moral wrongdoing. A *nolo* plea also serves as a "face-saving" device for a person like Spiro T. Agnew, who was allowed to plead *nolo contendere* to bribery and corruption charges in Maryland in exchange for his resignation from the vice-presidency in October 1973. If for any reason the defendant should refuse to enter a plea, the judge will merely enter a not-guilty plea on his or her behalf.

The discovery process in the criminal process is different from the one we saw in the civil process. Recall that in a civil proceeding, either party may request a deposition or send questions, in the form of interrogatories, to the other party. In a criminal case, on the other hand, the accused may not be forced to answer interrogatories or give a deposition because the Fifth Amendment protects him against self-incrimination. The accused does not have to prove his innocence, nor may he be forced to assist the state in proving its case against him. The accused is entitled to know what evidence of his guilt the prosecutor has, however, so that his lawyer can prepare an adequate defense. This is another example of how the rules of criminal procedure are tilted in favor of the defendant. Given the resources that the state may bring to bear to secure the defendant's conviction, this small advantage is somewhat justified.

The pretrial conference in a criminal case is similar to that in a civil suit. The defendant's lawyer and the prosecutor hammer out with the judge the basic issues of the case and any facts that can be agreed upon beforehand. If, for example, the defendant is pleading not guilty by reason of insanity in a murder case, the defense may be willing to stipulate that the accused killed the victim. The real issue is the question of the defendant's sanity, and the trial will revolve primarily around that issue. Once these ground rules have been agreed upon, the trial stage begins.

Criminal trial stage. The trial process for civil and criminal cases is very similar, so we will highlight only significant differences between the two. One such difference is in jury selection. Criminal procedure usually allows more peremptory challenges than are allowed in civil cases. In Texas, for example, each side is allowed 15 peremptory challenges in a capital case and 10 in a noncapital felony case.[11] Once the *voir dire* process is completed and the jury is impanelled, the defendant is said to be *in jeopardy.* The significance of being placed in jeopardy is that the Fifth Amendment to the U.S.

Constitution declares that no person shall "be twice put in jeopardy of life or limb." In other words, if the defendant is acquitted or the charges are subsequently dropped, he may not be tried again for the same offense.

Another important difference between a civil trial and a criminal trial is the standard of proof required for each. Under the rules of civil procedure, in order for the plaintiff to prevail, he must show that the weight, or preponderance, of evidence favors his version of the facts. In a criminal case, however, the State, as the plaintiff, must meet a higher standard—beyond a reasonable doubt. One way to think of the beyond-a-reasonable-doubt standard is to consider and then reject all other possible explanations for the crime except the conclusion that the defendant did indeed commit the crime for which he is being tried. All alternative or feasible explanations as to who might have committed the crime other than the defendant are considered and discarded. In presenting evidence, the prosecutor seeks to establish that the conclusion that the defendant is guilty of committing the crime is the only conclusion a reasonable person could reach. The job of the defendant's lawyer is to create a reasonable doubt in the minds of the jurors in order to avoid a guilty verdict. If state law requires a unanimous verdict, a single juror may cause a *hung jury.* In the event of a hung jury, the State retains the right to either retry the defendant on the same charge or on a lesser (but not greater) charge without violating the double-jeopardy clause. Finally, the prosecutor may decide that a new trial will not result in a conviction and drop the charges against the defendant.

A third difference between the civil and criminal processes involves the directed verdict. After each side has presented its case, the defense may request a directed verdict from the judge. While the defense may ask the judge to direct the jury to return a not-guilty verdict, the State may not request a directed guilty verdict. This is another example of how the rules of criminal procedure tend to favor the defendant. The presumption is that the defendant, who is without the vast resources possessed by the State, must be given some advantages to offset the power that the State is capable of marshalling against him.

After the closing statements and the charge, the men and women of the jury begin their deliberations. In routine cases, the jury will reach a verdict in a relatively short period of time. In highly publicized cases, the judge may order the jury *sequestered* from the time the first juror is selected or when the jury panel is complete. The jury is then isolated until they either reach a verdict or inform the judge that they are hopelessly deadlocked. The judge must be very careful about how long he allows a deadlocked jury to deliberate. Naturally, the judge (and perhaps the parties) would prefer a definite verdict in order to avoid another trial. However, the jury may not be pressured to bring in a verdict, especially if it turns out to be a guilty verdict. The defendant, on appeal, could argue that the lengthy deliberation indicated reasonable doubt among some of the jurors and that these "holdouts" were pressured to change their votes to "guilty" in order to avoid prolonging their ordeal. Such undue pressure could constitute reversible error, resulting in a new trial for the defendant.

A final way in which criminal and civil cases differ is in the right of appeal. The defendant, of course, is free to appeal his conviction based on errors made during the trial. The State, however, can appeal an acquittal only on rare occasions. Generally speaking, the State may appeal an acquittal only to clarify a matter of law. That is, if the prosecutor believes that the judge has rendered an incorrect legal ruling, the State may appeal the ruling to clarify the point of law for future reference. The defendant actually tried in the case involving the disputed ruling cannot be retried without violating the double-jeopardy clause.

The appellate process in a criminal case can be long and arduous if the defendant is willing to pursue it. Conviction for a crime in a state court allows the defendant to avail himself of the state's appellate procedure. If unsuccessful at the state level, the defendant may seek further review in a federal court under federal *habeas corpus* procedures. Habeas corpus review, in effect, allows federal courts to reopen a case on the grounds that a right secured by the U.S. Constitution has been abridged by the State. The Burger and Rehnquist Courts have shown a reluctance to allow lower federal courts to review allegations of violations of constitutional rights if the allegations have already been reviewed extensively by state courts.[12]

By mid-1995, at least one-quarter of the states and Congress were considering methods of sharply curtailing death-row inmates' use of the habeas proceedings. The favored plan seemingly is one that would limit the prisoner to one habeas petition that would be considered simultaneously as the direct appeal. These habeas petitions challenge the constitutionality of the conviction rather than the issue of guilt or innocence that is the subject of the direct appeal.[13] The federal courts under the Supreme Court's direction have conducted their own review and made suggestions for streamlining the policy. The message that the Supreme Court wants to limit its involvement in death-penalty matters is bolstered by holdings in cases such as *Herrera* v. *Collins*.[14] There the Court held that while executing someone with a truly persuasive claim of actual innocence would be unconstitutional, federal habeas relief would be available only if there were no state avenues open to process such a claim. Justices Scalia and Thomas's concurring opinion declared that if the innocence claim were truly persuasive, then the state's governor would issue a pardon and the matter would not be in the courts at all.

RULES OF EVIDENCE

As previously noted, the submission of evidence is the most crucial part of a legal proceeding. In this section we will examine the rules of evidence in greater detail, providing examples from both civil and criminal cases. Specifically, we will discuss the types and forms of evidence, the hearsay rule, and the exclusionary rule. We begin our discussion with some general observations about evidence.

Trials are perhaps the ultimate contests in our competitive society. Even the names of cases, such as *Smith* v. *Jones,* reflect the adversarial nature of our judicial system. Each party bears the responsibility of persuading the trier of fact, whether judge or jury, to accept its version of the case, in much the same manner that it is the responsibility of a baseball team to move the batters around the bases in order to score runs and win. Each party is charged with structuring the facts it presents to persuade the fact-finder, although certain "rules of the game" govern the introduction of evidence in legal proceedings.

The umpire of the match is the judge. He or she decides whether a particular piece of evidence is relevant—that is, whether it tends to establish a material fact in the case.[15] The parties involved in the trial elect to have either a judge alone or a jury act as the fact-finder and render the decision in the case. The fact-finder hears the statements of the witnesses, observes their demeanor, and examines the physical evidence. They decide the credibility of each witness and assess the weight of the evidence. Suppose that X testifies that she saw the accused assault Y, but the defense produces other witnesses who say that X was not present at the scene. The jury may choose to disbelieve X and, therefore, not rely on her testimony, while giving full weight to the testimony of the defense witnesses. In other words, the "weight" of the evidence depends on the credibility of the statement in the fact-finder's mind as well as on the amount of influence the evidence has on the final verdict.[16]

Everyone is familiar with the concept of evidence, whether the exposure comes from television dramas, media coverage of sensational trials, or actual involvement in a hearing. Evidence introduced at trials includes not only physical evidence but also the statements of witnesses who testify on the stand. It ranges from simple declarations, such as "I saw the yellow car run the light and smash into the other car," to sophisticated scientific evidence relating to design weaknesses in product-liability cases. Evidence that was once considered exotic—bitemarks, DNA, various body fluids (blood, saliva, semen), and fabric fibers—is becoming commonplace in criminal trials and often forms the basis for a conviction.

Direct and circumstantial evidence. Evidence may be classified as either direct or circumstantial, depending on the nature of the facts. *Direct evidence* is derived from one's five senses—taste, touch, smell, sight, and hearing. The following statements are examples of direct evidence: "I smelled alcohol on her breath," or "I saw the accident." Direct evidence proves the facts without the introduction of additional testimony. Although direct evidence may stand alone as proof, the fact-finder may decide to give little weight to it for a variety of reasons, such as the unreliability of the witness or contradictory testimony from another witness.

In contrast, *circumstantial evidence* requires the fact-finder to fit pieces of evidence together to complete the picture, just as one might fit a jigsaw puzzle together. The lawyer carefully provides the necessary pieces of evidence to construct a credible and viable case.[17] To illustrate, suppose the State presents a series of witnesses who testify to the following: (1) Sebastian and Osborn had a disagreement at a party; (2) the two of them went alone into a windowless room with only one exit and locked the door behind them; (3) eavesdroppers loitering outside the room heard a loud bang and decided to investigate; and (4) upon breaking down the door, they found Sebastian holding a revolver and Osborn stretched out on the floor with a neat, circular wound in his arm. Although none of the witnesses actually saw Sebastian shoot Osborn, the fact-finder at Sebastian's trial can easily use the building blocks of testimony provided by the State to infer Sebastian's guilt and convict him.

Forms of evidence.   Evidence may be presented in the form of *tangible evidence* (physical exhibits such as weapons or charts), evidence that comes under *judicial notice* (facts that are commonly known or are verifiable by referring to some widely accepted reference book), or *oral testimony.* First, tangible evidence is evidence that the fact-finder can touch or observe in the courtroom. This category is subdivided into two groups: real evidence and demonstrative evidence. Real evidence is a physical object that is involved in the case, such as a murder weapon or the cocaine allegedly sold by the defendant to an undercover police officer. Demonstrative evidence is a visual or audiovisual aid, such as a chart of the intersection where an automobile accident occurred, a skeleton in a personal injury case, or a videotape of the incident.[18] Lawyers are becoming increasingly creative in the use of these visual aids. For example, a fairly common practice is to present a videotape of an average day in the life of a person who is paralyzed because of a defendant's negligence to raise the jury's sympathy and thus the amount of damages awarded. Prosecutors and the police have also adopted video technology. Police routinely videotape allegedly intoxicated drivers taking sobriety tests of various kinds, and then those tapes are introduced at trial. In *Pennsylvania v. Muniz,* the Supreme Court ratified the admission of such tapes taken before the *Miranda* warnings were given to the accused, although they held that before asking questions which go beyond the routine booking queries, the warnings should be given.[19]

A second form of evidence is judicial notice, which allows the judge to recognize that certain facts are commonly known within the community (it is very cold in the Arctic) or can be ascertained by reference to a highly reliable source such as a calendar (December 25, 1983, was a Sunday). The parties are then relieved of the obligation to provide formal proof through witnesses or exhibits.[20] Judicial notice is particularly useful when the case involves the law of several jurisdictions. For example, several states may claim an extremely wealthy person as a resident of their states upon her death in order to enrich their state treasuries through the inheritance tax. The crux of the case is the interpretation of the laws of the various states regarding the definition of legal residency. In such a case, the court could accept the statutes into evidence by judicial notice without calling the state official who is charged with publishing the official version of the laws to testify.

The third and most common form of evidence is oral testimony, which is given by a witness on the stand in open court or in a deposition under oath. Each party has the opportunity to question the witness and to test his veracity, either on direct examination or on cross-examination. This right to observe the witnesses and their demeanor is guaranteed in criminal trials by the Sixth Amendment to the U.S. Constitution, which states that "the accused shall enjoy the right . . . to be confronted with the witnesses against him; to have compulsory process for obtaining witnesses in his favor." The opportunity to cross-examine opposing witnesses and to present one's own witnesses is entrenched as firmly in the civil law as in the criminal law, but face-to-face confrontation of the witnesses is not an absolute rule. For example, the Supreme Court has permitted the use of one-way closed-circuit television in child-abuse cases in which the victim and the defendant were in separate rooms but the child was subject to cross-examination.[21] A *subpoena,* a written order from the court, may be served on a prospective witness demanding that he or she either appear in court to testify or be subject to a penalty, often contempt of court. As previously noted, a *subpoena duces tecum* requires the witness to bring to court any records in his or her possession related to the case. These legal tools are available in civil and criminal cases to both parties in order to enable them to command the presence of witnesses.[22] A party may not compel an out-of-state witness to appear in the absence of a statute, but states have acted to create procedures to allow service of subpoenas on out-of-state residents.[23]

Presentation of evidence.   Evidence is presented to the fact-finder through the testimony of witnesses. Generally, one of the first orders of business in a trial is to segregate the witnesses from the courtroom proceedings in order to prevent them from tailoring their testimony to fit the evidence that has already been presented. Obviously, this procedure is not followed for party-witnesses, who have a right to be present throughout the proceeding.[24] Witnesses may also be sequestered for the duration of the trial, although this is rather rare. During the trial, the attorney identifies the person to be called to testify and the oath is administered.

Information is elicited from the witness through a series of questions and answers. The lawyer calling the witness first questions the person in direct examination, and then the opposing lawyer cross-examines the same witness. The process continues until one or the other counsel informs the judge that there are no more questions for this witness. The successive questions are limited to topics in the previous statements and thus are narrowed on each round of questioning.[25]

As previously noted, an attorney generally may not lead his own witness. However, the Federal Rules of Procedure have altered the traditional rule to allow leading questions on direct examination "as necessary to develop the witness' testimony" while continuing to accept their use for *adverse witnesses* or parties.[26] To impeach a witness is to put his credibility at issue in the minds of the triers of fact. Many methods are used to implant doubts about the witness's testimony. One is to show that the witness is biased or has a monetary interest in the case. (Expert witnesses are often challenged on the basis that they are being paid for their testimony. In fact, they are selling their time and knowledge to one party or the other, but in a perfectly acceptable manner.) Another method is to show that the person has a poor reputation for truth and veracity in the community. A third way is to present conflicting testimony from other witnesses.[27]

Even tangible evidence is introduced into the trial through oral testimony. In other words, a witness on the stand must identify the tangible evidence and explain its significance to the case. However, the parties may agree on certain evidence by stipulation beforehand, and it is then presented to the fact-finder by the attorneys. To present tangible evidence of all types requires that *foundation,* or basic information, be provided about the item before the court will admit it into evidence, this is called *laying a predicate.*[28] Assume, for example, that a contract case involves the records of the XYZ Corporation and that these records are essential to the plaintiff's case. The custodian of the corporation's records is called to the stand and is required to testify to the following before the records are admissible: (1) that the record was made during the regular course of business; (2) that the record was made at or near the time of the event in question; and (3) that the record was made by an employee with personal knowledge or as a regular part of business activities based on information from someone who did have personal knowledge. Different requirements are set forth for items such as photographs, weapons, and other pieces of tangible evidence.[29]

The judge is the umpire who decides on the admissibility of evidence. The opposing party has the opportunity to object to the testimony or tangible evidence as it is introduced, and the party who introduced the evidence then has to explain why the evidence should be admitted. Failure to enter a timely objection often constitutes a waiver of the objection for purposes of appeal.[30] Evidence that might be inflammatory, such as gory pictures of a murder victim, or otherwise prejudicial might be the subject of a *motion in limine.* Such a motion is filed and considered before trial or outside the presence of the jury. The judge may forbid the introduction of such evidence and even prevent the attorneys from referring to such evidence.[31] Many jurisdictions allow the parties to exclude evidence that the defendant's insurance company will actually pay the damages if the defendant is found to be at fault.[32] The obvious intent is to prevent juries from assessing heavier or lighter damages because of the ultimate source of funds.

Rule against hearsay. When a witness is testifying about information based on his own sensory perceptions, the jury and the parties to the lawsuit have the opportunity to observe the witness's demeanor. This is not the case when the witness quotes someone else, however. For example, statements like "I know he forged the check because he told me he did," or "Dick said that the defendant admitted it was all his fault" are deemed *hearsay* because the person who initially made the statement is not in the courtroom and cannot be cross-examined. Courts have, therefore, developed the *rule against hearsay*, which prevents such statements from being admitted as evidence.

Hearsay includes not only spoken and written comments but also conduct. To illustrate, suppose a police officer testifies that he conducted a lineup of suspects and that the victim pointed out the defendant as the perpetrator of the crime. The victim did not orally identify the defendant, but the officer is relaying her nonverbal assertion that the defendant is the one who committed the crime. The definition of hearsay is three-pronged: (1) it is an assertion (by verbal, written, or assertive conduct), (2) made by someone other than the testifying witness, which (3) is offered to prove the truth of the matter stated. If an assertion meets all three of these conditions, it is hearsay and *must be excluded from trial.*[33] Not all out-of-court statements are offered to prove the truth of the matter stated, however. For example, an ambulance driver's testimony that "Henry told me that the driver of the green car ran the light and was at fault" is not admissible to show which driver was at fault, but it is admissible to show that Henry was conscious following the accident.

The most celebrated case of a conviction based on hearsay, and one which contributed to the development of the rule against hearsay, is that of Sir Walter Raleigh. Raleigh, founder of the American colony of Roanoke, is famous for swirling his cloak to the ground to prevent Queen Elizabeth I from stepping into the mud. He was later charged with treason on the basis of two out-of-court statements. A ship's pilot told the court that a Portuguese gentleman reported to him that Raleigh had expressed an intention of cutting the queen's throat. Lord Cobham declared in his sworn statement that Raleigh and he had plotted to dethrone Elizabeth and put Arabella Stuart in her place. Although Cobham was imprisoned only a few feet away from the site of the trial, he did not appear in person at the proceedings. Thus, Raleigh was convicted on the accusations of two people who did not appear in court and whose veracity was never questioned by the trier of fact. In fact, Cobham later recanted his allegations. Public disgust with the decision spurred the development of a new rule of law—hearsay evidence should be excluded from trials.[34]

There are three primary reasons for the exclusion of hearsay evidence. First, it is very possible that the statement has not been repeated accurately. A popular party game called "gossip" illustrates this possibility. The first person whispers a comment to the next person and so on until everyone in the group has heard the statement. The final statement often does not even resemble the beginning comment. The same may be true for a statement that is being offered as evidence. Second, the person who has made the statement is not in court and therefore is not subject to cross-examination. As we have already discussed, the right to confront witnesses is one of the mainstays of our legal tradition. In addition, the trier of fact, whether judge or jury, is not given the opportunity to observe the declarant and his demeanor in order to determine his veracity. Nor can the fact-finder determine the basis of the declarant's information, whether personal observation or casual rumor. The third reason for excluding hearsay, and perhaps the most obvious, is that the declarant was not under oath when he made the original statement and was therefore not compelled to tell the truth.[35]

Over the years the courts have backed away from the absolute stand that hearsay is never admissible, and certain exceptions have developed. An example is the exception that permits dying declarations to be admitted as evidence on the questionable theory that a person who is dying will be truthful because he will soon be facing his Maker. Three basic requirements must be met before such a statement will be admitted: (1) the declarant was aware of his pending death; (2) the declarant had direct and accurate knowledge; and (3) the statement contains facts and not opinions or guesses. Traditionally, there has also been a requirement that the person must actually be deceased at the time of trial; however, that has been abandoned by some jurisdictions including the federal courts.[36]

The Federal Rules of Evidence approach the problem of hearsay and the various exceptions by creating three categories of such statements. First, the Rules declare that prior statements by the witness which were given under oath and were subject to cross-examination are not hearsay and neither are admissions by the party opponent. If the statements are not hearsay, then obviously the rule against hearsay does not apply. Second, the Rules list a set of circumstances when hearsay can be admitted even when the declarant is available and could be called to testify himself or herself. The 23 or so exceptions include the following: (1) contemporaneous statements made while under the stress of a startling event or of one's impressions about the event; (2) statements made about the then existing mental, emotional, or physical conditions of declarant or for purposes of medical diagnosis; (3) records of regularly conducted activities or the absence of such entries; (4) various public records; (5) widely published and accepted market reports and learned treatises; (6) statement of personal or family history; and (7) reputation as to character or judgment of previous conviction (there are additional rules limiting the admissibility of both). Third, the Rules provide for admission of hearsay for former testimony, for statements under belief of impending death, and for statements against one's pecuniary or proprietary interest or which would subject one to civil and/or criminal liability when the declarant is unavailable. The unavailability of the declarant may stem from death, from a refusal to testify despite a court order to do so, from the witness's testimony as to lack of memory of events, from mental or physical illness, or from absence from the proceeding after a showing by the party that he tried to locate the declarant and could not.[37]

The witness.   One of the main issues at any trial is the credibility of the witnesses. In other words, can and will the trier of fact believe the witness's statements? The chief method of presenting a case in our adversarial system is through the witnesses. The party calling the witness to the stand claims the witness as his own. It is imperative that the attorneys have an accurate picture of what the witness will say before calling him to the stand.

People who observe the same event do not always perceive it in the same way. A fan of one football team may deem an interception by his team as a great defensive play, while the other team's fans might call it a horrible offensive play. A husband and wife are both parties to the same marriage and the same events. When each is called to the witness stand in a divorce action, however, the testimony often sounds as if they are talking about two different marriages and totally different people. The spouses are not intentionally distorting the truth, but one's perceptions color the testimony given. Police reports abound with eyewitnesses giving conflicting information about a crime. It is the responsibility of the fact-finder to sort through the information in order to arrive at an accurate assessment of the situation.

The first question about any witness is his or her competency to testify. Adults are presumed to have the necessary attributes of competency: the ability to perceive and understand what they are testifying about, the ability to remember the event, and the ability to communicate their knowledge to the fact-finder. This presumption may be challenged for a variety of reasons; the witness's having been intoxicated or hard-of-hearing are two examples. Even a witness who has been adjudged insane may be a competent witness if the court finds that he is able to give an accurate description of the event and that he or she understands the consequences of lying on the stand.[38] The latter requirement is the same for infant witnesses. The question for children is whether they understand the difference between right and wrong and whether they know what it means to lie. The trial judge has a great deal of discretion in deciding whether a child is competent to testify.[39]

An issue similar to competency is that of qualifying someone as an expert witness. The general rule prevents the opinions and conclusions of laypersons from being admitted as evidence. There are two reasons for this rule. The first is that the jurors themselves, given the same facts, can form a conclusion just as well as the witness can (and it is their job to do so). The second reason is that the witness lacks the necessary training, skill, or experience necessary to be considered an expert and is therefore unqualified. On the other hand, experts are permitted, and even encouraged, to testify as to their conclusions. The main criteria are (1) that the opinions to which the expert is testifying were formed because of special knowledge, skills, education, experience, or training that is not within the ordinary experiences of jurors and (2) that the witness is truly an expert. Qualification as an expert does not require formal training.[40] For example, a mechanic who has worked in his field for 20 years may be qualified as an expert just as easily as would a mechanical engineer.

Although a witness may be competent, she may not be credible. The judge or the jury has the opportunity to observe the witness to detect any telltale signs that she is lying. They are assisted in this task by the opposing counsel, who may try to impeach the other party's witnesses. Four primary tactics are used in impeaching witnesses: (1) showing bias or prejudice, (2) using prior inconsistent statements, (3) proving a sensory deficiency, and (4) providing evidence of prior behavior that casts doubt on the witness's veracity.

A lawyer can show a witness to be biased by eliciting information that the other party is paying him for his testimony or that his expenses are being paid during the trial (a frequent and proper arrangement for expert witnesses). A second method of impeachment is through the use of prior inconsistent statements. Suppose that Smith testifies on the stand that it was foggy on the day of the accident, but she had said in her deposition that it was clear. Another method is to challenge the witness's ability to perceive the event. For example, Pasternacki testifies that his glasses were broken but that he clearly saw the accident from two blocks away, while his optometrist testifies that Pasternacki's vision would have been blurry and that he could not possibly have seen the accident clearly.[41] A fourth way to cast doubt on veracity is to show prior felony convictions or a bad reputation in the community for truthfulness. Frequently, states delineate both the types of crimes and the time period since the conviction before allowing admission of such evidence. The federal system will not permit impeachment through use of a conviction more than ten years old and requires that the crime was one which could result in imprisonment of one year or more or involved dishonesty or false statements. In addition, the probative value of the evidence must outweigh the prejudice. Parties may also challenge the witness's reputation in the community for untruthfulness, and evidence to support the evidence of a truthful character is admissible only after untruthfulness has been alleged.[42] The object is to create doubts as to the witness's credibility in the minds of the jury.

Privileges.   Certain communications are considered privileged; that is, the witness does not have to reveal the contents of the conversation. The *privilege* is based on the relationship of those having the discussion. As a society, we have decided that maintaining confidentiality in certain relationships is more important than having the relevant information in a particular trial. Examples of privileges are those between attorneys and clients, physicians and patients, and clergy and penitents. The states are split with regard to the marital privilege; some states treat it as a privilege of one spouse not to have the other testify against him, while other states treat it as a privilege of the spouse not to give testimony against the other. In other words, some states treat it as a privilege belonging to the defendant to prevent the spouse from testifying against him, while others treat it as a privilege of the witness-spouse to elect not to testify. Obviously, government officials do not have to reveal military or state secrets if they can show that disclosure would be harmful to national defense; there is also a privilege that allows police officers to refuse to reveal the name of an informer. Some states have enacted *shield laws* which allow journalists to protect the identity of their sources from being disclosed without fear of being held in contempt themselves.[43]

The exclusionary rule. As we repeatedly discuss, our legal system places a premium on due process and the fairness of the procedures used for conviction. The courts have outlined procedures to be followed in the course of gathering evidence and preparing for trial. Just as we are aware of the rules we must obey in order to avoid entanglement in the legal system, so the police are aware of the rules that govern the gathering of evidence. When the police violate those rules, the courts decline to accept the improperly collected evidence into the trial. This refusal to accept such "tainted" evidence is called the ***exclusionary rule.***

The exclusionary rule was established in the case of *Weeks* v. *United States*,[44] wherein the Supreme Court argued that if there were no exclusionary rule, "the protection of the Fourth Amendment . . . might as well be stricken from the Constitution." Although the *Weeks* rule initially applied only to cases in federal courts, the Supreme Court extended the rule to state cases in *Mapp* v. *Ohio*.[45] Evidence uncovered as a result of improper police conduct, called "the fruit of the poisonous tree," is inadmissible at trial. The Supreme Court has somewhat eroded the strong protection of the rule through the enunciation of limited exceptions in recent cases. The exclusionary rule continues to be controversial, and we will say more about it in Chapter 7.

Scientific evidence in criminal trials. Technological advances have been made in every societal endeavor, and police work is no exception. For years, courts have given credibility to certain pieces of scientific evidence, such as firearms identifications through ballistics tests, chemical tests for intoxication, fingerprints, handwriting samples, and photographs, just to name a few. However, courts still do not routinely accept the use of evidence gathered through hypnosis, and the results of polygraph tests usually come in as evidence only if both parties agree to the admission.[46] Courts do not rush to endorse technological advances, but today cases are decided by microanalysis of fibers, analysis of bitemarks, and neutron activation analysis of evidence. As in civil cases, the credibility of this evidence depends on the party's ability to show the fact-finder that the test was conducted in a fair manner by a qualified person.

Each party in a lawsuit has the responsibility to convince either the judge or the jury to accept its version of the case. They do so through the presentation of evidence. Evidence is classified by types: real evidence, evidence admitted by judicial notice, and oral testimony. All evidence is presented by witnesses who testify under oath either in open court or in depositions about the matters within their personal knowledge or by stipulation by the parties. Statements that fall under the hearsay rule or improperly seized evidence in criminal trials will not be admitted at trial.

ALTERNATIVE DISPUTE RESOLUTION

Abraham Lincoln, that practical lawyer, once offered a piece of advice to law students: "Discourage litigation. Persuade your neighbors to compromise whenever you can. Point out to them how the nominal winner is often a real loser—in fees, expenses and waste of time."[47] In the 140 years since, little has changed on the American legal scene, and Lincoln's advice is as pertinent today as it was then. When wronged or cheated, we stampede to the courthouse to file civil lawsuits, seeking both retribution and omnipotent judges to ratify our certain belief that we are right. However, there are several roadblocks in our path—overcrowded dockets with very long delays in hearing civil cases; very high expenditures in the form of attorney's fees, court costs, and discovery; no assurance of winning in the end or recouping our costs; further estranged relations with the opposing party with whom we may have an ongoing relationship, such as a former spouse; and perhaps most importantly, the "stress, trauma and sagging spirits" as well as the incredible investment of time and effort involved in a lawsuit.[48]

Disillusionment and disgruntlement with the civil justice system has led to the burgeoning attention given to alternatives for resolving disputes. The need for timely and affordable justice has provided the impetus for the creation of a multidimensional approach to public justice—involving both formal and informal means. Nearly all states have hopped on the bandwagon and have made provisions for some type of alternative dispute resolution (ADR), either through the private sector or through administrative agencies or the courts. These programs cover the gamut in terms of organization, from the so-called "rent-a-judge" program in which the neutral party (often a retired judge) hears the evidence which would be presented in court before reaching a decision, to neighborhood justice centers where a trained (the term is used advisedly) mediator assists the parties in reconciling their differences in a much more informal setting which encourages participation of the parties and discourages the participation of lawyers. The most effective use of ADR for individuals seems to be in the areas of landlord-tenant, domestic relations, contracts, motor vehicles, and consumer transactions.[49]

Utilizing neutral third parties to settle disputes without resorting to litigation is a commonly mandated practice in contracts, especially those relating to labor, employment, and construction contracts. *Mediation* is the intervention by a neutral third party between two contending parties "with a view to reconcile them or persuade them to adjust or settle their dispute."[50] When the parties agree in advance to be bound by the decision of the mediator, then it is called *arbitration.* Arbitration has been an integral part of the legal system for years and is codified on the federal level in the Arbitration Act, Title 9 of the United States Code.

One trend in ADR is court-annexed arbitration. Courts have had the power to refer cases to arbitration for centuries, but there is a new emphasis on its use at both the state and national level. In 1988, Congress created a pilot project for ADR on the national level in 20 district courts, which has twice been renewed. In those courts, parties may agree to consensual arbitration, or in 10 named districts, the judges may require submission of the case to arbitration if the amount in controversy is less than $100,000 (exclusive of interests and costs) *and* if the case does not involve violation of the Constitution, civil rights claims under 42 U.S.C. §1985, or equal protection claims. The arbitrator has the power to conduct the hearing, to administer oaths, and to issue subpoenas. Once the arbitrator has rendered a decision, it is final and binding on the parties unless a motion for a *trial de novo* or new trial is filed with the district court within 30 days; otherwise, there is no appeal from the decision.[51] Parties in federal court today may be subjected to ADR under local rule or by statute; however, arbitration as described here is only one form of federally accepted ADR.

Justice Sandra Day O'Connor has stated, "The courts of this country should not be the places where the resolution of disputes begins. They should be the places where the disputes end—after alternative methods of resolving disputes have been considered and tried."[52] Proponents argue that not only does ADR relieve the burden on the courts, but it also provides expeditious and swifter public justice in many instances. However, not all see neighborhood justice as a panacea. They point out that the wealthy will still have access to the courts while poor people will be forced into lesser forums and that it promotes uncertainty—while one of the legal system's goals is predictability—because ADR is a somewhat ad hoc system of justice in that the case outcome may not follow legal norms.[53] Despite the criticisms, it appears likely that ADR will continue to flourish and grow as an alternative to full-blown litigation.

CONCLUSION

Procedural due process of law, whether civil or criminal, is fundamental to American law. As we have seen, the rules of civil procedure provide the standard by which essentially private disputes are settled in a just and orderly fashion. Before a person is willing to put his case before a court of law for resolution, he must believe that the ground rules are fair to both sides and that the dispute settler will be impartial. The rules must be spelled out clearly and in advance. All of this is necessary so that citizens will accept the legitimacy of the judicial process.

Procedural due process in the area of criminal law presents an additional problem. There is little doubt that government possesses awesome power to deprive individuals of life, liberty, or property. Consequently, due process places strict procedural requirements on government to ensure that public officials do not abuse their power. Although sometimes criticized for favoring the accused, procedural due process is necessary for liberty in a free society. The requirement that government obtain the deprivation of a person's life or liberty "by the book" is considered by many to be an essential safeguard of freedom. Even a cursory examination of repressive and totalitarian governments reveals that denial of fundamental principles of due process is a common element. In a democratic society, *how* the government deprives a person of life, liberty, or property is every bit as important as *why* it does so.

NOTES

1. The opening scene in the film *The Godfather* illustrates this point. The undertaker, whose daughter has been brutally beaten, seeks "justice" from the Godfather when his daughter's attackers receive only a suspended sentence.

2. In rare instances, the disputing parties might be able to work out a last-minute negotiated settlement before the jury returns its verdict. However, such a settlement is highly unlikely.

3. Fed. R. App. P. 3–12.

4. Administrative Office of the United States Courts, *Annual Report of the Director of the Administrative Office of the United States Courts: Judicial Business of the United States Courts, 1993* (Washington, D.C.: Government Printing Office, 1993), p. A-1.

5. *Humphrey's Executor* v. *United States*, 295 U.S. 602 (1935).

6. Herbert L. Packer, "Two Models of the Criminal Process," in George F. Cole, *Criminal Justice: Law and Politics*, 4th ed. (Monterey, Calif.: Brooks/Cole, 1984), pp. 15–29.

7. *Miranda* v. *Arizona*, 384 U.S. 436 (1966).

8. *Mallory* v. *United States*, 354 U.S. 449 (1957).

9. Herbert Jacob, *Justice in America: Courts, Lawyers, and the Judicial Process*, 4th ed. (Boston: Little, Brown, 1984), p. 188.

10. James V. Calvi, "Plea Bargaining: An Empirical Study of Participant Perspectives" (unpublished Ph.D. dissertation, University of Missouri, 1977), pp. 2–3.

11. Tex. Code Crim. Proc., Art. 35.15

12. *Stone* v. *Powell*, 482 U.S. 465 (1976).

13. Mark Ballard, "Fast-Moving Habeas Bill Sets Up Quicker Executions, Counsel Pay," *Texas Lawyer*, April 10, 1995, p. 6.

14. *Herrera* v. *Collins*, 61 U.S.L.W. 4108 (1993).

15. Edmund Morris Morgan, *Some Problems with Proof under the Anglo-American System of Litigation* (Westport, Conn.: Greenwood Press, 1975), p. 86.

16. Milton D. Green, *Basic Civil Procedures* (Mineola, N.Y.: Foundation Press, 1972), pp. 164–165.

17. Paul B. Weston and Kenneth M. Wells, *Criminal Evidence for Police* (Englewood Cliffs, N.J.: Prentice-Hall, 1976), pp. 185–186.

18. Jon R. Waltz, *Introduction to Criminal Evidence* (Chicago: Nelson-Hall, 1983), pp. 14–15.

19. *Pennsylvania v. Muniz*, 58 U.S.L.W. 4817 (1990).

20. William Farnum White, *Winning in Court on the Law of Facts* (Englewood Cliffs, N.J.: Prentice-Hall, 1976), pp. 122–125; Fed. R. Evid. 201.

21. *Maryland v. Craig*, 58 U.S.L.W. 5044 (1990).

22. Weston and Wells, pp. 55–56.

23. 81 Am. Jur. 2d Witnesses § 8.

24. Fed. R. Evid. 615.

25. Edward W. Cleary, ed., *McCormick's Handbook on the Law of Evidence*, 2nd ed. (St. Paul, Minn.: West Publishing Co., 1972), p. 6; Fed. R. Evid. 611.

26. Fed. R. Evid. 611.

27. Weston and Wells, pp. 64–66.

28. Waltz, pp. 30–35.

29. Rolando del Carmen, *Criminal Procedure and Evidence* (New York: Harcourt Brace Jovanovich, 1978), pp. 117–118; Fed. R. Evid. 803 (6) and (7).

30. Morgan, pp. 86–88.

31. Fed. R. Evid. 403.

32. Cleary, p. 479; Fed. R. Evid. 411.

33. Cleary, p. 584.

34. Sir Walter Raleigh's Case as cited in David W. Louisell, John Kaplan, and Jon R. Waltz, *Cases and Materials on Evidence* (Mineola, N.Y.: Foundation Press, 1972), pp. 51–52.

35. Morgan, p. 112.

36. del Carmen, pp. 113–114; Fed. R. Evid. 804.

37. Fed. R. Evid. 801–804.

38. Waltz, pp. 303–305.

39. Weston and Wells, p. 57.

40. Andrea A. Moenssens, Ray Edward Moses, and Fred E. Inbau, *Scientific Evidence in Criminal Cases* (Mineola, N.Y. Foundation Press, 1973), pp. 1–4; Fed. R. Evid. 702.

41. Waltz, pp. 105–133.

42. Fed R. Evid. 608.

43. del Carmen, pp. 105–110.

44. *Weeks v. United States*, 232 U.S. 383 (1914).

45. *Mapp v. Ohio*, 367 U.S. 643 (1961).

46. Waltz, pp. 337–432.

47. Edward J. Kemp, *Abraham Lincoln's Philosophy of Common Sense*, Vol. I (New York: New York Academy of Sciences, 1965), p. 346.

48. Fletcher Knebel and Gerald S. Clay, *Before You Sue: How to Get Justice Without Going to Court* (New York: William Morrow and Company, Inc., 1987), p. 15.

49. Council of State Governments, *The Book of the States 1988–89 Edition* (Lexington, Ky.: The Council of State Governments, 1988), pp. 148–149.

50. Henry C. Black, *Black's Law Dictionary,* 4th ed. (St. Paul, Minn.: West Publishing Company, 1968), p. 1133.

51. Judicial Improvements and Access to Justice Act, 28 U.S.C.A. §§ 651–658.

52. Janice Roehl and Larry Ray, "Toward the Multi-Door Courthouse—Dispute Resolution Intake and Referral," *NIJ Reports* SNI 198 (July 1987), pp. 2–7.

53. Jonathan B. Marks, Earl Johnson, Jr. and Peter L. Szanton, *Dispute Resolution in America: Processes in Evolution* (Washington, D.C.: National Institute for Dispute Resolution, 1985), pp. 51–56.

5

Limitations

The judicial branch of government, although immensely influential, is not unrestrained. The powers of courts and judges are circumscribed by barriers emanating from a variety of sources, including the judicial system itself. The doctrine of *stare decisis*, or following the precedent of prior court decisions, evolved through judicial custom. Courts are confined by constitutional provisions and the procedural guarantees of the Bill of Rights. Although statutes are often merely legislative enactments of established court procedure, they serve to establish boundaries for courts. The procedure for selecting judges, particularly election, also acts to constrain the power of the judicial branch. This chapter will further describe some of the limitations on the power of courts; other limitations, both substantive and procedural, will be discussed elsewhere in this book.

JUDICIAL RESTRAINT

Despite the widely held belief that judges, like fools, rush in "where angels fear to tread," courts have established rules of procedure that allow them to avoid many of the hard cases that lawyers claim make bad law. Courts, especially appellate courts, have considerable discretion over the cases they hear and use that discretion to engage in what is often referred to as *judicial gatekeeping.* As Alexis de Toqueville observed in *Democracy in America*, virtually every issue of public policy comes before the courts sooner or later. The reason usually given for this propensity to litigate is the legalistic nature of the American people. Americans tend to have strong feelings about their rights, and courts of law are the logical forums for vindicating those rights. Consequently, every schoolchild kicked off the football team or dismissed from the cheerleading squad seeks judicial protection of what is perceived to be, at the very least, a God-given right.

While there is much disagreement among judges, lawyers, and legal scholars about the degree to which courts should intervene in such disputes, the heart of the debate centers around the question of *access* to courts as appropriate forums for the resolution of societal conflict. One school of thought holds that the formal adjudication of conflict should be limited to those issues that are important and worthy of a court's time. Issues such as those raised by our football player and cheerleader are too trivial to warrant a court's time and are a waste of taxpayers' money. Other issues are viewed by this school of thought as inappropriate for judicial resolution. This argument holds that courts are ill-equipped to resolve some issues and that other political bodies, usually legislatures, should handle them. Finally, some believe that courts should not allow themselves to become embroiled in issues that might bring the stature of the courts into disrepute. Those who take the positions just listed wish to close the judicial gates—that is, to limit access to the courts as forums for the resolution of certain conflicts.

Another school of thought would prefer to see the judicial gates opened wider. Proponents of this position argue that the courts are often the last resort for persons whose rights have been violated. Courts are frequently the last hope of the poor, the elderly, or any other group unable to achieve its goals in the larger political system. If courts are established to ensure that justice is done, then every issue, no matter how seemingly trivial, is worthy of judicial resolution. Proponents of opening the judicial gates concede that there are limits to the courts' ability to resolve every societal conflict. They also concede that certain issues are best resolved by the more traditionally political branches of our government. However, proponents of greater judicial involvement argue that courts have a constitutional duty "to say what the law is," and that to avoid thorny issues entirely is a dereliction of judicial duty.

In this section we will examine a number of judicial doctrines relied upon by courts to either open or close their judicial gates to conflict. Although there are numerous examples illustrating both of these doctrines, we will focus on those aspects of each doctrine that reveal the *political* nature of judicial gatekeeping. Let us begin our discussion with the issue of standing.

Standing. The term *standing* refers to the right of a litigant to "stand" before a court. In general, standing refers to the litigant's right to bring a cause of action before a court for judicial resolution. Issues of standing often turn on whether or not the party bringing the case before the court is the appropriate one to do so. For example, in most cases one cannot sue to protect the rights of another because only the party who has actually been injured may bring a lawsuit.[1] A court may close the judicial gates by denying standing to persons wishing to raise issues that the court would prefer to avoid.

Standing is the major bar to so-called *taxpayer's suits.* A taxpayer's suit is a suit filed by someone claiming standing solely on the basis of status as a taxpayer. Taxpayer's suits often involve government programs or policies that a taxpayer, or even a group of taxpayers, disapproves of as a waste of money. In other words, the taxpayer claims that a continuation of the government program being challenged is injurious to the taxpayer because it increases the tax burden. Someone might conclude, for example, that the space program is a waste of taxpayers' money and ask a court to enjoin the government from continuing to finance it. Since there is hardly a government program that does not offend someone, acceptance of the right of a taxpayer *qua* taxpayer to sue would open a big can of worms, requiring courts to review virtually every government program enacted. Such a prospect has caused courts to bar taxpayer's suits in all but a few limited instances.

The first case to raise the issue of taxpayer's suits was *Frothingham* v. *Mellon*.[2] Congress had enacted the Maternity Act of 1921, which encouraged states to create special health programs for mothers and infants in an attempt to reduce the infant mortality rate. The act provided federal funds as an incentive to states that created such programs. Frothingham, a taxpayer, claimed that the act increased her tax burden and deprived her of her property without due process of law. The Supreme Court ruled against Mrs. Frothingham, stating that the amount of tax an individual taxpayer contributes to the program is so small that it is indeterminable. In addition, the Court realized that to permit Frothingham to challenge the expenditures under the Maternity Act would conceivably allow every disgruntled taxpayer to challenge every program of which he or she disapproved. Because the injury to the individual was so slight and the consequences so potentially damaging, *Frothingham* barred most taxpayer's suits for over 40 years.

In 1968, however, the Supreme Court opened the judicial gates to taxpayer's suits just a crack in the case of *Flast* v. *Cohen*.[3] Conventional wisdom held that *Frothingham* served as an absolute bar to taxpayer's suits; in *Flast*, however, the Court held that although a taxpayer could not challenge federal spending solely on the basis of status as a taxpayer, neither could a taxpayer be barred from showing sufficient personal stake in the outcome of a case to meet the requirement of adversariness that courts demand. If such a showing could be demonstrated, standing could be granted.[4] *Flast* held that the taxpayer must first establish a link, or nexus, between taxpayer's status and exercises of congressional taxing and spending powers *only*. Second, the taxpayer must establish a link between taxpayer's status and a specific constitutional limitation on the taxing and spending powers of Congress. In

Flast, the petitioners filed suit to enjoin the expenditure of federal funds for parochial schools as a violation of the Establishment Clause of the First Amendment. Consequently, the Court ruled that the petitioners in *Flast* had met both conditions. Mrs. Frothingham had met only the first condition; she merely alleged that the Maternity Act exceeded the general powers of the national government without linking the act and expenditures to a specific constitutional limitation, thus failing to meet the second condition set forth in *Flast*.

Subsequent cases[5] involving the war in Vietnam, the secret budget of the Central Intelligence Agency, and other controversial government spending programs have retreated from *Flast* somewhat, leaving the exact status of taxpayer's suits in limbo. Such a situation does illustrate the political nature of the standing issue, however. If a court, especially the Supreme Court, wishes to open the gate to litigants or their claims, *Flast* may serve as a precedent for granting standing. If, on the other hand, a court wishes to dodge a controversial issue, it can merely rule that the litigants have not demonstrated the links outlined in *Flast*. As mentioned at the beginning of this section, this leaves the courts free to exercise their discretion to open or close the judicial gates on issues of standing.

Mootness and ripeness.   Two judicial doctrines that also permit courts to avoid controversial issues, at least in the short run, are ***mootness*** and ***ripeness***. One requirement that American courts insist upon is that a case be a "real case or controversy" within the meaning of Article III of the Constitution. Because American law is based upon the adversary system, courts will refuse to hear cases in which one party lacks a personal stake in the outcome or in which the controversy originally at issue has somehow resolved itself. The question of mootness involves both situations. If a situation that gave rise to the lawsuit in the first place somehow resolves itself, then a court will rule that the issue is moot. A case is rendered moot not only because the problem is no longer a problem, but also because the party who brought the suit has lost the personal stake in the outcome that the adversary system demands.

Perhaps the best illustration of the Supreme Court's use of mootness to avoid a controversial issue is *DeFunis* v. *Odegaard*,[6] a case which involved affirmative action. Marco DeFunis applied to law school in the state of Washington but was denied admission. The law school to which DeFunis applied had an affirmative action program which admitted members of certain minority groups, some of whom had lower grades and Law School Admission Test (LSAT) scores than did DeFunis. DeFunis brought suit, alleging "reverse discrimination," and won in the lower court. The trial court granted DeFunis temporary admission to the law school pending the outcome of the school's appeal. By the time the case reached the Supreme Court, DeFunis was enrolled in his last quarter of law school. Officials of the law school indicated that regardless of the Court's decision, DeFunis would be allowed to finish the current quarter in which he was enrolled. The Court ruled that, inasmuch as DeFunis had won what he had set out to win and since whatever the Court ruled would have no bearing on DeFunis's rights, the case was now moot.

The dissenting justices in *DeFunis* argued that the case should not have been declared moot. They pointed out that even though DeFunis was in his last quarter, he could become ill, flunk out, or otherwise fail to complete his final quarter. Should that happen, DeFunis might be barred from reenrolling and completing his law degree. More important, the dissenters believed that the Court should address the issue of affirmative action raised by the case. They argued that it was inevitable that the Court would have to rule on the constitutionality of affirmative action programs and that to delay resolution of the issue would only result in further waste of time and money. In fact, the dissenters proved to be correct. Four years later the Supreme Court faced the issue again in *Regents of the University of California v. Bakke*.[7] As the dissenters had predicted, the Court had merely succeeded in postponing the inevitable. On the other hand, the Court had four more years to reflect on one of the most controversial issues to come before it in recent years. Use of a doctrine like mootness can provide the Court with the time it needs to prepare itself for difficult and controversial issues.

The Supreme Court cannot always demand strict adherence to the mootness requirement. One quick example will illustrate why. Except under the most unusual circumstances, it takes about three years for a case to reach the Supreme Court. Recall that DeFunis was in his third year of law school before his case reached the High Court. A pregnant woman wishing to challenge the constitutionality of a state's abortion law would be unable to do so because the gestation period of humans is only nine months; the issue would thus be moot before it could ever reach the Court. Naturally, the Court could not be expected to adhere to the mootness doctrine since the woman would either have to have the baby or have an illegal abortion. In *Roe v. Wade*,[8] the Court said as much by agreeing to hear the case notwithstanding the issue of mootness.

Whereas mootness involves a situation in which an issue has waited too long before reaching a court, ripeness involves a situation in which an issue reaches a court too soon. A case is said to be "not ripe for review" when a court feels that judicial resolution of the controversy would be premature. The Supreme Court, for example, requires litigants to exhaust all of their lower remedies before bringing a case before it. If the issue is at all capable of being resolved below, the Court wants it to be. Since the nine justices can review only a small percentage of the total number of cases the Court is asked to review, it wishes to handle only those difficult questions incapable of being resolved by the lower courts.

The requirement for ripeness can postpone the necessity of resolving a difficult issue for the Court. The Court can sit back, wait, and hope that, in effect, the problem will go away. Although we saw with the case of affirmative action that some issues just will not go away, the requirement that an issue be ripe for review may, like mootness did in *DeFunis*, buy the Court enough time to reflect on how to resolve a difficult issue.

Political questions.   Perhaps the clearest indication of the unwillingness of courts to become embroiled in controversial issues is the *political question* doctrine. The exact nature of what constitutes a legitimate political question is open to debate. For example, the Supreme Court has agreed to hear cases involving such highly charged issues as busing, abortion, school prayer, reverse discrimination, and Watergate. These are certainly "political" questions within any ordinary meaning of that word. Why, then, does the Court choose to label some issues "political questions," thereby avoiding them, while agreeing to hear cases involving some of the most political issues imaginable? The answer, as we have already suggested, is that the "political question" label is a convenient way for courts to avoid issues they would rather not address. Unlike standing, mootness, and ripeness, however, political questions tend to put courts on a collision course with one of the other branches of government, and those are confrontations that courts have a tendency to lose. Consequently, courts, preferring discretion over valor, defer (some say surrender) the resolution of controversial issues to Congress or the president.

An early example of the use of the political question doctrine is *Luther* v. *Borden*.[9] In that case, Chief Justice Taney refused to decide which of two competing governments in Rhode Island was the legitimate one. Taney ruled that either Congress or the president should decide whether a state has a "republican form of government" within the meaning of Article IV of the Constitution. In *Luther*, since Congress had not refused to seat the members of the House elected from Rhode Island under the Charter Government and since President Tyler had promised to send federal troops to support the Charter Government, the Supreme Court did not believe that its decision could or should countermand the decisions of the two political branches of government.

In reaching its decision in *Luther*, the Court did not necessarily remain neutral. Indeed, by refusing to decide the issue, the Court implicitly backed the Charter Government. By adopting a hands-off policy, the Court may actually be supporting the status quo, as the case of *Colegrove* v. *Green*[10] demonstrates. After many years of failure to redraw the lines of congressional districts, Illinois was severely malapportioned. Some Illinois congressional districts had as much as eight times as many people as others. This left the people in the large districts severely underrepresented. Colegrove, living in one of the disfavored districts, sought an injunction against further congressional elections in Illinois until the district lines had been redrawn to reflect equal populations. The Supreme Court ruled against Colegrove for several reasons. First, the Court was unsure about whether it could provide an appropriate judicial remedy. If the Court did rule that the existing lines were unconstitutional, it could do nothing if the state still refused to redraw them. Second, if the Illinois delegation was elected in violation of the Constitution, Congress could refuse to seat the state's representatives. Third, if malapportionment was a problem in Illinois, it was not for the Court, but for the people—through the ballot box—to correct it. Finally, the Court took note of the highly partisan nature of reapportionment and ruled that courts ought not to enter this "political thicket."

Colegrove did not put an end to the issue of reapportionment as a political question. In 1962 the Court was faced with the issue again, except this time the case involved the malapportionment of *state* legislative districts. In *Baker* v. *Carr*,[11] the Supreme Court ruled that federal courts could take jurisdiction in reapportionment cases. In reversing itself on whether reapportionment was a "political question," the Court outlined six criteria for determining whether an issue raises a political question. The Court ruled that a case raises a political question: (1) if the issue has clearly been left to a coequal branch of the national government by the Constitution; (2) if a judicial decision would embarrass the nation in its foreign relations; (3) if the Court lacks manageable judicial standards by which to decide the case; (4) if the Court's decision would demonstrate a lack of respect for a coequal branch of government; (5) if there is a need to adhere to a decision already made; or (6) if the issue involves a policy determination clearly left to nonjudicial policymakers.[12] In ruling that reapportionment cases were not political questions, the Court opened the door to numerous challenges of legislative and nonlegislative districts that did not conform to the "one person, one vote" standard of equal population.

The most recent applications of the political question doctrine have involved some of the most controversial issues of our times. In *United States* v. *Nixon*,[13] lawyers for former President Richard Nixon argued that the use of "executive privilege" was a political question left to the president's discretion. The Supreme Court disagreed, ordered the Watergate Tapes released, and the rest is history. In *Massachusetts* v. *Laird*,[14] the Court refused to hear a case on the constitutionality of the war in Vietnam. Finally, in *Powell* v. *McCormack*,[15] the Court was asked to decide whether the refusal by Congress to seat a member of the House was a political question. The Court agreed to hear the case despite arguments that the decision to seat members was clearly left to the Congress by the Constitution.

In this section we have attempted to demonstrate how courts can use doctrines such as standing, mootness, ripeness, and political questions as tools of judicial policymaking. If the Supreme Court wishes to enter a particular "political thicket," it seldom has trouble finding a way to do so. On the other hand, these doctrines serve as a convenient excuse for the Court if it wishes to avoid controversy. An important point to remember is that the decision *not* to get involved in a controversy can have as many policy implications as the decision *to* get involved. By not involving itself, the Court supports the status quo. Similarly, a decision to rush in where angels fear to tread can put the Court in the forefront of policymaking in the United States. The decision as to which road to take is itself a highly charged political question.

LEGAL LIMITATIONS

The previous section dealt with political limitations that are invoked by judges to avoid having to resolve certain questions. Those same limitations may also be regarded as legalistic in nature. To illustrate, standing may be employed to restrict access to courts, but it may also be used to prevent those without a stake in the matter from meddling in a lawsuit while allowing those with an interest to participate in the proceedings. For example, you cannot intercede in a lawsuit brought by a creditor against your best friend merely because the debtor is such a good person and you think it is harsh that she must pay the debt. On the other hand, a statute might grant standing to grandparents to intervene in their child's divorce (a lawsuit in which the grandparents would otherwise not have standing) in order to protect visitation rights with their grandchildren. Just because we arbitrarily categorize these limitations on judicial power as either political or legalistic does not imply that they are exclusively one or the other.

Jurisdiction.   The threshold question in any lawsuit is to determine which court or courts have jurisdiction in the matter. Judicial *jurisdiction* can be defined as the power or authority of a court to decide a particular case. As discussed in Chapter 3, jurisdiction stems from constitutional or legislative provisions, and the boundaries of each court's jurisdiction is carefully delineated. The concept of jurisdiction appears fairly simple in its initial definition but is infinitely complex in its application.

Jurisdiction has three facets: (1) geographic limitations, (2) subject matter limitations, and (3) personal or *in rem* jurisdiction. All three requirements must be met before a court may decide a case. Every tribunal in our system is limited by geographic boundaries. Decisions of the U.S. Supreme Court are operative everywhere in the United States, but they are both irrelevant and ineffective in Brazil. The same principle holds true for state and local courts as well; municipal courts lack power to decide cases that arise outside the city boundaries and that do not involve city ordinances. The Supreme Court succinctly explained the principle in the following excerpt:

> The authority of every tribunal is necessarily restricted by the territorial limits of the State in which it is established. Any attempt to exercise authority beyond those limits would be deemed in every other forum . . . an illegitimate assumption of power.[16]

In addition, jurisdiction is defined topically. Courts are assigned particular types of lawsuits to handle. Misdemeanors are generally heard by courts of limited jurisdiction, while felonies are heard by trial courts of general jurisdiction in the state systems. In civil matters such as tort or contract litigation, jurisdiction is commonly determined by the amount in controversy or the monetary damages sought by the parties. Cases involving relatively smaller amounts, perhaps less than $1,000, can be heard by county or JP courts, while suits involving $5,000 or more can be heard in superior courts. As you may remember from Chapter 3, the amount in controversy must be at least $50,000 in order for federal courts to consider diversity suits,[17] and may be raised to $75,000 soon.

The third element is that the court must have either *in personum* or *in rem* jurisdiction. "Every state possesses exclusive jurisdiction and sovereignty over persons and property within its territory.[18] *In rem jurisdiction,* which arises in suits affecting property interests, stems from the physical location of the property inside state boundaries and under the control of the court. Technically, suits *in rem* are filed against the property itself—for example, a suit to seize an obscene film or to determine ownership of an abandoned cache of jewels—but the term is also used generically to describe suits affecting the property interests of the parties. Probate proceedings or suits to partition land would fall into this category.

In personum jurisdiction is the power of the court to "determine the personal rights and obligations of the defendants."[19] Personal jurisdiction may be founded on presence, domicile, consent, and certain activities within the state. Those who reside in a state or who are physically present within the territorial limits of a state are subject to the *in personum* jurisdiction of the state's courts; however, a caveat must be added in that the other prerequisites must be met for a court to have jurisdiction to render an effective decree. Out-of-state residents come under the jurisdiction of the court either by voluntarily consenting to be sued in that state (a common provision in contracts) or because of jurisdictional statutes. Specific legislative enactments, commonly referred to as *long-arm statutes,* extend the power of state courts over nonresident parties. The long-arm statutes are based on a form of implied consent; that is, if one is doing business in the state or commits a tort therein, one is deemed to have consented to be sued in the state courts.

> Due process requires only that in order to subject a defendant to a judgment in personam, if he be not present within the territory of the forum, he have certain *minimum contacts* [emphasis added] with it such that the maintenance of the suit does not offend "traditional notions of fair play and substantial justice."[20]

Remember that the defendant, whether a natural person or a corporation, must receive adequate notice of the proceedings and an opportunity to be heard. That notice may be in the form of either personal or substituted service. **Personal service** occurs when the party is officially notified of the pending litigation in accordance with the statutory requirements, generally by mail or by personal delivery of the petition by the process server. **Substituted service** frequently occurs through publication in the local newspaper. Personal service is the preferred method of advising the defendant of the pending litigation, and substituted service is ineffective in certain instances. These are rather technical rules, and reference to applicable state rules would be needed to determine whether substituted service is acceptable in a given lawsuit.[21]

Quasi-in-rem jurisdiction allows the court to exercise judicial jurisdiction over land, chattels, and intangibles to satisfy a personal obligation such as a debt of the owner, even if the owner is not personally subject to the court's jurisdiction.[22] For example, a state statute may allow a nonresident to be sued in the state's courts, even if the accident occurred elsewhere, on the basis that his insurance company is incorporated in that state. This type of jurisdiction is not employed as frequently. A defendant who wishes to challenge the jurisdiction of the court generally must either do so in the initial pleading or forfeit the right to question the authority of the court. Similarly, any effort to change the location of a trial must be filed as a pretrial motion.[23]

Venue.   Venue must be distinguished from jurisdiction, or the power to adjudicate. **Venue** refers to the site or geographic location where a trial takes place. A court may have jurisdiction to hear a particular case, but venue may not be proper with the particular court. District courts may have the prerequisites of jurisdiction to hear felony cases, but the venue statute will limit the venue to the county in which the crime occurred. Venue is thus a further limitation on the power of the court.[24]

Venue provisions are deemed so important that they appear in the U.S. Constitution: "The trial of all crimes . . . shall be held in the State where the said crimes shall have been committed."[25] The social policy is that the parties to a lawsuit, whether civil or criminal in nature, should not be hauled into far distant forums and forced to defend lawsuits in a place inconvenient for them and for their witnesses. Such inconvenience might seriously prejudice the case in that the witnesses might be unable to travel to the new location; in addition, transporting and lodging the necessary personnel can be expensive. A particular concern in criminal cases is that the defendant be tried in the community in which the crime was committed for at least two reasons: (1) the defendant is entitled to be tried before peers who are applying contemporary community standards; and (2) the community has a vested interest in the trials of those accused of committing crimes in their neighborhoods.

Venue is generally governed by statutory provisions and may be based on the issues involved in the lawsuit. In litigation concerning land, for example, venue is proper in the county in which the land is located. Litigants have a limited opportunity to modify the venue of the proceeding, but such a move requires court approval. The most common ground for transfer in a civil case is *forum non conveniens,* a doctrine which allows the court to decline jurisdiction if in the interest of justice and for the convenience of the parties the case should be moved.[26] Much more frequent, however, is the motion in a criminal case to change venue because of prejudice and bias in the community that would prevent a fair trial. This perceived prejudice or bias is often attributed to pretrial publicity in a particularly newsworthy case.[27] The issue for the court and potential jurors is not whether they have heard about the case, but rather whether they have already formed an opinion about the matter to the extent that they would be unable to listen to the evidence and render a fair and impartial verdict. In other words, the jurors do not have to be recluses who know nothing about community events, but they must have open minds about the guilt or innocence of the accused despite having heard the pretrial publicity.[28] Courts are hesitant to grant motions to move trials because of the community's interest in resolving local matters and because it may be a very expensive proposition. Moving the trial may be especially costly in criminal cases, in which the original forum has to pay all travel and lodging expenses for court personnel, attorneys, and witnesses.

Statutes of limitation.   An additional legislative restriction on the court's power to hear a particular matter is statutes of limitation. *Statutes of limitation* are temporal in nature and prescribe the time periods in which actions must be brought. The plaintiff must file within the time limit or be forever barred from seeking relief; violation of the statute of limitations is a defense to the suit.[29] The purpose is to ensure that the action is brought within a reasonable time and while the evidence is still fresh. As time proceeds, valuable information could be lost or destroyed, and witnesses' memories of the event fade.[30]

Again, statutes of limitation vary according to the type of lawsuit. The basic rule in civil cases is that the statute begins to run when the cause of action accrues—at the time of injury, for example.[31] However, determining the time of injury is not always as easy as it might first appear. A medical condition caused by an automobile accident or by malpractice might not manifest itself immediately; similarly, a psychological problem caused by a traumatic event such as child molestation may surface years after the event. Some statutes allow tort victims leeway by extending the limit from the date of injury to the date that the injury was discovered or should have been discovered; the latter provision protects a defendant from perennial potential for suit. Criminal laws also include statutes of limitation. The limits for misdemeanors are usually shorter than those for felonies, whereas there is rarely a statute of limitations for the crime of murder.

To mitigate the possible harshness of the statute of limitations, there are provisions allowing the statute to be tolled, or suspended.[32] Conditions such as infancy or insanity might cause the statute to be tolled. It is the time of filing the petition, and not the time of judgment, which is critical. In other words, the statute is tolled with the initiation of the legal action.

Conflict of laws.   Americans live in a mobile and interconnected society. For business or for pleasure, we frequently cross state lines or even cross the country, and we think nothing of entering into contracts with companies located across the continent from us. We often change our domiciles from one state to another. We seek assistance from experts in cities and institutions far from home. We purchase goods produced in factories in other regions of the country. We do all of these things without fully appreciating the ease with which we do them and the legal safeguards that are afforded to us as we move around the nation.

This mobility poses special legal problems. If our extraordinary communications and transportation systems failed and we were isolated within our own states, an entire subfield of law would be eradicated. But we are not confined and unable to communicate, and conflict of laws is therefore a flourishing branch of law. The area of conflict of laws involves three subsidiary issues: (1) selection of the court with the correct jurisdiction; (2) choice-of-law questions; and (3) effect of judgments under the Full Faith and Credit Clause of the U.S. Constitution. The former was discussed in the section on jurisdiction, and the latter two are the topics here.

Each of the 50 states and the national government is a sovereign entity with its own unique laws and procedures. Plaintiffs naturally gravitate to the forum in which the laws are likely to be most beneficial and in which they are likely to be most successful. Jurisdiction and choice-of-law rules limit plaintiffs' ability to "forum shop" in order to find the best deal. *Choice-of-law* questions arise in ascertaining which law the forum will apply when some or all of the operative events occurred in a jurisdiction other than the forum state. To illustrate, assume that Roberts and Golden, both Michigan residents, are involved in an automobile accident in Santa Fe. The other driver, Ellison, is from California. Due to diversity jurisdiction, Roberts and Golden could file suit in their home state of Michigan, in New Mexico, in Ellison's home state of California, or in federal court in any of the three states if the amount of controversy exceeds $50,000. It would certainly be more convenient for the pair to pursue the lawsuit on their home ground, but Ellison can make the same argument about California. The witnesses are in New Mexico. (This may be the ideal time for using the discovery techniques discussed in Chapter 4.) It appears, then, that there is no one place that is truly convenient for all.

The choice of the forum in which to pursue this matter is very important. Like all good bargain hunters, the plaintiffs are seeking the best deal. Such situations also generate "races to the courthouse" because as long as all other prerequisites are met, the party who files first (and in our example it could be Ellison) typically determines the location. If the plaintiff seeks relief in federal courts, the federal court is obligated to enforce the law of the state in which it is located, unless the matter is governed by the U.S. Constitution or by federal statutes.[33] Our accident case involves neither, and the applicable law will be that of one of the states.

If the suit is filed in either Michigan or California, we have the classical choice-of-law problem, in which the operative facts occurred elsewhere. Generally, when a state applies the law of a sister state (foreign law), it applies the *internal* law, or the law that the sister state would use if there were no conflicts issue. The theory that would allow the use of the sister state's *whole* law, including choice-of-law rules, is *renvoi;* renvoi is seldom used in this country because it often exacerbates the problem of determining which law applies. Procedural matters, such as pleading and venue, are normally governed by the local law of the forum, whereas substantive matters, loosely interpreted to mean any matter determinative of outcome, are governed by the appropriate foreign law. Again, however, classifying a particular aspect of a case as one or the other can be rather complex.[34] Foreign law must be proven at trial, and in the absence of proof, it is presumed to be the same as the law of the forum.[35] Most states allow judicial notice of foreign law or provide some method to facilitate its introduction and proof.

There are fairly standard rules for determining which state law will be applied in choice-of-law questions; like many other legal standards, however, they are riddled with exceptions. In a tort case, the place of injury determines the applicable law, although many courts are applying a more flexible significant-relationship rule; that is, the court determines which state has the most significant contacts and then applies that state's rule.[36] Questions involving title or interest in land are governed by the laws of the state in which the land is located.[37] The most confused area is that of contract law, and a number of approaches have been used by courts. These include the place of making; the place of performance; the intention of the parties, which may be expressed in a specific contractual clause; and the newer balancing approach of applying the law of the state with which the parties and the contract have the greatest relationship or most significant contacts.[38]

The concept of *domicile* is important because the law to be applied in many controversies is the law of the party's domicile, or home. Domicile involves more than mere physical presence; it requires intent to retain permanent ties with the locale. Nonresident college students living in dormitories are classic examples of those whose residence may not coincide with their domicile. Domicile is likely to be the controlling factor in the following areas: (1) probate matters; (2) divorce, including child custody and property matters; (3) political rights and privileges, such as voting; (4) federal diversity jurisdiction; and (5) *in personum jurisdiction*, which automatically accrues to the state courts of the party's domicile.

The mobility of our society and the complexity of our transactions complicate the courts' job of resolving conflicts. The Framers of the Constitution were concerned about the orderly flow of commerce and business among the various states and about state courts discriminating against residents of other states, as exemplified by the inclusion of diversity jurisdiction, which provides a neutral forum in federal courts. In addition, Article IV, Section 1 provides that "Full faith and credit shall be given in each State to the public acts, records, and judicial proceedings of every other state." Remember that state law, standing alone, has no force outside the state's geographic boundaries, but the Full Faith and Credit Clause expands the effective reach of state law. This does not mandate automatic and immediate acceptance. Before it will be recognized by the receiving state,[39] the party wishing to enforce the court order must file suit in the new state and prove the foreign judgment which is presumed to be valid and final. Equity decrees apparently do not fall under the Full Faith and Credit Clause, but they may be recognized on a *comity,* or courtesy, basis. The same holds true for international judgments and decrees, although there may be special treaty provisions relating to the reciprocal recognition of court judgments among sovereign nations.

Stare decisis.   Another precept which limits the judges' power in resolving cases is *stare decisis,* which, as you remember, is the doctrine of applying precedents from previous case law to the case at bar. Precedent is developed from examining the facts and applying the appropriate law to reach the decision. It adds stability and predictability, in that cases are decided in the same way when the material facts are the same.[40] In part, it is a result of the itinerant justices who traveled England and employed the same principles to decide similar cases, thereby developing the common law.

The general rule is that *stare decisis* is mandatory, and judges are bound to follow precedent. However, the same judicial innovators who developed the doctrine also determined how to circumvent it. One of those ways is to distinguish the present case from the prior one. This is usually done on the basis that the material facts in the current case are not the same as those in the preceding case. To illustrate, let us examine two dog-bite cases. The first case, or the precedent, occurred when a casual passerby was bitten by the dog, and the owner was held fully responsible and ordered to pay all damages. The second situation varied in that the person who was bitten had been beating the dog. The injuries are the same: The dog, under the control of his owner, bit the stranger. Employing the legal formula of precedent, the results should also be the same; that is, the owner should pay in both instances. In the second case, however, the court could consider that the provocation offered the dog was a material fact, differentiate the two cases on that basis, and relieve the owner of all or partial liability.

Decisions rendered by the highest courts within the same state are binding on lower courts; that is, the lower court must follow the precedent. In order to avoid that obligation, however, the court may determine that the relevant section of the precedent was *obiter dictum*—statements by the judge that were not essential to the resolution of the particular case and are therefore ineffective as precedent. Those points and the reasoning critical to the case are known as *ratio decidendi*, which is binding.[41] In addition, a certain hierarchy exists in the organization of U.S. court systems, and judges are exempt from complying with orders of courts not in their particular hierarchy. Every court must follow the decisions of the Supreme Court and their own state's highest courts. In regard to intermediate courts of appeals, which generally have only regional jurisdiction, judges are bound only by the decisions of their own regional courts, and opinions of other courts are only persuasive, not mandatory.[42]

CONCLUSION

Courts are extremely powerful institutions; however, they are not unencumbered by restrictions. Some of these restraints are judicially created and serve to protect the integrity of the judicial branch by providing mechanisms for the court to avoid confrontations with the more "political" branches. Others stem from constitutional provisions or statutes ratifying long-standing judicial practices and are rather technical in application. Both the "gatekeeping" aspects and the legalistic rules affect access to the courts and the availability of relief for those seeking assistance from the judicial branch.

NOTES

1. As is the case with most rules, there are exceptions, such as those for minors and the mentally incompetent.

2. *Frothingham* v. *Mellon,* 262 U.S. 447 (1923).

3. *Flast* v. *Cohen,* 392 U.S. 83 (1968).

4. Peter Woll, *Constitutional Law: Cases and Comments* (Englewood Cliffs, N.J.: Prentice-Hall, 1981), pp. 40–42.

5. See *U.S.* v. *Richardson,* 418 U.S. 166 (1974); *Schlesinger* v. *Reservists' Committee to Stop the War,* 418 U.S. 208 (1974); *Warth* v. *Seldin,* 422 U.S. 490 (1975); and *Simon* v. *Eastern Kentucky Welfare Rights Organization,* 426 U.S. 26 (1976).

6. *DeFunis* v. *Odegaard,* 416 U.S. 312 (1974).

7. *Regents of the University of California* v. *Bakke,* 438 U.S. 265 (1978).

8. *Roe* v. *Wade,* 410 U.S. 113 (1973).

9. *Luther* v. *Borden,* 7 Howard 1 (1849).

10. *Colegrove* v. *Green,* 328 U.S. 549 (1946).

11. *Baker* v. *Carr,* 369 U.S. 186 (1962).

12. Otis H. Stephens and Gregory J. Rathjen, *The Supreme Court and the Allocation of Constitutional Power: Introductory Essays and Selected Cases* (San Francisco: W. H. Freeman & Company Publishers, 1980), p. 90.

13. *U.S.* v. *Nixon,* 418 U.S. 683 (1974).

14. *Massachusetts* v. *Laird,* 400 U.S. 886 (1970).

15. *Powell* v. *McCormack,* 395 U.S. 486 (1969).

16. *Pennoyer* v. *Neff,* 95 S. Ct. 565 (1877), at 573.

17. 28 U.S.C. § 1332.

18. *Pennoyer* v. *Neff,* 95 S. Ct. 565 (1877), at 568.

19. Ibid., p. 570.

20. *International Shoe Co.* v. *Washington,* 326 U.S. 310 (1945), at 316.

21. Fed. R. Civ. P. 4.

22. *Freeman* v. *Alderson,* 119 U.S. 185 (1886).

23. Fed. R. Civ. P. 12.

24. Milton D. Green, *Basic Civil Procedure* (Mineola, N.Y.: Foundation Press, 1972), pp. 50–51.

25. U.S. Constitution, Art. III, § 2.

26. Green, pp. 51–55.

27. *Sheppard* v. *Maxwell,* 384 U.S. 333 (1966).

28. *Murphy* v. *Florida,* 421 U.S. 794 (1975).

29. *Christmas* v. *Russell,* 5 Wall. 290 (1866).

30. *Weber* v. *State Harbor Commissioners,* 18 Wall. 57 (1873).

31. *Maytin* v. *Vela,* 216 U.S. 598 (1909).

32. *Amy* v. *Watertown,* 130 U.S. 320 (1889).

33. *Erie R. Co.* v. *Tompkins,* 304 U.S. 64 (1938).

34. 16 Am. Jur. 2d *Conflict of Laws* § 4.

35. *Loebig* v. *Larucci,* 572 F.2d 81 (2nd Cir. 1978).

36. *Guillory on Behalf of Guillory* v. *United States,* 699 F.2d 781 (5th Cir. 1983).

37. *Sunderland* v. *United States,* 266 U.S. 226 (1924).

38. *Duncan* v. *Cessna Aircraft Co.,* 665 S.W.2d 414 (Tex. 1984).

39. *Christmas* v. *Russell,* 5 Wall. 290 (1866).

40. Lief H. Carter, *Reason in Law,* 3rd ed. (Boston: Little, Brown, 1988), pp. 36–39.

41. Mark W. Cannon and David M. O'Brien., eds., *Views From the Bench* (Chatham, N.J.: Chatham House Publishers, 1985), pp. 123–124.

42. Carter, p. 36.

6

Constitutional Law

In Chapter 1 we introduced constitutional law, along with case law, statutory law, and several others, as one of the many kinds of law comprised by the American legal system. We noted that the U.S. Constitution and the laws and treaties of the United States are the supreme law of the land. However, we also noted in Chapter 1 that the language of the Constitution tends to be ambiguous, employing such phrases as "due process of law," "equal protection of the law," and "cruel and unusual punishment" without clearly defining them. This ambiguity presents a problem: How can the Constitution be our supreme law if we don't know what it means? Also, how can we ever learn the meaning of the Constitution when those who wrote it have long since died? The answer lies in judicial interpretation of the Constitution, which is the main, but not exclusive, responsibility of the U.S. Supreme Court. As Chief Justice John Marshall wrote in the famous case of *Marbury* v. *Madison*, "It is emphatically the province and duty of the judicial department to say what the law is."[1] Chief Justice Charles Evans Hughes, in the same vein, remarked, "We are under a constitution but the constitution is what the judges say it is."[2]

This ability to be the final arbiter of the meaning of the Constitution has given the Supreme Court tremendous power to affect not only the laws of the nation, but its politics as well. As the final interpreter of the Constitution, the Supreme Court has the ability to rule on the constitutionality of the actions of the other two branches of government as well as those of the states and other governmental entities. Through judicial elaboration of the meaning of the Constitution, the Court can broaden or limit the powers of the president and the Congress. In so doing, the Court breathes life into the Constitution, making it a "living" document that changes as the nation changes, and giving it as much relevance in the late twentieth century as it had when it was written in 1787.

The study of constitutional law, then, becomes a study of the development of a nation. In a sense, constitutional law is a political history of the United States. While it is not possible in an introductory text to afford extensive coverage to any kind of law, we will attempt to provide our readers with sufficient background to acquaint them with at least some of the major areas of interest to constitutional law scholars. In this chapter we will examine several facets of constitutional law. First, we will discuss the doctrine of judicial review, its origin and significance. Next, we will analyze several approaches to constitutional interpretation. Finally, we will look at some major constitutional doctrines, such as federalism, separation of powers, and equal protection to provide a better understanding of our constitutional system.

JUDICIAL REVIEW

Judicial review is the power of a court to review the actions of other government bodies in order to determine whether or not those actions are consistent with the Constitution. If, in the opinion of the court, an act is not consistent with the Constitution, the court will declare the act invalid. Judicial review is usually associated with the court's determination that a law passed by Congress or a state legislature is unconstitutional, but judicial review is much broader than that. It extends to all actions taken by the president, administrative agencies, or any other government body. Justice Owen Roberts, in *United States* v. *Butler,* wrote the following famous passage describing judicial review:

> The Constitution is the supreme law of the land ordained and established by the people. All legislation must conform to the principles it lays down. When an act of Congress is appropriately challenged in the courts as not conforming to the constitutional mandate the judicial branch of the Government has only one duty—to lay the article of the Constitution which is invoked beside the statute which is challenged and to decide whether the latter squares with the former.[3]

Although many constitutional scholars view Justice Roberts's description of the process as overly simplistic, it does capture the essence of judicial review.

Having defined judicial review as a court's ability to declare unconstitutional the actions of government bodies, we need to understand how the courts acquired this important power. To do so we must understand the case of *Marbury* v. *Madison*, in which the Supreme Court, in effect, gave itself the power of judicial review.

Marbury v. Madison. Constitutional scholar Craig R. Ducat has written, "There is scarcely a casebook on constitutional law that does not begin with *Marbury* v. *Madison*."[4] Ducat's observation underscores the importance of *Marbury*, for without the power of judicial review, the Supreme Court would be unable to transform the Constitution into a living document. Understanding *Marbury* is therefore essential to understanding not only judicial review, but also our entire constitutional development. We will begin our discussion of this important case with some historical background.

Marbury v. *Madison* really begins with the election of 1800. The two dominant political parties of that era were the Federalists, led by President John Adams and Alexander Hamilton, and the Democratic-Republicans, led by Thomas Jefferson and James Madison. In the election of 1800, the Federalists suffered a tremendous defeat. Jefferson, in an election which was eventually decided by the House of Representatives, defeated Adams for the presidency. At the same time the Jeffersonians, as the Democratic-Republicans were called, had also won control of both houses of Congress. The Jeffersonians had dealt the Federalists a defeat from which the latter would never recover. In those days, however, a new president was not inaugurated until March 4 of the following year, so Adams remained in office as a "lame duck" president from late 1800, when the election was held, until March 4, 1801, when Jefferson was inaugurated.[5] During the same period, the "lame duck" Congress was also controlled by the Federalists.

The Federalists realized that they were on the ropes politically, but they did not intend to take their defeat lying down. Instead, they devised a plan to entrench themselves in the one branch of government they still controlled—the federal judiciary. On February 3, 1801, the Federalist Congress passed a law creating 16 new circuit-court judgeships, and a few weeks later it passed another law creating 42 new justice-of-the-peace positions for Washington, D.C. President Adams promptly nominated, and the Federalist Senate confirmed, the individuals chosen to fill the positions. The Jeffersonians were outraged at this blatant attempt by the Federalists to entrench themselves in the judicial branch, but there was nothing they could do about it until they came to power.

At this point the events that led to the *Marbury* case began to unfold. Because of the hurried manner in which the judgeships were created and in which the judges were nominated and confirmed, the Adams administration was actually still trying to complete the appointment process late on the evening of March 3, 1801.[6] The person responsible for delivering the judicial commissions to the appointees was Adams's secretary of state, John Marshall. Since Secretary Marshall was too busy to deliver the commissions personally, he asked his brother James to deliver them for him. James was unable to deliver 12 of the commissions, so he merely placed the undelivered commissions (including William Marbury's) on the secretary of state's desk. The next day, however, Jefferson's secretary of state, James Madison, took office, and the undelivered commissions came into his possession. Because of the blatantly partisan way in which the judgeships had been created and because he believed the positions were unnecessary, President Jefferson ordered Secretary Madison not to deliver the 12 commissions. The stage was now set for a dramatic confrontation between Jefferson and the Federalist-dominated Supreme Court.

William Marbury and three others decided to sue to recover their commissions. In 1789, Congress had passed the Judiciary Act, which established the federal court system for the United States. Section 13 of the act authorized the Supreme Court "to issue . . . writs of *mandamus* . . . to . . . persons holding office under the authority of the United States."[7] A writ of *mandamus* is a court order directing a government official to perform a nondiscretionary act. Therefore, under Section 13 of the Judiciary Act of 1789, Marbury had the right to bring an original action suit in the Supreme Court against James Madison. Marbury's suit asked the Supreme Court to order Madison to deliver his commission since Madison had no legal authority to withhold it from him. Because of some retaliatory legislation on the part of the Jeffersonians once they took power, the case was not decided until the 1803 term of the Court.

The Chief Justice of the United States in 1803 was none other than John Marshall. The *Marbury* case presented Chief Justice Marshall with a number of problems. First, as the person responsible for the failure of Marbury to receive his commission, Marshall probably should have recused himself in the case. Second, Marshall's own appointment to the Supreme Court was under a cloud. As part of the Federalist "court-packing" scheme, the previous chief justice, Oliver Ellsworth, had been persuaded to resign so that President Adams could appoint the younger Marshall to be Chief Justice. Third, the highly partisan case threatened the integrity of the Supreme Court itself. If the Court denied the writ, the public might question the validity of all of the Federalist appointments to the federal bench. If the Court ruled in favor of Marbury, it would leave itself open to charges that it had based its decision solely on partisan issues. Finally, President Jefferson had made it clear that he would not comply with a writ of *mandamus* coming from the High Court. He would instead defy a direct order from the Supreme Court, and, given Jefferson's popularity, the Chief Justice knew that the Court would be unable to do anything about the defiance. Marshall appeared to be in a classic no-win situation, which is why *Marbury* v. *Madison* is a masterpiece of judicial decision making.

Chief Justice Marshall's decision revolved around the answers to three questions posed by the Court. The first question was, "Has Marbury a legal right to the commission he demands?" Marshall answered that Marbury was indeed entitled to the commission since the positions had been legally created by the Congress and Marbury had been nominated by the president and confirmed by the Senate in accordance with the law. Marbury, the Chief Justice ruled, unquestionably had a legal right to the commission. (At this point one could imagine a smile forming on William Marbury's face.)

The second question was, "If Marbury has a legal right to the commission and if that right has been violated, does the law afford him a legal remedy?" Again, Marshall answered affirmatively by indicating that a legal right is useless if it is without a legal remedy. Marshall proceeded to discuss the writ of *mandamus* and concluded that the delivery of a judicial commission was not a discretionary power of the secretary of state; that is, the secretary had no authority to refuse to perform what is essentially a ministerial or clerical task. Therefore, the writ of *mandamus* was the appropriate legal remedy in this case. (The smile on William Marbury's face broadened as victory seemed ever more apparent.)

It was with the third question, however, that Chief Justice Marshall dropped his bombshell. The question was, "If the law affords Marbury a legal remedy, is it a *mandamus issuing from the Supreme Court?*" To this Marshall answered no. The key to Marshall's negative answer is the phrase "issuing from the Supreme Court." Marshall, in effect, threw out Marbury's suit on a technicality: The Supreme Court, according to Marshall, lacked jurisdiction to hear Marbury's case. But did not Section 13 of the Judiciary Act of 1789 specifically authorize the Supreme Court to issue writs of *mandamus* to persons holding office under the authority of the United States? Yes, Marshall conceded, but Section 13 was unconstitutional and therefore invalid. According to the Constitution, the Supreme Court has only two types of jurisdiction: original and appellate. Any case that comes before the Court must do so under either its original or appellate jurisdiction. But the Constitution limits the Supreme Court's original jurisdiction to cases involving foreign ambassadors and cases involving states. By enacting Section 13, Congress had created, whether intentionally or not, a third category of original jurisdiction—that is, suits involving the writ of *mandamus.* This, Marshall ruled, Congress could not do. The only way to either increase or diminish the original jurisdiction of the Supreme Court was to amend the Constitution in the manner prescribed in the Constitution itself. To allow Congress to change the Court's original jurisdiction by ordinary statute (as Section 13 was) would defeat the purpose of having a written constitution as fundamental law. Since the law under which Marbury brought his suit was invalid, the Supreme Court had no authority to hear the case, and Marbury's suit was dismissed.

With the decision in *Marbury* v. *Madison,* Chief Justice Marshall appropriated for the Supreme Court (and all courts) the power of judicial review. We must remember that there is no specific reference to judicial review in the

Constitution. Marshall used a logical reasoning process first to deduce that the power to invalidate unconstitutional legislation actually exists, and second to conclude that the power to decide when and if legislation conflicts with the Constitution belongs to the judiciary. Marshall accomplished his first goal by arguing that a written constitution must be considered to be superior to ordinary legislative acts; otherwise, having a written constitution would be senseless. Next, he argued that the Constitution implicitly recognizes that Congress could inadvertently pass a law that conflicts with the Constitution. Article VI declares that the Constitution and the laws of the United States *made in pursuance of the Constitution* are the supreme law of the land. Marshall argued that laws *not* made in pursuance of the Constitution were *not* the supreme law of the land. Someone or some group, then, must determine which laws are and which laws are not made in pursuance of the Constitution.

Having established the fact that laws passed in violation of the Constitution were invalid, Marshall next appropriated the power to determine their invalidity for the judiciary. With a sweep of the pen, Marshall declared, "It is emphatically the province and duty of the judicial department to say what the law is." Marshall argued that judges take an oath to uphold the Constitution and that it was their duty, when confronted with a law that clearly violated the Constitution, to declare that law null and void.

Chief Justice Marshall accomplished a number of goals with his decision in *Marbury*. First, he extricated himself from a serious dilemma that he, through his failure to deliver the commissions personally, had created. The Federalist Supreme Court could not be accused of partisan politics since it had not ruled in Marbury's favor. In addition, the Court had avoided a potentially dangerous confrontation with President Jefferson. The president could hardly refuse to obey an order the Court had declined to issue; thus, the president had no need to openly defy the Court's authority. Second, Marshall, in answering the first two questions he posed, scolded the president for refusing to deliver to Marbury that which was legally his. Third, the Court increased its own prestige by showing that it was "above politics." Fourth, and most important, Marshall secured for his Court and future courts the power of judicial review. Since the federal judiciary was heavily dominated by the Federalists, the Jeffersonians were put on notice that laws passed by them in Congress might someday be subjected to Federalist scrutiny. Despite this veiled threat, having once acquired the power of judicial review, the Supreme Court would not use it again for another 54 years.[8]

Judicial review and constitutional law.   The Supreme Court's power of judicial review enables it to interpret the meaning of the Constitution and, in so doing, give substance to the Constitution's ambiguous phrases. But the Supreme Court is not free to roam at will, handing down constitutional decisions like some self-proclaimed prophet interpreting the meaning of the stars. There are real limits to the Court's use of judicial review, some of which are self-imposed[9] and some of which are political.[10] Our primary concern, however, is in understanding how the Supreme Court has used its power to interpret the Constitution and has thereby shaped what we have called constitutional law.

As we have noted, the Supreme Court is not free to issue constitutional pronouncements on its own. It cannot, in other words, issue what are commonly called "advisory opinions." If the president proposed to take an action of dubious constitutionality and wanted to clear it with the Court first, the justices would simply refuse to do so. That is because the Court will rule on the constitutionality of acts only if there is a real "case or controversy." If the president proceeded to take the same action, and if his action were later challenged in court by a person with proper standing, the Court could properly hear the case. Other reasons that the Court might refuse to hear certain cases are because they raise "political questions," because a controversy has become moot, or because the Court feels that the issue is not "ripe" for judicial review.[11] It is important to remember that the availability of judicial review does not mean that the justices will always use their power "to say what the Constitution is."

A second important aspect of constitutional law is that it tends to be evolutionary. Recall that in Chapter 1 we defined case law as law that develops when judges make interpretations of the meaning of constitutions, statutes, or other forms of written law.[12] Case law develops over a long period of time and tends to be an ongoing process. Let us look at the right to counsel as an example.

The right to counsel was included in the Bill of Rights because of the British practice of refusing the accused the right to have an attorney in certain cases, even if the accused could afford one. Throughout most of our constitutional history, the Sixth Amendment's guarantee of the right to counsel meant only that the accused was entitled to an attorney *if he could pay for one.* Beginning in 1932, the Supreme Court began to change the meaning of the right. In the Scottsboro Boys Case,[13] a number of African-American youths were accused of raping two white women near Scottsboro, Alabama, in March 1931. Because of what the Court termed an atmosphere of "great hostility," the local sheriff had to call in the state militia to protect the defendants. At the trial the judge appointed the entire Scottsboro bar as the defendants' counsel and, to no one's surprise, all the youths were convicted. The Supreme Court overturned the convictions on the grounds that the defendants had been denied effective counsel. In addition, because of their youth, their illiteracy, and the hostile environment, the defendants had been denied due process of law as a result of their lack of effective counsel. With the Scottsboro Boys Case, the Supreme Court began the "special circumstances" rule, which stated that when special circumstances were present (youth, illiteracy, low mentality), the state had an affirmative duty to provide counsel for persons accused of serious crimes.

For the next ten years, the Supreme Court wrestled with the problem of which "special circumstances" required the state to appoint counsel for indigent defendants. In 1942, the Court ruled that indigency alone was insufficient grounds for requiring court-appointed counsel. In that case, *Betts* v. *Brady*,[14] an indigent defendant named Betts was forced to defend himself and was convicted. The Supreme Court said that Betts was a man of average education and intelligence, capable of understanding the proceedings and protecting his own interests. They allowed Betts's conviction to stand, ruling that indigency alone did not constitute a "special circumstance."

The next major step in the development of the right to counsel was the *Gideon* v. *Wainwright*[15] case. Gideon was charged with a felony in Florida, and because he was indigent, he asked for court-appointed counsel. Under Florida law, a judge was permitted to appoint counsel for indigent defendants only in capital cases, so the trial judge denied Gideon's request. Gideon proceeded to defend himself but was convicted and sent to prison. Gideon appealed his case to the U.S. Supreme Court *in forma pauperis,* and in a rare occurrence, the Court agreed to hear his case. The Court ruled 9–0 that the due process clause of the Fourteenth Amendment requires states to provide free counsel to indigent defendants in all noncapital felony cases. At his new trial, this time with the assistance of court-appointed counsel, Gideon was found not guilty. A few years later the Court extended its ruling to include misdemeanor cases in which the possibility of a jail term exists.[16] By its interpretation of the meaning of the Sixth Amendment and due process of law, the Supreme Court changed the meaning of the right to counsel. Instead of merely not denying a defendant who can afford to hire a lawyer the right to have that lawyer with him in court, the state has an affirmative duty to provide counsel to those who cannot afford to hire their own. Later cases, such as the *Escobedo*[17] and *Miranda*[18] decisions, addressed the question of when a person accused of a crime has the right to consult with an attorney, and even today the Supreme Court continues to struggle with the problem of right to counsel.

The final aspect of the nature of constitutional law is related to the one just discussed. If constitutional law has an evolutionary character, then it is also true that the resolution of constitutional issues is seldom final. Recall that in Chapter 1 we discussed the sociological theory of law, which holds that law changes as a society changes. As a society's view of what constitutes fairness or justice changes, those views will slowly be incorporated into its system of law. The previously discussed issue of the right to counsel illustrates this point. Prior to the 1963 *Gideon* decision, many well-intentioned people saw nothing unfair about requiring an indigent defendant to argue his own case without the assistance of a lawyer. But today a majority of people would probably agree with Justice Hugo Black, author of the *Gideon* decision, who wrote that "lawyers in criminal courts are necessities, not luxuries."[19] Yet as our society continues to change and the makeup of the Supreme Court changes, "settled" issues such as the right to counsel are raised again and again. Although unlikely, it is possible that a future generation will return to the pre-*Gideon* view of the right to counsel. As unfortunate as that may be, that is a fundamental characteristic of the American legal system.

The changing face of constitutional law is apparent in virtually every aspect of the field. In the next section we will see how the way in which the Supreme Court interprets the Constitution influences its evolution over time. Then in the following section we will examine five major areas of constitutional law in order to increase our understanding of this important field.

CONSTITUTIONAL INTERPRETATION

Constitutional law provokes a tremendous amount of controversy in our political system. This is, in part, because constitutional law is a struggle over which values shall predominate in our society. Legal battles over gun control, school prayer, abortion, and the death penalty are in reality battles over whose sets of values shall govern our law. Everyone who gives law any thought would like to see the law reflect his or her value system as much as possible. Since constitutional law is the supreme law of the land, it follows that the values it embodies are also supreme. The stakes being so high, it is small wonder that so much has been written about the proper way to interpret the Constitution.

Constitutional interpretation can be viewed in terms of both *who* and *how*. In Chapter 3, we discussed judicial selection, which focuses on how a person becomes a Supreme Court justice. Just as important is *who* the person interpreting the Constitution will be. For example, when President Reagan nominated Robert Bork to the Supreme Court in 1987, liberals were very concerned about how he would interpret, if confirmed, the right of privacy. Bork's defeat was due less to who he was as a person than how he would rule as a Supreme Court justice, but both factors were present in the decision to reject his nomination.

How to properly interpret the Constitution leads us to consider another side of judicial review. Because judicial review permits judges to say what the law is, it has become an object of controversy. Critics of the Supreme Court claim that judicial review permits judges to inject their own values into the Constitution. The Constitution means what a majority of the Supreme Court at a given point in time wants it to mean. These critics assert that judges should not inject their personal values into the Constitution but should merely interpret the intentions of the Founding Fathers. Another school of thought holds that if the Constitution is to solve contemporary legal problems, it must be interpreted in terms of contemporary values. The thinking of the Framers who accepted slavery as proper can hardly dictate race relations as we near the end of the twentieth century.

In the remainder of this section, we shall examine several of the leading theories or methods of constitutional interpretation. Each theory has its strengths and weaknesses, which we will try to denote. To a certain extent, each theory reflects the values of the persons who espouse it. For example, conservatives like Robert Bork have been accused of favoring reliance on the original intentions of the Framers because it "can consistently be made to support the conservative position."[20] Finally, each will have to be evaluated by the reader who should determine for oneself which is the "proper" way to interpret the Constitution.

Original intention.   The predicament posed by the theory of original intention (or original intent as it is sometimes called) can be revealed by a modern controversy: Did the Framers intend flag burning to be protected by the First Amendment? If your answer is "No," how do you know that? Many of the members of the First Congress who submitted the First Amendment to the states for ratification were also delegates who helped frame the original Constitution. Many were leaders of the American Revolution. Perhaps some were flag burners themselves, although the flag they might have burned was probably the Union Jack, not the Stars and Stripes. If your answer is "Yes," how do you know that? The First Amendment protects freedom of *speech* but flag burning is an action, not speech. Perhaps the Framers intended merely to protect words, not the actions that accompany words. To the Supreme Court, this is no theoretical debate. In *Texas* v. *Johnson*,[21] the justices had to decide an issue that touches the very soul of our constitutional government. That answer, like previous decisions involving abortion, school prayer, and desegregation, sparked a heated, ongoing debate.

Original intention is the name given to the doctrine that asserts that the only proper way to interpret the Constitution is in conformity to the intentions of the Framers. Its supporters claim that the original intentions of the Framers can be ascertained by either the plain language of the Constitution itself or from the debates and writings of the Framers. James Madison, for example, kept copious notes of the debates of the Constitutional Convention. Extensive historical research has uncovered letters, diaries, and contemporary newspaper accounts written about the Convention by actual participants and observers. *The Federalist Papers* by Madison, Hamilton, and Jay are yet another valuable source of insight into the thinking of the Founding Fathers.

Supporters of original intention argue that once the meaning of a constitutional provision has been determined, judges should merely rule accordingly. For example, if one wishes to determine if capital punishment is "cruel and unusual punishment," forbidden by the Eighth Amendment, one need only decide the Framers' position. Since all 13 states permitted capital punishment at the time of the Constitution's adoption, it is inconceivable the Framers thought capital punishment was "cruel," and it certainly was not "unusual."

Proponents of original intention give several reasons for this theory of constitutional interpretation. First, they argue that it just makes common sense to give weight to the intentions of the persons who wrote the Constitution. The Framers could not have intended to forbid capital punishment when it was an acceptable form of punishment at the time. To rule otherwise is simply nonsense. Second, adherence to original intention constrains the abuse of judicial review. Requiring judges to stick to the intent of the Framers limits judicial discretion and prohibits judges from introducing their personal values into the Constitution.[22] Third, reliance on original intention also provides a certain amount of consistency over time.[23] The "true" meaning of the Constitution does not change as the makeup of the Supreme Court changes.

A frequent criticism of original intention is that it often fails to provide answers for contemporary legal issues. For example, while capital punishment *per se* may be constitutional, is death by electrocution "cruel and unusual punishment"? Since death by electrocution was unknown to the Framers, how can we know their position on its use? Supporters of original intention respond that the solution is simple: The Constitution was never intended to address every conceivable manner of punishment. The Constitution does, however, provide for a Congress and state legislatures composed of the people's representatives to decide contemporary issues. Since the Framers' views cannot be determined, the collective judgment of elected officials should decide the issue. Judges should prohibit death by electrocution only if there is a clear constitutional ban against it.

A variation of original intention is what one author has termed "moderate originalism." This approach states that interpreters should concern themselves with the general purpose of a constitutional provision rather than its exact purpose.[24] Judges should ascertain the underlying purpose of the "cruel and unusual punishment" clause and rule accordingly. If the clause was intended to prohibit inhumane punishment, then the real issue is whether electrocution is inhumane.

Critics find original intention objectionable for a variety of reasons. First, they maintain that it is impossible to discover original intention. They point out that the records of the Constitutional Convention are incomplete and unofficial. Although James Madison took notes on the various positions of the delegates, estimates are that only about one-tenth of what was said was actually recorded.[25] A second problem surrounds the question of who should be included among "the Framers." Should original intention be limited to those who attended the Philadelphia Convention, those who signed the Constitution, or both? Should the delegates who ratified the Constitution in the state ratifying conventions also be included? Only six states had complete records of their deliberations while the remainder had either incomplete or no records. Finally, how can we assume there was a consensus among the Framers, regardless of how they are identified, on the meaning of a constitutional provision? As the debates at the Convention reveal, there was widespread disagreement on what the Constitution meant. For example, despite assurances from Hamilton in *The Federalist Papers* that a citizen of one state could not sue a state in a federal court, the Supreme Court later ruled just the opposite.[26] This has led one constitutional scholar to conclude, "So no jurisprudence of original intention is possible, because original intention is undiscoverable."[27]

Critics of original intention also claim that it is too narrow to be the overriding consideration of constitutional interpretation. Society, they argue, changes its attitudes and opinions on subjects such as capital punishment. Are we, they ask, to be bound forever by the opinions of the Framers? Although it is possible to amend the Constitution to reflect the changes in societal values, such an approach is tedious and impractical. Finally, many critics claim that reliance on original intention is merely a smokescreen used by conservatives to implement a conservative agenda now that conservative justices command a majority of the Supreme Court.[28]

Is original intention an honest attempt to return to our constitutional roots, or is it a covert attempt to activate a conservative agenda? As noted earlier in the chapter, constitutional issues are seldom final in their resolution. So, it should come as no surprise that the extent to which judges should rely on the intentions of the Framers will probably never be conclusive.

Interpretivism.   Closely related to original intention is the doctrine of *interpretivism*. This doctrine holds that the persons who wrote and ratified the Constitution selected certain principles they deemed fundamental and incorporated them into a written Constitution.[29] These principles, such as the Bill of Rights, were regarded as so fundamental that they were even to be protected from majority rule. Freedom of speech, being so essential to the maintenance of democratic government, was not to be abridged by laws passed at the whim of a mere majority. Only through the passage of constitutional amendments, which require extraordinary majorities, could these fundamental principles be altered.

Interpretivism, then, holds that the task of the judge is to apply new facts to these fixed and binding principles recognized by the Framers.[30] A jurist adopting this approach can disclaim injecting his own values into the Constitution. Instead, the values being upheld are those of the Founding Fathers. For example, in his concurring opinion in the Texas Flag Burning Case, Justice Anthony Kennedy wrote that the invalid Texas flag desecration law had to be "judged against a pure command of the Constitution."[31] Implicit in this statement is the assertion that Justice Kennedy's position reflected not his personal views of flag burning, but a directive of the Framers themselves.

Justice Hugo L. Black was one of the foremost proponents of interpretative theory. Justice Black never accepted substituting the term "freedom of expression" for freedom of speech. Black was critical of the notion that certain actions termed "symbolic speech" were protected by the First Amendment. For Justice Black wearing black armbands to protest the war in

Vietnam was not "speech" within the meaning of the First Amendment.[32] Thus, Black would disagree with Justice Kennedy that the decision to permit flag burning was a "pure command" of the Constitution. On the contrary, since flag burning constitutes action, not speech, Black probably would have held that it is unprotected. At the same time, Black often took the words of the Constitution literally. For example, he interpreted the First Amendment's command that "Congress shall make no law" abridging freedom of speech to mean that all speech, even obscene speech, was protected.

Interpretivism differs slightly from original intention. The advocate of interpretivism realizes the intent of the Framers cannot always be ascertained. However, the interpretivist does not necessarily defer to legislative bodies if original intention cannot be determined. For example, in deciding whether the Eighth Amendment prohibits persons from being electrocuted, proponents of original intent would defer to legislative bodies. The interpretivist would try to determine if death by electrocution violates the spirit of the provision prohibiting cruel and unusual punishment. In other words, although the interpretivist might agree with the advocate of original intent that capital punishment is constitutional, he would not necessarily agree that electrocution as a method of capital punishment is. The interpretivist, consequently, is less willing to relinquish the justices' right to "say what the law is."

One of the major criticisms of judicial review is that it is inherently undemocratic. The nine justices of the Supreme Court can strike down a law passed by the elected representatives of the people. Interpretivism can be viewed as a form of judicial restraint. As we have seen, it is the Framers' values, not the justices', that are being respected. As one scholar has noted, "The chief virtue of this view is that it supports judicial review while answering the charge that it is undemocratic."[33]

Noninterpretivism. *Noninterpretivism* espouses the position that the Framers never intended to create a Constitution frozen forever in the eighteenth century. Instead, they intended to write a "living Constitution" which would endure for all time. The most prominent champion of this position was Chief Justice John Marshall, who wrote in *McCulloch* v. *Maryland*, "This provision is made in a constitution intended to endure for all ages to come, and, consequently, to be adapted to the various crises of human affairs."[34] Noninterpretivism calls for the Supreme Court to serve as an ongoing constitutional convention constantly modifying, revising, and reinterpreting the Constitution to meet the needs of the current generation of Americans.

Noninterpretivists claim that their approach is the only one that makes sense. No one, not even the Framers, could have anticipated the changes that have occurred over the last 200 years. The Constitution has to be flexible enough to meet the exigencies of modern America. To paraphrase Chief Justice Marshall, as long as the Supreme Court's decisions are consistent with the spirit of the Constitution, they are constitutional.

An example will illustrate the noninterpretivist approach. When the Fourteenth Amendment was added to the Constitution, segregation laws and laws prohibiting interracial marriages were common in the states. Does that fact preclude a modern Court from striking down such laws as violations of equal protection? Of course not, claim the noninterpretivists. The Constitution is full of phrases such as "equal protection," "due process," and "liberty," which are evolutionary, not stagnant, concepts. These concepts must constantly be reassessed to reflect today's morals. Should the public's attitudes about interracial marriages and segregation change, the Constitution must be free to change with them. The Supreme Court, in a sense, acts as both the conscience of the nation and the guardian of its constitutional values.

Critics of noninterpretivism are less concerned about innovative interpretations of existing constitutional provisions than the practice of pulling constitutional rabbits out of a hat. In *Griswold* v. *Connecticut*,[35] for example, the Court struck down a law banning the use of contraceptives by married couples on the basis of the right to privacy. Similarly, in *Roe* v. *Wade*[36] the majority based the right to have an abortion on privacy. Although there is an acknowledged common law right to privacy, there is no explicit constitutional reference to privacy. Defenders of the noninterpretivist approach point out that many constitutional doctrines, including executive privilege, federalism, separation of powers, and even judicial review itself, are not specifically mentioned in the Constitution. However, no one would deny that these doctrines are woven into the very fabric of the Constitution.

MAJOR CONSTITUTIONAL DOCTRINES

The field of constitutional law is so immense that it is virtually impossible to cover it in a single textbook much less in one chapter of an introductory text. Consequently, we have chosen to focus on five major doctrines of constitutional law—federalism, separation of powers, due process of law, equal protection, and civil liberties—which we believe will increase your understanding of constitutional law. Each doctrine will be presented separately with an attempt to identify some of the problems it poses and some of the approaches the Supreme Court has adopted in resolving the issues raised by it.

Federalism.   It may come as a surprise to some people that the word "federalism" never appears in the Constitution. That is because the Framers did not deliberately set out to create a federal form of government. The 13 states that comprised the United States each had a viable state government in the summer of 1787. Most of the delegates who met in Philadelphia had one major concern: to strengthen the ineffective national government without unnecessarily weakening the existing state governments. To achieve this goal, they devised a plan that divided governmental powers between the national government and the states. A typical textbook definition of federalism defines it as a "Constitutional arrangement whereby power is divided by a constitution between a national government and constituent governments, called states in the U.S."[37]

Under our federal system, the Constitution assigns some powers, like the power to declare war and to regulate interstate commerce, to the national government. The so-called "police power," or the power to regulate health, safety, and morals, is one of the powers reserved to the states. Still other powers, like the taxing power, may be exercised by both levels of government. Although it may appear to be a simple task of assigning a power to one or the other level of government, actually defining the boundaries of the national government's and the states' powers has been one of the most perplexing problems in our constitutional history.

The commerce power of the national government and the police power of the states serve to illustrate the problem. Congress may regulate interstate commerce or commerce among the states. Consequently, any commercial activity involving two or more states comes under congressional authority. If, however, the activity is internal to the state, it constitutes *intrastate commerce* and falls within the state's police power.

An early approach to federalism, called dual federalism, was based on the premise that governmental and commercial activities could be placed into neat, discrete categories. The major task of the Supreme Court was to decide if a particular activity belonged to the national government or to the states. To assist it in deciding to which level of government the power to regulate a given activity belonged, the Court devised certain tests it could apply. For example, the "direct-indirect effect test" held that if the activity had a direct effect on interstate commerce, it fell within the power of the national government, but if the effect was only indirect, the states were free to regulate the activity. Of course, the determination of what was a direct or indirect effect on interstate commerce was left to the subjective judgment of a majority of justices.

An example should clarify this dual federalism approach. In 1916, Congress passed the Child Labor Act which banned goods manufactured with child labor from interstate commerce. Congress considered this to be a legitimate use of its commerce power. Although states had their own child labor laws, some states, like North Carolina, permitted children as young as 12 to work full time. In striking down the Child Labor Act, the Supreme Court found that child labor practices had only an indirect effect on interstate commerce.[38] The Supreme Court took similar positions when Congress tried to regulate monopolies[39] and set minimum wages and maximum hours for workers.[40] Even though, for all practical purposes, these decisions have been reversed or superseded, they serve to illustrate the rigid, legalistic approach dual federalism brought to constitutional law.

The modern approach to federalism has been that of cooperative federalism. Unlike dual federalism, which portrays the two levels of government as antagonistic competitors for power, cooperative federalism stresses the need for states to work with the national government to solve the nation's problems. Cooperative federalism also stresses the interplay of politics in our federal system. Instead of the Court serving as a referee of jurisdictional disputes between the two levels of government, it assumes that the states have the political skills to protect their interests both in and out of Congress. The reasoning behind this approach is that members of Congress represent states and they must be presumed to have the states' best interests at heart.

Cases involving the commerce power may again help to illustrate the cooperative federalism approach. By the late 1960s, the Supreme Court had adopted a broad, expansive view of the commerce power permitting Congress to regulate wages and hours of workers,[41] labor relations,[42] farm production,[43] and even race relations.[44] However, these uses of the commerce power were all aimed at regulating the commercial practices of private companies and individuals. A different question of federalism arose as to whether the commerce power could be used to regulate the activities of the states themselves. That is, while Congress may unquestionably require the local McDonald's to pay its employees a minimum wage, may it require the states to pay their employees the federal minimum wage?

The Supreme Court has equivocated somewhat on the issue of using the commerce power to regulate the activities of states. Initially, the Court ruled that Congress could require public as well as private hospitals to pay their employees the minimum wage.[45] However, when Congress attempted to extend the provisions of the Fair Labor Standards Act to include other state employees, the Supreme Court declared the attempt unconstitutional.[46] Surprisingly, only nine years later the Court reversed itself again, ruling that Congress could require the City of San Antonio to pay its transit authority workers the prevailing minimum wage. The majority opinion in this latest decision, *Garcia* v. *San Antonio Metropolitan Transit Authority*,[47] incorporates many of the cooperative federalism arguments. The Court noted that San Antonio receives millions of dollars from the federal government under the Urban Mass Transportation Act of 1964. The national government may place certain conditions on the states, such as requiring them to pay their employees the minimum wage, in exchange for federal subsidies. Finally, the Court noted that the states have ways to protect their interests in Congress and that it is unlikely Congress would pass legislation harmful to the states' interests. With the election of a Republican Congress in November 1994, the future course of federalism is unclear. Republicans generally favor returning power to the states in such areas as welfare reform and environmental regulation. Undoubtedly the Supreme Court will be required to rule on the changes that will occur in state-federal relationships. It seems clear that the debate over federal regulation of state activities is entering a new phase. It is equally clear that, as we enter a third century of constitutional development, the issue of federalism is not dead.

   Separation of powers.   Just as the Framers sought to divide power between the national government and the states, they also wanted to prevent the concentration of power into the hands of one individual, or even one group of individuals, within the national government. The Framers reduced all governmental functions to essentially three: legislative, executive, and judicial. They believed that the very root of tyranny was to allow these three essential governmental functions to be exercised by one person or group. Consequently, they deliberately set out to divide the three functions into three separate and distinct institutions. Congress was to exercise the legislative power while the president and his subordinates would exercise the executive power. Finally, the Supreme Court, with any inferior courts created by Congress, would possess the judicial power of the United States.

   It is very difficult to discuss *separation of powers* without mentioning the corresponding doctrine of checks and balances. The Framers believed that one branch of government would invariably seek to encroach upon and to usurp the powers of the others. In fact, given the ambiguous language describing the powers of each branch, they almost guaranteed there would be such attempts. The Framers anticipated that one branch would resist attempted encroachments of its powers, but they also realized that safeguards were needed to help each branch protect its powers against attacks. As James Madison wrote:

> But the great security against a gradual concentration of the several powers in the same department consists in giving to those who administer each department the necessary constitutional means and personal motives to resist encroachments of the others.[48]

   The "necessary constitutional means" of which Madison writes form the basis for the doctrine of checks and balances.

   The president's veto is the most common example of checks and balances. Ordinarily, we think of the president's veto as a check on legislation he considers to be unwise. While this is certainly a valid and frequent reason for using the veto, the Framers also expected the president to use his veto to strike down any law which encroached upon his prerogatives. For example, in 1973 when President Richard Nixon vetoed the War Powers Act, he did so mainly because he believed the law encroached upon his powers as commander-in-chief. Even though Congress passed the War Powers Act over Nixon's veto, several of his successors, especially President Reagan, share his doubts about its constitutionality. The point is, however, that each branch possesses constitutional weapons to defend itself from the other two.

   It is easy to overemphasize the "separateness" of the doctrine of separation of powers. Similarly, it is easy to overemphasize the adversarial nature of checks and balances. But the Framers did not create three separate institutions operating in their different spheres oblivious to one another. Nor did they create circumstances under which the three branches would be constantly battling in a permanent struggle for power. On the contrary, the Framers created a system of interdependency among the three branches, and in doing so created one of the greatest paradoxes of American government. That paradox is this: Despite the tendency for the three branches to confront one another, in order for our national government to work, they must cooperate with one another. Laws must be passed by the Congress, signed and enforced by the president, and upheld by the federal courts. This need for cooperation is especially true if the Republicans continue to dominate Congress and if the Democrats maintain control of the White House.

As with federalism, there are too many facets of separation of powers to explore extensively. Therefore, we have chosen to concentrate on the relationship between the president and Congress. With the Supreme Court in its customary role as referee of our constitutional system, we will focus on some of the major controversies that have divided the two great political branches of our government.

As previously noted, constitutional disputes often arise because of the vagueness of constitutional language or because the Constitution is silent about a particular topic. When both the president and Congress have a constitutional role to play, the potential for conflict is increased. For example, the Constitution states that the president, "shall nominate and by and with the advice and consent of the Senate, shall appoint . . . officers of the United States, . . . "[49] Clearly, both the president and Congress are involved in the *selection* of executive branch members subordinate to the president. Unfortunately, the Constitution is silent about which branch has the power to *dismiss* members of the executive branch. Lesser executive officials, just like the president, are subject to impeachment, but the Framers did not intend for it to be used for routine removals since impeachment is only for "treason, bribery, or other high crimes and misdemeanors."[50]

During our constitutional history several landmark cases about questions of appointment and removal of executive officials have surfaced. Early in our history it was assumed that executive officers, especially Cabinet members, served entirely at the pleasure of the president. Nevertheless, in 1867 Congress enacted the Tenure of Office Act which prohibited the president, without Senate permission, from removing officials from office who had previously received Senate confirmation. In other words, the act required Senate permission to remove as well as appoint Cabinet officers. When President Andrew Johnson tried to remove his secretary of war, Edwin M. Stanton, the Radical Republicans in Congress were angered. In 1868 the House of Representatives impeached Johnson in part for violating the Tenure of Office Act. Although saved from conviction in the Senate by a single vote,

Johnson's acquittal did not fully settle the issue of removal of executive officers.

The issue of removing executive officials arose again when President Woodrow Wilson removed a Portland, Oregon, postmaster from office. An 1876 statute held that certain classes of postmasters served four-year terms of office and could only be removed with the consent of the Senate. In *Myers* v. *United States*,[51] Chief Justice William Howard Taft, himself a former president, declared the 1876 law to be an unconstitutional restraint on the removal power and consequently a violation of separation of powers. However, when President Franklin D. Roosevelt removed a member of the Federal Trade Commission (FTC), the Supreme Court ruled the removal unconstitutional. In *Myers*, the Court said, the removed official was performing purely executive functions. In this case, *Humphrey's Executor* v. *United States*,[52] on the other hand, the Court noted that the FTC performs "quasi-legislative" and "quasi-judicial" functions as well as executive functions. Congress, in establishing the FTC, sought to insulate it from partisan politics. Its membership was, by law, to be bipartisan and the terms of its members were also set by law. In addition, removal of FTC members could only be done for a reason specified in the Federal Trade Commission Act. For these reasons, the Court ruled that President Roosevelt's removal of Humphrey was illegal.

Two more recent Supreme Court decisions illustrate the continuing problem of shared responsibility for the appointment and removal of government officials. Following the Watergate Scandal, Congress passed the Federal Election Campaign Act of 1974. The act created the Federal Election Commission (FEC) whose membership consisted of two persons appointed by the president, two appointed by the speaker of the House, and two appointed by the president *pro tempore* of the Senate. All six members were subject to Senate confirmation. In *Buckley* v. *Valeo*,[53] the Supreme Court ruled that the composition of the FEC usurped the president's appointment power and caused the FEC to be restructured.[54]

In 1985, Congress passed the Gramm-Rudman-Hollings Act, which was designed to reduce the annual deficit of the federal government to zero by 1991. Under the act, the comptroller general, after a complicated process, was to make specific budget cut recommendations to the president. The Supreme Court struck down key provisions of the act on separation of powers grounds. The Court noted that the comptroller general is nominated by the president and confirmed by the Senate from a list of three persons submitted by the speaker of the House and the president *pro tempore* of the Senate. From the legislative history of the office, the Court concluded that the comptroller general was intended to be a legislative officer. The Gramm-Rudman-Hollings Act assigned executive functions to the comptroller general, which the Court found unconstitutional under the doctrine of separation of powers.[55]

Another source of constitutional friction between the president and

Congress has been the *legislative veto.* As mentioned in Chapter 1 and explained more fully in Chapter 8, Congress passes general laws and then permits executive agencies to promulgate regulations that have the force of law. This practice, known as *delegation,* has been upheld by the Supreme Court as a necessary practice of modern government. It permits the more knowledgeable executive officials to fill in the details of legislation after Congress has written the general guidelines.

The legislative veto is Congress's attempt to have the last word on public policy. Suppose an executive agency promulgated a rule which had an effect Congress never really intended. Congress could always amend the original statute to clarify its intention, but the legislative process is cumbersome and tedious. Also, minor "housekeeping" changes in legislation often get lost in the onslaught of other, more important bills. Consequently, Congress has employed the legislative veto to ensure its will is obeyed. The legislative veto permits either one or both houses of Congress to nullify a proposed regulation. If an agency proposes a rule contrary to the intent of the statute, Congress by legislative resolution may veto the proposed rule.

Presidents have complained that the legislative veto is an encroachment upon their executive power. On the other hand, bills containing legislative vetoes have been signed into law by several presidents. Over the years Congress and the president have reached an accommodation over legislative vetoes, and literally hundreds of them have been enacted.

In 1983 the Supreme Court muddied the constitutional waters by its ruling in *Immigration and Naturalization Service* v. *Chadha.*[56] The Immigration and Nationality Act permits the attorney general to suspend the deportation of an alien. The attorney general had decided to suspend the deportation of Jagdish Rai Chadha, a native of Kenya living in the United States. Section 244 (c) (2) of the act permitted either house of Congress to cancel the attorney general's suspension of deportation, which the House of Representatives did in Chadha's case. Chadha then challenged the constitutionality of § 244 (c) (2).

In striking down the legislative veto, the Supreme Court found that the cancellation of the attorney general's suspension of deportation contained in § 244 (c) (2) was a legislative action. Under the Constitution, legislative actions must be presented to the president for his signature or veto. Since legislative vetoes are not sent to the president, they violate the Presentment Clause and are therefore unconstitutional. The Court also ruled that the Constitution requires legislative actions to be passed by both houses of Congress. Since legislative vetoes can be effected by one house, they violate the bicameralism requirements of the Constitution as well as the doctrine of separation of powers.

One final area of conflict involving separation of powers which will be covered is the doctrine of *executive privilege.* Executive privilege is the president's claim to be able to withhold information from Congress.[57] The term "executive privilege" does not appear in the Constitution but is maintained by some to be grounded in the doctrine of separation of powers. George Washington set the precedent for executive privilege when, in 1792, the House sought information about a failed Indian expedition in the Northwest led by General St. Clair. After discussing whether he should comply with the request with his Cabinet, President Washington gave the House the papers it requested.[58]

Essentially, the issue of executive privilege is over access to information needed by Congress and possessed by the president. Congress claims that the information in the president's hands is needed for its lawmaking function. There are times when the information Congress seeks is politically embarrassing to the administration and Congress wants it exposed for partisan political reasons. Historically, Congress has not insisted that the president reveal information if public disclosure would harm national security or generally not be in the public interest. The main problem, of course, is who—the president, Congress, or the Court—should decide when the president may withhold information that Congress feels it has a legitimate right to see.

The most famous conflict over executive privilege involved the Watergate tapes. A burglary at the headquarters of the National Democratic Party in June 1972 touched off a series of events that led to the resignation of President Richard M. Nixon. Although President Nixon denied any knowledge of the break-in or subsequent attempt to cover up White House involvement, investigations into the Watergate affair kept getting closer to the Oval Office. When it was discovered that President Nixon had installed a voice-activated taping system in his office to record presidential conversations, the crisis intensified. In the summer of 1973, the Senate Watergate Committee began investigating the 1972 presidential campaign. In the summer of 1974, the House Judiciary Committee began hearings on whether the House should impeach the president. Both committees wanted copies of the tapes containing conversations between the president and key Watergate figures. President Nixon, claiming that the release of the tapes would damage the presidency, invoked executive privilege and refused to surrender the tapes.

Ultimately, however, it was not Congress but a member of the president's own executive branch who succeeded in securing release of the tapes. The Watergate special prosecutor, Leon Jaworski, asked federal judge John Sirica to issue a *subpoena duces tecum* to the president ordering him to produce the tapes as evidence in the criminal prosecution of the Watergate defendants. When Judge Sirica complied, the president challenged the issuance of the subpoena. Jaworski then appealed to the Supreme Court.

The Court ruled unanimously 8–0 (Justice William Rehnquist did not participate) that the president had to release the tapes.[59] The Court recognized the constitutional basis for executive privilege, but held that the president's right to decide when it is invoked is not absolute. The Court found the need to balance the president's admitted right to protect his confidential conversations with the need of the Watergate defendants to have all relevant evidence in their trial. The Court found that absent a compelling national security interest, a president's claim of executive privilege, standing alone, was insufficient to overcome the defendants' right to a fair trial.

This brief discussion of separation of powers illustrates that the concept, like federalism, is neither archaic nor static. Cases like Watergate serve to remind us that constitutional doctrines are both relevant and dynamic concepts. Future disputes over the powers of the three branches will undoubtedly arise simply because of the nature of our constitutional arrangement of shared powers. That is because, as Madison predicted so long ago, such struggles are inherent in the governance of human beings.

Due process.   The U.S. Constitution actually contains two due process of law clauses. The Fifth Amendment reads, "No person shall . . . be deprived of life, liberty, or property without due process of law; . . . " Due to an early Supreme Court ruling which held that the Bill of Rights restricts only the actions of the national government,[60] a second due process clause was included in the Fourteenth Amendment which was adopted shortly after the Civil War. That Amendment reads, ". . . nor shall any State deprive any person of life, liberty, or property without due process of law; . . . " There was widespread belief that another due process clause was needed to protect the newly freed slaves from vindictive actions at the hands of southern state governments.

Due process is one of the most elusive and complex concepts in law. In simple terms it means that before government can take away a person's life, liberty, or property, certain procedures must be followed. Due process is the individual's major defense against despotic and arbitrary government. It prevents government interference with the basic rights of its citizens. Due process has real significance only in a system of government where the people are truly sovereign, for it means that not even the government itself is above the law. The government itself must respect certain rights and conform to accepted standards of behavior.

It is important to clarify two common misconceptions about due process. Due process does not mean that government may *never* take away one's life, liberty, or property. When the state executes a convicted murderer, it takes life; when it drafts a person into the armed forces, it takes liberty; and when it confiscates land to build a new highway, it takes property. All that is required for due process is that the law be properly followed and the "takings" not be arbitrary or capricious. The second misconception is that due process is reserved for citizens. However, the Fifth and Fourteenth Amendments refer to persons, not just citizens. Anyone, including both legal and illegal aliens, within the jurisdiction of the United States are entitled to due process. This is because the Framers of these two amendments regarded life, liberty, and property as basic human or natural rights that do not depend upon citizenship for protection against government abuse.

Previously, due process was described as an elusive concept. It is certainly one of the most elastic and controversial in American law. Persons attempting to capture the essence of due process frequently resort to such phrases as "fundamental fairness" or "canons of decency." Violations of due process are said to "shock the conscience" or "offend a sense of justice."[61] The major problem with due process is that it is a highly subjective concept: How much process is due? To one person our legal system provides too many loopholes which allow criminals to elude justice. To another, life, liberty, and property are sacred and every safeguard is essential. As is often the case, where one stands depends on where one sits; due process may have different connotations for a person facing confiscation of his property than for a highway contractor.

Due process of law has two interesting dimensions: procedural and substantive. *Procedural due process* stresses the policies or procedures government must observe when depriving someone of life, liberty, or property. Virtually everyone agrees, for example, that someone should not be imprisoned without first having a trial. But in Anglo-American law we also speak of a "fair trial," which implies there is more to a trial than mere adherence to a set of procedures. The phrase "fair trial" also implies some subjective evaluation of whether the judge was impartial and the jury unbiased. The evaluation of the fairness of a judicial proceeding or law is the essence of *substantive due process.*

Substantive due process, in effect, permits judges to decide what is "fundamentally unfair," "unreasonable," or "shocking" to the conscience of society. Substantive due process exposes justices to charges of injecting their personal policy preferences into the due process clause. Early in this century, the Supreme Court was accused of imposing its economic views on the nation by striking down laws regulating the number of hours bakers could work[62] and minimum wages for hospital workers.[63] Although substantive due process is generally conceded to be a discredited constitutional doctrine, modern courts have been accused of resurrecting substantive due process, especially in the area of the right to counsel. Critics of the *Miranda* v. *Arizona*[64] decision contend it is a prime example of the Court extending the right to counsel far beyond the original intent of the Framers. It is not always easy to keep procedural and substantive due process separate. The *Miranda* decision outlines a procedure that police must follow when making an arrest, but it also contains a subjective evaluation of the fairness of informing the accused of his or her constitutional rights.

In the remainder of this section we will focus on the constitutional doctrine known as *incorporation.* Although incorporation has been applied to First Amendment freedoms and other provisions of the Bill of Rights, we will limit our discussion to those provisions concerning the rights of the accused. An understanding of the incorporation process should shed light on the interplay between procedural and substantive due process of law.

As noted at the outset of this section, there are two due process clauses in the Constitution. When the Supreme Court ruled that the Bill of Rights applied only to the national government, it meant that only the national government had to observe due process. Since, as we saw in Chapter 3, the vast majority of criminal cases are tried in state, not federal, courts, it meant that for most criminal defendants the Bill of Rights might just as well not exist. Theoretically, at least, each state was free to define the meaning of due process for itself affording or withholding procedural rights as it saw fit. Although state constitutions contained bills of rights with similar protection, due process often varied from state to state.

As we have seen, the Fourteenth Amendment was passed in part to ensure that southern states would not oppress the newly freed slaves. Consequently, states were also forbidden to deny persons within their jurisdictions due process of law. The problem, of course, is what is meant by due process of law? Is due process whatever is required of the federal government, or could states continue to define due process independently? Does due process require the states to adopt some, all, or none of the provisions of the Bill of Rights? These questions and others complicate the already confusing issue of due process.

Three theories emerged as a result of the debate over which provisions of the Bill of Rights apply to the states. The first theory, known as *Total Incorporation,* holds that all of the procedural safeguards in the Bill of Rights were made applicable to the states through the Due Process Clause of the Fourteenth Amendment. This process, also known as *absorption,* maintains that the Fourteenth Amendment's Due Process Clause, like a sponge, absorbs the Bill of Rights. Due process is merely a shorthand summary of the Bill of Rights. Without the right to counsel, protection against self-incrimination, and the other procedural safeguards, due process has no meaning. Advocates of Total Incorporation would include Supreme Court decisions which interpret procedural safeguards, but they would limit the definition of due process to the Bill of Rights.

A second theory, known as *Selective Incorporation,* holds that some, perhaps most, but certainly not all of the Bill of Rights are applicable to the states through the Fourteenth Amendment. Selective Incorporation holds that the Supreme Court should decide on a case-by-case basis whether a particular provision of the Bill of Rights is essential to due process. For example, the Fifth Amendment requires that a person charged with a federal offense be indicted by a grand jury. Selective Incorporationists argue that the Due Process Clause of the Fourteenth Amendment does not require the states to use grand jury indictment. In our federal system, states should be free to employ other methods of indictment and, in fact, about half of the states indict by information, not by grand jury.

Over the years the Supreme Court has favored Selective Incorporation. By the end of the 1960s, under former Chief Justice Earl Warren, most of the major provisions of the Bill of Rights had been incorporated. There is still some disagreement over the extent to which the states must follow federal procedural rules. For example, in *Duncan* v. *Louisiana,* the Court ruled that due process requires a jury trial where the maximum punishment possible is two years' imprisonment. Although Justice Abe Fortas agreed that due process required a jury trial, he did not believe that states should have to observe other federal requirements, such as a unanimous verdict.[65] Later, the Supreme Court did in fact rule that unanimous verdicts are not essential to due process in all criminal cases.[66]

The third theory, which we might label "due process plus," holds that due process is not limited to the provisions of the Bill of Rights. Using the language of the noninterpretivists, advocates of this position argue that limiting due process to the Bill of Rights is too restrictive and too narrow. Due process evolves as society evolves and is not limited to how it was conceived by the eighteenth-century Framers nor to how it is interpreted by twentieth-century Supreme Courts.

In this section we have tried to cover some of the basic ideas behind due process of law. If due process is in fact an evolving concept, then it will probably never be fully understood. Another problem is that due process depends heavily on individual notions of fairness and justice. For these reasons due process will continue to elude a clear definition. We can only hope that this brief exposure to due process will assist the reader in coming to terms with this fascinating concept of law.

Equal protection. Like the Due Process Clause, the Equal Protection Clause of the Fourteenth Amendment was designed to prevent discrimination against the newly freed slaves. The Fourteenth Amendment reads, "No State shall . . . deny to any person within its jurisdiction the equal protection of the laws." The general thrust of the Equal Protection Clause is that government must treat people "similarly situated" alike. This does not mean that government may never classify people or never treat them differently. A state may classify people into those 16 years of age and older for the purpose of issuing driver's licenses. Similarly, a state may provide special benefits for farmers, veterans, or low-income people. Depending on the criteria, these benefits may be extended to some people and denied to others without violating the Equal Protection Clause.

If equal protection permits government both to classify and to treat people differently, what then does it mean? The Supreme Court has approached equal protection analysis by weighing two major factors. The first is the nature or basis of the classification. In the past, states have classified people on the basis of race, age, sex, height, and other physical characteristics. States have also classified people according to wealth, IQ or some other test score, occupation, and education. In deciding if a classification is constitutional or not, the Court determines whether there is a rational basis for the classification and whether the classification has some rational relationship to a legitimate government concern or goal.

Suppose, for example, a college professor decides to categorize everyone in her class according to his or her eye color; those with brown eyes in one group and those with nonbrown eyes in the other group. Suppose further that she decrees that those with brown eyes will be allowed to earn extra credit points but those with nonbrown eyes may not. The professor has denied the nonbrown-eyed students equal protection because her classification scheme is arbitrary and has no basis in logic or reason. Furthermore, there is no rational relationship between eye color and class performance as reflected in grades.

Suppose, on the other hand, that the same professor decides to permit students to earn extra credit points based on good class attendance. She again divides the students into two groups: attenders and nonattenders. In the first place, this classification is based on objective criteria, that is, the number of absences a student has. Second, it may be reasonably assumed, though not necessarily proven, that good attendance and class performance are related. Although it is possible that someone with perfect attendance will fail the class, it is still sensible to assume that class attendance will help the performance of most of the students in the class. In conclusion, while a classification based on eye color is irrational and subjective, one based on attendance is objective and reasonable.

Over the years the Supreme Court has developed criteria for determining whether classifications are reasonable. In the process the Court has created a category containing what it calls *suspect classifications.* Race and alienage are examples of suspect classes. Any law that classifies on the basis of race or alienage is immediately "suspect" and presumed unconstitutional. The Court decides whether a classification is suspect by first determining whether its members constitute a "discrete and insular minority." That is, if the group members are readily identifiable, distinct, and separate from the majority of citizens, it may qualify as a suspect class. Second, the Court ascertains if there has been a history of past discrimination against the group. Finally, the Court looks at the relative political power of the group. A group possessing relatively little ability to affect the political process may qualify for suspect status. These groups may need judicial protection from the majority that groups with political power do not require.

Race is a good example of a suspect class because it is difficult to justify the use of racial classifications. We do not mean, of course, that government census takers may not ask a person's race or record it on a census form. We do mean that race may not generally be a factor in how a person is treated under the law. Racial classification can be used if the state can suggest a compelling reason why it is justified. For example, affirmative action advocates maintain that the state's interest in overcoming past discrimination against blacks is compelling enough to justify favorable treatment of blacks. Some people view this as "reverse discrimination" and contend that affirmative action programs are unconstitutional.

The Court has recognized a second category of classes which are commonly called "near-suspect" classes. Near-suspect classes include sex, illegitimacy, disability, and age. These groups, for one reason or another, fail to meet the criteria necessary for suspect status but still deserve some protection from possible discrimination at the hands of the majority. Women are a good example of a near-suspect class because numerically they constitute a majority of Americans. Yet few would deny that there has been a history of discrimination, especially in terms of employment opportunities, based on sex in the United States. On the other hand, since women received the right to vote in 1920 there has been no serious attempt, as in the case of black Americans, to keep them from exercising voting rights.

Finally, there are classifications based on criteria that the Court considers "nonsuspect." As we have already noted, laws that bestow benefits on farmers, veterans, poor people, college students, and other special interest groups are generally considered to be reasonable and will usually survive judicial review.

Thus far we have focused entirely on the first major factor of equal protection analysis, the nature of the classification. The second major factor is whether the law or practice being challenged involves a fundamental interest or right. When a state enacts legislation that infringes upon a fundamental right, the Court considers the nature of the right, the interest of the state, and the hardship to the individual in its analysis. If a constitutional or statutorily created right is involved, the Court is more likely to strike down the law. For example, in *Sherbert* v. *Verner,* the Court ruled that a Seventh-Day Adventist could not be denied unemployment benefits because her refusal to work on Saturdays (her Sabbath) made her unemployable. The Court found that the denial of benefits placed an unfair burden on her free exercise of religion.[67]

A major problem, of course, is determining exactly what is a fundamental right or interest. Consider the following situations: (1) a state law denies aliens the opportunity to become notaries;[68] (2) a County Bar Association refuses to allow a noncitizen to take the bar exam even though she is qualified in every other respect;[69] and (3) a state law prohibits the certification of noncitizens as public school teachers.[70] In each example the person involved is a noncitizen and the issue is whether a state may deny access to these occupations to noncitizens. The Court must decide whether a person has a fundamental right to pursue a particular occupation.

As in the case of suspect classifications, a state may overcome an infringement of a fundamental right by showing it has a compelling interest in enacting the law. Also, if the state can demonstrate that the law is carefully tailored to minimize the burden on a fundamental right, the statute may be constitutional. In our three examples, the Court found no compelling reason to deny noncitizens the opportunity to be notaries and lawyers, but did find cause to deny noncitizens certification as public school teachers.[71] The Court held that the citizenship requirement "was rationally related to the State's interest in furthering the goal of educating students to be good citizens."[72] The Court also held that since the law made exceptions for noncitizens who intended to apply for citizenship, it was carefully tailored to serve its purpose without placing an unnecessary burden on noncitizens.[73]

We finally come to the interrelationship between classification schemes and fundamental interests. In determining whether the Equal Protection Clause has been violated, the Supreme Court has employed a two-tier approach. If the law involves a suspect class, a fundamental right, or both the Court applies "strict scrutiny" to the law. In such instances, the Court presumes that the law is unconstitutional and the state bears the burden of overcoming this presumption. As we have seen, that is done by the state showing a compelling reason to justify the law.

The second tier is when the Court applies its reasonable basis analysis. If a law involves neither a suspect class nor a fundamental right, the Court merely determines whether there is a reasonable basis for the law. The burden is on the person challenging the law to show that it violates equal protection. Earlier we referred to the minimum age for receiving a driver's license. Since persons under 16 are not a suspect class and since most legislatures do not consider driving a fundamental right, the Court would simply determine if the state had a reasonable or rational basis for setting the age limit at 16. Since driving a car requires a certain degree of maturity, it is easy to see that the law does not violate equal protection to 16-year-olds no matter how unfair they believe it to be.

Some constitutional law scholars and Supreme Court justices have advocated a middle-tier approach to equal protection analysis. This would allow judges to employ more than a reasonable basis analysis but less than strict scrutiny in close cases. For example, the Court could use this middle-tier analysis in cases in which near-suspect classifications are involved. In any case, the degree of scrutiny is a function of the amount of deference the Supreme Court is willing to afford legislative bodies. As our earlier discussion of judicial review indicated, the degree of deference to legislative bodies is critical to understanding the role of the courts in our constitutional system.

Civil liberties.   The field of civil liberties concerns one of the most controversial areas of constitutional law because it involves the fundamental question of the rights of the individual versus the rights of society. Most people agree that order and stability are necessary for personal freedom to exist and that individuals must sacrifice some freedom for the good of society. However, we do not wish to sacrifice more freedom than is absolutely necessary to achieve the desired level of stability. But how much stability is enough and how much freedom must be sacrificed to achieve it? Unfortunately, there is no easy answer. This is an especially difficult question in a democratic society that simultaneously values individual freedom and majority rule. Nor is the tension between the rights of the individual and the rights of a democratic society easily reconciled. In the American political system it is the job of the Supreme Court to strike a balance between the two. The times and the circumstances of society will determine the extent of personal liberty. At times we seem to enjoy tremendous freedom and at other times there seems to be a "chilling effect" on the exercise of individual freedom. As a result, civil liberties are in a constant state of fluctuation in which the amount of freedom we enjoy will depend on the willingness of society and the Court to tolerate our exercise of freedom.

Civil liberties are not rights conferred upon citizens by government as they are often misperceived to be. John Brigham has written that liberties "are rights held against authorities" that "limit interference with a variety of activities deemed worthy of special protection."[74] In other words, certain liberties, such as freedom of speech and religion, are considered to be so fundamental that they are protected from majority rule. The field of civil liberties is traditionally divided into First Amendment freedoms and the rights of the accused. First Amendment freedoms include freedom of religion, speech and assembly, and freedom of press. Since the rights of the accused, such as the right to counsel, are addressed in other sections of this book, we will limit our discussion here to First Amendment freedoms. We begin with freedom of religion.

There are actually two clauses in the First Amendment that pertain to freedom of religion: the Establishment Clause and the Free Exercise Clause. The Establishment Clause reads, "Congress shall make no law respecting an establishment of religion. . . ." One theory of the Establishment Clause is that it was designed to erect a "wall of separation" between church and state. This theory holds that the majority will attempt to use the power of government to promote or advance a particular religion. To prevent that from happening, civil libertarians must be vigilant about any attempt to use state power to promote religion in any manner. In other words, the wall should be kept high. A second theory asserts that erecting a wall of separation results in government hostility toward religion, which was never the intent of the Constitution's Framers. Instead, the Establishment Clause was designed to ensure that all religions received equal treatment from government. As long as government shows no preference for one religion over others, the Establishment Clause is not violated.

Cases involving the Establishment Clause have entailed those in which government financial aid is at issue and those in which some form of religious exercise is challenged. The first category consists of cases in which the government sought to provide financial aid to parochial schools, for example. In the early cases,[75] the Supreme Court was asked to rule on the constitutionality of providing bus transportation, school books, and other forms of assistance to students attending religiously affiliated schools. In some instances the Court allowed such government aid and in others the aid was denied. The Court formulated the much-criticized *Lemon* test to resolve issues of financial aid. The *Lemon* test states that in order to survive judicial scrutiny the policy (1) must have a secular legislative purpose, (2) may neither advance nor inhibit religion, and (3) must avoid excessive entanglement between church and state. If any one of the three components is not met, the Establishment Clause is violated.

The second category of establishment cases includes those in which some form of religious exercise involving government is challenged. The prayer-in-school controversy that continues to surface in political debate is such an example. Beginning with *Engel v. Vitale*[76] in 1962, which banned the use of a nondemoninational prayer in New York public schools, the Supreme Court has been faced with a multitude of religious exercise cases. The Court has been asked to rule on the posting of the Ten Commandments in public school classrooms,[77] an Alabama law authorizing a period of silence for "silent meditation or prayer,"[78] and prayers at high school commencement ceremonies.[79] To illustrate the complexity of these issues, the Supreme Court held in its 1994 term that the University of Virginia's refusal to pay for the publication of a Christian student magazine from student fees violated the students' freedom of *speech*. The university had refused to pay for the publication on the grounds that to do so would violate the Establishment Clause. However, the Court ruled 5–4 that freedom of speech, not the Establishment Clause, was the critical issue involved.[80]

The second great clause of the First Amendment that deals with religion is, of course, the Free Exercise Clause. After admonishing Congress not to establish a religion, the Constitution forbids it to prohibit "the free exercise thereof." A common thread that runs through the free exercise cases is this fundamental question: Should an individual or group be exempt from some general law or obligation for religious reasons? The Supreme Court confronted this very question in *Reynolds v. United States*, better known as the Mormon Polygamy Case.[81] Reynolds argued that because polygamy was a tenet of the Mormon religion, he and other Mormons should be exempt from laws that make multiple marriages a crime. The Supreme Court refused to grant the exemption and drew a distinction between holding a religious belief and acting on that religious belief. Mormons were free to believe in polygamy but the state may punish actions that violate the norms of society. "Suppose," Chief Justice Morrison Waite asked, "one believed that human sacrifices were a necessary part of religious worship, would it be seriously contended that the civil government [could] not interfere to prevent a sacrifice?"[82]

In addition to the polygamy issue, religious groups have sought exemptions from general laws in a variety of other cases. Jehovah's Witnesses have challenged laws that require reciting the Pledge of Allegiance in public schools,[83] and that require licenses for religious door-to-door solicitation.[84] In *Wisconsin v. Yoder*, Amish parents successfully challenged compulsory school attendance beyond the eighth grade for their children.[85] Finally, in *Employment Division, Department of Human Resources of Oregon v. Smith*, the Supreme

Court ruled against two Native Americans who claimed that their use of peyote was for religious purposes.[86] As in other areas of civil liberties, the Supreme Court fluctuates on its willingness to protect free exercise claims.

Freedom of speech is the second great area of civil liberties protected by the First Amendment. Although freedom of speech can be defended on the need to protect the dignity of all persons, it is absolutely essential for a democratic society. Justice Oliver Wendell Holmes, Jr., said that free speech in a democratic society was essential to the "marketplace of ideas."[87] Freedom of speech, like other liberties, requires the Supreme Court to balance the rights of the speaker against the rights of society. For our purposes, we will examine the following areas: pure speech, symbolic speech, and speech plus action.

Pure speech is the use of language alone to communicate one's ideas. Pure speech becomes a problem when the speaker urges his or her audience to do something that is illegal. In one sense, the person responding to the speech is responsible for his or her response. For example, if a person is urged to participate in a lynching, each member of the mob is guilty of the crime. On the other hand, the person who exhorts others to illegal actions is equally guilty in the eyes of many people. In an early free speech case, the Supreme Court formulated the "clear and present danger test" to help determine when government may punish speech.[88] The clear and present danger test held that if a person's speech presented a clear and present danger of bringing about an evil which the government had a right to prevent, then the speaker could be punished. Another area in which pure speech has raised problems is in the category of "fighting words" or "words likely to cause an average addressee to fight."[89] Fighting words would include but are not limited to obscene words that would provoke the average person to engage in a confrontation. In general, the Supreme Court is willing to permit government to impose these and other reasonable "time, place, and manner" restrictions on even pure speech.

A second and even more controversial area of free speech is symbolic speech. Symbolic speech involves the nonverbal conveyance of an idea or opinion, such as burning an American flag. Although not the first case to raise the issue of symbolic speech, *Tinker v. Des Moines Independent School District*[90] is one of the best known. High school students opposed to the war in Vietnam wore black armbands to protest that war in violation of a school policy. The Supreme Court upheld the students' right to engage in nondisruptive protest under the First Amendment. Burning of the American flag has aroused debate over the concept of symbolic speech. The Supreme Court ruled in *Texas v. Johnson*[91] that states could not punish flag burning. The Court reaffirmed its commitment to this form of freedom of expression by declaring the Flag Protection Act of 1989 (passed in response to *Johnson*) unconstitutional in *United States v. Eichman*.[92]

The final type of free speech constitutional issue is speech plus action, which combines pure speech and symbolic speech. If a person makes a speech while burning a draft card, is the speech protected even if the draft card burning is not? In other words, is it possible to separate forbidden act (draft card burning) from the protected speech? In *Street* v. *New York,* the Supreme Court overturned Street's conviction for flag burning on the grounds that it was impossible for the jury to separate the action from his accompanying speech.[93] However, the year before *Street* in *United States* v. *O'Brien,* the Supreme Court held that O'Brien could be punished for burning his draft card to protest the war in Vietnam even though a speech in opposition to the war was protected.[94] In any event it is difficult for some people to understand why burning a draft card may be punished but burning a flag may not be.

Freedom of press is the last great area of civil liberties to be discussed in this section. Freedom of press is less important to us as individuals than freedom of religion or speech, which are personal liberties. Freedom of press involves the rights of someone else, that is, the press. In a sense, however, freedom of press is about a citizen's right to receive information. Just as a speaker has a right to air his or her views, an individual has a right to hear the views of others. This makes a free press vital to a democratic society.

Problems with freedom of press fall into three general categories: prior restraint, libel, and obscenity. Under a system of *prior restraint,* the government requires the press to submit to a preclearance procedure whereby officials can check a publication for problems and eliminate them before the publication can reach its audience. For example, articles for high school newspapers frequently are submitted to the paper's faculty sponsor for such preclearance and the Supreme Court approved the practice in *Hazelwood School District* v. *Kuhlmeier.*[95] Issues involving questions of national security is another area where prior restraint is sometimes justified. Libel is the punishment of an author or publisher after something has been printed and distributed. Libel is a form of defamation in which the person libeled seeks damages from the author or publisher for inflicting the alleged harm, usually to a person's reputation. While private persons may avail themselves of the protection from libel, the Supreme Court has held that a higher standard of malice exists for public officials and those who deliberately seek to become public figures, such as movie stars.[96] Finally, in *Roth* v. *United States,*[97] the Supreme Court ruled that "implicit in the history of the First Amendment is the rejection of obscenity as utterly without redeeming social importance."[98] As a result, it became necessary for the Court to fashion some sort of test to determine which materials were obscene and unprotected and which were protected. Not only the printed word, but also motion pictures,[99] radio broadcasts,[100] and even nude dancing[101] have sought the protection of the First Amendment. To the consternation of the justices, finding an acceptable definition of obscenity and the scope of freedom of expression have proven elusive.

Civil liberties are important because they reinforce the rule of law in society. There are some activities that are so vital to democratic society that even the government must respect them. Civil liberties are also important because they provide the freedom necessary for individuals to express themselves without government interference. Democracy strives to ensure that each person can reach his or her full potential. Civil liberties are the guarantees the Constitution provides to meet this ideal.

CONCLUSION

This chapter has tried to introduce the field of constitutional law within the limits of an introductory text. We have examined judicial review, introduced several approaches to constitutional interpretation, and analyzed five major constitutional doctrines. Yet we have only covered the tip of the iceberg. Constitutional law is a vast and fascinating area of law because it deals with ideals, hopes, and rights for which some people are willing to die. In a real sense, our Constitution says a lot about who we are as a people and a nation. The Constitution is the foundation of American law, for in the final analysis, all our law must conform to its principles.

NOTES

1. *Marbury* v. *Madison,* 1 Cranch 137 (1803).
2. Arthur A. North, *The Supreme Court: Judicial Process and Judicial Politics* (New York: Appleton-Century-Crofts, 1966), p. 3.
3. *United States* v. *Butler,* 297 U.S. 1 (1936), at 62.
4. Craig R. Ducat, *Modes of Constitutional Interpretation* (St. Paul, Minn.: West Publishing Company, 1978), p. 1.
5. The date of the president's inauguration was not changed to the twentieth of January until the passage of the Twentieth Amendment in 1933.
6. This is why those appointed came to be known as the "Midnight Judges."
7. Alfred H. Kelly, Winfred A. Harbison, and Herman Belz, *The American Constitution: Its Origins and Development,* 6th ed. (New York: W. W. Norton & Co., Inc., 1983), p. 180.
8. In 1857, the Supreme Court invalidated the Missouri Compromise in the *Dred Scott Case.*
9. See, for example, Henry J. Abraham, *The Judicial Process,* 3rd ed. (New York: Oxford University Press, 1975), pp. 354–376.
10. See, for example, Sheldon Goldman and Thomas P. Jahnige, *The Federal Courts as a Political System,* 3rd ed. (New York: Harper & Row, Pub., 1985), pp. 224–229.
11. See Howard Ball, *Courts and Politics: The Federal Judicial System* (Englewood Cliffs, N.J.: Prentice-Hall, 1980), Chapter 4.
12. Chapter 1, p. 13.
13. *Powell* v. *Alabama,* 287 U.S. 45 (1932).
14. *Betts* v. *Brady,* 316 U.S. 455 (1942).

15. *Gideon* v. *Wainwright*, 372 U.S. 335 (1963).

16. *Argersinger* v. *Hamlin*, 407 U.S. 25 (1972).

17. *Escobedo* v. *Illinois*, 378 U.S. 478 (1964).

18. *Miranda* v. *Arizona*, 384 U.S. 436 (1966).

19. *Gideon* v. *Wainwright*, 372 U.S. 335 (1963), at 344.

20. Judith A. Baer, "The Fruitless Search for Original Intent," in *Judging the Constitution: Critical Essays on Judicial Lawmaking,* ed. by Michael W. McCann and Gerald L. Houseman (Boston: Scott, Foresman and Company, 1989), p. 63.

21. *Texas* v. *Johnson*, 57 U.S.L.W. 4770 (1989).

22. Paul Brest, "The Misconceived Quest for the Original Understanding," in *Modern Constitutional Theory: A Reader,* ed. by John H. Garvey and T. Alexander Aleinikoff (St. Paul, Minn.: West Publishing Co., 1989), p. 60.

23. Ibid.

24. Brest, pp. 60–61.

25. Baer, p. 53.

26. *Chisholm* v. *Georgia*, 2 Dallas 419 (1793).

27. Baer, p. 59.

28. Baer, p. 62; Lief H. Carter, *Contemporary Constitutional Lawmaking: The Supreme Court and the Art of Politics* (New York: Pergamon Press, 1985), p. 42.

29. Thomas C. Grey, "Do We Have an Unwritten Constitution?" in *Modern Constitutional Reader,* ed. by John H. Garvey and T. Alexander Aleinikoff (St. Paul, Minn.: West Publishing Co., 1989), p. 29.

30. Ibid.

31. *Texas* v. *Johnson*, 57 U.S.L.W. 4770 (Kennedy, J., concurring), at 4776.

32. *Tinker* v. *Des Moines Independent Community School District*, 393 U.S. 503 (1969) (Black, J., dissenting).

33. Grey, p. 28.

34. *McCulloch* v. *Maryland*, 4 Wheaton 316 (1819).

35. *Griswold* v. *Connecticut*, 351 U.S. 479 (1965).

36. *Roe* v. *Wade*, 410 U.S. 113 (1973).

37. James MacGregor Burns, J. W. Peltason, and Thomas Cronin, *Government by the People,* 14th ed. (Englewood Cliffs, NJ.: Prentice Hall, 1990), p. 819.

38. *Hammer* v. *Dagenhart*, 247 U.S. 251 (1918).

39. *United States* v. *E.C. Knight Co.*, 156 U.S. 1 (1895).

40. *Schechter Poultry Corp.* v. *United States*, 295 U.S. 495 (1935).

41. *United States* v. *Darby Lumber Co.*, 312 U.S. 100 (1941).

42. *National Labor Relations Board* v. *Jones & Laughlin Corp.,* 301 U.S. 1 (1937).

43. *Wickard* v. *Filburn*, 317 U.S. 111 (1942).

44. *Heart of Atlanta Motel* v. *United States*, 379 U.S. 241 (1964).

45. *Maryland* v. *Wirtz*, 392 U.S. 183 (1968).

46. *National League of Cities* v. *Usery*, 426 U.S. 833 (1976).

47. *Garcia* v. *San Antonio Transit Authority*, 469 U.S. 528 (1985).

48. James Madison, "Federalist No. 51," in *The Federalist Papers,* ed. by Clinton Rossiter (New York: New American Library, 1961), pp. 321–322.

49. U.S. Constitution, Art. II, § 2, para. 2.

50. U.S. Constitution, Art. II, § 4.

51. *Myers* v. *United States,* 372 U.S. 52 (1926).

52. *Humphrey's Executor* v. *United States,* 295 U.S. 602 (1935).

53. *Buckley* v. *Valeo,* 424 U.S. 1 (1976).

54. Herman Pritchett, *The American Constitution,* 3rd ed. (New York: McGraw-Hill Book Co., 1977), p. 234.

55. *Bowsher* v. *Synar,* 478 U.S. 714 (1986).

56. *Immigration and Naturalization Service* v. *Chadha,* 462 U.S. 919 (1983).

57. Raoul Berger, *Executive Privilege: A Constitutional Myth* (New York: Bantam Books, 1974), p. 1.

58. Arthur M. Schlesinger, Jr., *The Imperial Presidency* (New York: Popular Library, 1973), p. 28.

59. *United States* v. *Nixon,* 418 U.S. 683 (1974).

60. *Barron* v. *City of Baltimore,* 7 Peters 243 (1833).

61. See generally, *Rochin* v. *California,* 342 U.S. 165 (1952) for an excellent discussion of the meaning of due process.

62. *Lochner* v. *New York,* 198 U.S. 45 (1905).

63. *Adkins* v. *Children's Hospital,* 261 U.S. 525 (1923).

64. *Miranda* v. *Arizona,* 384 U.S. 436 (1966).

65. *Duncan* v. *Louisiana,* 391 U.S. 145 (1968) (Fortas, J., concurring).

66. See *Johnson* v. *Louisiana,* 406 U.S. 356 (1972) and *Apodaca* v. *Oregon,* 406 U.S. 404 (1972).

67. *Sherbert* v. *Verner,* 374 U.S. 398 (1963).

68. *Bernal* v. *Fainter,* 467 U.S. 216 (1984).

69. *In re Griffiths,* 413 U.S. 717 (1973).

70. *Ambach* v. *Norwick,* 441 U.S. 68 (1979).

71. Norman Redlich, Bernard Schwartz, and John Attanasio, *Constitutional Law,* 2nd ed. (New York: Matthew Bender & Co., 1989), pp. 844–852.

72. Ibid., p. 852.

73. Ibid.

74. John Brigham, *Civil Liberties and American Democracy* (Washington, D.C.: Congressional Quarterly Press, 1984), p. 6.

75. See *Everson* v. *Board of Education,* 330 U.S. 1 (1947); *Board of Education* v. *Allen,* 392 U.S. 236 (1968); and *Lemon* v. *Kurzman,* 403 U.S. 602 (1971).

76. *Engel* v. *Vitale,* 370 U.S. 421 (1962).

77. *Stone* v. *Graham,* 449 U.S. 39 (1980).

78. *Wallace* v. *Jaffree,* 472 U.S. 38 (1985).

79. *Lee* v. *Weisman,* 112 S.Ct. 2649 (1992).

80. *Rosenberger et. al.* v. *Rector and Visitors of University of Virginia et. al.,* 63 U.S.L.W. 4702 (1995).

81. *Reynolds* v. *United States,* 98 U.S. 145 (1879).

82. Quoted in Gerald Gunther, *Constitutional Law: Cases and Materials,* 10th ed. (Mineola, N.Y.: Foundation Press, 1980), p. 1582.

83. *Minersville School District* v. *Gobitis,* 310 U.S. 585 (1940) and *West Virginia State Board of Education* v. *Barnette,* 319 U.S. 624 (1943).

84. *Murdock* v. *Pennsylvania,* 319 U.S. 105 (1943) and *Martin* v. *City of Struthers,* 319 U.S. 141 (1943).

85. *Wisconsin* v. *Yoder*, 406 U.S. 208 (1972).

86. *Employment Division, Department of Human Resources of Oregon* v. *Smith*, 494 U.S. 872 (1990).

87. *Abrams* v. *United States*, 250 U.S. 616 (1919) (Holmes, J., dissenting).

88. *Schenck* v. *United States*, 249 U.S. 47 (1919).

89. *Chaplinsky* v. *New Hampshire*, 315 U.S. 568 (1942) at 573.

90. *Tinker* v. *Des Moines Independent School District*, 393 U.S. 503 (1969).

91. *Texas* v. *Johnson*, 491 U.S. 397 (1989).

92. *United States* v. *Eichman*, 496 U.S. 310 (1990).

93. *Street* v. *New York*, 394 U.S. 576 (1969).

94. *United States* v. *O'Brien*, 391 U.S. 367 (1968).

95. *Hazelwood School District* v. *Kuhlmeier*, 484 U.S. 260 (1988).

96. See *New York Times Company* v. *Sullivan*, 376 U.S. 254 (1964) and *Time Inc.* v. *Firestone*, 424 U.S. 448 (1976).

97. *Roth* v. *United States*, 354 U.S. 476 (1957).

98. Ibid., p. 484.

99. *Kingsley International Corporation* v. *Regents of University of New York*, 360 U.S. 684 (1959).

100. *Federal Communications Commission* v. *Pacifica Foundation*, 438 U.S. 726 (1978).

101. *Barnes* v. *Glen Theatre, Inc.*, 501 U.S. 560 (1991).

Criminal Law

7

Of all the subfields of American law, criminal law is perhaps the most controversial. As we noted in Chapter 1, criminal law deals with activities that have been formally forbidden in a society by its government.[1] The controversy surrounding criminal law centers around both the substance or content of criminal law and the procedures by which we deprive accused persons of their life, liberty, and property. Substantive criminal law asks questions such as what should be made a crime, what is the appropriate punishment for committing a particular crime, and what specific behavior constitutes a crime. The first question focuses on the kinds of activities that may or should be forbidden by government. Certain actions, like murder, are inherently evil and universally condemned as criminal behavior. Other activities, such as gambling, are questionable as "criminal" since there is not universal consensus on their immorality, as there is with crimes like murder and rape.

Even if there is general agreement within a society that a certain activity should be banned, there is often disagreement over how severe the punishment should be. For example, some states impose long sentences on persons convicted of possessing marijuana. Many people, while still believing that marijuana use should be forbidden, believe that the penalty is excessive for the crime. Making the punishment fit the crime, then, is an important concern of criminal law.

As controversial as substantive criminal law is, it pales in comparison with the controversy generated by procedural law. Procedural criminal law is closely associated with the concept of due process of law. Due process of law refers to the process or procedures that must be followed before a person can legally be deprived of "life, liberty, or property." In criminal law, procedural due process sets forth the procedures that government must observe before it can execute, imprison, or fine an individual. Although not really a game, procedural due process can be thought of as the "rules of the game" that the State must adhere to before it imposes punishment. Some people argue that government has "gone too far" in protecting the rights of those accused of crimes, while totally ignoring the rights of their victims. Critics of procedural due process argue that most persons accused of crimes are indeed guilty and that they should not be allowed to escape punishment because of a "technicality" in the law. Justice, after all, requires that persons committing crimes be punished.

Defenders of procedural due process offer a number of rationales for supporting the rights of persons accused of crimes. First, our system of justice is based upon the assumption that a person is innocent until proven guilty; thus the State bears the burden of proof in a criminal case. Under our legal system, the accused is not required to assist the State in securing his own conviction. Consequently, safeguards, such as protection against self-incrimination, ensure that the State has evidence other than the accused's own testimony to secure a conviction.

A second reason for procedural safeguards is the possibility of unjustly convicting an innocent person. No system of justice is infallible, so we believe that we should take whatever precautions are needed to ensure that, ideally, the innocent person is always freed and the guilty person is always convicted. Overall, most defenders of procedural due process would argue that it is better for ten guilty persons to go free than for one innocent person to be imprisoned.

A final rationale for protecting the rights of the accused is political. Since time immemorial, governments have used their criminal justice systems as a means of repressing certain groups in society. Governments have used the criminal justice system against religious, racial, and political dissidents throughout history. The argument, then, is that if government can use the law against one unpopular group today, it may very well use it against a group to which I belong tomorrow. Therefore, citizens must remain vigilant to ensure that punishment for criminal activity is never used as a pretext for persecuting an individual or a group for its religious or political beliefs. Only by guaranteeing that government obeys "the rules of the game" can we be certain that religious or political persecution does not occur under the pretext of law and order.

This chapter will focus on both the substance and procedures of criminal law. First, it will discuss the characteristics of criminal law and the elements of a crime. Second, it will examine the parties to a crime. Third, it will examine three areas of criminal procedures to highlight our previous discussion of this controversial topic. Next, we briefly focus on the juvenile justice system. Finally, we will look at two case studies, one substantive and one procedural, to illustrate the complexities of criminal law.

CHARACTERISTICS OF CRIMINAL LAW

What is the nature of criminal law? In Chapter 1, we noted that one of the functions of law is to proscribe certain activities. In so doing, a society is defining exactly what is and what is not acceptable behavior. In a democratic society, it is the function of legislative bodies, as the elected representatives of the people, to decide what behavior will be made criminal and what penalties will be attached to violations of the law. In this section, we will attempt to define the nature of criminal behavior more precisely, with an emphasis on how criminal law reflects the society that creates it.

In Chapter 1 we introduced two terms: *malum in se* and *malum prohibitum. Malum in se* means "wrong in itself" and is applied to behavior that could be considered inherently wrong or evil. Murder and rape are two examples of acts that are criminal because they are inherently wrong in themselves. Murder (as opposed to killing in self-defense, for example) is inherently wrong because there can be no legitimate justification for it. Rape is another example: What possible justification could exist for a man to force himself sexually on a woman? Crimes that are considered *malum in se* have two primary characteristics: They tend to have highly moral overtones, and there is nearly universal consensus that the type of behavior involved cannot be tolerated in a civilized society. The latter characteristic does not mean that every person agrees that rape should be a crime; obviously, the rapist may not think so. It means that acts of murder and rape have been universally condemned by most civilized societies throughout history. In a sense, then, crimes that are *malum in se* are the easiest to define because they are universally condemned.

A much more complex problem surrounds the second category of crimes—those defined as *malum prohibitum.* Some behavior has been labeled "criminal" not so much because it is inherently wrong or universally condemned, but merely because a legislative body has deemed it undesirable. As we noted in Chapter 1, parking in a "No Parking" zone is not the kind of behavior that arouses moral condemnation or social ostracization, but it is a crime, albeit a minor one. It is a crime because a city council has chosen to make it one. Crimes defined as *malum prohibitum* may have rational justifications, such as public safety or traffic control, but they are hardly inherently evil. What, then, makes the classification of *malum prohibitum* so complex? It is the fact that society is sometimes in disagreement over whether an activity is criminal because it is immoral or because it is just undesirable. In this chapter's introduction, we used gambling to illustrate this problem. Why is gambling a crime? Is it because it is a morally reprehensible activity? If so, then why do millions of presumably moral people bet on the Super Bowl? Is it because the compulsive gambler may gamble away his family's grocery money? Is it because gambling is an activity that brings "the wrong element" into a community? Any or all of these could be reasons that a legislature might choose to prohibit gambling. However, the success of places like Las Vegas and Atlantic City indicates that some people see no harm in it.

In addition to gambling, activities such as prostitution, illegal use (as opposed to the illegal sale) of drugs, and even homosexuality have been declared criminal partly because they are considered immoral and partly because they are offensive to the majority. The prohibition of these activities is sometimes justified on the grounds that while morally debatable, they lead to other serious crimes or create other problems. Prostitution, for example, can spread AIDS and venereal disease, exploit women, lead to drug addiction, and result in violence against women. Drug addiction may lead its victims to commit crimes, such as burglary, to feed their habit. Finally, prohibiting so-called victimless crimes is justified on the grounds that the State has the right to safeguard the quality of life in a community. Prostitution, gambling, and drug addiction rely on baser human needs. The State should uplift the human spirit by prohibiting activities that debase it and society. In the final analysis, then, activities labeled *malum prohibitum* may be considered immoral or just a nuisance, but either way, in a democratic society, legislatures may make them criminal.

One final aspect of the *malum prohibitum* category is worth mentioning. Given the debatable nature of the morality of such activities as gambling, what is the appropriate penalty? At one time some states allowed sentences of ten or more years for mere possession of marijuana, regardless of the amount. Many people believed that such penalties were excessive given the nature of the crime. Still others argue that only a "get-tough" policy will eradicate the undesirable activity. Today, many of the crimes we have been discussing are classified as misdemeanors. Prostitution, possession of small amounts of marijuana, and so forth receive small fines and light sentences. Laws dealing with the purveyors of crime are harsher. Selling marijuana will result in a stiffer sentence than mere possession, and acting as a pimp is generally considered more serious than prostitution itself. In attempting to get at the source of the crime, the law has made the drug dealer, the pimp, and the bookmaker more criminally liable and therefore more susceptible to harsher penalties. Whether such tactics are effective in the "war on crime" is another matter.

As may already be apparent from the foregoing discussion of *malum in se* and *malum prohibitum*, criminal law is a reflection of the society that produces it. In an Islamic theocracy, such as Iran, criminal law will reflect the religious teachings of the Koran; in a Catholic country, it will reflect the tenets of Catholicism. In addition, the law will change to reflect changes in society, especially attitude changes. As noted, use of marijuana was once considered a serious crime with harsh penalties, whereas today the penalties in most states are relatively light. As public tolerance of marijuana use grew, the severity of the penalties was reduced. As a society advances, its judgments about crime and punishment change. Thomas Gardner has written:

> The criminal punishments used 200 years ago in England and Europe were severe. In England alone, more than 200 offenses were punishable by death. Condemned criminals were usually hanged, although occasionally they were beheaded, quartered, or drawn (dragged along the ground at the tail of a horse).[2]

Obviously, both the number of capital offenses and the penalties have been changed in modern England. The point is that attitudes about what should be made a crime and what penalty should be assessed vary from one society to another and from one historical era to another. In 1903, the first Justice John Marshall Harlan, quoting an earlier case, wrote of lotteries:

> ". . . [they] infest[s] the whole community; it enters every dwelling; it reaches every class; it preys upon the hard earnings of the poor; it plunders the ignorant and the simple."[3]

Today many states are turning to lotteries as a means of relieving their financial problems. Law does and should change with the needs and attitudes of the society it serves.

ELEMENTS OF A CRIME

In this section we will examine a very important aspect of substantive criminal law: the elements of a crime. Specifically, we will focus upon the type of behavior that an individual must engage in to be guilty of a crime. Obviously, different crimes require different behavior, but there are common elements necessary for proving all crimes, and identifying these common elements will be our primary concern.

The first element of a crime is the **actus reus**. *Black's Law Dictionary* defines *actus* as "an act or action"[4] and *reus* as "a person judicially accused of a crime."[5] Therefore, *actus reus* is literally the action of a person accused of a crime. David W. Neubauer has defined *actus reus* simply as "the guilty act."[6] All this means is that a criminal statute must clearly define exactly what act is deemed "guilty"—that is, the exact behavior that is being prohibited. This is done so that all persons are put on notice that if they perform the guilty act, they will be liable for criminal punishment. Courts will occasionally nullify a law that is "void for vagueness." Justice William Brennan, quoting an earlier case, defined an unconstitutionally vague law as "a statute which forbids or requires the doing of an act in terms so vague that men of common intelligence must necessarily guess at its meaning and differ as to its application."[7] Unless the *actus reus* is clearly defined, one might not know whether or not one's behavior is illegal.

In addition to adequate notice of the proscribed behavior, another characteristic of *actus reus* needs clarification. The guilty act might not just be what one does; it might also be what one fails to do. Criminal laws not only prohibit certain behavior; in some cases they require action. That is, a person can be held criminally liable for failure to act. Thomas J. Gardner has listed examples of when failure to act is a crime, including failure to come to the aid of a police officer when requested to do so and failure to submit to a breathalyzer test when requested to do so.[8] Gardner cites two famous examples of when failure to act might have constituted a crime. In 1964, a young woman was brutally murdered on a New York street in an attack that lasted 35 minutes. Despite her repeated cries for help, no one called the police. In 1983, a woman was gang raped in a Boston bar while onlookers watched and cheered. No one came to her aid or called the police.[9] These are but two examples of when the failure to act is, or should be, a crime. Such crimes are crimes of omission as opposed to crimes of commission, but both may be considered morally reprehensible under the circumstances.

Finally, *actus reus* should be understood to mean that in order to be guilty of a crime, a person must do or not do something rather than just *be* something. The State may choose to make homosexual acts illegal, but it may not make being a homosexual a crime. Homosexuals have not committed a crime unless or until they engage in the specific behavior the State has forbidden. As common sensical as that might seem, some states have passed laws making one's status a crime. In *Robinson* v. *California*,[10] the Supreme Court struck down a California law that made status of narcotics addiction a crime. Under the law there was no need to provide evidence that Robinson had actually used narcotics in California—only that at some time he had been addicted to narcotics. In contrast, in *Powell* v. *Texas*,[11] the Court ruled that a chronic alcoholic could be punished even though the alcoholism was a disease. Powell had been convicted for being drunk in public, not for being an alcoholic.

Mens rea.   A second element of a crime is **mens rea**. Black defines *mens rea* as "a guilty mind; a guilty or wrongful purpose; a criminal intent."[12] *Mens rea*, then, refers to an individual's state of mind when a crime is committed. Criminal statutes employ terms such as *knowingly, willfully, intentionally,* and *purposely* to describe the state of mind one must have in order to possess "a guilty mind." While the *actus reus* is proven by physical or eyewitness evidence, *mens rea* is more difficult to ascertain. The jury must determine for itself whether the accused had the necessary intent to commit the act, and that raises a number of difficult problems.

Mens rea requires the accused to have the requisite intent to commit an illegal act. Some crimes require proof of *specific intent*. As indicated, specific-intent acts must be carried out "knowingly" and "willfully." Under coercion, an individual might "knowingly" commit an illegal act without doing so "willfully." Patty Hearst, for example, claimed that she was coerced into robbing banks by her kidnappers, but the jury refused to believe her.

Another type of intent is *general intent*. General intent "is sufficient for crimes for which a voluntary performance of the prohibited act constitutes an offense, regardless of whether the person intended to violate the law."[13] In other words, the prosecutor does not have to prove that a motorist "willfully" ran a red light, only that the act itself was voluntarily performed and witnessed by a police officer. Otherwise, every motorist would argue that he ran the light inadvertently, thus not having the necessary "guilty mind."

Finally, *mens rea* includes an element called *scienter*, which refers to the degree of knowledge one must have to be guilty of a particular crime. One aspect of scienter is simply the knowledge that a certain activity is illegal. People of common intelligence know that murder, burglary, and arson are illegal. But certain crimes require additional knowledge on the part of the accused. In Texas, for example, the murder of a police officer is a capital offense, but the prosecutor must prove that the defendant knew that his victim was a police officer. For example, a drug dealer might claim he did not know his murder victim was an undercover narcotics officer. The crime of receiving stolen property requires that the buyer know the property has been stolen.[14] These crimes require additional proof beyond the fact that the accused knew his actions were illegal.

The requirement of *mens rea* is one reason that insanity is a legal defense for some persons accused of crimes. In an insanity defense, the accused typically does not deny that he performed the *actus reus*, but merely asserts that because of his insanity he was incapable of distinguishing right from wrong. Under U.S. law, persons cannot be punished for a crime unless they are able to distinguish right from wrong. A similar rationale applies to children below a certain age: The law assumes that children are incapable of understanding that their acts are wrong and therefore they cannot be punished. Even if someone is found not guilty by reason of insanity, the law may require that he or she be institutionalized until such time as psychiatrists deem them mentally competent. John W. Hinckley's assassination attempt on the life of President Ronald Reagan in March 1981, and the verdict in that case, has reopened the debate on the insanity plea in our legal system, illustrating once again that controversial legal issues are seldom, if ever, settled for good.

Causation. The next element of a crime is *causation*. To *cause* an event is to bring it about or to make it happen. Often the phrase "but for" is used to determine whether causation has occurred. For example, we might say "Cain killed Abel," by which we really mean "Cain caused Abel's death." In other words, "But for Cain's act, Abel would still be alive." Causation, then, means that "but for" the actions of A, B would not have been harmed. In criminal law, causation is an element that must be proven beyond a reasonable doubt.

One type of causation is *direct causation,* which means that nothing intervenes between cause and effect. In a modern version of the Biblical story, let's say Cain shoots Abel, causing Abel's immediate death. Cain is clearly the direct cause of Abel's death. But suppose Cain shoots Abel, inflicting what is normally a nonfatal wound. Then Abel is dropped by the ambulance attendants as he is being loaded into the ambulance, receives an infection from an unsterile blood-transfusion needle, and ultimately dies. Did Cain kill Abel? May Cain be charged with murder? Certainly Cain caused the bullet wound that necessitated the ambulance call and the blood transfusion that ultimately resulted in Abel's death, but did Cain "cause" Abel's death, or did other factors cause it? What, if any, is the extent of Cain's criminal liability in the death of Abel?

The foregoing example illustrates what is known as *proximate cause.* We see a chain of events that leads to Abel's death, but can Cain be held legally responsible? Cain is undoubtedly guilty of *something,* but is it the crime of murder? One might argue that but for the gunshot wound, Abel would not have been taken to the hospital, where he received the fatal blood transfusion. But can Cain be held responsible for the unsterile needle? Obviously, an intervening variable (the needle) has entered the equation contributing to Abel's death. In order to prove murder or even manslaughter, the prosecution must prove that Cain's actions were the proximate cause of Abel's death; otherwise, a lesser offense, such as assault with a deadly weapon, must be charged. The determination of causation under circumstances much more complex than those we have described is one of the most difficult tasks in criminal law.

Standard of proof. Under the U.S. system of law, the person who brings the cause of action before the court bears the burden of proof. That is, the plaintiff is responsible for proving the truthfulness of his allegations. Under the rules of civil law, the plaintiff must usually meet only the *preponderance-of-evidence* standard in order to win. Under that standard, the weight of evidence, however slight, must favor the plaintiff's version of the dispute. If the plaintiff fails to meet this standard of proof, the defendant will prevail. In criminal law, a different standard of proof, called *beyond a reasonable doubt,* is required. This standard places a greater burden on the State, which is the plaintiff, in a criminal case. "Beyond a reasonable doubt" essentially means that all possible alternative explanations for what happened have been considered and rejected except one—the one that concludes that the accused committed the crime for which he is charged. Note that the standard means not beyond all doubt, but only beyond "reasonable" doubt. Courts employ the "reasonable person" standard, which holds that if 12 reasonable persons, after hearing the relevant evidence, conclude beyond a reasonable doubt that the accused committed the crime, the burden of proof has been met.

The law requires a higher standard of proof in criminal cases than in civil cases for a number of reasons. One is that the stakes are much higher in a criminal case. A person convicted of a crime may be stripped of his liberty or even his life. The taking of a person's life or liberty is so serious that it may be done only if there is a high degree of certainty that the person committed the crime. Imagine the case of a person wrongfully convicted of a crime who serves five years in prison before the error is discovered. Now consider the mental anguish of such a person, who alone knows that he is innocent. How can such a person or his family ever be compensated for those five years of mental anguish? How can the State give back five years of a person's life? The beyond-a-reasonable-doubt standard seeks to minimize the chances of the innocent person's conviction, but even then we know that some innocent people are still convicted.

A second reason for the greater standard of proof in criminal cases is the relative strength of the two parties involved. The criminal defendant is usually David to the State's Goliath. The State has tremendous human and financial resources at its disposal to try to prove the defendant's guilt. Even with the requirement of court-appointed counsel, the poor person is at a distinct disadvantage. Since most defendants are poor, the higher standard of proof evens the odds somewhat.

A third reason for the higher standard is one mentioned earlier in this chapter. Since the criminal justice system is capable of becoming a means of repressing persons who hold unpopular political views, the higher standard of proof guarantees that the State will not use its awesome power to "railroad" an innocent person simply because she holds unpopular views. Although it is impossible to absolutely guarantee that the criminal justice system will not be used as a tool of repression, the higher standard of proof reduces the risk that it will be.

The beyond-a-reasonable-doubt standard places a heavy burden on the State in a criminal case. It is important to remember that the accused does not have to prove anything. The defendant does not have to take the stand in his own defense, call any witnesses to testify, or present any evidence in his own behalf. The defendant may do nothing, and if the State has failed to prove its case beyond a reasonable doubt, the defendant must be acquitted. That is why, in the technical sense, an accused is not found "innocent." Innocence implies that the defendant is blameless. The accused may be *factually* guilty of the crime, but unless the State proves its case, the accused is not *legally* guilty. Therefore, a verdict of not guilty may mean that the State was unable to prove its case to the satisfaction of the jury, not that the defendant was innocent or morally blameless.

Let us now summarize the elements of a crime. First, the prohibited behavior designated as a crime must be clearly defined so that a reasonable person can be forewarned that engaging in that behavior is illegal. Each criminal statute has certain elements that distinguish that crime, and the state must prove each element. Second, the accused must be shown to have possessed the requisite intent to commit the crime. Third, the State must prove causation. Finally, the State must prove beyond a reasonable doubt that the defendant committed the crime. Understanding these essential elements of a crime can provide added insight into the substantive and procedural nature of criminal law discussed later in the chapter.

PARTIES TO A CRIME

Culpability is another important characteristic of criminal law. *Culpability* is the degree of blame involved in the commission of a crime—that is, how much legal responsibility a person bears for the commission of a crime. At common law, two categories of persons—*principals* and *accessories*—were considered to be parties to a crime but received disparate sentences based on the level of their involvement. Today that distinction has been blurred, and by statute, most states hold persons involved in a crime to be equally liable despite the varying degrees of involvement.[15] For example, if the intended crime is robbery of a liquor store and the perpetrator kills the owner, the driver of the getaway car is equally guilty of felony murder even though the murder was never intended. If there is a "common design to commit an unlawful act to which all the defendants agreed, whatever is done in furtherance of the criminal plan is the act of all if it is a natural and probable consequence of the intended crime."[16] However, in death-penalty cases, the U.S. Supreme Court has set a higher standard that only those "with major participation in the felony committed combined with reckless indifference to human life" are subject to execution.[17] Criminal responsibility is not contingent upon one's physical presence at the scene, that is, a conspirator who assisted in the planning of the crime is guilty both of the conspiracy and the principal crime even though he or she was not actually present at the time of the event.

An *accessory after the fact* is "one who receives, relieves, comforts, or assists another knowing that he has committed a felony."[18] An accessory after the fact must know that another person has committed a felony and must have personally assisted the felon. The basis for condemning someone as an accessory after the fact is obstruction of justice.[19] Actions commonly attributed to an accessory after the fact include hiding a felon, lying to police officers about a felon's whereabouts, and helping a felon cover up his or her criminal activity.

Under the common law, it was the rule that an accessory could not be prosecuted until the principal had been convicted. Today most states follow the federal case of *Standefer* v. *United States*,[20] which permits conviction of any aider or abettor regardless of whether the perpetrator was acquitted or even prosecuted.[21] Accessories may be subjected to the same punishment as principals. Although an accessory is as legally culpable as the principal, the sentencing authority, whether judge or jury, frequently assesses lighter sentences upon accessories after the fact.

PROCEDURAL CRIMINAL LAW

In Chapter 4 we discussed criminal procedures primarily from what might be termed a "cookbook" approach; that is, we followed the steps of the criminal process from arrest to appeal, much as one might follow the steps of a recipe. Our purpose in Chapter 4 was to provide the reader with an overview of criminal procedures without getting bogged down in details. In this section we wish to discuss in greater detail some of the procedural safeguards guaranteed by the Constitution. We will look at three controversial areas of constitutional law: search and seizure, the right to counsel, and the protection against self-incrimination. Our purpose in focusing on these three topics is to provide the reader with an understanding of the history of these procedural safeguards, the philosophical basis of each, and the complexity of the issues involved with each. As noted in the introduction to this chapter, our concern about procedural due process is motivated by our desire to ensure that government "plays by the rules," by our anxiety about convicting the innocent, and by our fear that government may use the criminal justice system to prosecute unpopular individuals or groups. With these considerations in mind, we turn our attention to the first topic: search and seizure.

Search and seizure. "A man's home is his castle" is a common adage. Although this adage fails to inform us of the status of a *woman's* home, we will proceed on the premise that under the English common law, even the humblest home in the realm was to be a haven from the outside world. The lowest of the king's subjects was entitled to the sanctuary of his own home. It is with this understanding that the Fourth Amendment was included in our Bill of Rights. The Fourth Amendment reads as follows:

> The right of the people to be secure in their persons, houses, papers, and effects, against unreasonable searches and seizures, shall not be violated, and no warrants shall issue, but upon probable cause, supported by oath or affirmation, and particularly describing the place to be searched, and the persons or things to be seized.[22]

Several things should be noted from the text of the Fourth Amendment. First, the amendment prohibits only "unreasonable" searches and seizures, thus implying that reasonable ones are permitted. What is reasonable and what is not ultimately becomes a question for the courts to decide. Second, search warrants are to be issued only "upon probable cause," another rather vague notion. Recent decisions of the U.S. Supreme Court indicate a growing willingness to substitute reasonableness for the probable-cause standard of the Constitution. For example, the Court has upheld searches of a public school student's purse,[23] highway sobriety checkpoints,[24] mandatory drug testing of railroad employees following a train accident,[25] and random searches of passengers on interstate buses.[26] Each of these searches failed to meet the probable-cause standard but were permitted without a search warrant anyway because the Court deemed each reasonable under the Fourth Amendment. Third, the warrant, if issued, must describe the place to be searched and the things to be seized. All three of these stipulations are of sufficient ambiguity to cause problems for the Supreme Court in interpreting the Fourth Amendment.

One might wonder why the Framers of the Constitution, and especially those who wrote the Fourth Amendment, were so concerned about the rights of criminal defendants. Were they a bunch of "knee-jerk" liberals who were "soft on crime"? On the contrary, we sometimes forget that the Framers were revolutionaries who had firsthand experience with a tyrannical government. They knew what can happen when government begins to ignore the rights of its citizens, and they were certainly familiar with the general warrants of George III authorizing British troops to search the homes of suspected patriots for powder and shot that might be used by the rebels. In other words, the Framers were not glassy-eyed idealists who failed to foresee the consequences of their actions. Instead they were pragmatists who, in balancing the rights of individuals against the need for law and order, made an initial determination that, in a free society, the former was more important. But, as noted in Chapter 6, constitutional law is constantly changing to meet the needs of new generations of Americans. The values underlying the protection against unreasonable searches and seizures, although important to our Founding Fathers, might not be shared by Americans in the late twentieth century. Or are they? Perhaps we should ask ourselves that question as we study the Fourth Amendment.

Historically, the items subject to seizure by government in a criminal case fell into three categories: contraband, fruits of the crime, and instrumentalities of the crime. *Contraband* is something the government has forbidden to be in a person's possession, such as illegal drugs, explosives, or obscene materials. *Fruits of the crime* include stolen goods or money. *Instrumentalities* of the crime are tools or weapons used in the commission of a crime. Even a getaway car could be classified as an instrumentality subject to seizure. In 1969, in *Warden* v. *Hayden*,[27] the Supreme Court created a fourth category it labeled "mere evidence." In *Hayden*, a jacket and a pair of trousers identified as being similar to those worn by the robber of a taxi company were found in Hayden's home after a warrantless search. After first deciding that the search was reasonable, the Court turned to the issue of whether the jacket and trousers were subject to lawful seizure. Rather than continue the legal fiction that the clothes were subject to seizure as "instrumentalities" of the crime, the Court ruled that the clothes, as "mere evidence," were also subject to seizure. The Court ruled that the purpose of the Fourth Amendment is the protection of privacy, not property, and noted, "Privacy is disturbed no more by a search directed to a purely evidentiary object than it is by a search directed to an instrumentality, fruit, or contraband."[28]

Besides the question of what may be seized as evidence, another issue is how evidence is obtained by the police. Under the common law, courts did not concern themselves about the methods used to obtain evidence, but only with the reliability of that evidence. That is, if the evidence was "good," it mattered not how the police acquired it. That common-law rule was changed for federal courts in *Weeks* v. *United States*.[29] Weeks was accused of running an illegal lottery through the mails. Local police and, later, a federal marshal conducted an illegal search and seized letters and papers as evidence. Weeks made a motion for the return of his property, which the trial court denied. The Supreme Court, in overturning Weeks's conviction, ruled:

> . . . If letters and private documents can thus be seized and held and used in evidence against a citizen accused of an offense, the protection of the 4th Amendment, declaring his right to be secure against such searches and seizures, is of no value, and, so far as those thus placed are concerned, might as well be stricken from the Constitution.[30]

Thus was born the exclusionary rule. The exclusionary rule states that evidence obtained in violation of a person's constitutional rights must be excluded from the trial of the accused person. Since Weeks's papers were seized by an illegal search and seizure, they could not be used as evidence against him. The *Weeks* rule initially applied only to the exclusion of evidence in cases in federal courts, but in 1961 the Supreme Court made the rule applicable to the states in the case of *Mapp* v. *Ohio*.[31] Although the exclusionary rule developed in the context of search and seizure, it was later extended to include other violations of a defendant's constitutional rights.

There has probably never been a more controversial issue in criminal law than the exclusionary rule. Proponents of the rule argue that there are a number of important justifications for its existence. First, proponents argue that the exclusionary rule preserves the integrity of the judicial system by excluding evidence "tainted" by illegal police activities. Most would agree that a confession extracted through torture is an improper way to obtain evidence even if the person is factually guilty. The argument, then, is that in accepting the "reliable" but coerced confession, the courts are aiding and abetting improper police tactics. Justice Louis Brandeis has written:

> If the Government becomes a lawbreaker, it breeds contempt for law; it invites every man to become a law unto himself; it invites anarchy. To declare that in

the administration of the criminal law the end justifies the means—to declare that the Government may commit crimes in order to secure the conviction of a private criminal—would bring terrible retribution. Against that pernicious doctrine this Court should resolutely set its face.[32]

Courts, according to Brandeis, should not close their eyes to the methods used to obtain evidence, but should see that law enforcers also obey the law.

A second justification for the exclusionary rule is one mentioned by Justice Day, author of the *Weeks* opinion. If evidence seized in violation of the Fourth Amendment is admitted, then the amendment has no meaning. Why should a police officer obey the amendment's command to secure a search warrant when it is easier to obtain evidence without one? As long as the courts close their eyes to police methods, the police will continue to collect evidence without warrants.

A third justification is the deterrent effect of the exclusionary rule. The assumption is made that what police want most is to secure convictions. If evidence seized illegally is excluded, resulting in the accused getting off, the police will no longer have an incentive to engage in unconstitutional practices. That is, if an officer knows that the evidence he obtains from an illegal search will be excluded from the trial, he is less likely to conduct illegal searches. As a practical matter, the officer's work will be for nothing, and the criminal defendant will go free in some cases. Thus, the police will take greater pains to secure proper search warrants rather than risk letting a guilty person go free.

A fourth justification for the exclusionary rule is that it is the only viable solution to the problem of abuses of constitutional rights. Unless the police are to be "above the law," they too must obey the Constitution. According to proponents, the exclusion of illegally obtained evidence is the only realistic solution. Other solutions, such as making the offending officer liable in a civil suit for violating the constitutional rights of the accused, are simply impractical. Suppose, for example, an officer conducts an illegal search that produces reliable evidence which is then used to secure the defendant's conviction. The defendant may sue the officer for violating his constitutional rights, but what jury is going to rule in favor of a convicted criminal under such circumstances? Suggestions that officers be fined or suspended for violating the rights of accused persons also raise problems. Would the police be afraid to make an arrest or search a car for fear of being fined or suspended later? Proponents argue that the exclusionary rule is the only effective way to deal with violations of constitutional rights.

Finally, proponents of the exclusionary rule argue that it is more important to keep the police in check than to worry about guilty persons being set free. This argument is similar to the "integrity of the judicial system" argument discussed earlier. Police must be made to understand that they too must obey the Constitution, the supreme law of the land. Those in authority must understand that the ends (convictions) do not always justify the means (illegal searches). As Justice Tom Clark wrote in *Mapp*, "The criminal goes free, if he must, but it is the law that sets him free."[33] If we are truly to be a nation of laws, not men, then we must make sure that those who enforce the law also obey the law.

The opponents of the exclusionary rule advance a number of valid counterarguments. First, they reject the "integrity of the judicial system" argument by pointing out that the purpose of a trial is to arrive at the truth. If illegally seized evidence is reliable, then what difference does it make how it was obtained? Only in extreme cases of police overzealousness—cases that "shock the conscience"[34] of the community—should the exclusionary rule be employed.

A second objection is that if the purpose of the Fourth Amendment is to protect privacy, then the exclusionary rule is a totally inadequate solution. The person's privacy has already been violated, so how does excluding the otherwise reliable evidence further any Fourth Amendment values? The damage to privacy interests has been done, so what purpose is served by perhaps letting a factually guilty person go free? Even if the State could get a conviction without the illegally seized evidence, why take the chance?

A third objection questions the deterrent effect of the exclusionary rule. Suppose a police officer makes what he believes to be a legal search, and the search is later ruled invalid. How could the officer have been deterred in his conduct? He made a "good-faith" error in conducting the search in the first place, so how could he have been deterred in making a search he believed to be valid?

A fourth objection is that the exclusionary rule punishes the wrong people. It is society that is being punished by the enforcement of the exclusionary rule because it allows some factually guilty defendants to go free just because "the constable blunders." The offending officers are not punished (except that they lose their "bust"), and the criminal reaps a bonus by getting away with no punishment in some cases.

Finally, opponents of the rule argue that the exclusionary rule itself "breeds contempt for the law." This argument holds that when law-abiding citizens see criminals set free on "technicalities," they become contemptuous of the law. Instead of protecting law-abiding citizens, the law seems to protect the lawless. For these reasons and others, the exclusionary rule continues to be one of the most controversial issues of criminal law.

In the remainder of this section we will focus on the instances of reasonable and unreasonable searches. We begin by asking: When is a search reasonable? Obviously, a search made pursuant to a valid search warrant falls within this category. The police officer goes before a judge or magistrate with sufficient evidence to establish probable cause, and the latter will decide if a search warrant is justified. This allows a neutral third party to independently decide whether the warrant should be issued. A second type of reasonable search is one that is made pursuant to a lawful arrest. The Supreme Court has recognized that searches made pursuant to lawful arrests are valid because of the need for the officer to uncover any weapons the suspect might have that could harm others or aid in his escape. In *Chimel v. California*,[35] however, the Court also made it clear that the search could only extend to the area within the immediate reach of the suspect. In *Chimel*, the police, while serving an arrest warrant, searched Chimel's entire house despite his objections. The Court ruled that since Chimel was already in custody, a warrantless search of the house was not "pursuant" to the arrest and therefore was unreasonable. The police should have secured a warrant and returned later to conduct the search.

A third category of reasonable searches are those in which permission to make the search is granted. This can lead to a number of problem situations. For example, what constitutes an "intelligent waiver" of one's constitutional rights? A police officer's *request*, such as, "Do you mind if I look in your trunk?" becomes a *command* to most people. When the teacher says to Johnny, "Will you please go to the blackboard?" no one in the class believes Johnny really has the right to refuse. Similarly, a polite request from a police officer takes on the air of an order one may not refuse. Is "permission" under such circumstances an intelligent waiver of constitutional rights?

Another problem concerns the question of who may give permission to police to conduct a search. In *Warden v. Hayden*, the "mere evidence" case, the Supreme Court ruled the search valid because Mrs. Hayden had given the police permission to enter her home (although one might question whether her waiver was an intelligent one). The general rule is that "The person giving the consent must have the capacity to consent."[36] The Supreme Court has ruled that if a person has authority over the area to be searched, that person's consent is valid.[37]

A fourth area of controversy is so-called stop-and-frisk searches, which by their nature are warrantless. The leading case in this category is *Terry v. Ohio*.[38] McFadden, a plainclothes police officer with 39 years' experience, observed Terry and two other men acting in a suspicious manner. The men repeatedly walked past a store window, peered in, then conferred with one another on a street corner. After observing the ritual for approximately 10 minutes, McFadden concluded that Terry and the others were "casing" the store for a robbery. McFadden approached the men, identified himself as a police officer, and patted them down. When he discovered a revolver in Terry's coat pocket, he arrested him for carrying a concealed weapon. Terry was convicted and appealed on grounds of an unreasonable search and seizure. The Supreme Court, aware of the potential abuse of stop-and-frisk searches by police, nevertheless ruled that Officer McFadden had sufficient probable cause to believe a crime was about to be committed and was therefore justified in conducting his limited "pat-down" search. The Supreme Court has recognized that probable cause must be more than "a hunch." In

Terry, the Court ruled that "in justifying the particular intrusion the police officer must be able to point to specific and articulable facts, which taken together with rational inferences from those facts reasonably warrant the intrusion."[39] Thus, probable cause requires "specific and articulable facts" along with "rational inferences" before a warrantless search is valid.

Another category of search and seizure that has caused problems is the search of automobiles and other movable vehicles. It is obvious that, in requirements for search warrants, an automobile cannot be treated like a house or a building since an automobile can be moved before the warrant can be obtained. The Supreme Court first recognized this problem in *Carroll* v. *United States.*[40] Since *Carroll,* many of the search-and-seizure cases involving automobiles have concerned the questions of whether police had enough probable cause to stop and search particular automobiles,[41] searches pursuant to an arrest for traffic violations,[42] and inventory searches of automobiles that have been impounded.[43] In 1990, the Supreme Court upheld a Michigan law allowing police officers to set up highway sobriety checkpoints to check for drunk drivers. Every car encountering the checkpoint was stopped. The Court held that given the danger of drunk driving to the public safety and the relatively minor inconvenience to motorists, the "seizure of law abiding citizens is reasonable."[44] Still unclear is the extent to which police may search for other criminal activity unrelated to drunk driving during the course of a sobriety checkpoint stop.

Two final areas of search and seizure are cases involving the "plain-view" doctrine and wiretaps. The plain-view doctrine holds that police may seize evidence in plain view without a search warrant if the police are where they legally have a right to be. For example, in *Harris* v. *United States,*[45] the police searched Harris's apartment pursuant to a valid *arrest* warrant. Harris was suspected of forgery, and the police were looking for two canceled checks. In the course of the search they found fake draft cards, which they seized and used as evidence against Harris. The Court ruled that the search was made pursuant to a lawful arrest (overturned by *Chimel*) and that the draft cards were subject to seizure as contraband. The Court reasoned that "the police are not required to close their eyes and need not walk out and leave the article where they saw it. Any other principle might lead to an absurd result and at times perhaps even defeat the ends of justice."[46] The discovery of evidence in "plain view" often turns on whether or not the police officer is where he has a right to be, for "if the officer does become a trespasser . . . his action then amounts to an illegal search and seizure. He cannot use information so obtained to procure a warrant, nor can he seize the evidence without a warrant."[47]

Since 1971 the Supreme Court had taken the position that the discovery of evidence in plain view had to be inadvertent, that is, by chance. However, in a 1990 ruling the Court held that evidence in plain view could be seized constitutionally even if the police officer had anticipated finding evidence not specifically listed in a search warrant. In *Horton* v. *California*[48] a search warrant listed jewelry stolen in a robbery but failed to list the weapons used. The search of Horton's residence failed to uncover the jewelry, but weapons similar to those described by the victim were in plain view. At Horton's trial the officer admitted that he had anticipated finding the weapons as well as the jewelry. The Court's majority found that no privacy interest is protected by the requirement that evidence seized in plain view be discovered inadvertently.

Wiretapping illustrates how advances in technology can affect the application of the Fourth Amendment. Is a wiretap a "search" or "seizure" within the meaning of the Fourth Amendment? It is obvious that the Court cannot rely on the intent of the Framers in such cases since telephones did not exist when the Constitution was written. The Supreme Court confronted the issue in *Olmstead* v. *United States*,[49] in which it ruled that a wiretap was not a "search" because there was no physical invasion of Olmstead's residence. In *Goldman* v. *United States*,[50] authorities used a listening device in an adjacent office to hear Goldman's conversations through the walls. Relying on *Olmstead*, the Court ruled again that the search and seizure of Goldman's conversations were valid since no physical intrusion had occurred. In *Katz* v. *United States*,[51] however, the Supreme Court ruled that a wire-tap on a public telephone booth did constitute an illegal search and seizure, thus overruling *Olmstead*. Today wiretaps are permitted only with a court order upon a showing of probable cause.

Olmstead, Goldman, and *Katz* raise the question of the underlying purpose of the Fourth Amendment. If one assumes that the amendment protects *property*, then the *Olmstead-Goldman* position is defensible. If, on the other hand, the purpose of the amendment is to protect people's *privacy*, then the *Katz* position is preferred. As technology provides new ways to invade our privacy, the courts must be vigilant that law enforcement officers, in their eagerness to fight crime, do not adopt a "Big Brother" mentality. The question of privacy or property will no doubt be a recurring one in the future.

Right to counsel.   Much of the background of the right to counsel was discussed in Chapter 6, so only a brief summary is needed here. Suffice it to say that the right to counsel was intended to guarantee the services of a lawyer for those accused who could afford to pay for one. In Chapter 6 we chronicled how the Supreme Court extended the privilege in *Powell* v. *Alabama, Gideon* v. *Wainwright,* and *Argersinger* v. *Hamlin*. As a result of these cases, no person must face a serious criminal offense without the presence of an attorney, either retained or court appointed.

Despite the fact that the right to counsel has been clearly established at trial, a more perplexing problem is *when* the accused has the right to counsel. An early federal case illustrates the problem of what can happen if the accused does not have access to an attorney in the early stages of the criminal justice process. Andrew Mallory was a young man of "limited intelligence" accused of raping a woman in a Washington, D.C., laundromat. Although Mallory was arrested early in the afternoon, he was detained and questioned by the police throughout the rest of the day. During the interrogation, Mallory confessed to the crime. The next day he was taken before a U.S. magistrate for arraignment, at which time he was informed of his right to remain silent and his right to an attorney. But it was too late for Andrew Mallory. Any advice an attorney could have given him was useless in light of his confession. Mallory was convicted of rape and sentenced to die for his crime. Attorneys for Mallory decided to appeal his case, however, on the grounds that police had delayed too long before bringing Mallory before the magistrate. To inform Mallory of his constitutional rights after his confession was a classic case of closing the barn door after the horse is gone. In *Mallory* v. *United States*,[52] the Supreme Court agreed. The Court noted that the magistrate was located in the same building where Mallory was being interrogated, and it would have been a simple task to bring him before the magistrate before intense questioning began. The Court considered the delay between Mallory's arrest and his arraignment unreasonable and overturned his conviction. In *Mallory,* the Supreme Court recognized that the exercise of constitutional rights, such as the right to counsel, can be critical long before the accused is brought to trial. Knowledge and understanding of one's constitutional rights are needed early in the process, especially in the case of someone like Mallory, who had a limited capacity to understand what was happening to him.

The Supreme Court continued to develop the question of when the accused has the right to counsel in the case of *Escobedo* v. *Illinois.*[53] Danny Escobedo was accused of murdering his brother-in-law. He was arrested, interrogated, and later released by the police even though he remained the prime suspect. When additional evidence implicating Escobedo turned up, he was arrested again. In the meantime, his family had retained a lawyer who went to the jailhouse to see Escobedo, but the police purposely kept Escobedo from seeing his lawyer. When Escobedo asked to see his lawyer, he was told that his lawyer did not want to see him. At the same time, Escobedo's lawyer was being told that he could not see his client until the police were finished interrogating him. Escobedo subsequently confessed, and his confession was used to convict him of murder. In overturning Escobedo's conviction, the Court stressed the importance of the "guiding hand of counsel"[54] noting that "The right to counsel would be hollow indeed if it began at a period when few confessions were obtained."[55] In other words, the advice of an attorney is needed most during the period between arrest and arraignment, when most confessions are made. The Court ruled that when the focus had shifted from a general inquiry into an unsolved crime to a particular suspect, that suspect must be informed of his right to remain silent. Otherwise, he has been denied the assistance of counsel guaranteed by the Sixth Amendment.[56]

In the controversial *Miranda* v. *Arizona*[57] decision, the Warren Court reaffirmed *Escobedo* and explicitly stated what police must do when making an arrest. The Court ruled that when a person is taken into custody or otherwise denied freedom of movement, the police must inform the accused of his constitutional rights before questioning. These rights include the right to remain silent, the right to an attorney either appointed or retained, and the right to know that anything he says may be used against him in court. The *Miranda* decision is perhaps the most controversial decision in criminal justice since the imposition of the exclusionary rule. The police argued that the decision would make it virtually impossible to gain confessions from criminals, and that because confessions are a major source of evidence, convictions would be more difficult to obtain. Studies have indicated that the worst fears of the police have not been realized.[58] The major reason that police still obtain confessions from accused persons is plea bargaining. Guilty persons are still willing to trade their confessions for a charge reduction or lighter sentence. Since confessions are seldom the only evidence the police have, criminal defendants prefer to plea bargain rather than take chances at trial. Despite its limited impact, *Miranda* remains controversial even 30 years after it was handed down and even though the predicted consequences never materialized.

The issues surrounding the right to counsel in *Miranda* have focused on when the *Miranda* warnings are required and what constitutes an intelligent waiver of one's rights. One of the first cases to decide when the *Miranda* warnings are required was *Mathis* v. *United States*.[59] While in prison for an unrelated offense, Mathis was "routinely" questioned by IRS agents about his 1960 and 1961 tax returns. The agents failed to give Mathis the *Miranda* warnings, and evidence elicited from Mathis was used to convict him of tax fraud. The Supreme Court ruled that because tax investigations can lead to criminal charges, the *Miranda* warnings are required.

Similarly, in *Orozco* v. *Texas*,[60] the Court ruled that suspects must be given the *Miranda* warnings when they are under arrest, even if the questioning is not in a "coercive environment." The police arrested Orozco at his boardinghouse and questioned him, without the *Miranda* warnings, while he sat on his bed. The Court ruled that Orozco had been deprived of his freedom of action in a significant way and therefore the warnings were required. In contrast to *Mathis* and *Orozco,* however, the Court ruled in *Beckwith* v. *United States*[61] that an interrogation by IRS agents in the home of the accused was not a custodial arrest requiring the specific *Miranda* warnings. It should be noted, however, that the IRS agents did advise Beckwith of his right to remain silent and his right to an attorney.

In *Oregon* v. *Mathiason*,[62] the Court ruled that a confession by a person who voluntarily appears at police headquarters and who is not under arrest may be used even though the *Miranda* warnings were not given. Although the interrogation of Mathiason took place in a "coercive environment," the

Court ruled that he was not denied his freedom of action in any significant way. Finally, in *Estelle* v. *Smith*,[63] the Court extended the *Miranda* requirements to include pretrial psychiatric examinations in which the psychiatrist is permitted to testify in the punishment stage of a capital case.

A second area of concern in right-to-counsel cases involves the intelligent waiver of constitutional rights after *Miranda* warnings have been given. Police may not rely on "trickery and deceit" nor do anything to overbear the defendant's will. For example, in *Brewer* v. *Williams*[64] (one of our case studies at the end of this chapter), police, after being warned not to question Williams, made statements designed to elicit incriminating information from him. Police, knowing of Williams's religious beliefs, talked of allowing the parents of his 10-year-old victim to give her a "Christian burial." The Supreme Court held that the "Christian burial" speech was psychologically calculated to coerce Williams into identifying the location of the girl's body, which he did. The *Brewer* v. *Williams* case and its aftermath will be examined at greater length at the end of this chapter.

In *North Carolina* v. *Butler*,[65] the Court again faced the issue of an intelligent waiver. Butler was arrested by the FBI on a North Carolina fugitive warrant. After agents determined that Butler had an eleventh-grade education, he was handed an FBI "Advice of Rights" card, which he read. Butler refused to sign the waiver at the bottom of the form but agreed to talk with agents, whereupon he made some incriminating statements. Butler neither requested counsel nor asked to terminate the questioning. The North Carolina Supreme Court ruled that Butler's statement could not be used as evidence without an explicit statement of waiver, but the Supreme Court reversed. The Court ruled that in agreeing to answer questions, Butler had implicitly waived his right to counsel and his protection against self-incrimination.

Two other cases merit mention. In *Rhode Island* v. *Innis*,[66] the Court faced a situation similar to that in *Brewer* v. *Williams*. Innis was arrested for the murder of a cab driver, but the murder weapon, a shotgun, was not found. After being given the *Miranda* warnings, Innis was driven to the police station. En route, one officer remarked about how it would be unfortunate if some child in the neighborhood discovered the weapon. Innis asked the police to return to the place where he was arrested. After being warned a third time of his rights, Innis told the police where they could find the murder weapon. Unlike *Brewer*, however, the Court ruled that the casual conversation of the officers did not constitute "express questioning" or its "functional equivalent" and ruled that Innis had intelligently waived his rights.

In *New York* v. *Quarles*,[67] the Court created a "public safety" exception to the *Miranda* rule. Police followed Quarles, a rape suspect, into a supermarket and arrested him. The victim had told police that Quarles was armed, but a search produced no weapon. When asked about the gun, Quarles replied, "The gun is over there." No *Miranda* warnings had been given. The Supreme

Court ruled that the gun posed enough danger to public safety to warrant an exception to the *Miranda* rule.

Finally, in *Illinois* v. *Perkins*[68] the Supreme Court held that incriminating statements made by a defendant to an undercover officer do not require a prior *Miranda* warning. While in jail on an unrelated offense, Perkins made incriminating statements to an undercover agent posing as an inmate about an unsolved murder in East St. Louis. The majority held that one underlying purpose of *Miranda* was to protect the defendant from being questioned in a coercive police environment. The Court ruled 8–1 that no coercion exists when a defendant voluntarily gives information to someone he believes to be a fellow inmate.

The cases examined here involving the right to counsel indicate an erosion of the *Miranda* decision and illustrate the game, or contest, approach to criminal justice. The police, for their part, try to devise clever ways to elicit incriminating evidence from defendants without violating the letter (but not the spirit) of *Miranda*. Criminal defendants try to devise clever ways to show how police tricked or otherwise deceived them into offering incriminating evidence. But criminal justice should not be a game of "Trickery and Deceit" or "Catch Us If You Can." Yet, as these cases illustrate, that is what the process often becomes.

Self-incrimination.   The privilege against self-incrimination was already well established as common law when the Bill of Rights was added to the Constitution. Under English law, individuals charged with crimes could not be compelled to testify against themselves at trial. The privilege reflects, in part, a reluctance to force individuals to provide the means of their own destruction. That is, we are opposed to forcing people to condemn themselves to prison or death. It also reflects our accusatory approach to law: The accused does not have to prove his innocence; the State must prove his guilt. Surely the accused cannot be expected to assist the State in making a case against him. Finally, the privilege reflects concern over the reliability of confessions, especially if any evidence of coercion is involved. Recall that in *Mallory* v. *United States*, the Supreme Court was concerned not only with the failure of the police to arraign Mallory, but also with Mallory's inability to make an intelligent confession because of his limited mental capacity. Of course, the Constitution does permit the accused to confess, but there must be an intelligent waiver of the right to remain silent.

Despite some valid arguments for protection against self-incrimination, the privilege is not without its critics. The major criticism centers around this argument: If the accused is innocent, why should he be afraid to take the stand in his own defense? If, the argument runs, the accused has nothing to hide, why should he be afraid to take the stand to deny his guilt or to explain away the State's evidence against him? The problem, of course, is that this argument shifts the burden of proof to the defendant. The defendant is told, in effect, that he must prove his innocence and should therefore be willing to take the stand in his own defense. This argument is valid, and some criminal defendants do take the stand in their own defense, but only voluntarily and only with the advice of counsel.

Until fairly recently, some states allowed a prosecutor to comment on a defendant's failure to take the stand even when state law protected the defendant's right to refuse to testify. In two early cases, *Twining* v. *New Jersey*[69] and *Adamson* v. *California*,[70] the Supreme Court ruled that the Constitution did not prohibit a state jury from drawing negative inferences from a defendant's failure to take the stand in his or her own defense. Nor is due process violated if a state judge calls the defendant's failure to testify to the attention of the jury, even though federal judges are not allowed to do so. In *Malloy* v. *Hogan*,[71] however, the Court overturned *Twining* and ruled that the same protections against self-incrimination apply to both state and federal prosecutions.

The privilege against self-incrimination is closely related to both the right to counsel and protection against unreasonable searches and seizures. After being placed under arrest, the accused is usually told of his right to remain silent and then informed of his right to have an attorney present during questioning. This is done so that the accused will not inadvertently admit something that incriminates him since, as we have seen, the right to the advice of counsel is useless if the accused has already made incriminating statements. Likewise, the privilege against self-incrimination is related to search-and-seizure issues. In *Boyd* v. *United States*,[72] for example, the police seized invoices that showed that Boyd had imported cases of plate glass without paying the duties on them. The Supreme Court overturned Boyd's conviction on both Fourth and Fifth Amendment grounds, saying, "... we have been unable to perceive that the seizure of a man's private books and papers to be used in evidence against him is substantially different from compelling him to be a witness against himself."[73] Although *Boyd* has been modified considerably since 1886,[74] private papers, such as diaries, cannot be used to incriminate the accused.

As we have seen with other constitutional rights of the accused, time and technology have forced the courts to reconsider and reinterpret the privilege against self-incrimination. Although it is clear that the accused cannot be forced to admit his guilt, does the privilege extend to nonverbal forms of communication? For example, in *Rochin* v. *California*,[75] the police saw Rochin swallow some capsules they believed to be morphine. They took Rochin to a hospital and ordered physicians to pump his stomach against his will. The contents did contain morphine, and Rochin was convicted of its possession, but the Supreme Court reversed. In addition to condemning the act as an unreasonable search and seizure, the Court considered the act tantamount to a coerced confession. Calling the stomach pumping a method "too close to the rack and the screw," the Court ruled that the actions of the police "shock the conscience." However, in *Breithaupt* v. *Abram*[76] and *Schmerber* v. *California*,[77] the Court allowed a blood test to be admitted as evidence of drunk driving. In *Breithaupt*, the accused was unconscious and the test was done under medical supervision. The Court contrasted the relatively painless blood test to the stomach-pumping procedure used in *Rochin*. In *Schmerber*, the Court ruled that a blood test could be required even over the objections of the accused. The Court stated:

> We hold that the privilege protects an accused only from being compelled to testify against himself, or otherwise provide the State with evidence of a testimonial or communicative nature, and that the withdrawal of blood and use of analysis in question in this case did not involve compulsion to these ends.[78]

The "testimonial and communicative nature" requirement has led the Court to permit the admission of a number of types of nonverbal incriminating evidence. The Court has ruled that the accused may be forced to give handwriting samples, fingerprints, voice identifications, and dental records. Although the Court has ruled that the accused must submit to a lineup, it has also ruled that the accused has the right to have counsel present at postindictment lineups to ensure that no irregularities occur.[79]

Pretrial publicity. Fundamental to the Anglo-American concept of justice is the notion that the accused is entitled to a public trial before an impartial jury. One way to ensure the impartiality of the jury is to limit access to prejudicial evidence which might influence prospective jurors. However, the news media maintain that in a free society the public has "a right to know," and they will sometimes publish material that inflames the community, making it difficult for the accused to get a fair trial. As a result, a common area of conflict has been the free press–fair trial controversy and the problem of prejudicial pretrial publicity.

One of the leading cases is *Sheppard* v. *Maxwell*,[80] a spectacular murder case in which a prominent Cleveland doctor was accused of killing his wife. Although Dr. Sheppard was not initially a suspect in the case, newspaper editorials implying special treatment prompted police officials to focus on him. Sheppard was eventually indicted, and during his trial the courtroom had what Justice Tom Clark later described as a "carnival atmosphere." Newspaper accounts of "evidence" never actually introduced at trial were made available to jurors, reporters were allowed to be inside the bar (an area normally restricted to lawyers and participants), and the trial judge made no effort to control the press. The Supreme Court, after severely criticizing the trial judge, reversed Sheppard's conviction, noting, "Due process requires that the accused receive a trial by an impartial jury free from outside influences."[81] On retrial, in a calmer atmosphere, Sheppard was acquitted of the murder charge.

Sheppard v. *Maxwell* implies a need for a balance between the right of the press to cover sensational trials and the right of the accused to a fair trial. *Sheppard* was one of the cases that began marking the parameters of the free press–fair trial dilemma. For example, in *Gannett Co. Inc.* v. *DePasquale*,[82] the defense made a motion to exclude the press in a pretrial preliminary hearing in which the trial judge would decide whether or not to exclude certain evidence in a murder case. The trial judge granted the motion, and the newspaper company quickly challenged its exclusion. The Supreme Court upheld the trial judge's decision on the grounds that the public (and therefore the press as part of the public) "have no constitutional right under the Sixth and Fourteenth Amendments to attend criminal trials."[83] The Court ruled that although the press does have a *First* Amendment right of access to trials, the trial judge correctly decided that the defendant's right to a fair trial outweighed the newspaper's right in this case.[84]

The Supreme Court's ruling in *DePasquale* that the public has no right to attend a criminal trial did not settle the issue. *DePasquale* involved the exclusion of the press/public from a *pretrial* hearing. In *Richmond Newspapers Inc.* v. *Virginia*,[85] the Court was asked to rule on whether or not the press/public could be excluded from the actual trial. After three previously unsuccessful attempts to try a defendant on a murder charge, a Virginia trial judge granted the defense lawyer's motion to exclude the public, including two reporters, from the courtroom. The Supreme Court, in a divided opinion, ruled that the public does have a First Amendment right to attend criminal trials. The Court ruled that the trial judge should have resorted to less restrictive measures to guarantee the defendant a fair trial. However, public access to criminal trials may be limited in cases involving juveniles and in certain rape and child abuse cases. The issue of public access to criminal trials is far from settled, since new cases with different circumstances are sure to arise.

One other issue associated with the public's right to know is that of television broadcasts of criminal trials. In *Estes* v. *Texas*,[86] the Supreme Court ruled that the bright lights and heavy equipment used in broadcasting disrupted criminal trials. In *Chandler* v. *Florida*,[87] however, the Court reversed itself, stating that *Estes* was not intended to impose an absolute ban on televised trials. Chief Justice Warren Burger noted that changes in television technology and greater sensitivity on the part of judges to the need for precautionary measures have made television less intrusive than it once was. *Estes* and *Chandler* illustrate how changes in technology can also affect changes in constitutional law. Concern over the televised proceedings in the O.J. Simpson murder trial has renewed the debate over media coverage of sensational trials. Although the Simpson jury was sequestered, some observers were concerned about the circus atmosphere that surrounded the trial. In addition, some critics maintain that the Simpson trial was not typical and viewers were left with a distorted picture of the legal system.

PUNISHMENT

Punishment is an integral (and controversial) part of the criminal justice system. We read shrieking headlines that persons committing heinous crimes were on parole or that a death-row killer has been given a stay of execution or a new trial. People become upset at such events, and each becomes an instant expert on the system. Certainly, no one likes to hear that someone has been injured by a parolee or probationer, but the solution to punishment is not easy. What punishment fits the crime? What modes of punishment are acceptable in a civilized society? What should the treatment of prisoners be like in a society dedicated to human rights? What is the appropriate balance between the rights of the convicted or accused vis-à-vis the victim? These are the questions that the legislative branch must answer in establishing the penalties for crimes and in funding various types of punishment, that the executive branch must answer in operating prisons and probation and parole programs, and that the judicial branch must consider in deciding cases which challenge the conditions and procedures involved in punishment.

Theories of punishment.   There are three primary models of punishment—retribution, deterrence, and rehabilitation. The earliest extant criminal codes—the Code of Hammurabi and the Old Testament—reflect the legal doctrine of *lex talionis* or "an eye for an eye, a tooth for a tooth." Retribution should be distinguished from vengeance; the former is done under authority of the state to enforce the law and maintain social order, whereas the latter is private and personal. Retribution is based on the premise that the perpetrator is a reasonable and rationale being who freely made the decision to violate the law. This theory advocates that the wrongdoer be punished in such a way that the punishment fits the crime.

Rehabilitation is the notion that punishment should rehabilitate or reform the behavior of offenders so that they will become law-abiders rather than lawbreakers This was the dominant theory of punishment from the 1920s to the 1970s in this country and is based on the premise that treatment programs may change behavior patterns. Many have abandoned the idea of meaningful rehabilitation for our penal institutions for a variety of reasons including lack of resources (which reflects lack of public support) and now recognize that prisons and jails are often merely "warehouses" and that while incarceration may be a learning experience, it is rarely a positive one.

Deterrence refers both to discouraging this particular offender from further illegal acts and to deterring others from criminal activity. The underlying theory is that people carefully weigh their actions and the attendant costs and benefits, and that the fear of punishment dissuades them from breaking the law. There has been a resurgence of interest in deterrence theory in the last three decades or so. Scholars and others have examined the deterrent effect in a variety of settings. For example, in the area of capital punishment, the more methodologically sound studies indicate that there is not a deterrent effect on others and may, in fact, encourage similar acts, although most scholars agree that more research needs to be done on this topic. In other areas, such as income tax evasion or fraud, prosecution of offenders does not seem to inhibit criminal activity. It appears that harsher penalties, longer sentences, and promptness of punishment may affect the individual, but unless sentences are well publicized, there is little deterrent effect on others who are likely to commit crimes of some magnitude.[88]

Types of punishment. There are various types of punishment for crimes ranging from the payment of a fine only through the death penalty. Every crime carries with it a penalty that is determined by the legislative body, and it is an element of due process that individuals are entitled to know the possible range of punishment. The assessment of punishment may come about through plea bargaining, in which the defendant agrees to accept the punishment, or through assessment by judge or jury depending on state law and the defendant's selection of a jury or bench trial (where that option exists).

The punishment defined by statutes is incarceration and/or fine or the death penalty and/or a fine. Misdemeanors usually carry time at the city or county correctional facility, whereas conviction of felonies usually means incarceration at either the state penitentiary for state crimes or the federal penitentiary for federal crimes. The national government not only has a separate set of laws and courts, but it also has a separate program for corrections including probation and prisons.

The form of punishment most frequently imposed is ***probation.*** Generally, the states impose various limitations on probation and reserve it for less serious crimes. With probation, the defendant is not confined in an institution but remains in the community subject to various conditions such as submitting to drug testing, staying away from certain people or places, and committing no other offenses. The probationer remains under the control of the court, and probation may be revoked for noncompliance with the probation terms as monitored by a probation officer.

Similar to probation is the ***suspended sentence,*** which is also known as deferred adjudication. Under this, either there is no conviction entered following the plea (suspension of imposition of sentence) or the sentence is prescribed but not carried out (suspension of the execution of the sentence). The result is the same; if the offender successfully meets the court's requirements, such as restitution, completion of a substance-abuse program, or community service, the defendant is unconditionally discharged. With suspension of the imposition of the sentence, there is no conviction on the offender's record. This practice came under attack in driving-while-intoxicated cases. Drivers would be arrested numerous times but would have no convictions on their record because of suspended sentences. To correct that problem, many states adopted laws barring such practices. However, deferred adjudication is still very useful in selected cases for certain offenders (for example, a college honor student who committed a relatively minor criminal indiscretion such as trespass) who have no prior involvement with the law and who are unlikely to err again. This allows the court to impose some punishment without marring the person's record with a conviction.[89]

Parole is release from imprisonment on the condition of good behavior; the terms of parole are similar to those required of probationers—to avoid persons and places of bad reputation, participate in treatment programs, and to regularly report to a parole officer, to name a few. The state systems vary so widely in terms of organization and in terms of eligibility standards that we can only generalize in the broadest of terms here. One common feature of parole organizations is that they are under the control of the executive or administrative branches of government rather than under the control of the judiciary. Parole is both granted and revoked by administrators rather than judges. Although these administrators have broad discretion, they are limited by some elements of due process even though the U.S. Supreme Court has determined that not all of the full panoply of procedural rights found in criminal trials must be afforded in parole hearings.[90]

Another common aspect of parole systems is the use of "good time." Good time is a classic example of the carrot-stick approach to control and management. The promise of early release (the carrot) is dangled in front of inmates as a reward for good behavior in prison, and if they do not conform to institutional rules and norms, they face the loss of good time (the stick), which results in longer incarceration. Different states take different tacks in regard to the use of good time and even parole. Some states bar parole for those offenders who commit certain crimes such as capital murder; some set minimum time periods (for example, one-fourth of the sentence) exclusive of good time which must be served for certain offenses; and some use *mandatory release,* which provides for automatic release when the calendar time and good time served equal the maximum time for which the inmate was sentenced.[91] Still others have adopted determinate sentencing and abandoned parole. In most *determinate sentencing* schemes, the legislature establishes a flat rate of punishment rather than a range of five to ten years for the crime, which removes judicial and jury discretion in the length of sentences along with abolishing parole.

Prisoner's rights. Courts have always guarded—sometimes zealously, sometimes not—the rights of prisoners to challenge the basis of their convictions through appeal and writs of *habeas corpus,* but prisoners seeking redress of other grievances have often been faced with closed courthouse doors. They were regarded as slaves of the state who lost all legal rights—regardless of whether they were first offenders for minor offenses or the most heinous of all offenders—and who were totally subject to the arbitrary and capricious (and often brutal) whims of their captors.[92] The courts maintained a "hands-off" policy in regard to prison management, deferring to the expertise of prison administrators.

However, federal courts became more receptive to inmate suits[93] challenging both prison practices and conditions with the advent of the civil rights movement and increased interest in all human rights and by such events as the 1971 Attica (N.Y.) Prison Riots where armed state troopers killed 29 inmates and 10 officer hostages in retaking control of the prison.[94] The vehicle for such suits was the newly rediscovered Civil Rights Act of 1871 (42 U.S.C. § 1983), which gave federal courts jurisdiction to hear civil actions for deprivation of constitutional rights; this meant that a more neutral forum was available than the state courts, which were generally not amenable, if not actively hostile, to this type of litigation.

Prisoner suits have revealed that, even within the last two decades, incarceration in this country amounted to "banishment from civilized society to a dark and evil world completely alien to the free world."[95] Conditions in both jails and penitentiaries are described by courts as "degrading and disgusting"[96] and as "violating the elemental concepts of decency,"[97] thereby creating cruel and unusual punishment in violation of the Eighth Amendment. Municipal and county jails have not escaped the courts' scrutiny, especially in light of the fact that many of those in jail have not been convicted of the crime for which they are being held and are technically innocent but yet are being subjected to horrible conditions. Courts intervened to mandate that steps be taken to relieve overcrowding and that basic living and sanitary conditions be improved for both the general prison population and those in administrative or punitive segregation.[98]

Inmates also sought protection of the court in arenas other than prison conditions. Recent courts have readily agreed that the Eighth Amendment draws "meaning from the evolving standards of decency that mark the progress of a maturing society"[99] and that "prison walls do not form a barrier separating prison inmates from the protections of the Constitution";[100] the difficulty is in balancing the security of the institution and the safety of staff and prisoners against the constitutionally protected interests of the inmates.

Under the First Amendment, courts were asked to examine the rights of prisoners in the areas of religious freedom, speech, access to the press, and assembly. Prisoners do maintain some semblance of these rights even though the reach of the rights may be circumscribed. For example, prison administrators cannot punish a prisoner or discriminate against him or her on account of the individual's religious faith.[101] They cannot arbitrarily prevent the practice of a religion because it is unpopular but instead must carefully weigh the security interest of the prison versus the prisoner's right to practice his or her religion, and mere speculation as to the danger or dislike of the religion's tenets will not suffice to prohibit a religion.[102]

Although most provisions of the Bill of Rights have been the subject of prisoner litigation, two are particularly noteworthy. One is the issue of access to courts "which is afforded special protection"[103] because "All other rights of an inmate are illusory without it."[104] Prisons are required to provide some system of legal services to inmates to challenge the grounds for their imprisonment.[105] This assistance may take a variety of forms including, but not limited to, state-provided attorneys, law students working in a clinic under supervision, or the assistance of other inmates, the "jailhouse lawyers." In addition, basic materials must be provided for legal research.[106] Prisoners who are perceived to be activists or troublemakers cannot be denied access to their attorneys or subjected to punishment for their activities.[107] Unlike other correspondence, mail to and from attorneys and courts is generally not to be read or even opened.[108]

Another fertile source of litigation is disciplinary proceedings and due process. Corporal punishment such as flogging or administering electric shocks was long used as the primary disciplinary tool in American penal institutions. However, in the late 1960s, courts recognized that corporal punishment "is easily subject to abuse in the hands of the sadistic and unscrupulous . . . generates hatred toward the keepers . . . is degrading to the punisher and the punished alike . . . [and] public opinion is obviously adverse."[109] Today, the use of force (except in emergency situations) to control inmates has been supplanted by the disciplinary hearing as the chief mechanism to maintain order. A hearing must be provided in nonemergency situations before punishment is assessed whether that punishment is denial of privileges or infringement of a constitutional right such as a prisoner's limited liberty interest in being in the general prison population versus solitary confinement or administrative segregation.

The courts have sought to prevent such hearings from merely being charades. In *Wolff* v. *McDonnell*,[110] the Supreme Court established minimal due process requirements for such hearings: (1) written notice of the charges at least 24 hours before the hearing; (2) the opportunity to call witnesses and present documentary evidence unless the institutional safety is put in jeopardy by calling such witnesses; (3) impartial hearing board; and (4) written statement of the evidence relied on by the board. While there is no right to an appointed attorney, an inmate who is illiterate or mentally handicapped is entitled to have the assistance of a counsel-substitute (another inmate or staff member).[111]

Capital punishment.   Contrary to what many think, the Supreme Court has never held the death penalty to be unconstitutional. Instead, the Court found that the procedures imposing the death penalty were unconstitutionally sound in that they allowed "arbitrary and capricious" actions on the part of the jury in sentencing a person to death,[112] but that the defect could be cured by carefully drafted statutes which gave the sentencing authority (whether judge or jury) adequate information and guidance.[113] The courts are concerned that the individual and the circumstances of this particular crime be scrutinized and considered by the jury or judge, and mandatory imposition of the death penalty without that consideration will not pass constitutional muster.[114] The morality and efficacy of the death penalty raises fascinating questions, but our discussion will focus on the legal aspects surrounding this most controversial topic.

Today, the death penalty is assessed only when the victim is murdered and then only in limited circumstances.[115] Strange as it may sound, not all murders are treated the same, and statutes define exactly what constitutes capital murder, such as a murder-for-hire scheme or killing a police officer in the line of duty. Although those only tangentially involved in capital murder (such as the driver of the getaway car) may not be given the death sentence,[116] those accessories "with major participation in the felony committed combined with reckless indifference to human life" may receive such punishment.[117] The Court has upheld the various methods of execution including hanging, firing squad, electrocution, and lethal gas, and many states now have adopted the use of lethal injections as the method of execution.

Various aspects of capital punishment—both procedural and substantive—continue to be troublesome for the Court. Human rights activists throughout the world are appalled that this nation imposes the death penalty on youthful offenders—those 16 and 17 years of age when they commit the crime[118]—and on those who, while having sufficient capability to form criminal responsibility, are mentally retarded.[119] The manner of jury selection has also provoked appeals. The Supreme Court has denied the state the right to exclude from the jury all those who oppose the death penalty[120] and has barred the racially discriminatory use of peremptory challenges by prosecutors as, for example, eliminating all African-American jurors from a jury when the defendant is African-American.[121] Concern still remains that the death penalty is applied disproportionately according to race, particularly when the victim is white and the offender is African-American. In *McCleskey v. Kemp*,[122] a sophisticated statistical study was introduced to show that African-Americans were more likely to be sentenced to the death penalty than whites in Georgia. The Supreme Court accepted the study and its conclusions but held that McCleskey, who is African-American, failed to show that discrimination affected the outcome in his particular case.

In addition to these types of issues, the Court also has practical concerns regarding the death penalty. The seriousness of the punishment and its irreversible nature mandates that the cases be carefully considered, but extensive scrutiny clogs the courts' dockets. The Court is continually examining methods of streamlining the appeals process while maintaining a strict standard of review. It is also worrisome to the Court and others that death-row inmates are not receiving adequate legal representation on appeal because many lawyers and law firms are reluctant to take on these cases with their attendant loss of profits because of the attention and resources diverted to such cases.

Other issues.   Punishment is one of those areas of the law where everyone sees the problems but no one has the solution. Conviction of the wrongdoer is not the end of the line; he or she does not drop off the face of the earth. Society must decide the appropriate level of punishment as well as the amount of resources it is willing to devote to punitive measures. The financial and human costs of the programs are immense, especially in terms of total institutions. Such costs have encouraged the use of diversionary tools such as electronic monitoring devices, house arrest, boot camps, halfway houses, and other innovative programs. The goal of such diversion is not only to limit the economic costs but also the human costs. The vast majority of inmates who are sentenced to prison do not die there but are released back into society after attending "The University of Crime" where their knowledge of crime has been greatly enhanced. Balancing the needs of society for retribution against the costs to society is a difficult and unenviable task for elected officials.

JUVENILE JUSTICE

Criminal law, like all law, reflects the attitudes of the society that produces it and this can be seen in the legal treatment of children. Under Roman law, for example, children were subject to the complete control of their father under the doctrine of *patria potestas,* or parental authority. The *paterfamilias,* who sometimes was a grandfather, exercised absolute authority, including the power of life and death, over his children. This absolute control was in part a reflection of the reluctance of the state to interfere in the privacy of the home. In keeping with the spirit of the maxim, "A man's home is his castle," the Roman state hesitated to intervene in the private affairs of its citizens. During the Middle Ages children were often treated as miniature adults who were expected to work when they were able. As part of a feudal society, children were viewed as property of their parents much as their own serf/parents were vassals of their feudal overlord. In our own society, children are not viewed as chattel subject to absolute control of their parents but as individuals with limited rights. Although there is still some reluctance by the state to intervene in family matters, states today have much greater latitude to act "in the best interests of the child."

In this section, we will examine the legal treatment of children in the United States. Like other aspects of criminal law, juvenile law has both procedural and substantive elements. Procedural law concerns the requirements that must be observed before the state denies a person life, liberty, or property. As we shall see, procedural safeguards for juveniles have been equivocal. Substantive law concerns the issues such as the age at which juveniles may be punished for criminal behavior. We begin with a look at procedural law and juvenile justice.

Procedural law. The prevailing philosophy of procedural due process, simply stated, has been that juveniles do not need the same procedural protection our system grants to adults. This is because the state, acting like a concerned parent, is only interested in the welfare of the child and intervenes only to help. The doctrine that permits the state to intervene on behalf of a child is known as *parens patriae.* Originally this doctrine applied to the king who, as "father of the country," had a paternalistic interest in the well-being of his subjects. In a modern sense, *parens patriae* holds that the state has an obligation to care for its innocents, that is, those who cannot care for themselves. *Parens patriae* imposes an affirmative duty on the state to intervene to protect the life or well-being of a child. This doctrine justifies the removal, if necessary, of the child from the parents' control.

Ironically, the *parens patriae* doctrine has resulted in the ambivalent treatment of children in the area of procedural law:

> From its origins, the juvenile court system denied children procedural rights normally available to adult offenders. Due process rights such as representation by counsel, a jury trial, freedom from self-incrimination, and freedom from unreasonable search and seizure were not considered essential for the juvenile court system because the primary purpose of the system was not punishment but rehabilitation.[123]

Unlike adult criminals who often were viewed as lost causes, many people believe that there is still hope of rehabilitating a child who has committed a crime. Society is less willing to give up on a child who may yet be saved from a life of crime. Oddly enough, this paternalistic approach has had some negative effects. Since the purpose of the juvenile justice system was to save rather than punish the child, the procedural safeguards afforded to adults were denied to children. Supreme Court Justice Abe Fortas explained this rationale in *In re Gault:*

> The right of the state, as *parens patriae,* to deny the child procedural rights available to his elders was elaborated by the assertion that a child, unlike an adult, has a right "not to liberty but to custody." He can be made to attorn to his parents, to go to school, etc. If his parents default in effectively performing their custodial function—that is, if the child is "delinquent"—the state may intervene. In doing so, it does not deprive the child of any rights, *because he has none.* [Emphasis added.] It merely provides the "custody" to which the child is entitled. On this basis, proceedings involving juveniles were described as "civil" not "criminal" and therefore not subject to the requirements which restrict the state when it seeks to deprive a person of his liberty.[124]

Gault and its immediate predecessor, *Kent* v. *United States,*[125] revealed the disturbing state of juvenile procedural law. Although *Gault* raised several procedural issues including right to counsel, notice of proceedings, and the privilege against self-incrimination, the most egregious issue concerned the penalty Gault received. As a delinquent accused of making obscene phone calls, Gault was subject to confinement until he reached age 21. An adult charged with the same offense would have received a maximum penalty of a $50 fine and two months in jail.[126] Although the Supreme Court made it clear that its decision "will not compel the States to abandon or displace any of the substantive benefits of the juvenile process,"[127] many observers heralded *Gault* as the dawn of a due process revolution for juvenile justice.

The Supreme Court extended the procedural rights of juveniles in the years following *Gault*. Three years later the Court ruled in *In re Winship*[128] that the "beyond a reasonable doubt" standard required for adult convictions also applied to juvenile cases. Before *Winship* the states applied the "preponderance of the evidence" standard used in civil proceedings. The use of the lesser civil standard in juvenile cases reflected the paternalistic, nonadversarial approach of the criminal justice system. Finally, the Court extended the Constitution's double-jeopardy provision to juveniles in *Breed* v. *Jones*.[129]

While the Supreme Court made great strides in protecting the constitutional rights of juveniles, the Court clearly does not intend to extend all provisions of the Constitution to juvenile justice. For example, in *McKeiver* v. *Pennsylvania*[130] the Court held that juveniles are not entitled to a jury trial. Similarly, in *Schall* v. *Martin*[131] it upheld a New York law that permitted pretrial detention of accused delinquents. Gregory Martin was detained 15 days, whereas an adult charged with the same offense would have been permitted to post bail.[132] In *New Jersey* v. *T.L.O.*,[133] the Court upheld the search of T.L.O.'s purse by an assistant principal despite insufficient probable cause. While recognizing student constitutional rights, the Court nevertheless approved such searches under a less stringent standard. A school official need have only a "reasonable suspicion" to search a student's possessions.

After several major advances in procedural due process for juveniles, the Supreme Court has retreated from extending further safeguards. This uncertainty about how to treat juvenile offenders is reflected in substantive juvenile law to which we now turn our attention.

Substantive law. Procedural law, as we have seen, centers on what procedures the law affords to juveniles. Substantive law raises questions such as when, or even if, a child should be punished for a criminal act. Another important issue is whether a young person should receive the same penalty for a crime as an adult would receive. Substantive juvenile law is like procedural juvenile law in that both raise the fundamental question whether a child should be treated the same as an adult.

Historically, the law has assumed that children below a certain age may not be punished for criminal behavior. Under Roman law, for example, a child under seven could not be punished for committing a crime. Seven was accepted during the Middle Ages because at that age children made their first confession in the Catholic Church.[134] The American colonies followed the common-law rule of the age of seven as well.[135] Today most states accept ten as the age at which children are liable for their criminal actions. This is not to say that children are treated as adults at this age, but only that they may be subject to the juvenile justice system.

The principal reason for exempting children from criminal liability is the belief that very young children lack the necessary criminal intent or *mens rea* to commit a crime.[136] The key issue is whether a child can distinguish right from wrong.[137] Similarly, the law recognizes the inability to distinguish right from wrong as an element of an insanity plea.[138] Society has concluded that it is simply wrong to punish a person, adult or child, who is incapable of understanding the consequences of his or her actions.

A second issue of substantive juvenile justice is the punishment a child should receive if convicted. The early practice was to treat a child over seven as an adult and apply the same penalty. As one legal scholar has noted:

> It was probably not until the time of Spigurnel, Edward II's judge, that it became the practice to ask whether the child could tell good from evil, and children of seven—the crucial age in Roman law—*were in danger of being hanged or burned.*[139] [Emphasis added.]

In the American colonies, 14 generally was the age at which a person could be sentenced to death.[140] In this century, the youngest person executed was 13 in 1927 by the state of Florida.[141]

Under American law today, the punishment of a child is tied to age and the nature of the offense. For certain crimes, a child may be punished as an adult if he or she is certified as an adult. A recent trend has been to lower the age at which a person may be certified as an adult. For example, in 1994 Congress passed the Omnibus Anti-Crime Bill, which permits a child of 13 to be certified as an adult for such crimes as murder, robbery, and rape.[142] If certified as an adult, the child is subject to the same punishment an adult may receive. The exception is that in *Thompson* v. *Oklahoma*[143] the Supreme Court ruled that states may not execute someone under 16. The Court held that to do so violates the Cruel and Unusual Punishment Clause of the Eighth Amendment.

As we have seen, the treatment of juveniles under the law has undergone considerable change. The legal treatment of juveniles charged with a crime ebbs and flows with public opinion. In this sense juvenile justice mirrors society's attitudes about crime in general. Too much reliance on differential treatment of juveniles could result in a return to the pre-*Gault* era. That, in turn, could result in the situation best described by Justice Fortas in *Kent*:

> There is evidence, in fact, that there may be grounds for concern that the child receives the worst of both worlds: that he gets neither the protections accorded to adults nor the solicitous care and regenerative treatment postulated for children.[144]

TWO CASE STUDIES IN CRIMINAL LAW

In the introduction to this chapter, we noted the controversial nature of both substantive and procedural criminal law. In this section we will examine two Supreme Court cases that illustrate that controversy. The first case, *Rummel* v. *Estelle*,[145] deals with a question of substantive law—specifically, when does the punishment fit the crime? The second case, *Brewer* v. *Williams*,[146] raises the difficult question of protecting the constitutional rights of a factually guilty person.

Rummel v. Estelle.[147]   Texas, like many other states, had a habitual-offender statute which imposed a mandatory life sentence on anyone who was convicted of three felonies. In addition to having been convicted, the defendant must also have actually served time in prison for the first two convictions. In 1964, William Rummel was convicted of fraudulent use of a credit card in the amount of $80 and was sentenced to three years in the state prison. In 1969, he was convicted of passing a forged check for $28.36, for which he received four years in prison. In 1973, Rummel was convicted of receiving $120.75 by false pretenses. The total value of all three of Rummel's crimes was less than $230. At Rummel's 1973 trial, the prosecutor chose to proceed under the Texas habitual-offender statute, and Rummel received a life sentence. Rummel challenged the constitutionality of the life sentence on the grounds that it "was so disproportionate to the crimes he committed as to constitute cruel and unusual punishment."[148] The district court rejected Rummel's claim of cruel and unusual punishment, but a panel of the Fifth U.S. Court of Appeals reversed the district court judge. The case was reheard *en banc,* and the full Court of Appeals reversed the panel; that is, it upheld the original judgment of the district court against Rummel's claim. The U.S. Supreme Court, in a 5–4 decision, also ruled against Rummel.

Then Justice William Rehnquist authored the Court's majority opinion. Rehnquist began by noting that Rummel was not challenging the Texas recidivist statute per se. Rummel challenged the act only as it applied to him. Nor did Rummel challenge the fact that he could constitutionally have received sentences totaling 25 years for his three crimes. Rummel challenged only the State's ability to impose a life sentence in his particular case. Rummel based his challenge both on *Weems* v. *United States*,[149] in which the Supreme Court reversed the conviction of a Philippine official imprisoned at hard labor for 12 years for the crime of falsifying public records, and on some of the Court's previous decisions in death-penalty cases.[150] The Court rejected both in ruling against Rummel.

Justice Rehnquist noted the uniqueness of the *Weems* case. In addition to the lengthy sentence, Weems was chained at the ankle and wrist and forced to do hard labor for the 12 years. When viewed in its totality—the minor crime of falsifying public records and the harsh sentence—the Court in 1910 found no difficulty in ruling that the sentence was disproportionate to the crime. In Rummel's case, because of the State's liberal "good time" policy, he could be eligible for parole in 12 years. The Court also refused to apply its rationale in death-penalty cases to Rummel's situation. Justice Rehnquist noted that the irrevocability of the death sentence gave the death penalty a uniqueness that did not apply to Rummel.

Having stripped Rummel of his precedents, Justice Rehnquist proceeded to explain why the Eighth Amendment was not offended in this case. First, exercising judicial deference, he noted that the length of prison sentences is a legislative prerogative and that the determination of appropriate punishments for various crimes is too subjective for courts to decide. If Rummel's crimes had totalled $5,000 instead of a mere $230, would the life sentence be fairer? That, Justice Rehnquist said, is for a legislature, not the courts, to decide. Second, Rehnquist rejected Rummel's argument that the life sentence was excessive because his crimes were nonviolent. The presence or absence of violence has nothing to do with society's interest in deterring crime. Pollution, for example, is nonviolent, but society may impose harsh penalties to deter it. Third, Justice Rehnquist noted that Rummel was *not* being punished just for receiving $120.75 under false pretenses. As a habitual offender, Rummel had shown an inability to conform to the norms of society. Fourth, the penalty imposed by Texas, though severe, is not grossly out of line with recidivist statutes in other states. Finally, the fact that Rummel would be eligible for parole after serving 12 years indicated the unlikelihood of his remaining in prison for the rest of his life. These factors led the majority to conclude that the life sentence did not constitute cruel and unusual punishment.

Justice Lewis Powell, joined by three other justices, wrote a dissenting opinion in *Rummel.* Justice Powell disagreed with the majority's analysis on a number of points. First, in the death-penalty cases, the Court ruled that the death sentence is an excessive punishment for certain crimes, such as rape.[151] Powell saw no reason that the disproportionality analysis of death-penalty cases should not apply to noncapital cases since there is no basis for such a distinction in Eighth Amendment jurisprudence. Powell also believed that the Court's restriction of *Weems* to its unique facts was not warranted. The *Weems* Court emphasized the number of years Weems received for a minor offense as much as the conditions of hard labor imposed. Nor did Powell accept the notion that society's interest in deterring repeat offenders justified a mandatory life sentence for Rummel's crimes. Powell observed, "A statute that levied a mandatory life sentence for overtime parking might well deter vehicular lawlessness, but it would offend our felt sense of justice."[152] In other words, the fact that Rummel's sentence might meet a societal goal does not make it less offensive to the Eighth Amendment.

Powell attacked the majority's reasoning on another point: the seriousness of Rummel's crimes. It is hard to imagine crimes that pose less danger to the safety of society than Rummel's, Powell argued. Forged checks, misuse of credit cards, and receiving money under false pretenses are hardly on a par with rape and murder. Yet under Texas law, the maximum sentence on a rape conviction is 20 years and the minimum is two years. At the time, the same sentence applied to a person convicted of involuntary manslaughter. The only first-time offense subject to a mandatory life sentence is capital murder. Powell noted that even Texas admits that Rummel's third offense was not a serious crime since in 1980 the state reduced it to a misdemeanor.

Finally, Powell argued that the fact that Rummel might become eligible for parole after 12 years should not be a consideration. Prison inmates have no legal right to a parole. Powell noted that in 1979, Governor William Clements of Texas denied parole to 79 percent of the inmates recommended by the state's pardon and parole board.[153] Therefore, Powell argued, the question of the disproportionality of Rummel's sentence should be judged independently of any hypothetical chance of parole.

The *Rummel* case did not end the debate over the practice of imposing life sentences on habitual offenders. Just three years later, in *Solem* v. *Helm*,[154] the Court reviewed the imposition of a mandatory life sentence on a person convicted of seven felonies. Helm's offenses, like Rummel's, were nonviolent property crimes, with the last one being the writing of a $100 "no account" check. However, this time the Court reversed its previous position somewhat. This time, with Justice Powell writing for the majority, the Court ruled that the imposition of a life sentence with no chance of parole did violate the Eighth Amendment's prohibition against cruel and unusual punishment. Making many of the same arguments he used in *Rummel*, Justice Powell asserted that the Eighth Amendment does forbid excessive punishment in noncapital as well as capital cases. Powell also argued that objective criteria could be developed to guide courts in determining whether a given penalty was excessive. These criteria include the gravity of the offense versus the harshness of the penalty, whether sentences imposed on others for more serious crimes are less harsh, and whether sentences imposed for the commission of the same crime in other jurisdictions are less harsh.[155] Applying the criteria to Helm's case, the majority concluded that the life sentence he received was excessive for the crimes he had committed. In addition, Powell emphasized that in *Rummel* the prisoner had a possibility of parole after 12 years, whereas in *Helm* the sentence contained no chance of parole unless the governor commuted the sentence, a possibility the Court considered unlikely.

The *Rummel* and *Helm* cases raise some of the questions about the nature of substantive criminal law discussed earlier in the chapter. Individuals disagree over the appropriate punishment for habitual offenders. They also disagree, as did the justices of the Supreme Court, over what constitutes excessive or cruel and unusual punishment. It is because reasonable people disagree over the substance of criminal law that one must understand the political nature of the criminal justice system and, as discussed in Chapter 6, the lack of finality of constitutional questions. Suffice it to say that the debate over life sentences for habitual offenders is far from over.

Brewer v. Williams. On Christmas Eve in 1968, a 10-year-old girl named Pamela Powers disappeared while attending a wrestling match at a Des Moines, Iowa, YMCA. A teenager opened the door of the YMCA for Williams, who was carrying a large bundle wrapped in a blanket. When the teenager opened Williams's car door, he noticed two "white and skinny legs" protruding from the bundle. Williams immediately became a suspect in the abduction of Pamela Powers. Later, Williams's car was discovered in Davenport, 160 miles east of Des Moines. A warrant was issued for Williams's arrest.

On December 26, a Des Moines lawyer named Henry McKnight informed police that he had been contacted by Williams from Davenport and that he had advised Williams to turn himself in to the Davenport police, which Williams did. Upon his arrest, Williams was given the *Miranda* warnings. In the presence of the Des Moines chief of police and a police detective named Leaming, McKnight informed Williams over the telephone that two Des Moines detectives were coming to Davenport to return him to Des Moines. McKnight also told Williams that he was not to discuss Pamela Powers with the detectives during the return trip. Williams was arraigned in Davenport and again given the *Miranda* warnings. Kelly, a Davenport attorney, also advised Williams not to say anything until he spoke with McKnight in Des Moines. When Detective Leaming arrived, he again gave Williams the *Miranda* warnings. At one point, Kelly asked Leaming for permission to accompany Williams back to Des Moines but was informed that the police department had a "no passengers" rule.

On the trip back to Des Moines, Detective Leaming made what was later termed "the Christian burial speech." Under the guise of giving Williams "something to think about," Detective Leaming pointed out that the weather was becoming worse and that snow was predicted before the day was over. Leaming pointed out that if it snowed, it might be impossible for anyone, even Williams, to find Pamela's body and that her parents were at least entitled to give their daughter a Christian burial. Williams asked if the police had found the girl's shoes, and when Leaming replied that he was unsure, Williams directed them to a service station where he claimed to have left them. However, a search failed to turn up the shoes. Later Williams inquired about the blanket and directed the detectives to a rest area, but the blanket was not found. Finally, Williams led the detectives to the body of Pamela Powers. Williams was later indicted for first-degree murder, and his motion to suppress all evidence resulting from his statements to Leaming was denied. The trial judge ruled that Williams had waived his right to counsel and his protection against self-incrimination.

The Supreme Court, in a bitterly divided vote, ruled that Williams had not waived his right to counsel and that Detective Leaming's "Christian burial speech" was a form of interrogation forbidden by the Sixth Amendment without the presence of counsel. Justice Potter Stewart, writing for the majority, found that Detective Leaming deliberately set out to elicit incriminatory information from Williams. Leaming, after reading Williams the *Miranda* warnings, said to Williams, "We'll be visiting between here and Des Moines."[156] Although Leaming had been warned not to interrogate Williams, the "Christian burial speech" was designed to appeal to Williams's deep religious beliefs. Moreover, at Williams's trial, Leaming admitted that was his purpose. In response to a question, Leaming replied, "I was sure hoping to find out where that little girl was, yes, sir."[157] More important, the Court ruled, the State bears the burden of proving that a defendant has waived his right to counsel. Williams repeatedly told police that he would tell everything when they reached Des Moines. The Court interpreted that to mean that Williams did not intend to waive his right to counsel until he had a chance to speak with his lawyer, McKnight, in Des Moines. Finally, the fact that Williams had called McKnight in Des Moines and had secured Kelly's services in Davenport provided further proof of his reliance on the assistance of counsel. In light of these factors, Justice Stewart found that the State had failed to meet the burden of proving that Williams had intelligently waived his right to counsel.

In a concurring opinion, Justice Thurgood Marshall shed additional light on Leaming's actions. If, as indicated, Williams promised to tell the whole story back in Des Moines, why didn't the police just wait? If Williams were allowed to tell McKnight the location of the body, McKnight could then have told the police and Williams would not have been forced to incriminate himself directly—that is, by "directly demonstrating his knowledge of the body's location."[158] If finding Pamela Powers's body were truly the main objective, "this scenario would accomplish all that Leaming sought from his investigation except that it would not produce incriminating statements or actions from Williams."[159] In other words, eliciting incriminating statements from Williams, and not finding Pamela's body, was Leaming's real objective. Justice Marshall defended the majority's decision by noting, "The heinous nature of the crime is no excuse, as the dissenters would have it, for condoning knowing and intentional police transgression of the constitutional rights of a defendant."[160] Justice Marshall concluded his opinion by quoting Justice Louis Brandeis's dissent in *Olmstead* v. *United States:*

> In a government of laws, existence of the government will be imperilled if it fails to observe the law scrupulously. Our Government is the potent, the omnipresent teacher. For good or for ill, it teaches the whole people by example. Crime is contagious. If the Government becomes a lawbreaker, it breeds contempt for law; it invites every man to become a law unto himself; it invites anarchy. To declare that in the administration of the criminal law the end justifies

the means—to declare that the Government may commit crimes in order to se-cure the conviction of a private criminal—would bring terrible retribution. Against that pernicious doctrine this Court should resolutely set its face.[161]

Lawyers like to say that "hard cases make bad law"; *Brewer* v. *Williams* is undoubtedly a hard case, but whether it made bad law depends on one's perspective. The dissenters in *Williams* saw Leaming's actions as "good po-lice work," while the majority condemned them. There can be no doubt that Williams killed Pamela Powers, but it is important to remember that the Supreme Court does not deal with questions of guilt or innocence per se. The Court is interested in due process of law and in making sure that government obeys its own laws. Although that point may be difficult to understand and to accept, especially when an innocent little girl has been brutally murdered, it may be, to paraphrase Justice Oliver Wendell Holmes, Jr., that due process of law is the price we pay for civilization.

If the reader is still troubled by the decision in *Williams*, there is more to the story. The Supreme Court's decision did not mean that Williams was set free, but only that the State must retry him without using the incriminating evidence secured by Leaming's unlawful interrogation. In 1977, Williams was again tried for first-degree murder and was again found guilty. The prosecution introduced evidence concerning the condition of Pamela Pow-ers's body when it was found, and the defense sought to suppress it as the "fruit" of Leaming's illegal interrogation. The trial court ruled that searchers would have come upon the body eventually even without Williams's help and that it would have been essentially in the same condition. Therefore, the trial judge allowed the evidence. Williams again appealed his case to the Supreme Court, but in *Nix* v. *Williams*,[162] the Court ruled against him and upheld his conviction and life sentence.

These two case studies, *Rummel* v. *Estelle* and *Brewer* v. *Williams*, were included in this chapter to illustrate aspects of substantive and procedural criminal law. In a real sense, justice prevailed in both cases. Rummel was paroled just eight months after his appeal was denied by the Supreme Court,[163] and Williams was sentenced to life in prison. However, the ques-tions raised by the two cases are fundamental ones that may never be an-swered because they deal with our sense of justice and fairness. The debate over these issues will continue, for, as Yogi Berra aptly observed, "It ain't over till it's over."

CONCLUSION

As noted in this chapter's introduction, no topic in law is as controversial as criminal law. There is perhaps nothing that tells as much about a society as the way it treats those who are accused of crime. In a sense, then, crime is not only a social problem but a political one as well. In this chapter we have discussed both substantive and procedural criminal law. Substantive criminal law concerns what constitutes criminal behavior, what the elements of a crime are, and what punishment is appropriate for a given criminal act. Procedural criminal law concerns the "rules of the game" by which government must abide before it can deprive one of its citizens of life, liberty, or property. Both topics raise difficult questions that have elusive answers. Perhaps in the final analysis we must determine the answers individually. The one certainty is that the questions will not go away, and it is our hope that we have added to the reader's understanding of an enormously complex area of law.

NOTES

1. Chapter 1.

2. Thomas J. Gardner, *Criminal Law: Principles and Cases,* 4th ed. (St. Paul, Minn.: West Publishing Company, 1989), p. 180.

3. *Champion* v. *Ames,* 188 U.S. 321 (1903) quoted in Gerald Gunther, *Constitutional Law: Cases and Materials,* 10th ed. (Mineola, N.Y.: Foundation Press, 1980), p. 130.

4. Henry C. Black, *Black's Law Dictionary,* 4th ed. (St. Paul, Minn.: West Publishing Company, 1968), p. 55.

5. Ibid., p. 1481.

6. David W. Neubauer, *America's Courts and the Criminal Justice System,* 2nd ed. (Monterey, Calif.: Brooks/Cole, 1984), p. 64.

7. Gerald Gunther, *Constitutional Law,* 11th ed. (Mineola, N.Y.: Foundation Press, 1985), p. 1157.

8. Gardner, p. 12.

9. Ibid.

10. *Robinson* v. *California,* 370 U.S. 660 (1962).

11. *Powell* v. *Texas,* 392 U.S. 514 (1968).

12. Black, p. 1137.

13. David Eliot Brody, *The American Legal System: Concepts and Principles* (Lexington, Mass.: Heath, 1978), p. 290.

14. Gardner, p. 45.

15. *State* v. *Williamson,* 282 Md. 100, 382 A.2d 588 (1978).

16. Thomas J. Gardner, *Criminal Law Principles and Cases,* 4th ed. (St. Paul, Minn.: West Publishing Co., 1989), p. 80.

17. *Enmund* v. *Florida,* 458 U.S. 782 (1982) and *Tison* v. *Arizona,* 481 U.S. 137 (1987), at 158.

18. Justin Miller, *Handbook of Criminal Law* (St. Paul, Minn.: West Publishing Company, 1934), p. 239.

19. Jesse R. Pistole, *Criminal Law for Peace Officers* (Reston, Va.: Reston, 1976), p. 144.

20. *Standefer* v. *United States,* 447 U.S. 10 (1980).

21. Gardner, p. 77.

22. U.S. Constitution, Amendment IV.

23. *New Jersey* v. *T.L.O.,* 469 U.S. 325 (1985).

24. *Michigan Department of State Police* v. *Sitz*, 496 U.S. 444 (1990).

25. *Skinner* v. *Railway Labor Executives' Association*, 489 U.S. 602 (1989).

26. *Florida* v. *Bostick*, 501 U.S. 429 (1991).

27. *Warden* v. *Hayden*, 387 U.S. 294 (1967).

28. *Warden* v. *Hayden* quoted in Lloyd L. Weinreb, *Leading Constitutional Cases on Criminal Law* (Mineola, N.Y.: Foundation Press, 1981), p. 187.

29. *Weeks* v. *United States*, 232 U.S. 383 (1914).

30. Quoted in Robert F. Cushman, *Cases in Constitutional Law*, 6th ed. (Englewood Cliffs, N.J.: Prentice Hall, 1984), p. 321.

31. *Mapp* v. *Ohio*, 367 U.S. 643 (1961).

32. *Olmstead* v. *United States*, 277 U.S. 438 (1928), at 485 (Brandeis J., dissenting).

33. *Mapp* v. *Ohio* quoted in Cushman, 6th ed., p. 326.

34. *Rochin* v. *California*, 342 U.S. 165 (1952).

35. *Chimel* v. *California*, 395 U.S. 752 (1969).

36. John C. Klotter and Jacqueline R. Kanovitz, *Constitutional Law for Police*, 3rd ed. (Cincinnati: Anderson Publishing Company, 1977), p. 213.

37. Ibid.

38. *Terry* v. *Ohio*, 392 U.S. 1 (1968).

39. *Terry* v. *Ohio* quoted in Weinreb, p. 330.

40. *Carroll* v. *United States*, 267 U.S. 132 (1925).

41. *Chambers* v. *Maroney*, 399 U.S. 42 (1970).

42. *United States* v. *Robinson*, 414 U.S. 218 (1973).

43. *South Dakota* v. *Opperman*, 428 U.S. 364 (1976); *Cady* v. *Dombrowski*, 413 U.S. 433 (1973).

44. *Michigan Department of State Police* v. *Sitz*, 496 U.S. 444 (1990).

45. *Harris* v. *United States*, 331 U.S. 145 (1947).

46. Klotter and Kanovitz, p. 226.

47. Ibid., p. 227.

48. *Horton* v. *California*, 58 U.S.L.W. 4694 (1990).

49. *Olmstead* v. *United States*, 277 U.S. 438 (1928).

50. *Goldman* v. *United States*, 316 U.S. 129 (1942).

51. *Katz* v. *United States*, 389 U.S. 347 (1967).

52. *Mallory* v. *United States*, 354 U.S. 449 (1957).

53. *Escobedo* v. *Illinois*, 378 U.S. 478 (1964).

54. *Escobedo* v. *Illinois* quoted in Harold W. Chase and Craig R. Ducat, *Constitutional Interpretation: Cases, Essays, Materials*, 2nd ed. (St. Paul, Minn.: West Publishing Company, 1979), p. 945.

55. Ibid.

56. Ibid., pp. 945–946.

57. *Miranda* v. *Arizona*, 384 U.S. 436 (1966).

58. See Richard H. Seeburger and R. Stanton Wettick, Jr., "*Miranda* in Pittsburgh: A Statistical Study," *University of Pittsburgh Law Review*, Vol. 29 (Oct. 1967), pp. 1–26.

59. *Mathis* v. *United States*, 391 U.S. 1 (1968).

60. *Orozco* v. *Texas*, 394 U.S. 324 (1969).

61. *Beckwith* v. *United States*, 425 U.S. 341 (1976).

62. *Oregon* v. *Mathiason,* 429 U.S. 492 (1977).

63. *Estelle* v. *Smith,* 451 U.S. 454 (1981).

64. *Brewer* v. *Williams,* 430 U.S. 387 (1977).

65. *North Carolina* v. *Butler,* 441 U.S. 369 (1979).

66. *Rhode Island* v. *Innis,* 446 U.S. 291 (1980).

67. *New York* v. *Quarles,* 467 U.S. 649 (1984).

68. *Illinois* v. *Perkins,* 58 U.S.L.W. 4737 (1990).

69. *Twining* v. *New Jersey,* 211 U.S. 78 (1908).

70. *Adamson* v. *California,* 332 U.S. 46 (1947).

71. *Malloy* v. *Hogan,* 378 U.S. 1 (1964).

72. *Boyd* v. *United States,* 116 U.S. 616 (1886).

73. M. Glenn Abernathy, *Civil Liberties Under the Constitution,* 2nd ed. (New York: Dodd, Mead, 1972), p. 112.

74. See *Matter of Grand Jury Empanelled,* 597 F. 2d 851 (3rd. Cir., 1979) and *United States* v. *Payner,* 447 U.S. 727 (1980).

75. *Rochin* v. *California,* 342 U.S. 165 (1952).

76. *Breithaupt* v. *Abram,* 352 U.S. 432 (1957).

77. *Schmerber* v. *California,* 384 U.S. 757 (1966).

78. Klotter and Kanovitz, p. 353.

79. *United States* v. *Wade,* 388 U.S. 218 (1967).

80. *Sheppard* v. *Maxwell,* 384 U.S. 333 (1966).

81. Ibid., p. 362.

82. *Gannett Co.* v. *DePasquale,* 443 U.S. 368 (1979).

83. Quoted in Sheldon Goldman, *Constitutional Law and Supreme Court Decision Making: Cases and Essays* (New York: Harper & Row, Inc., 1982), p. 583.

84. Ibid.

85. *Richmond Newspapers Inc.* v. *Virginia,* 448 U.S. 555 (1980).

86. *Estes* v. *Texas,* 381 U.S. 532 (1965).

87. *Chandler* v. *Florida,* 449 U.S. 560 (1981).

88. John E. Conklin, *Criminology,* 2nd ed. (New York: Macmillan Publishing Company, 1986), pp. 380–456.

89. James A. Inciardi, *Criminal Justice,* 2nd ed. (San Diego: Harcourt Brace Jovanovich, 1987), pp. 629–632.

90. *Greenholtz* v. *Inmates of Nebraska Penal and Correctional Complex,* 422 U.S. 1 (1979).

91. Inciardi, pp. 646–659; see, for example, Tex. Code Crim. Proc. Art. 42.18(b).

92. *Ruffin* v. *Commonwealth,* 62 Va. (21 Gratt.) 790 (1871), at 796.

93. *Inmates of the Attica Correctional Facility* v. *Rockefeller,* 453 F.2d 12 (2d Cir. 1971).

94. Inciardi, p. 591.

95. *Holt* v. *Sarver,* 309 F. Supp. 362 (E.D. Ark. 1970), at 381, *aff'd* 442 F.2d 304 (8th Cir. 1971).

96. Ibid.

97. *Jordan* v. *Fitzharris,* 257 F. Supp. 674 (N.D. Cal. 1966), at 679.

98. For further study of prison conditions, see *Holt* v. *Sarver,* 300 F. Supp. 825 (1969) and 309 F. Supp. 362 (1970); Steve J. Martin and Sheldon Ekland-Olson, *Texas Prisons: The Walls Came Tumbling Down* (Austin, Tex.: Texas Monthly Press, Inc., 1987); Ben M. Crouch and James W. Marquart, *An Appeal to Justice: Litigated Reform of Texas Prisons*

(Austin, Tex.: University of Texas Press, 1989); and Roger Morris, *The Devil's Butcher Shop: The New Mexico Prison Uprising* (New York: F. Watts, 1983).

99. *Trop v. Dulles*, 356 U.S. 86 (1958), at 101.

100. *Turner v. Safley*, 482 U.S. 78 (1987), at 84.

101. *Cooper v. Pate*, 382 F.2d 518 (7th Cir. 1967).

102. *Banks v. Havener*, 234 F. Supp. 27 (E.D. Va. 1964).

103. *Taylor v. Sterrett*, 532 F.2d 462 (5th Cir. 1976), at 470.

104. *Adams v. Carlson*, 488 F.2d 619 (7th Cir. 1973), at 630.

105. *Johnson v. Avery*, 393 U.S. 483 (1969).

106. *Younger v. Gilmore*, 404 U.S. 15 (1971).

107. *Cruz v. Beto II*, 603 F.2d 1178 (5th Cir. 1969).

108. *Wolff v. McDonnell*, 418 U.S. 539 (1974); *Thornburgh v. Abbott*, 57 U.S.L.W. 4517 (1989).

109. *Jackson v. Bishop*, 404 F.2d 571 (8th Cir. 1968), at 579–580.

110. *Wolff v. McDonnell*, 418 U.S. 539 (1974).

111. *Baxter v. Palmigiano*, 425 U.S. 539 (1976).

112. *Furman v. Georgia*, 408 U.S. 238 (1972).

113. *Gregg v. Georgia*, 428 U.S. 153 (1976).

114. *Woodson v. North Carolina*, 428 U.S. 280 (1976).

115. *Coker v. Georgia*, 433 U.S. 583 (1977).

116. *Enmund v. Florida*, 458 U.S. 782 (1982).

117. *Tison v. Arizona*, 481 U.S. 137 (1987), at 158.

118. *Stanford v. Kentucky*, 57 U.S.L.W. 4973 (1989).

119. *Penry v. Lynaugh*, 57 U.S.L.W. 4958 (1989).

120. *Witherspoon v. Illinois*, 391 U.S. 510 (1968).

121. *Batson v. Kentucky*, 476 U.S. 79 (1986).

122. *McCleskey v. Kemp*, 481 U.S. 279 (1987).

123. Larry J. Siegel and Joseph J. Senna, *Juvenile Delinquency: Theory, Practice and Law*, 5th ed. (St. Paul: West Publishing Company, 1994), p. 443.

124. *In re Gault*, 387 U.S. 1 (1967) at 17.

125. *Kent v. United States*, 383 U.S. 541 (1966).

126. LaMar T. Empey and Mark C. Stafford, *American Delinquency: Its Meaning and Construction*, 3rd ed. (Belmont, Calif.: Wadsworth Publishing Company, 1991), p. 334.

127. *In re Gault*, at 21.

128. *In re Winship*, 397 U.S. 358 (1970).

129. *Breed v. Jones*, 421 U.S. 519 (1975).

130. *McKeiver v. Pennsylvania*, 402 U.S. 528 (1971).

131. *Schall v. Martin*, 467 U.S. 253 (1984).

132. Ibid., p. 259.

133. *New Jersey v. T.L.O.*, 469 U.S. 325 (1985).

134. Nigel Walker, *Crime and Insanity in England* (Edinburgh: Edinburgh University Press, 1968), p. 40.

135. Empey and Stafford, p. 50.

136. Frederick B. Sussman and Frederic S. Baum, *Law of Juvenile Delinquency*, 3rd ed., (Dobbs Ferry, N.Y.: Oceana Publications, 1968), p. 2.

137. In his Commentaries, William Blackstone asserts that a male under 14 was presumed to be physically incapable of rape and therefore exempt from prosecution. See William Blackstone, *Commentaries on the Laws of England: Of Public Wrongs* (Boston: Beacon Press, 1962), p. 238.

138. Walker, p. 40.

139. Ibid., p. 28.

140. Empey and Stafford, p. 50.

141. James A. Inciardi, *Criminal Justice*, 2nd ed. (New York: Harcourt, Brace Jovanovich, 1987), p. 707.

142. *Congressional Quarterly*, Vol. 52, No. 11 (March 19, 1994), p. 672 and Vol. 52, No. 34 (August 27, 1994), p. 2490.

143. *Thompson* v. *Oklahoma*, 487 U.S. 815 (1988).

144. *Kent* v. *United States*, at 556.

145. *Rummel* v. *Estelle*, 445 U.S. 263 (1980).

146. *Brewer* v. *Williams*, 430 U.S. 387 (1977).

147. Unless otherwise noted, all facts pertaining to the case are taken from the Supreme Court's written opinions.

148. *Rummel*, at 267.

149. *Weems* v. *United States*, 217 U.S. 349 (1910).

150. See *Furman* v. *Georgia*, 408 U.S. 238 (1972); *Gregg* v. *Georgia*, 428 U.S. 153 (1976); and *Coker* v. *Georgia*, 433 U.S. 584 (1977).

151. *Coker* v. *Georgia*, 433 U.S. 584 (1977).

152. *Rummel*, at 288.

153. Ibid., at 294.

154. *Solem* v. *Helm*, 463 U.S. 277 (1983).

155. Ibid., at 292.

156. *Brewer*, at 391.

157. Ibid., at 399.

158. *Brewer* v. *Williams*, 430 U.S. 387 (1977), at 408 (Marshall, J., concurring).

159. Ibid.

160. Ibid.

161. *Olmstead* v. *United States*, 277 U.S. 438 (1928), at 485.

162. *Nix* v. *Williams*, 104 S.Ct. 2501 (1984).

163. *Solem*, footnote 25 at 297.

8

Administrative Law

The twentieth century has seen a tremendous growth in the number and power of bureaucratic organizations in the United States. Despite the attempts of the Reagan and Bush administrations to deregulate the U.S. economy and to shift governmental power from the national government to the states, bureaucracies continue to flourish, seemingly immune from the forces that would weaken them. For better or worse, bureaucratic government is a political and legal fact of life. The growth of administrative government can be attributed primarily to two of its strongest features: expertise and efficiency.

As the U.S. economy became more complex, there developed a greater need for expertise in the management of our economic system. The victims of the abuse of unchecked economic power by the railroads and other monopolies turned to government for relief. The first federal regulatory agency, the Interstate Commerce Commission (ICC), was created by Congress in 1887 to regulate railroads and to protect farmers from unjust rates and other unfair practices. Similarly, when the labor movement became politically strong enough, workers demanded some form of government protection for the rights of workers. As a result, the National Labor Relations Board (NLRB) was created to regulate labor relations and to prevent such practices as blacklisting, yellow-dog contracts, lockouts, and union-busting. The Great Depression taught us how damaging the consequences of an unregulated economy can be. The realization developed that government must guarantee the existence of the free-enterprise system by regulating banks and the stock market to prevent the recurrence of conditions that led to the Depression. In each of these areas of economic activity—monopolies, labor relations, banking, and stocks—the issues had become so complex that experts were needed to regulate them effectively. These activities, as well as many others, require public administrators with sufficient expertise to handle the myriad of problems associated with each. Thus, Congress responded to the demands for more government regulation by establishing agencies staffed by experts who were better qualified to deal with the problems of a modern industrial society. Administrative expertise soon became the justification for leaving major policy decisions to those most familiar with the problems—the administrators themselves.

The need for administrative expertise was paramount due to another aspect of our society. As Lief Carter has noted, "We live surrounded by very dangerous things—elevators, cars, airplanes, industrial wastes and chemical products, and recombinant DNA."[1] As technology provided us with new products and inventions, it also provided new ways to injure and kill people. People understandably wanted guarantees that airplanes and elevators were safe to use. The private sector, concerned more with profits than with safety, could not be trusted to take the necessary steps to ensure safety. Hence, people again turned to government to guarantee the safety of dangerous products through regulation. Similarly, people wanted guarantees that their food was pure, their prescription drugs safe, their workplaces safe, and their environment clean. Once again government responded to these demands by calling upon public administrators who possessed the expertise to handle the problems of our modern society. In short, then, abuses and changes in our economy and technology led to increased demands for government action, which in turn resulted in the growth of administrative government based upon expertise.

A second feature of administrative government that has contributed to its growth is its efficiency. In a sense, efficiency is related to expertise because expertise increases a government agency's efficiency. However, efficiency has another dimension. Because of the growth of the welfare system in the United States, the government receives hundreds of thousands of applications for Social Security benefits, veterans' benefits, food stamps, Aid to Families with Dependent Children (AFDC) benefits, and workers' compensation claims each day. In addition, the government issues licenses, ranging from liquor licenses at the state level to licenses for nuclear power reactors at the national level. Each year, thousands of students apply for student loans from state-supported colleges and universities. Without highly trained personnel to process these claims and applications, the system would quickly break down. Thus, a bureaucracy must be created to handle the large numbers of applications as expertly and efficiently as possible.

What do the need for expertise and efficiency have to do with administrative law? One often hears of Mussolini's Italy that "at least the trains ran on time." This comment is normally used to illustrate a political system that has sacrificed other values such as freedom, justice, and human dignity for efficiency. While administrative expertise and efficiency are important, we must be careful that they do not outweigh other cherished values such as justice and fundamental fairness. Anglo-American law tends to view justice and fairness in terms of what is called "due process of law." Our Constitution guarantees that "no person shall be denied life, liberty, or property without due process of law."[2] But problems arise, as they often do, with constitutional guarantees. What is a property right? Does a person have a "right" to public employment? Food stamps? Welfare? How much "process" is "due"? How many rights is a person entitled to? What kind of hearing is required before welfare benefits can be terminated? These and other issues are questions of administrative law. Administrative law concerns itself with the prevention of arbitrary and capricious action at the hands of public administrators. It is concerned with the abuse of official power and the overstepping of official authority. It is also concerned with the rights of citizens in a modern welfare state. In the constitutional language of checks and balances, administrative law deals with how the political system checks the exercise of discretion by public administrators and balances the rights of citizens with the rights of government. Without an understanding of this fundamental aspect of administrative law, we may find ourselves in a bureaucratic state in which the trains run on time, but in which there is little emphasis on human dignity or fundamental fairness.

In this chapter we will examine several facets of administrative law. Specifically, we will examine the legal source of administrative law, some procedural aspects of administrative law, and the role of judicial review. Finally, we will take a closer look at one substantive area of administrative law: public employment. We begin with the legal source of administrative authority.

DELEGATION THEORY

As previously noted, bureaucratic growth has occurred because of the need for expertise and efficiency in handling the problems posed by an increasingly complex economic system, new technology, and the advent of the modern welfare state. Throughout most of American history, the federal bureaucracy was small for a very simple reason: The federal government did not do very much. The New Deal period, as we have seen, sparked increased demands for positive government action in the management of the economy. This resulted in public pressure to create agencies for the regulation of everything from nuclear energy to the safety of the workplace. In so doing, Congress has created what is often termed the "fourth branch of government."

The influence of bureaucratic government has become so pervasive that virtually no aspect of the average American's life is unaffected. In order to understand the role of the bureaucracy in our political system, we must first have an understanding of what is known as *delegation theory.*

Under the American Constitution, all sovereignty ultimately resides in the people. In drafting and ratifying the Constitution, the people of the United States have collectively vested their sovereignty in the hands of their government. In so doing, however, the American people created three distinct branches of the national government—legislative, executive, and judicial—allocating to each certain powers presumably to be exclusively exercised by each. As we learned in Chapter 6, this doctrine is known as separation of powers.

It was the decision of the people to vest the Congress with the lawmaking power. The people, through the Constitution, delegated to the Congress the power to make the laws of the nation on their behalf. Congress thus became the agent of the people, exercising only the powers that the people thought proper to give it. At common law there is a maxim, *Delegatus non protest delegare*—"a delegate cannot delegate." What this means in terms of constitutional law is that Congress may not redelegate the powers that have been delegated to it by the people. There are some very good reasons for adhering to this doctrine. Suppose Congress wished to relieve itself of the burden of deciding when a state of war exists between the United States and another nation. Could the Congress enact legislation authorizing the president to declare war? Certainly not, since such an act would be a clear violation of the Constitution. If the people had wanted the president to be the one to decide whether or not to go to war, they would have given the president that power in the Constitution. Instead, the people chose to let Congress make the decisions concerning war and peace. To allow such a law to stand would undermine the doctrine of separation of powers since, theoretically, Congress could transfer all of its power to the president, thus achieving a result that the people sought to avoid—the concentration of governmental power in the hands of a single individual.

Despite the theory that Congress may not redelegate powers delegated to it under the Constitution, the reality of the situation is that Congress is simply incapable of making the countless governmental decisions that must be made on a daily basis. Consequently, Congress has developed the practice of authorizing administrative agencies and executive officials to act on its behalf. Such authorization consists of allowing administrative agencies to "fill in the details" of a general law. Congress will enact legislation setting forth its policy goals in very broad language and allow an administrative agency to deal with specifics. For example, Congress has authorized the Federal Communications Commission (FCC) to regulate the broadcasting industry "in the public interest." The FCC, staffed by professionals familiar with the workings of the broadcasting industry, makes rules governing the licensing of stations as well as numerous other aspects of the industry. Acting as the agent of Congress, the FCC makes rules and regulations that are just as binding on broadcasters as if Congress itself had enacted them. Realistically, then, Congress must either delegate its lawmaking authority to administrative agencies or abandon altogether any attempt to regulate highly complex and technical industries.

If delegation is a political reality, how does our legal system get around the constitutional prohibition against delegation? It does so by simply maintaining the legal fiction that delegation does not occur. In modern constitutional law, the myth of nondelegation is circumvented by the assertion that the Constitution forbids only "excessive delegation." The Supreme Court has ruled that although some delegation is desirable and permissible under the Constitution, there is a line which may not be crossed in delegating power to administrative agencies. Once the line is crossed, delegation is termed "excessive," in violation of the constitutional doctrine of separation of powers. Unfortunately, the line to be crossed is not always a bright one, and Congress can never be sure when it has crossed it.

The Supreme Court, in determining issues of excessive delegation, decides when the line has been crossed on a case-by-case basis. In the 1930s, for example, the Supreme Court ruled in a series of cases[3] that Congress had crossed the line in delegating excessive legislative authority to either the president or his subordinates. In still other cases, the Court has upheld very broad delegations of legislative power to the very same individuals. In the final analysis, the Court's approach to excessive delegation is similar to that of Justice Potter Stewart's view of obscenity—that is, the Court "knows it [excessive delegation] when it sees it."

In the performance of its duties as an agent of Congress, an administrative agency is primarily bound by two legal authorities. First, administrative agencies are subject to the same constitutional restraints as the general government. That is, anything the Congress or the president is forbidden to do, an administrative agency is also forbidden to do. Just as the Congress may not force people to attend church, neither may a government welfare agency require church attendance as a condition for receiving welfare. Similarly, if the national government is forbidden to deny any person of "life, liberty, or property without due process of law," neither may a government agency deny due process. As we will learn later, much controversy in administrative law centers around how much process is due.

A second constraint on administrative agencies is their authorization statute, which is the law that creates and empowers an administrative agency. Although some state administrative agencies are provided for in their state's constitution, federal administrative agencies are the creations of Congress. It is Congress that determines the structure, personnel, and powers of all administrative agencies and executive departments of the federal government. Consequently, an administrative agency may exercise only those powers given to it by Congress. When an agency attempts to exercise powers beyond its statutory authorization, it is said to be acting *ultra vires.* If an agency is allegedly acting *ultra vires,* those wishing to challenge the agency's action may seek judicial review. The court will be asked to decide whether the agency is acting within the limits of its legislative authority. The legislative authority is often vague, resulting in a judicial interpretation which attempts to ascertain the "intent of Congress." Should a court wrongly interpret the intent of Congress, the lawmakers can simply amend the authorization statute in such a way as to clarify their intentions. Also, despite its dubious constitutionality, Congress has relied on legislative vetoes to ensure administrative adherence to its will. Ultimately, then, Congress possesses the authority to curb *ultra vires* actions of administrative agencies and incorrect judicial interpretations of congressional intent.

Delegation of power to administrative agencies takes three forms. As we have already noted, Congress may authorize an agency to promulgate rules and regulations on behalf of Congress by filling in the details of legislation. This is called *rule-making.* Second, Congress may authorize the employees of the agency to enforce the rules made by the agency. For example, Federal Aviation Administration (FAA) inspectors may make periodic safety checks to ensure that FAA safety regulations are being obeyed by the airlines. This is referred to as *rule enforcement.* Finally, disputes over the promulgation or enforcement of the agency's rules may necessitate *adjudication.* Adjudication may occur, for example, if an airline believes that it has been wrongly fined for violating FAA regulations. Each of the three types of delegation brings into play questions of administrative law. Therefore, let us examine each type separately to see just how each shapes administrative law.

Rule-making.   Modern administrative law accepts the practice of allowing Congress to delegate its rule-making authority in general and sweeping terms. The first regulatory agency, the Interstate Commerce Commission (ICC), was authorized to set "just and reasonable rates" for railroads, and the definition of "just and reasonable" was left to the ICC itself. Similarly, other agencies are allowed broad delegations of authority. The FCC may issue licenses to broadcasters if doing so is "in the public interest." The Occupational Safety and Health Administration (OSHA) may adopt rules that are "reasonably necessary to provide safe and healthful employment and places of employment." Finally, the Consumer Product Safety Commission (CPSC) may make rules "reasonably necessary to prevent or reduce risk of injury" to consumers. Literally thousands of rules are promulgated each year by the myriad of administrative agencies. In fact, the number of rules passed by administrative agencies each year far surpasses the number of laws enacted by Congress. As already noted, the rules thus promulgated are just as binding on citizens as if they had been passed by Congress itself.

Administrative law develops in the realm of rule-making in primarily two ways. First, reviewing courts must ascertain whether the agency has the authority to promulgate the rule in question. That is, was the agency acting *ultra vires* by promulgating a rule that it had no authority to issue? Recall our discussion of *Bob Jones University* v. *United States*[4] in Chapter 1. Bob Jones University argued that the IRS had no authority to promulgate Revenue Ruling 71–477 without specific authorization from Congress. Although the Supreme Court ruled that 71–477 was valid, *Bob Jones University* illustrates how the authority to issue a rule can be the basis for challenging that rule.

The second way in which administrative law develops in regard to rule-making centers around the procedures used to promulgate the rule. The question here is, Did the agency follow the statute's procedures for enacting administrative rules? The rules of administrative procedure require (1) that proposed rules be published in advance of their consideration, (2) that interested and affected parties be allowed to comment either orally or in writing on the proposed rule, and (3) that any decision on the rule be based on the findings of "the whole record." These procedural requirements seek to prevent agencies from arbitrarily passing rules without giving opponents of the rules a fair opportunity to be heard. There is a certain "process" which is "due," and it is for the courts to determine whether the procedural rules were followed. It is not only important that the rules themselves be fair, but also that the rules be enacted in a fair manner.

In order to facilitate what is known as informal rule-making, Congress passed the Negotiated Rule-Making Act of 1990.[5] The purpose of the act is to encourage the promulgation of new rules through negotiation and consensus rather than in an adversarial setting. The act allows the head of an agency to create a negotiated rule-making committee composed of agency employees and representatives of interested parties. This committee

> shall consider the matter proposed by the agency for consideration and shall attempt to reach a consensus concerning a proposed rule with respect to such matter and any other matter the committee determines is relevant to the proposed rule.[6]

For example, if an agency proposes a new rule for automobile safety, the negotiated rule-making committee might be composed of industry representatives, labor union representatives, and consumer group representatives in addition to agency employees. Congress reasoned that if the interested parties could arrive at a consensus on a proposed rule, the persons or industries affected would be less likely to challenge the new rule in court.[7] Finally, the negotiated rule-making committee is experimental and will expire under federal sunset rules on November 29, 1996, unless renewed by Congress.[8]

Rule enforcement. A second way in which administrative agencies exercise authority delegated by Congress is through rule enforcement. Once an administrative agency has promulgated rules that deal with the substantive area within the agency's jurisdiction (for example, aviation, food and drugs, broadcasting), the agency may promulgate rules for the enforcement of its substantive rules. For example, OSHA has established regulations designed to ensure the safety of the workplace. OSHA has also established rules of procedures governing the inspection of factories and other workplaces to ensure compliance with its regulations. Failure to comply with OSHA regulations can result in civil penalties for the company involved. Thus, the agency responsible for issuing the original regulations is also responsible for the enforcement of those regulations. The procedures used in the enforcement of agency regulations are concerns of administrative law. As we have noted in relation to rule-making, procedures employed in rule enforcement must be within the agency's power to enact; otherwise the agency is proceeding *ultra vires*. In addition, the agency's procedures may not violate the Constitution.

Administrative enforcement may take a variety of forms.[9] Some regulatory agencies require their regulatees to keep records for inspection. The FAA, for example, requires airlines to keep maintenance records of their airplanes. The Equal Employment Opportunity Commission (EEOC) requires certain industries to keep employment records for the enforcement of job discrimination laws. Finally, the IRS requires individuals to keep records of income. Physical inspections constitute another type of administrative enforcement. As previously noted, OSHA inspectors may conduct physical inspections for safety violations, and the Mine Safety and Health Administration (MSHA) inspects mines to ensure safety. At the local level, public health officials may inspect dwellings for potential health hazards, fire inspectors may inspect for fire hazards, and welfare workers may investigate the home environment of welfare recipients. Finally, even such individuals as airline passengers are required to submit to X-ray and metal detector searches.

Rule enforcement by administrative agencies tends to raise the same kinds of constitutional questions common to other fields of law enforcement. In terms of mandatory record keeping, the question of self-incrimination can be raised. That is, does a law that requires a person or company to keep certain records allow them to be used as evidence in an administrative procedure? Suppose, for example, that an airline's maintenance record revealed that the airline was in violation of FAA regulations. Can the maintenance records be used to assess a fine against the airline? Suppose the IRS required persons engaged in illegal gambling to report the earnings from their illegal occupation. Would such persons, by paying the tax, be incriminating themselves by admitting their participation in an illegal activity?

The Supreme Court has ruled that administrative agencies may require record keeping under certain conditions. First, the records must be "of a kind customarily kept." Second, the records must be reasonably related to a public concern. Third, the records must pertain to a noncriminal area of activity. Thus, in the case of the airlines, because maintenance records are routinely kept, air safety is a public concern, and the records pertain to a noncriminal activity, the airline's maintenance records may be used to uncover violations of FAA regulations.[10] In the case of the gambler, however, the Supreme Court ruled in *Marchetti* v. *United States*[11] that the IRS requirement violates the Fifth Amendment's prohibition against mandatory self-incrimination. Marchetti was being forced to choose between reporting the gambling income, thereby subjecting himself to prosecution for state gambling violations, or not reporting the income, thereby subjecting himself to charges of federal income tax evasion. The Constitution, the Court ruled, forbids forcing a person to make such a Draconian choice.

The Fourth Amendment's prohibition against unreasonable searches and seizures is another area of special relevance to administrative enforcement. In regular law enforcement, searches require a search warrant issued by a magistrate upon probable cause. The search warrant must describe the places to be searched and the persons or things to be seized. Not all searches require search warrants, however. The Supreme Court has upheld numerous exceptions to the warrant requirement (warrantless searches) when it was shown that a particular search was not "unreasonable" within the meaning of the Fourth Amendment.

There are a number of problems associated with warrantless searches in administrative enforcement. First, it is almost impossible for an administrative agency to meet the probable-cause standard required for search warrants. When OSHA agents go out to check factories for safety violations, they almost never have probable cause to believe that a particular factory is in violation of OSHA rules. Similarly, when fire marshals inspect neighborhoods for fire hazards, they have no way of knowing which individual residences may constitute a fire hazard. Second, unlike other forms of law enforcement, administrative searches do not always have as their objective the detection of a "crime." OSHA agents and fire marshals are more concerned about correcting a dangerous situation than about punishing the offender. While it is true that civil and even criminal liabilities are possible, administrative enforcement of the type we are discussing is meant to be preventive and corrective rather than punitive. Finally, administrative enforcement often involves issues of public safety. Public health inspections and FAA inspections of airplanes are two notable examples. Because of the grave danger to the public posed by unsafe airplanes and unchecked health hazards, warrantless searches may be "reasonable" even if they do not meet the strict probable-cause standards necessary for the issuance of a search warrant.

The Supreme Court's solution to warrantless administrative searches has been to take a middle-ground approach. The Court recognizes that requiring administrative agencies to meet the probable-cause standard required in criminal cases would defeat the purposes of administrative enforcement.

However, the Court has also been aware of the need to protect the privacy rights of businesspeople and individuals. Consequently, the Court's middle-ground approach is to uphold, at least initially, the individual's right to privacy. That is, when a person is first asked to submit her home or business to a warrantless search, permission may be denied. After a refusal, however, administrative officials may seek a search warrant from a court without meeting the probable-cause standard. If the agency can show that a particular dwelling or business is being searched as part of an overall administrative plan to enforce the agency's regulations, then a search warrant may be issued without probable cause.[12] The practical effect of this approach is that the individual might merely delay a search until a warrant has been secured. The Court has ruled that concern over public health and safety outweighs any absolute right of privacy of an individual.

A final area of Fourth Amendment rights that has been somewhat controversial involves mandatory home visits in welfare cases. *Wyman* v. *James*[13] illustrates the problem. New York state law required welfare recipients to allow welfare workers to conduct home visits in order to determine the recipient's continuing eligibility. Barbara James, a welfare mother receiving AFDC, refused to allow such visits on Fourth Amendment grounds. Ms. James agreed to provide any information the welfare agency requested but refused to allow the home visit. The Supreme Court, in ruling against Ms. James, found that the home-visit requirement was not "unreasonable" within the meaning of the Fourth Amendment. According to the Court, the purpose of the AFDC program is to ensure that the children of welfare recipients are receiving adequate care, and assessment of the home environment is crucial to that end. The purpose of the visit was not to detect welfare fraud, since the welfare worker was not a law enforcement officer and the visits were announced in advance. Despite the finding of reasonableness, critics of the *Wyman* decision claim that it is just another example of discrimination against welfare recipients.

The problems with administrative enforcement point to a continuing concern of students of administrative government. As more agencies—state, local, and national—are created, there is an increasing number of "faceless bureaucrats" with authority over our lives and happiness. The delicate balance between the rights of individuals and the rights of society is a constant concern of courts responsible for curbing overzealous administrative enforcement.

Administrative adjudication.   The final type of delegation takes the form of what has been termed the "quasi-judicial" function of administrative agencies. In the normal course of an agency's duties, disputes will arise over the application of agency rules to a particular individual. For example, welfare laws and agency rules set forth the criteria for welfare eligibility. When an individual applies for welfare, agency personnel must make an initial determination of the person's eligibility based upon the agency's guidelines. Suppose that the person is denied benefits and wishes to appeal the denial. The agency usually has a procedure specifying the steps to be followed in appealing a denial of benefits, and the aggrieved person will be required to follow the procedure. This constitutes an adjudicatory procedure. Or, suppose a person who has already been receiving welfare benefits is informed that he is no longer eligible. If he appeals the loss of benefits, that too is an adjudicatory procedure. Similarly, a loss or denial of a license, loss of public employment, or even a denial of a passport can lead to an adjudicatory procedure.

As in other areas of administrative law, the main thrust of administrative adjudication is the prevention of arbitrary and capricious action at the hands of an administrative agency. Many people believe that they have been the victim of an unfair and arbitrary decision made by someone in authority over them. Administrative law seeks to reduce the risk of arbitrary decisions by requiring administrative agencies to observe fair rules of procedure in settling disputes that arise under their jurisdiction. In recent years, administrative law has seen what has been termed a "due process explosion." With increasing frequency, individuals who once meekly accepted the adverse actions of administrative agencies are demanding and receiving hearings on their complaints. Administrators who were once able to make decisions without fear of being questioned now find that their decisions are, in poker parlance, being "called" more frequently. While some observers applaud this more aggressive assertion of rights, others fear that too much emphasis on adjudication will bog down administrative agencies, leaving them unable to perform their functions adequately.

Administrative adjudications run the gamut from a simple disciplinary action in school to the dismissal of a public employee. The range of formality in adjudication also spans a wide range. At the informal end there is the unilateral decision of a person in authority; the more formal process involves adjudication by an administrative law judge. In this section, we will focus on the more formal aspects of adjudication in order to ascertain how administrative law is brought to bear on this "quasi-judicial" function.

One of the leading cases in administrative adjudication is *Goldberg* v. *Kelly*.[14] Kelly, a New York welfare recipient, was notified that her benefits were being terminated. Although several New York welfare administrators reviewed Kelly's eligibility before her benefits were actually terminated, Kelly was given no opportunity to present her side of the issue until *after* her benefits were terminated. At that point Kelly was entitled to a posttermination evidentiary hearing. If she prevailed at the posttermination hearing, her benefits would be restored and she would receive back payments. Pending the hearing, however, Kelly's benefits were cut off and she was practically destitute. Kelly argued that she should be granted a hearing before the termination of benefits, and the Supreme Court agreed. In the process of deciding the case, the Court outlined the "Goldberg ingredients" essential for due process of law.

Justice William Brennan, author of the *Goldberg* decision, outlined ten "ingredients" required to meet the minimum standard of due process of law in an administrative procedure.[15] The first *Goldberg* ingredient is (1) *adequate and timely notice.* A person subject to an agency action must be given notice of a change in status. For example, if an agency is preparing to terminate a benefit or suspend a license, the person affected (called the "person aggrieved") has a right to be informed in advance of the nature of the adverse action. Two related *Goldberg* ingredients are (2) the *right to confront adverse witnesses* and (3) the *right to cross-examine adverse witnesses.* Suppose a liquor retailer has been notified that her license is being suspended for selling liquor to a minor. The retailer has a right to confront the witnesses against her and to cross-examine them concerning their testimony.

The next two *Goldberg* ingredients are also related. The person aggrieved has (4) the *right to present arguments orally* and (5) the *right to present evidence orally.* Under the American system of law, persons aggrieved are not required to stand silently before their accusers. They have the right to present orally any relevant arguments or evidence in their favor. This ensures that those who are entitled to a "hearing" do indeed enjoy the right to be "heard."

(6) *Disclosure of opposing evidence* is the next *Goldberg* ingredient. In Chapter 4, a process called *discovery* was introduced. Discovery is the process whereby each party "discovers" the evidence upon which the other party plans to rely in presenting a case. In an administrative procedure, the person aggrieved has the right to know what evidence the agency is using to make its decision. For example, a person faced with the loss of welfare benefits has the right to see the evidence upon which the agency is basing its decision to terminate benefits. Disclosure of opposing evidence places the person aggrieved in a better position to present his or her case to the agency.

The next *Goldberg* ingredient is (7) the *right to retain an attorney.* Although administrative adjudications are not criminal in nature, the loss of a privilege or benefit can cause the person affected a great deal of emotional and financial hardship. Therefore, the person aggrieved has the right to have an attorney present to assist in the presentation of his or her case.

The last three *Goldberg* ingredients are (8) the *right to an impartial decision maker,* (9) a *determination on the record,* and (10) an *explanation of the decision.* The requirement of an impartial decision maker may seem self-evident. However, public administrators, like other humans, may prejudge a case or have a conflict of interest. An administrator is guilty of prejudgment if her mind appears to be made up even before the evidence is presented. Conflict of interest means that an administrator has a personal stake in the outcome of a case. Determination on the record is designed to ensure that no extraneous or impermissible evidence is used to make the decision. In criminal cases, for example, lawyers are often concerned that pretrial publicity in a sensational case will influence prospective jurors. That is, lawyers do not want prospective jurors to be influenced by newspaper or television reports containing evidence that is inadmissible in court. Newspapers may report hearsay evidence which is inadmissible at trial. Determination on the record seeks to ensure that only relevant, permissible evidence forms the basis for the decision.

Finally, the person aggrieved is entitled to a written explanation of the reasons for an adverse decision, the evidence upon which the decision was based, and the reason that other evidence was not relied upon by the decision maker. Basically, this ingredient serves to inform the person aggrieved why he or she lost. The written explanation can serve as the basis of further administrative appeal or even judicial review by an appellate court.

A cautionary note is in order here. The ten *Goldberg* ingredients represent an "ideal" model of administrative due process. A person aggrieved by an administrative agency may find all or none of the *Goldberg* ingredients in place. How is this possible? Lief Carter provides an answer, writing that "the bureaucratic world hardly marches in lockstep with the occasional pronouncements of the Supreme Court."[16] In other words, an administrative agency may continue on its merry way, adjudicating disputes as it has always done, totally oblivious to Supreme Court rulings. Even though *Goldberg* v. *Kelly* serves as a precedent for future cases, if an agency's procedures go unchallenged, the agency may never have to adopt the *Goldberg* ingredients for its own procedures. This situation serves to remind us that the law is an evolutionary process that sometimes proceeds at an excruciatingly slow pace.

JUDICIAL REVIEW AND ADMINISTRATIVE LAW

In Chapter 6, judicial review was defined as the power of a court to review the actions of other governmental bodies in order to determine whether or not those actions are consistent with the Constitution. The actions of administrative agencies are, of course, included among those subject to judicial review. However, judicial review of administrative agencies poses problems for courts that may not be present in other areas of the law. First, administrative agencies are highly specialized bodies with highly specialized personnel. Members of the Nuclear Regulatory Commission (NRC), for example, are experts in a highly technical field. It would be presumptuous for a judge to try to second guess the NRC's decisions about nuclear power. Similarly, most judges are not in a position to question the expert judgment of the FAA or the FCC. Second, as noted in the introduction to this chapter, some government agencies process hundreds of thousands of applications for all kinds of government benefits and programs. Excessive judicial meddling into the operations of an agency may paralyze it and undermine its efficiency. In *Goldberg* v. *Kelly*, for example, the Supreme Court ruled that Kelly must receive an evidentiary hearing prior to the termination of her benefits instead of after termination, as had previously been the welfare agency's practice. Although at first glance it might not seem to make any difference whether the hearing preceded or followed the termination of benefits, consider the possible consequences. If someone is receiving benefits to which he is not entitled, the benefits must continue to be paid until after a hearing is held. If every ineligible recipient chooses to exercise the right to a hearing, it might tax the ability of the welfare agency to conduct timely hearings, resulting in long delays. Meanwhile, recipients who may eventually prove to be ineligible for benefits continue to receive, at the taxpayers' expense, benefits to which they are not entitled. Consequently, the number of termination hearings increases for agency employees, and the government continues to pay benefits to ineligible recipients.

Despite the problems associated with judicial review of administrative agencies, supporters of judicial review in administrative law argue in favor of it. First, supporters argue that public administrators are just as susceptible to abuse of discretion as any other public official. Indeed, because most administrators are not elected, the potential for abuse of discretion may be even greater. The courts should serve as checks on public administrators to guard against arbitrary and capricious actions. Second, supporters of judicial review argue that an administrative agency is frequently "captured" by the agency's clientele group. Capture occurs when an agency begins to place the interests of the regulated industry above the public interest. Critics of the now defunct Civil Aeronautics Board (CAB) complained that airfares were set more to guarantee the airlines a profit than to keep the consumer's traveling costs down. In light of such charges, supporters of judicial review argue that judicial intervention may be necessary to protect the public interest. Finally, supporters of judicial review argue that bureaucrats tend to see problems from a narrow perspective, while judges tend to see the "big picture." In *Goldberg,* for example, Justice Brennan's opinion tended to stress the bigger picture of the role of welfare in our society, whereas a welfare worker might see only that the decision will increase the number of termination hearings for the agency. In the rest of this section we will examine some of the limits of judicial review in administrative law.

Preclusion of judicial review.   There are some areas in which the courts are precluded from reviewing the decisions of administrative agencies. Congress, for whatever reasons, has chosen to take the review of some administrative decisions out of the jurisdiction of the courts. One such area is veterans' benefits. Consider the preclusion language of this statute concerning veterans' benefits:

> [t]he decisions of the Administrator [of Veterans' Affairs] on any question of law or fact concerning veterans' benefits or payments under any law administered by the Veterans' Administration shall be final and conclusive and no other

official or any court of the United States shall have power or jurisdiction to review any such decision.[17]

This section of the statute clearly precludes judicial review of a *denial* of veterans' benefits. However, in *Wellman v. Whittier*[18] and several other cases, appellate courts held that although courts were precluded from reviewing denials of claims, the statute did not preclude judicial review of the *termination* of claims. In other words, a person denied veterans' benefits could not seek judicial review, whereas a person already receiving benefits could appeal a decision to terminate benefits.

As a general rule, a determined Supreme Court can find a way to get around most preclusion language. The Court is able to do this because, as we discussed in Chapter 6, it is the final arbiter of the meaning of the Constitution. For example, Congress amended the above statute on veterans' benefits:

[t]o make it perfectly clear that the Congress intends to exclude from judicial review all determinations with respect to noncontractual benefits provided for veterans and their dependents and survivors.[19]

In *Johnson v. Robison*,[20] however, Johnson was a conscientious objector who performed alternate service in lieu of his military obligation. Johnson sought veterans' education benefits but was denied under a law passed by Congress. Johnson challenged the denial of benefits on First Amendment and equal protection grounds, and the Supreme Court agreed to hear the case. Since Johnson was challenging the *statute* which denied benefits to all conscientious objectors and not the *decision* of the VA administrator, the Court said that it was not precluded from exercising judicial review. The Court ultimately ruled against Johnson's claim for benefits, but at least it agreed to hear the case on the merits. *Johnson* makes clear that no statutory language can preclude judicial review of an administrative decision when a constitutional right or issue is at stake.

Judicial restraint. Although courts can and do intervene in the administrative process, they are often reluctant to do so and tend to show great deference to administrative expertise when intervention is necessary. Courts have traditionally practiced judicial restraint when exercising the power of judicial review. Requirements of standing, ripeness, and mootness (as discussed in Chapter 5) are just a few of the methods used by courts to avoid the use of their judicial power. In addition to these traditional methods, courts have adopted several other procedural devices to prevent premature judicial intervention into the administrative process. The first of these is the *exhaustion of administrative remedies doctrine*. Courts prefer that formal litigation be looked upon only as a last resort for settling disputes. Consequently, courts insist that a person avail himself of all administrative remedies before seeking judicial ones. For example, a person who has had a license revoked must follow the agency's procedure for appealing the revocation before initiating a lawsuit against agency officials. Similarly, a student who has received an unsatisfactory grade must exhaust all university appeals before turning to a court for relief. Courts feel that the individual agency is better equipped to handle these disputes and that judicial intervention should be limited to those few cases that cannot be resolved at the agency level.

A doctrine related to exhaustion of remedies is the ***primary jurisdiction doctrine.*** Primary jurisdiction holds that litigants should take their disputes to the agency that has primary responsibility for the dispute rather than to a court of law. In *Texas Pacific Railway Co.* v. *Abilene Cotton Oil Co.*,[21] for example, the cotton oil company sued the railroad to recover $1,951.83 in unreasonable overcharges. Even though the Interstate Commerce Act specifically permitted the company either to file a complaint with the ICC or to file a suit in a federal district court, the Supreme Court ruled that the ICC had primary jurisdiction and that the cotton oil company should have filed its complaint with the ICC first. The Court believed that uniformity and fairness could best be achieved by allowing the ICC to make the initial decisions about the reasonableness of rates.[22]

The difference between primary jurisdiction and exhaustion of administrative remedies is subtle but important. Primary jurisdiction requires a party with a dispute that falls within an agency's jurisdiction to go to the agency before taking the dispute to court. Exhaustion of administrative remedies states that a party already subject to the jurisdiction of a governmental agency must give the agency an opportunity to resolve the dispute before taking it to court.

One final way that courts practice judicial restraint is by observing the ***substantial evidence rule.*** This rule states that conclusions of fact, if supported by substantial evidence based on the whole record, are to be regarded as final. In other words, an agency's finding of fact is considered final if there is substantial evidence to support it. In *Consolidated Edison* v. *National Labor Relations Board*,[23] the Supreme Court stated that substantial evidence "... means such relevant evidence as a reasonable mind might accept as adequate to support a conclusion."[24] In other words, if there is any plausible evidence to support an agency's conclusion of fact, the court has a duty to defer to the judgment of the agency.

A recent Supreme Court decision, *Sullivan* v. *Zebley*,[25] might indicate a shift away from judicial deference to agencies. In a 7–2 ruling, the Court held that the Social Security Administration had interpreted the intent of Congress too narrowly in the former's administration of Supplemental Security Income benefits to disabled children.[26] While it is too early to say whether further limits on administrative discretion are forthcoming, *Zebley* at least illustrates a greater willingness on the part of the Court to review more closely the decisions of administrative agencies.

Judicial review of the actions of administrative agencies is still relatively new compared with other areas of the law. It should be recalled that the modern administrative state is a fairly recent development in the United States, so it is not surprising that many areas of administrative law are as yet undeveloped. In the next section we will focus on one particular area of administrative law—the law of public employment—to illustrate some of the features we have discussed thus far.

THE LAW OF PUBLIC EMPLOYMENT

Throughout most of the nineteenth century, public employment in the federal government was based upon the so-called *spoils system.* The spoils system was an outgrowth of democratic theory, which held that any reasonably intelligent person could perform satisfactorily in most government jobs. Therefore, after each election, the winning candidate would remove the former officeholder's appointees from their jobs and replace them with his own supporters. Since most government jobs were clerical to begin with, it was not necessary to have highly skilled people in most positions. The winning candidate used these jobs—called patronage jobs—to reward his supporters for their help in winning public office. Thus the saying "To the victor go the spoils" was applied to political campaigns as well as military ones.

American presidents, although the chief beneficiaries of the spoils system, found the task of filling patronage positions tedious. Supporters tended to exaggerate their importance in helping the president win office. President William Howard Taft once remarked that every patronage appointment created "nine enemies and one ingrate." When President James A. Garfield was assassinated in 1881 by a disgruntled office-seeker, public opinion turned against the spoils system. In 1883, Congress enacted the Pendleton Act, which created the first civil service positions in the United States. Since the passage of the Pendleton Act, more and more government jobs have been added to the list of civil service positions, until today all but a few thousand of the 2.8 million federal jobs are civil service. Civil service jobs are characterized by merit selection, tests for promotion, and job security. Under civil service, public employees are chosen on the basis of merit, not party affiliation, and do not have to worry about losing their jobs after each election.

The initial approach to the rights of public employees was basically that they had none. As Justice Oliver Wendell Holmes, Jr., remarked in *McAuliffe* v. *Mayor of New Bedford,* "The petitioner may have a constitutional right to talk politics, but he has no constitutional right to be a policeman."[27] Holmes went on to say that all employees agree to forfeit some of their rights as a condition of their employment, and public employees were no exception to that rule. However, public attitudes about the rights of public employees have changed since Holmes's day, and there is greater recognition of their rights. For example, the Supreme Court ruled in 1987 that a deputy constable in Houston, Texas, could not be fired from her job for comments she made following the assassination attempt on the life of President Ronald Reagan in March 1981. Ardith McPherson stated to a coworker, "If they go for him again, I hope they get him." The Court held that however ill-considered the remark might be, it was protected speech within the First Amendment.[28] In the rest of this section we will examine several constitutional questions associated with the rights of public employees. The reader is cautioned to remember that we are discussing *public* employment and that many of the restrictions that apply to public employees do not apply to persons employed in the private sector.

The right to public employment.   One problem associated with public employment centers around the right/privilege distinction. That is, is public employment a right which cannot be denied without due process of law, or is it a privilege granted or withheld at the pleasure of the government? The answer, as is often the case in law, is somewhere in between. While it is still true that no one has an affirmative right to a government job, it is also true that certain rights can accrue *after* one has been hired by the government. It should not come as a surprise that many of the cases concerning public employment are ones surrounding the dismissal of public employees. In the language of due process, a public employee who is dismissed must assert and show either a property interest or a liberty interest. In other words, a public employee must show that her public job is her property which has been denied to her without due process or that her dismissal has infringed upon some liberty interest. To illustrate, let us examine some of the case law surrounding the rights of public employees, keeping in mind administrative law's special concern for questions of due process.

Board of Regents of State Colleges v. *Roth*[29] raised important questions of employees' rights. Roth was hired as an assistant professor of political science at Wisconsin State University–Oshkosh, under a one-year contract. Roth was on a "tenure track," which meant that after a probationary period—in this case, four years—he would receive tenure and be subject to dismissal only for cause. At the end of the academic year, however, he was informed that he would not be rehired. Roth filed suit against the University, alleging that his outspoken criticism of the University's administration was the real reason for his dismissal. Thus, Roth claimed that his right to freedom of speech had been abridged, constituting a denial of his "liberty" without due process of law. Second, Roth claimed that failure to afford him an opportunity for a hearing also violated due process.

The major issue before the Supreme Court was whether Roth was entitled to a hearing, and the Court ruled that he was not. In terms of his "liberty" claim, the Court noted that Roth had received no injury because he had no legal right to reemployment by the University. If Roth had been terminated during the term of the contract, he would have had a right to a hearing. But both Roth and the University upheld their ends of the contract for the specified one-year period. In addition, Roth was not precluded from seeking employment at another public university in Wisconsin. Finally, the Court ruled that Roth never proved that his dismissal was based on his free-speech activities. As for any "property" interest, the Court ruled that Roth had none. A property interest requires more than Roth's unilateral expectation of reemployment. Consequently, Roth was not entitled to a hearing when the University decided not to renew his contract.

On the same day that *Roth* came down, the Supreme Court decided *Perry* v. *Sindermann*.[30] Sindermann had taught at a community college in Odessa, Texas, for four years. Although the college had no formal tenure policy, the faculty handbook stated that an instructor should feel that he has "permanent tenure" as long as his work is satisfactory and "he is happy in his work."[31] Sindermann was terminated after he made a number of public statements that were highly critical of the college's Board of Regents. No official reasons for nonrenewal of his contract were given, and no hearing was held. Sindermann argued that the college's unofficial tenure policy vested him with a property right and entitled him to a hearing. The Supreme Court ruled that Sindermann must be given the opportunity to prove his claim to a property right. If Sindermann could prove that he had such a right, he was entitled to a hearing before being dismissed. The Court remanded the case to the lower court with orders that Sindermann be allowed to prove his claim to a property right. Sindermann ultimately prevailed, receiving a $48,000 judgment from the college in November 1972.[32]

A third case dealing with the right of public employment is *Bishop* v. *Wood*.[33] Bishop was a police officer on the Marion, North Carolina, police force. He began his employment in June 1969 and, after serving a six-month probation, became a permanent employee. He was dismissed by the city manager in March 1972 without a hearing. Bishop alleged that, as a permanent employee of the city, he was entitled to a hearing, that the grounds for his dismissal were false, and that his ability to seek future employment as a police officer was jeopardized by his illegal dismissal, thus abridging his liberty. The Supreme Court ruled against Bishop on all counts.

Bishop lost on the first issue, that of employment as a property right, on a technicality. Although the Supreme Court indicated that Bishop might have a legitimate claim, interpretations of North Carolina's public employment laws by state courts ran counter to Bishop's position, and the Supreme Court was obligated to abide by North Carolina's precedents. On the falsity of the grounds for his dismissal, the Court took the unsympathetic view that it was not their function to correct every personnel mistake made by public administrators. Finally, the Court ruled that he had no liberty claim. At most, Bishop could claim that his reputation had been damaged, reducing his chances of employment. But the Court noted that the charges against Bishop were not made public until he himself forced them to be made public during the pretrial discovery process. Consequently, any damage to his reputation as a result of the charges becoming publicly known was self-inflicted.

Finally, there is the question of freedom of association guaranteed by the First Amendment for public employees. As we have seen, under the spoils system it was accepted that the victorious party had the right to oust the other party's supporters from public jobs. Contemporary attitudes have altered this view and the Supreme Court has concurred. The Court has ruled that a public employee may not be dismissed from employment for partisan political reasons as long as the job is not a policy-making position.[34] In a recent expansion of public employees' rights, the Court held in *Rutan* v. *Republican Party of Illinois* that "Promotions, transfers, and recalls based on political affiliation or support are an impermissible infringement on public employees' First Amendment rights."[35] The case was brought by Cynthia Rutan, a rehabilitation counselor, who alleged she was repeatedly denied promotions because of her failure to support the Illinois Republican Party and Republican Governor James Thompson.

Roth, Sindermann, Bishop, and *Rutan* illustrate that, depending on the circumstances, public employment may or may not be viewed as a "right." It is clear that public employees may not be dismissed for exercising constitutional rights such as freedom of speech. However, it is often difficult to prove violations of constitutional rights. The existence of a property right will depend on whether a court feels there is some entitlement. In *Roth* and *Bishop,* the Court ruled, for different reasons, that no entitlement existed, whereas in *Sindermann* and *Rutan,* it did. As is so often true with case law, the unique circumstances of individual cases make it difficult to generalize. These four cases merely scratch the surface of a very complicated area of administrative law.

Loyalty oaths.   One of the most difficult areas of public employment law is the issue of loyalty oaths. Many states require its employees to sign a loyalty oath as a condition of their employment. The typical oath requires employees to swear that they have never been a member of a subversive organization. A major problem of such oaths is vagueness. As we saw in Chapter 7, the Supreme Court will invalidate legislation that is too vague. How is an employee to know which organizations are subversive? The government itself admits that some organizations are "fronts" for communist organizations. If someone innocently joins a communist-front organization, has he violated his loyalty oath?

The Supreme Court has struck down loyalty oaths that are overbroad. Some states required their employees to list every organization to which they had belonged. The Court found that such a requirement had a "chilling effect" on freedom of association. The Court did uphold prospective loyalty oaths in *Cole* v. *Richardson.*[36] A prospective loyalty oath obligates the employee to promise only future, not past, loyalty. Finally, in *Torcaso* v. *Watkins,*[37] the Court struck down a Maryland law that required all public officials to express a belief in God in order to hold public office.

Other issues. A number of issues surrounding the rights of public employees involve the exercise of rights enjoyed by employees in the private sector. Public employees argue that what they do on their own time is not the business of their governmental employer. For example, most private employers do not care where their employees live, but cities and school districts often require their employees to live within the city limits. The Supreme Court upheld the right of cities to make residency a condition of city employment in *McCarthy* v. *Philadelphia Civil Service Commission*,[38] although many cities have done away with the requirement. The Supreme Court has also upheld regulations prohibiting the cohabitation of unmarried employees. In *Kelley* v. *Johnson*,[39] the Court ruled that a city could require its male police officers to keep their hair cut short. The Court said that the general public has an image of police officers as clean-cut and that it is reasonable for the city to maintain that image.

It is clear that future battles over the rights of public employees will involve the increased use of mandatory testing for drug and alcohol abuse. Former President Ronald Reagan was an outspoken supporter of drug testing, even submitting to the test himself. Issues have ranged from requiring drug tests as a precondition of public employment to the testing of persons who are already public employees. Public employees argue that mandatory drug testing violates their constitutional right to privacy. Proponents of mandatory tests maintain that, especially in cases where the public safety is endangered, public employees have no right to refuse. As of this writing the issue of mandatory drug testing has not been fully resolved. However, it is almost certain that the courts will continue to play an important role in this controversial area of law and public policy.

CONCLUSION

Administrative law is one of the most fascinating and fastest growing areas of American law. As government gets bigger, the chances for government intrusion in our daily lives increases. If we are to remain "a nation of laws, not men," then we must keep vigilant watch over the rapidly growing government bureaucracy. Administrative law is the law that governs the people in government. We must not let those in government lose sight of the fact that they are the servants of the people, not their masters. Administrative law is one method we use to accomplish this goal.

NOTES

1. Lief H. Carter, *Administrative Law and Politics: Cases and Comments* (Boston: Little, Brown, 1983), p. 11.
2. U.S. Constitution, Amendments V and XIV.

3. See *Schechter Poultry Co.* v. *United States*, 295 U.S. 495 (1935); *Carter* v. *Carter Coal Co.*, 298 U.S. 238 (1936); and *Panama Refining Co.* v. *Ryan*, 293 U.S. 388 (1935).

4. *Bob Jones University* v. *United States*, 461 U.S. 574 (1983).

5. Pub.L. No. 101-648.

6. 5 U.S.C.A. § 566 (A).

7. Pub.L. No. 101-648, § 2 (5).

8. Ibid., § 5.

9. See Florence Heffron and Neil McFeeley, *The Administrative Regulatory Process* (New York: Longman, 1983), pp. 173–197.

10. In *Oklahoma Press Publishing Co.* v. *Walling*, 327 U.S. 186 (1946), the Supreme Court ruled that Fifth Amendment rights do not apply to corporations.

11. *Marchetti* v. *United States*, 390 U.S. 39 (1968).

12. See *Marshall* v. *Barlow's Inc.*, 436 U.S. 307 (1978).

13. *Wyman* v. *James*, 400 U.S. 309 (1971).

14. *Goldberg* v. *Kelly*, 397 U.S. 254 (1970).

15. Carter, p. 125.

16. Ibid., p. 124.

17. Walter Gellhorn, Clark Byse, and Peter L. Strauss, *Administrative Law: Cases and Comments*, 7th ed. (Mineola, N.Y.: Foundation Press, 1979), p. 943.

18. *Wellman* v. *Whittier*, 259 F. 2d 163 (D.C. Cir. 1958).

19. Gellhorn, Byse, and Clark, p. 944.

20. *Johnson* v. *Robison*, 415 U.S. 361 (1974).

21. *Texas Pacific Railway Co.* v. *Abilene Cotton Oil Co.*, 204 U.S. 426 (1907).

22. Heffron and McFeeley, pp. 308–309.

23. *Consolidated Edison* v. *National Labor Relations Board*, 305 U.S. 197 (1938).

24. Heffron and McFeeley, p. 277.

25. *Sullivan* v. *Zebley*, 58 U.S.L.W. 4177 (1990).

26. Tony Mauro, "Child Aid Decision Shows Why Court Matters," *Texas Lawyer*, Vol. 6, No. 1 (March 26, 1990), p. 25.

27. Quoted in William W. Van Alstyne, "The Demise of the Right-Privilege Distinction in Constitutional Law," *Harvard Law Review*, Vol. 81, No. 7 (May 1968), p. 1439.

28. *Rankin* v. *McPherson*, 483 U.S. 378 (1987).

29. *Board of Regents of State Colleges* v. *Roth*, 408 U.S 564 (1972).

30. *Perry* v. *Sindermann*, 408 U.S. 593 (1972).

31. Ibid, p. 600.

32. Gellhorn, Byse, and Clark, p. 464, footnote 3.

33. *Bishop* v. *Wood*, 426 U.S. 341 (1976).

34. See *Elrod* v. *Burns*, 427 U.S. 347 (1976) and *Branti* v. *Finkel*, 445 U.S. 507 (1980).

35. *Rutan* v. *Republican Party of Illinois*, 58 U.S.L.W. 4886 (1990), p. 4872.

36. *Cole* v. *Richardson*, 405 U.S. 676 (1972).

37. *Torcaso* v. *Watkins*, 367 U.S. 488 (1961).

38. *McCarthy* v. *Philadelphia Civil Service Commission*, 424 U.S. 645 (1976).

39. *Kelley* v. *Johnson*, 425 U.S. 238 (1976).

Torts

9

A _tort_ is a private, or civil, wrong in which the defendant's actions cause injury to a person or to property. Tort law provides redress for wrongs between individuals, while criminal law seeks to punish offenses against the public at large. A tort lawsuit involves only the persons involved in the tort; the state is neutral in regard to the outcome (unless, of course, the state is a party to the lawsuit). There are elementary dissimilarities between torts and crimes: (1) In the civil action of tort, the injured person himself initiates and maintains the lawsuit, whereas in criminal trials, the State prosecutes; and (2) the goal of each differs. Criminal law seeks to prevent wrongdoing and to punish the miscreant (by incarceration and/or fine), while tort law aims to place the victim in the same position he would have been in if the tort had not occurred (by assessment of monetary damages).

The same act often spawns both civil and criminal sanctions. Suppose that you are loitering in the hall before class when, without provocation, Joe suddenly comes up and hits you in the face. Joe is subject to criminal sanctions for this attack. However, you will also wish to file a tort action against Joe to recover money to pay for your new front teeth, your dentist's bill, your pain and suffering, and your mental anguish. The purposes of the two suits, which will be heard separately, are different. Society is punishing Joe for his antisocial behavior in the criminal trial, while you are seeking money from him. The usual remedy for tort liability is monetary reimbursement for the harm suffered.[1]

Tort law is fluid; it changes as society's values shift. New torts are today being recognized where no cause of action had previously existed, and the boundaries of tort liability are constantly in flux. One example is the expansion of liability in regard to drivers who injure someone while intoxicated. Traditionally, only the drivers themselves were responsible, but courts are now finding liable for damages employers who release their intoxicated employees to go home as well as drinking establishments whose customers leave and subsequently injure someone.[2] Generally, only the person who acts in an intentionally violent way is held civilly liable for the consequences of that act. However, juries have determined that the gun dealers who sell guns and ammunition to intoxicated buyers, underage purchasers, or those exhibiting signs of mental instability violate affirmative common-law duties to conduct their business to prevent sales of firearms to high-risk people. This liability has been imposed even without a statutory violation or on the principles of negligence (both of which will be discussed later in this chapter).[3] New causes of action may be created by the people directly acting as jurors in courtrooms or through their elected representatives in various legislative bodies as new statutes are written. The goal in each instance is to provide remedies for perceived wrongs.

Tort law establishes certain legal standards of conduct by which all members of society must abide and then provides a remedy when such a standard is violated. It is primarily designed to protect three types of interests: (1) the person, (2) tangible property, and (3) intangible interests, including relational interests such as business, family, and social relations. The person who breaches the standard of conduct is known as the ***tortfeasor.*** Generally, the tortfeasor cannot be held liable for damages unless he has violated the prescribed standard of conduct.

The plaintiff in the suit decides on the theory of tort recovery and draws the complaint to reflect the theory. Each theory contains certain elements that the plaintiff must prove in order to collect damages from the defendant. It is not unusual for a plaintiff to plead alternative theories of recovery, which may contain contradictory elements, in the complaint. Then, through discovery, it can be determined which is the strongest, and the plaintiff then proceeds to trial on that theory. The only requirement is that defendants be given adequate notice in the complaint of the possible causes of action in order that they may properly prepare the defense. In our discussion of tort law, we will look at the theories of negligence, intentional torts, strict liability, and product liability.[4]

NEGLIGENCE

Negligence is the reckless or careless failure of the tortfeasor to exercise the degree of care that the law deems appropriate in a particular situation. A common example is that of an automobile accident in which a driver recklessly drives too fast on an icy road, loses control, and slams into another car, causing both personal injuries and property damage. The driver was imprudent and did not exercise the usual standard of care. However, she did not set out to inflict injury; this absence of malicious intent is one of the characteristics of negligence cases. Recovery in negligence cases is not predicated on proving the tortfeasor morally at fault. Liability is imposed only for those things which the law requires to be done (commissions) or to be not done (omissions); it is not imposed for "moral" duties, those which are merely voluntary or are dictated by humane considerations or ethics only.[5] The elements that the plaintiff must prove in order to win at trial are the following: (1) that the defendant owed a duty of care to the plaintiff; (2) that the standard of care was breached; (3) that defendant's action was the proximate cause of the injury; and (4) that the plaintiff suffered some compensable damage as a result of defendant's actions. These four elements compose the *prima facie* case in a negligence cause of action; that is, the plaintiff is required to prove each of the elements in order to win the case.[6] The issue of negligence is primarily a question of fact, and it is therefore a matter to be decided by the jury.[7]

Duty of care. The plaintiff must initially show that the defendant owed a legally recognized duty of care. There are two subsidiary issues involved: what is the level of care the defendant must exercise, and to whom is the duty of care owed. In most cases, the test for the appropriate level of care is whether, under the circumstances of the case, the defendant acted as a "reasonably prudent person" would have acted to prevent the injury. The **reasonably prudent person** is a fictitious individual who has been created by the courts as an objective standard by which to measure a defendant's actions. This cautious and careful person is considered to be of ordinary intelligence and to have a normal memory and normal sensory perceptions. This ubiquitous paragon of virtue has been humorously described by one commentator, A. P. Herbert, in the following manner:

> He is an ideal, a standard, the embodiment of all those qualities which we demand of the good citizen. . . . He is one who invariably looks where he is going, and is careful to examine the immediate foreground before he executes a leap or bound; who neither star-gazes nor is lost in meditation when approaching trapdoors or the margin of a dock . . . who never mounts a moving omnibus and does not alight from any car while the train is in motion . . . and will inform himself of the history and habits of a dog before administering a caress . . . who never from one year's end to another makes an excessive demand upon his wife, his neighbors, his servants, his ox, or his ass . . . who never swears, gambles or loses his temper; who uses nothing except in moderation . . . this excellent but odious character stands like a monument in our Courts of Justice vainly appealing to his fellow citizens to order their lives after his own example.[8]

The fact-finder considers the events of the case and decides whether the defendant exhibited the due care that a person of ordinary intelligence would have. A child is not held to as high a standard of care; each is judged against a child of like age, intelligence, and experience.[9] On the other hand, a person who has a special skill or knowledge is judged by a higher standard of care. For example, architects, engineers, and physicians must exhibit the same skills and care that others in the profession do.[10] Certainly one expects a higher degree of medical knowledge and skill from a physician than one does from a layperson. The physician is required by law to act as a reasonably prudent *physician* would in providing treatment. If the professional does not act in accordance with the standard, the usual result is a malpractice suit. Typically, the only way to prove negligence in this type of action is through the use of expert testimony, and professionals are often hesitant to testify against each other.

Another issue in regard to the standard of care is the relationship between the plaintiff and defendant. It is this relationship which determines just how careful one must be toward another person. Generally, the law does not impose a duty on a person to go to the aid of someone who is in danger, even though there may be a moral duty to do so. However, such a duty may be imposed when there is a special relationship. Although a stranger is probably not *legally* required to assist a drowning child, the parent might well be expected to do so in the eyes of the law.[11] Similarly, occupiers of land may owe different levels of care to trespassers and to business visitors, although there are circumstances when liability accrues regardless of the status of the injured party—for example, when there is willful, wanton, or careless conduct such as the use of a life-threatening device to discourage trespassers. The occupier must extend the greater level of care to business visitors or *invitees*—the duty of ordinary care. Social guests or *licensees* and trespassers, those on the land without the owner's consent, are owed a lesser degree of care—the duty to refrain from willful or wanton misconduct. Some states now treat licensees and invitees alike in terms of the duties of the landowner.[12] Suits involving property owners and their guests are quite common, and most people buy insurance to protect themselves financially in case of such accidents.

Breach of duty. The second element the plaintiff must establish is that the standard of care owed to her was violated by the defendant. There are two prongs to this element of a negligence action. The plaintiff must convince the fact-finder (1) that the act or omission actually occurred and (2) that such action was a breach of the standard of care owed to this particular plaintiff. Such a breach can be through commission or through omission—that is, through a positive act of the defendant or through a failure of the defendant to act. An example of a positive act is someone dropping a flowerpot from a third-story window without regard for the passerby below; an example of an omission is the failure of a store clerk to pick up a banana peel from the floor after seeing it.

Courts have provided shortcuts for plaintiffs in proving the lack of ordinary care in limited circumstances. The first of these is *negligence per se.* In a typical case, the legislature passes a statute regulating certain activities in the interest of safety—for example, traffic or working conditions in industries or dealing in guns. The plaintiff alleges that the defendant violated such safety standard and that the plaintiff's injury is a result of such violation. If the judge agrees that the defendant violated the safety regulation, the decision is conclusive and the issue of negligence does not even go to the jury. The jury is then called upon only to decide the amount of damages.[13]

The second of these shortcuts is the doctrine of *res ipsa loquitur*—"the thing speaks for itself." Here the plaintiff is required to prove that the accident is of a type that ordinarily would not occur without negligence (an airplane crash) *and* that all instrumentalities that would probably cause the accident were under the control of the defendant at the time (crew of airplane and aircraft maintenance were under the control of the airline). This doctrine resembles circumstantial evidence in that the trier of facts is asked to infer the result from separate pieces of evidence. Again, the jury's task is limited to determining the truth of these allegations rather than actual negligence. If the jury agrees with the plaintiff on these two points, they find for the plaintiff.[14]

Proximate cause. The plaintiff must also show that the defendant's action was the proximate cause of his injury. In other words, there must be some reasonable connection between the negligent act of the defendant and the plaintiff's injury. Suppose that Sue and her husband have an argument at breakfast; that Sue unjustifiably criticizes her secretary, George, during the day; and that George is upset and, as a result, is careless while driving home and has an accident. In one sense, it is possible to trace the cause of the accident back to the spat between Sue and her husband because "in a philosophical sense, the consequences of an act go forward to eternity and the causes of an event go back to the discovery of America and beyond."[15] However, courts have declined to enter into this hornet's nest and have limited liability to "those causes which are so closely connected with the result and of such significance that the law is justified in imposing liability."[16]

This concept of legal responsibility based on a reasonable connection between the tortfeasor's action and the victim's injury is known as *proximate cause*. The plaintiff must establish not only that the defendant's conduct was *factually* one of the causes of the injury, but also that the defendant should be *legally* responsible for his actions. Additional limitations on liability have been developed. If the defendant could not reasonably have foreseen any injury to the plaintiff as a consequence of the act, there is no liability.[17] For instance, a tortfeasor involved in an automobile accident could not reasonably foresee that the sirens of the emergency vehicles would startle someone into dropping a pot of boiling water and scalding herself. Also, a defendant will be relieved of liability if there is an independent force intervening between the action and the injury.[18] To illustrate, assume that Sanders Gravel constructs a fence around its lake that is adequate to prevent the neighborhood children from straying in; however, a tornado strikes and blows down the fence, and a child drowns in the lake later that day. The tornado is considered to be an independent intervening cause in such a case.

There are often several contributing causes in a single accident, which will result in shared liability among the various tortfeasors. Consider a fairly typical automobile accident. Charles is driving east, is speeding, and is trying to get through the intersection before the light changes to red so that he does not slow down. Daniel, who is traveling west on the same street, is obeying all the traffic laws; however, his attention is diverted by his two children, who are squabbling in the back seat. Richard is going north on the intersecting street. The three cars collide at the intersection; personal injuries and property damage result. In addition to the foregoing facts, eyewitnesses will testify at the trial that the light was malfunctioning and was showing green on all sides. The trio will sue one another and the city for failing to properly maintain the traffic control device, the light. Each of them contributed to the accident, and it will be the jury's responsibility to apportion responsibility for the accident.

Damages.   The fourth element the plaintiff must prove is that of **damages,** a sum of money which the law imposes as pecuniary compensation. The plaintiff is required to establish both the nature of the injury and an amount that would fairly recompense him for the injury. The emphasis is on placing the plaintiff in the same position, insofar as is possible, as he was in before the accident. Of course, it is difficult to place a monetary value on pain and suffering or on the loss of an arm or leg or to predict a person's lifetime earnings; however, juries, utilizing the precedents of previous awards and the evidence adduced at trial, decide these formidable questions each day in rendering verdicts in tort cases.

Plaintiffs' attorneys have been successful in having courts recognize the various ramifications of an injury and in thereby expanding the recovery in tort actions. Assume that John is a football player who has signed a contract to play professional ball when he is paralyzed in an automobile accident. He would likely sue to recover for his pain and suffering, his medical expenses (which will be ongoing), his present loss of wages, his loss of future earnings, loss of value of his car, and mental anguish (if the state courts have recognized the latter).[19]

Assume that Peter died in the same accident. His estate would have a common-law action for personal injury resulting in death and could recover for his consciousness of impending death, physical pain and suffering, and medical and funeral expenses. Peter's family—wife, children, and/or parents—could also file a wrongful death suit for damages for the loss of emotional support as well as the loss of economic benefits that they could reasonably have expected to receive from Peter if he had not been killed. Wrongful death suits are suits to compensate the survivors and are not derived from the decedent's interests. They are generally founded on statutory enactments which define who may claim such benefits.[20]

The monetary value of these losses is quite troublesome for juries. The easier questions are those involving the loss of value to property such as automobiles, livestock, or buildings. Putting a price tag on someone's pain and suffering or anticipating the amount of future earnings of a child is subjective. Juries rely heavily on the testimony of experts, particularly economists, to assist them. Lawyers work throughout the trial to educate the jurors about the issue of damages; the plaintiff's counsel seeks to demonstrate how horrific the injury is and how only a large sum will adequately recompense the victim, while the defense seeks to minimize the possible award. The same kinds of damages are available for all torts including intentional torts and those involving product liability.[21]

Defenses. Once the plaintiff has established a *prima facie* case by presenting the four elements, the defendant has the opportunity to present his case and to rebut the plaintiff's arguments. Several methods of attack are available to the defendant, including challenging the plaintiff's proof on the four elements of negligence, claiming that the plaintiff was aware of the risk, or establishing that the plaintiff himself was negligent and thereby contributed to his own injury. For instance, a common defensive tactic is to dispute the seriousness of plaintiff's injury, thereby reducing damages; but the same approach, that of controverting fact questions, may be directed to each prong of the plaintiff's case. In addition, the defendant may also employ the affirmative defenses of contributory negligence and voluntary assumption of risk. In utilizing the defense of ***voluntary assumption of risk***, the defendant attempts to prove that the plaintiff was cognizant of the danger and voluntarily chose to encounter it. A typical example is a person who, with knowledge that she may be hit by a flying puck, attends an ice hockey game. In other words, the plaintiff, either expressly or impliedly, consented to the risk of possible injury.

In contrast, the defense of contributory negligence alleges that the plaintiff's actions contributed to his own injury. Every person is charged with the legal duty to avoid exposing oneself to injury—that is, to exercise due care in regard to one's safety as would the reasonable, prudent person in the community. The defendant bears the burden of proof to establish that the plaintiff acted in violation of this standard. The common-law rules of *contributory negligence* barred the plaintiff from *any* recovery if he was found to have contributed, even slightly, to his own injury. Modern courts and legislatures have tempered the harshness of this legal precept, however, through the adoption of *comparative negligence*. Under the doctrine of comparative negligence, the negligence is apportioned between the plaintiff and the defendant, with the result that the plaintiff may recover a certain portion of the damages even if he contributed to his own injury. Various jurisdictions have adopted one of three approaches to comparative negligence. The first, the "pure" approach, allows the plaintiff to recover if he contributed to his own injury, but there is a proportional reduction in the amount of the damages. If he was 30 percent liable, then his award is reduced 30 percent. The second, the "equal-to-or-greater-than" approach, permits recovery so long as the defendant's negligence was equal to or greater than the plaintiff's. The third, the "slight-gross" rule, allows a plaintiff to recover when her negligence is slight in comparison to the defendant's negligence.[22] Again, the burden rests on the defendant to prove that the plaintiff's own actions caused the injury.[23]

INTENTIONAL TORTS

Unlike torts based on negligence, which involve recklessness or a breach of the standard of care, intentional torts are based on willful and knowing misconduct. The tortfeasor knows or is substantially certain that her actions will result in injury either to a person or to property. To hold the defendant liable for damages, tort law does not require the tortfeasor to harbor a malicious desire to harm someone; instead, courts will imply the requisite intent if the harm suffered was the predictable result of the defendant's actions.

Intentional torts, such as assault and battery and false imprisonment, are often repeated in criminal statutes, and the tortfeasor may also be subject to criminal penalties in a separate lawsuit. Because intentional torts are more culpable than negligence, the defendant faces the possibility of greater liability. Again, the key for distinguishing intentional torts from negligence is that the tortfeasor *intentionally* performed the acts *knowing* that injury would be likely to occur.

Assault and battery.   To paraphrase a popular song, assault and battery go together like love and marriage. However, the two are separate and distinct intentional torts. **Battery** is a harmful or offensive contact with another, whereas **assault** is the apprehension of an unwanted contact with another. The former is the actual physical touching; the latter is the mental awareness of the unwanted invasion. A battery may be committed without an assault and vice versa. A person struck in the back of the head may not be aware of the attacker's presence (battery without assault), and someone who throws a punch and misses has committed assault without battery. Technically, one cannot be assaulted by words alone; there must be an accompanying physical act that places one in apprehension of impending contact.

Consent is the primary defense for the torts of assault and battery. A boxer agrees or consents to have the opposing fighter touch him during the bout. Similarly, you might accept the contact as a caress from one person and yet be highly offended if a stranger touched you in the same manner.[24] Certain persons are deemed to have a privilege to touch another; examples are a police officer making a valid arrest or a physician giving emergency treatment.[25]

False imprisonment. The social policy underlying the tort of false imprisonment is concern about one of the most treasured of American rights—the freedom to move about freely, or, in constitutional terms, one's liberty interest. The plaintiff's *prima facie* case must include proof that the defendant intentionally restrained the plaintiff's freedom against the plaintiff's will and that the plaintiff was aware of such restraint. The victim need not necessarily be incarcerated or locked behind physical barriers; impediments of the freedom to proceed on one's way, including holding one's property, are included. Moral pressure or threats of future action alone are insufficient to create the required restraints. Store security personnel who prevent an alleged shoplifter from leaving the premises are treading a very fine line, although there is some statutory and case-law guidance available. Police personnel who exceed their authority in making arrests or who do so maliciously are also subject to suit for false imprisonment, but it is a defense that the defendant had legal authority to restrain the plaintiff.[26]

Infliction of mental distress. A person who willfully and intentionally causes *serious* mental distress to another can be held liable for his actions. This tort is limited to cases involving extreme misconduct—for example, telling a mother that her child had been killed when, in fact, the tortfeasor knows the child is fine. It involves more than hurt feelings, disappointment, or worry; there must be actual and severe mental anguish. Courts have traditionally required that mental distress be linked with some other tort and actual physical harm; however, the trend is away from both these requirements. Many jurisdictions now recognize the infliction of mental distress as a separate tort.[27]

Invasion of privacy. The concept of privacy is zealously guarded in the United States; it is protected by the courts against invasion from either the government or the private sector. In today's world, in which personal information about all persons is listed on computers that are subject to being tapped, the right to privacy is assuming even more importance. Two related torts deal with the right to be shielded from the public eye and the right to preserve one's reputation. The first, *invasion of privacy*, covers three broad areas: (1) the intentional invasion of privacy by wiretapping a phone or shadowing a person, (2) the appropriation of a person's name or likeness without permission for advertising purposes, and (3) the unwarranted publication of information about an individual's private matters.

The test that courts use to gauge the tortfeasor's actions is whether a reasonable person would find the act to be highly objectionable.[28] For example, Jones is having difficulty collecting a debt from Smith, so Jones creates a billboard sign that informs the world, "Smith owes me $1,000 and will not pay it." Most people (who are also debtors) find this obnoxious, and Smith would likely succeed in a tort action for invasion of privacy.

The second action, *defamation,* also concerns the issue of one's reputation in the community. Defamation is the injury of one's reputation in the community by derogatory or defamatory comments. There are two distinct branches of defamation: *slander,* in which the comment is usually spoken; and *libel,* in which it is written or is in some permanent form. The underlying public policy is the strong emphasis on protecting people from malicious or untrue attacks on their good name in the community.[29] Hefty damages are frequently awarded. For example, GTE Corp. received $100 million from Home Shopping Network and entertainer Wayne Newton received $19 million from NBC.[30]

In order for the plaintiff to recover in a slander suit, he must establish that the statement was made in the presence of a third party, that it subjected him to ridicule or contempt, and that he suffered pecuniary damages as a result of the tortfeasor's statements. Libel is easier to prove in that the defamation is in writing, pictures, videotape, or something of a permanent nature. Public figures, those in the public eye, must prove an additional element— that the defendant made the statement either with knowledge that it was false or with a careless disregard for its truth. The defendant may rely upon one of three primary defenses: (1) that the statement is true; (2) that the defendant was protected by a privilege to speak, such as that given legislators speaking on the floor of the legislature; or (3) that the plaintiff consented to the statement.[31]

Intentional torts against property.   Although property damage can and does result from negligence, the law also recognizes intentional torts directed against property interests; among these are conversion, trespass, and nuisance. *Trespass to land* occurs when a person enters the land or building of another without consent. This intrusion must be physical; that is, the trespasser must actually walk on the ground or poke a stick through a fence. But even though the damage might be as minimal as a bent blade of grass, the owner can recover because of the interference with possession of the property.[32]

Nuisance is the use of the *defendant's* land in such a way that it interferes with the *plaintiff's* use of his land. Suppose, for example, that the defendant owns a quarry where blasting occurs and the shock waves shatter the windows in plaintiff's home; or, the defendant runs a chemical plant that produces a noxious odor. Courts must balance each party's right to use his own land as he chooses against the injury sustained by the other landowner. Factors to be considered in nuisance suits include the frequency of the intrusion, the value to society of the defendant's action, and the plaintiff's knowledge, if any, of the nuisance when he bought the property.[33] Even though nuisance is included here under intentional torts, the nuisance could be caused by the negligent or hazardous activities of the defendant, and therefore the plaintiff could proceed under the theories of negligence or strict liability. In addition to damages, the plaintiff in a nuisance suit may also be awarded the equitable remedy of injunction.

Personal property, as distinguished from real property or land, may also be damaged. A second type of trespass, *trespass to chattel,* occurs when the tortfeasor damages a *chattel,* which is an item of tangible, personal property such as jewels, money, or automobiles. For instance, Bill Bully intimidates his classmate, Stephen, into allowing Bill to ride Stephen's bicycle by breaking the headlight. Bill has damaged or impaired the bicycle, which is trespass to a chattel, and has also committed conversion by interfering with Stephen's possession of the bicycle. *Conversion,* then, is defined as depriving an owner of possession of tangible property. The person who borrows an item without permission or an employee who sells copies of the company's bid on a new construction project to a competitor has interfered with the owner's possession of the property and is subject to tort liability (that is, damages) as well as criminal penalties.[34]

Unfair competition or interference with commercial or economic relations. This ancient tort dating from Roman law involves interference with contractual relationships or prospects for economic advantage. Courts favor free competition among businesses and individuals; however, there are certain activities that are not legally accepted business practices. These include trademark infringement by using another company's trademark as one's own or by designing one's product container so as to mislead the consumer into believing your product is actually that of another, established company. Improperly obtaining trade secrets (items not in the public domain) by industrial espionage or by breach of confidence is also actionable.[35]

This tort may be filed whenever there is intentional and unjustified interference with the business relationships of another and such interference results in an injury to the present or future economic relationships of others. For example, a professional New York ballet company which improperly entices a premier ballerina to leave the Salt Lake City ballet company may be liable for the resulting loss of profits due to poor ticket sales.[36] The courts have held that labor is a "property" interest within the constitutional provision of "life, liberty, and property," although there is no constitutional right to have a job. Employers who act improperly in regard to current or past employees may be liable under this tort. To illustrate, an employer who retaliates against an employee who refuses social contact or who is a so-called whistleblower may be liable for interference with economic relations.[37]

Defenses to intentional torts. There are many other causes of action in tort law—including fraud, malicious prosecution, and alienation of affection—which permit the plaintiff to recover damages for the defendant's intentional infliction of injury. Each theory carries with it specific defenses that are applicable only to it. However, there are defensive tactics that are common to some, if not all, intentional torts. The defendant will initially attack and seek to rebut the plaintiff's *prima facie* case—those facts and elements that the plaintiff must prove in order to succeed at trial. The second front on which the defendant will do battle is the presentation of the general defenses; for example, the defendant would allege that the plaintiff consented to the action (that the football player agreed to be struck during the game) or that the defendant had a privilege to take the action (that the fireman trespassed on the land in order to put out a fire which was threatening other property). The third line of attack is the particular defense that is linked to a specific tort. For example, the defendant in an assault and battery case may counter with the argument that he struck the plaintiff only to protect and defend himself or another against the plaintiff's aggression.

STRICT LIABILITY

We have previously used the concept of fault as one of the distinguishing marks between intentional torts and negligence. In the former, the tortfeasor who knows and intends the consequences of the act is found liable for the injury it causes; and in the latter, the person who fails to exhibit ordinary care or who is reckless toward the welfare of others is required to make good on the damage that was inflicted. However, *fault*, in the eyes of the law, is not synonymous with moral blame. Instead, it implies that the actor has not lived up to the standard of conduct imposed by society.

Originally, the law would not impose liability on the tortfeasor unless it found "fault." However, courts, in the familiar traditions of common law, have developed a new doctrine of "strict liability" whereby the tortfeasor may be responsible for the loss or injury of another even if there has been no violation of the reasonable standard of conduct. Legislatures ratified the theory through statutory enactment.

The concept of strict liability was initially applied against the owners of animals that escaped and damaged another's property, but it has been expanded to cover hazardous activities, such as blasting or moving explosive and inflammable liquids. Questions involved in such suits include the locale of the dangerous activity, the customs of the community, and the fitness of the premises or machinery for these purposes. In these situations in which neither party is at fault, society, through the courts, imposes the costs for the loss on the party who is most able to afford it.[38]

An expanding area of recovery is that of *product liability,* wherein the manufacturer, seller, or supplier of a defective product or instrumentality is responsible to purchasers, users, and bystanders for any injuries caused by the product. Permitting recovery in tort based on foreseeability of harm to the consumer, rather than founding the recovery in contract only, follows the same principles as strict liability. Those who profit from the dangerous product should assume liability for damages sustained by those injured.[39] The plaintiff must prove that the product was defective as marketed in one of the following ways: (1) There was a defect in the construction of the product; (2) There was a defect in the design of the product; or (3) There were inherent dangers in the product about which the ultimate purchaser was not warned. A plaintiff who suffered serious injuries as a result of food poisoning because the food was improperly canned might allege the first, whereas those suing an automobile company because the gasoline tank of their cars exploded upon minimal impact would probably proceed on the second premise. An example of the third cause of action would be a patient who is suing a pharmaceutical company because the company did not warn that a certain medicine aggravated high blood pressure even though it was aware of the problem.

Other remedies are also available to a person who is injured because of a malfunction of a product. The first of these is negligence, but there is the practical problem of establishing the failure to exercise the proper standard of care. Another possibility is to proceed on a breach of warranty under contract law. The seller of a product is deemed by the law to have either expressly or impliedly warranted that the product is fit for its intended use. A plaintiff may wish to file suit against the seller for breach of the warranty and against the manufacturer for a defective product under tort law, thereby enhancing the possibility of establishing liability and obtaining damages. Jurors are consumers too, and they are awarding increasingly larger judgments against manufacturers and sellers of defective products although recently legislatures have been passing laws limiting liability.[40]

GENERAL TORT DEFENSES

Two basic premises of American jurisprudence are that no one is above the law and that one is not liable for someone else's actions. This is not absolutely true in tort law, however. Tort liability may be moved from the actual tortfeasor to another (innocent) party under the theory of *vicarious liability;* thus, parents are responsible for some torts committed by their children, and employers are responsible for the torts of their employees committed during the course of employment. The legal theory for shifting the responsibility from the employee to the employer is known as ***respondeat superior***. Vicarious liability is actually a "rule of policy, a deliberate allocation of a risk."[41] It places the monetary punishment on the person or organization with the "deep pockets," the one who is profiting from the enterprise or who is able to pay larger judgments. In police misconduct cases, the plaintiff typically sues the city as well as the individual officer because the city has the deeper pockets.

One of the largest employers in the country has limited liability for the torts of its employees, however. The U.S. government is subject to suit only for the negligent torts of its employees and not for intentional torts. This is an offshoot of the traditional sovereign immunity of governments, a concept which dates from the absolute monarchies in Europe. Congress and many state legislatures recognize the injustice of this immunity and have passed statutes designed to permit tort actions to be filed against the government. These same legislative bodies may also adopt special legislation allowing a particular plaintiff or class of plaintiffs to petition for redress from the courts even in the face of the immunity laws.[42] Other immunities exist as well. Public officials who are acting in the performance of their duties, such as judges, are also shielded from tort liability. Of course, these officials are not absolved from liability for personal torts or for torts outside the scope of job responsibility. In order to be protected from liability, the official must show that he is acting as a public official *and* that the activities fall within his job responsibilities.

CONCLUSION

The cry for tort reform has resonated throughout the land and has fallen upon receptive ears, both in state legislatures and in Congress. Those who claim that the explosion of tort suits is unwarranted, that Americans are too inclined to sue on frivolous claims, and that all this litigation is too burdensome on business have successfully fought to limit the types of suits brought and to impose ceilings on judgments, particularly on punitive damages. Those plaintiffs who do file the so-called "frivolous" lawsuits will essentially be fined by being required to pay the other party's court costs and attorney's fees.

Opponents of such reforms argue that innocent parties, the victims, should not be uncompensated for the wrongs done to them and that the wrongdoers should be forced to assume responsibility for their actions. They point to enhanced safety in consumer products that is the direct result of tort litigation as well as protection of personal autonomy in such areas of privacy. Furthermore, businesses too benefit from tort law through recoveries for loss of trade secrets and interference in employee relationships.

Tort law closely resembles criminal law in its effort to avenge the victim. In criminal law, the punishment as set by the state is incarceration or a fine, which is funneled into state coffers; in tort law, however, the money flows to the victim. Tort law involves intentional wrongdoing as well as negligence. It seeks to protect the consumer from wrongful acts by manufacturers. The social policy that is the foundation for tort law focuses on compensating the innocent victim, in a personal way, for injuries caused by third parties, a goal most find admirable. The public debate centers primarily on who should set that policy—the juries in the courts that are deciding individual cases or the legislature that is setting broad social policy but is more subject to lobbying by those with vested interests. Some view the trend of tort reform with horror, some with rejoicing, and some with neutrality regarding it as merely a midcourse adjustment in the fluid field of tort law.

NOTES

1. William P. Statsky, *Torts: Personal Injury Litigation* (St. Paul, Minn.: West Publishing Company, 1982), pp. 1–8.
2. *Otis Engineering Corp.* v. *Clark*, 668 S.W.2d 307 (Tex. 1984).
3. Dennis Henigan, "Gun Control Through Tort Law," *Texas Lawyer*, September 9, 1991.
4. Statsky, pp. 1–8.
5. Martin Weinstein, *Summary of American Law* (Rochester, N.Y.: The Lawyer's Cooperative Publishing Co./Bancroft-Whitney Co., 1988), pp. 503–504.
6. W. Page Keeton, Dan B. Dobbs, Robert E. Keeton, and David G. Owen, *Prosser and Keeton on The Law of Torts* (St. Paul, Minn.: West Publishing Company, 1984), pp. 164–165.
7. Ibid., pp. 235–236.
8. A. P. Herbert, *Uncommon Law* (London, Meuthen, 1935; reprint, London: Bibliophile Books, 1986), pp. 2–3 (page references are to reprint edition).
9. *Rudes* v. *Gottschalk*, 159 Tex. 552, 324 S.W.2d 201 (1959).
10. *Cook Consultants Inc.* v. *Larson*, 700 S.W.2d 231 (Tex. App.—Dallas, 1985).
11. Statsky, pp. 313–315.
12. Keeton et al., pp. 412–434.
13. *Richardson* v. *Gregory*, 281 F.2d 626 (D.C. Cir. 1960).
14. *Sweeney* v. *Erving*, 228 U.S. 233 (1912).
15. William L. Prosser, *Handbook of the Law of Torts*, 4th ed., (St. Paul, Minn.: West Publishing Company, 1971), p. 236.
16. Keeton et al., p. 264.
17. *Palsgraf* v. *Long Island R. Co.*, 248 N.Y. 339, 162 N.E. 99 (1928).
18. *Garner* v. *Prescott*, 234 S.W.2d 704 (Tex. Civ. App.—Eastland, 1950).
19. Statsky, p. 380.
20. Keeton et al., pp. 945–960.
21. Statsky, pp. 380–394.
22. Keeton et al., pp. 470–474.

23. Statsky, pp. 380–394.

24. Keeton et al., pp. 41–42.

25. Ibid., p. 117.

26. Statsky, pp. 521–527.

27. Ibid., pp. 510–517.

28. P. Allan Dionispoulos and Craig R. Ducat, *The Right to Privacy* (St. Paul, Minn.: West Publishing Company, 1976), pp. 19–30.

29. Raymond L. Yasser, *Torts and Sports* (Westport, Conn.: Quorum Books, 1985), pp. 87–89.

30. Michael P. McDonald, "It's Alive! Libel Law Arises from the Dead," *Texas Lawyer,* June 11, 1990, p. 38.

31. Yasser, pp. 89–90.

32. Keeton et al., pp. 67–84.

33. *Commerce Oil Refining Corp.* v. *Miner,* 281 F.2d 465 (1st Cir. 1960).

34. Keeton et al., pp. 85–107.

35. Ibid., pp. 978–1023.

36. Weinstein, pp. 531–532.

37. Ibid., pp. 324–329.

38. Keeton et al., pp. 536–538.

39. *McPherson* v. *Buick Motor Co.*, 217 N.Y. 382, 111 N.E. 1050 (1916).

40. Keeton et al., pp. 677–694.

41. Prosser, p. 459.

42. Peter H. Schuck, *Suing Government* (New Haven, Conn.: Yale University Press, 1983), pp. 29–53.

Contracts

10

Contracts are binding agreements that have legal consequences and can be enforced in court. Noted contract scholar Samuel Williston defines a contract as "a promise, or set of promises, for breach of which the law gives a remedy, or the performance of which the law in some way recognizes as a duty."[1] Contracts provide stability and allow society to carry out its transactions in an orderly fashion; however, contracts are not limited to serious business ventures. For example, siblings who enter into bargains to divide the household chores between them are creating contracts. While some contracts are rather elaborate and formal, others are informal and even implied.

Ensuring stability and certainty is the quintessential goal of contracts. Those who enter into these agreements do so with the knowledge that failure to live up to one's part of the bargain may result in a court order for specific performance or for monetary damages as well as damage to one's reputation in the community. The importance of contract stability is emphasized by Article I, § 10 of the U.S. Constitution, which provides that "No State shall . . . pass any . . . Law impairing the Obligation of Contracts." In earlier days, freedom of contract was virtually uncircumscribed by government restrictions; people contracted as they pleased, with the only real restraint being that contracts for illegal purposes were not enforceable by the courts. For example, government contracts secured by bribing a public official cannot be enforced by the corporation offering the bribe. That rule is still valid; however, other restrictions have been added. Consider, for example, employment

243

contracts, which are governed by regulations barring discrimination, requiring minimum wages, limiting hours, and providing workers' compensation, to name only a few. As society becomes more complex and more litigious, legislatures, administrative agencies, and courts at all levels of government are placing greater restrictions on the freedom to contract. Contract law permeates our daily lives in such diverse areas as sales, credit, employment, and various other commercial transactions.

CONTRACTUAL TERMS OF ART

The field of contracts is an area of law in which mysterious terms of art abound. Contracts may be characterized as express or implied; bilateral or unilateral; executory or executed; and void, voidable, and unenforceable. It will be helpful for you to have some understanding of these terms as you learn about contracts.

An *express contract* is one in which the terms are stated by the parties; it may be either an oral or written contract. An example would be your agreement to buy a class ring for the sum of $200 under a written contract. An *implied contract* is one which is inferred from the conduct of the parties. Your conduct in entering a restaurant and ordering a meal gives rise to an implied contract that you will pay the price stated on the menu for the food even though you may not expressly say so to the waiter when you order. In each case, you have entered into a contract, and the only difference is in the type of evidence necessary to establish the contract.

A *bilateral contract* is one in which the parties exchange promises to do some future act. You agree with the car dealer that you will pay for your new Jaguar when you take delivery next week. Each of you has promised to do something in the future: the dealer to deliver the car and you to pay for it. In contrast, a *unilateral contract* is one in which one party acts immediately in response to the offer. Assume that you tender a monetary reward for the return of your much loved, but lost, dog—Sebastian. Vincent finds Sebastian and returns him. The response is in the form of immediate action rather than a mutual exchange of promises.

An *executory contract* is one in which some or all of the terms are uncompleted—our car deal, for example. An *executed contract* then is one in which all the terms have been completed. You have eaten your meal and paid your bill at the restaurant or paid Vincent for returning Sebastian to his happy home.

The terms "void, voidable, and unenforceable" are relevant in situations where there is a breach of contract or when the one party fails to comply with the terms of the agreement. A *void contract* is a nullity from its beginning, and damages do not result. For example, a contract to murder someone is void, and the person making the "hit" could not successfully maintain a lawsuit to collect her salary. On the other hand, a *voidable con-*

tract is one which is binding until it is disaffirmed or canceled by the party with the authority to do so. In many ways, marriage is a contract which either party may rescind by obtaining a divorce. Other contracts are deemed to be unenforceable. *Unenforceable contracts* are those which meet the basic common law elements for contracts but lack some other additional legal requirement such as being signed in front of a notary public.[2]

FORMATION OF CONTRACTS

The requirements for formulating a contract appear relatively uncomplicated. First, there must be two or more parties, each of whom have the legal *capacity* to enter into an agreement. Second, there must be an *offer* and *acceptance*, or consent, which reflects a mutual understanding between the parties as to the essential elements of the contract. Third, the agreement must be supported by *consideration* or obligation.[3] Determining the existence of each of these elements is not as simple as it might appear at first glance.

Parties.   Two or more parties must be involved in a contract.[4] One cannot enter into a legally enforceable contract with oneself. Parties to such agreements include both natural and *artificial persons* (corporations). The law creates a legal fiction that corporations are persons.[5] This allows corporations to sue and be sued and to conduct business transactions as entities without involving individual shareholders.

Each party involved in the contract must have the legal capacity to enter into the agreement.[6] Incapacity may result from the age of the individual or from a party's being mentally incapable of understanding the ramifications of the contract. At common law, a person under the age of 21 was considered an infant, or minor. Today many states establish the *age of majority* at 18, the age at which citizens may vote. State laws often provide that minors may enter into contracts but that they retain the ability to withdraw from the agreement.[7] Assume that Patricia, age 17, buys a $750 stereo, but upon bringing it home and discussing the matter with her parents, she decides to return the stereo to the store. As a minor, she may disaffirm the contract, and the store must take the stereo back if there is a timely disclaimer on her part. Minors are under an obligation to return any consideration received under the contract. The fact that minors may avoid contracts causes many people to refuse to contract with them. Minors who contract for necessities such as food, shelter, and clothing are not usually permitted to avoid such agreements after the goods or services have been delivered; however, the minor is liable only for the reasonable value of the goods or services, which may not be the same as the contract price.[8] *Emancipation,* or the removal of one's disabilities as a minor, can occur by reaching the statutory age of emancipation, by court order, by entry into the armed forces, or by marriage, according to state law provisions regarding emancipation.

Mental competency is another issue relating to capacity. The mental capacity to contract can be defined as the ability to understand the nature and effects of the business being transacted. Some people, such as the severely mentally retarded, are not capable of understanding the effects and obligations of contracts. These people are generally released from any contract they enter.[9] On the other hand, courts are hesitant to intervene in contractual relationships and are reluctant to release people from contracts merely because they were foolish for entering into them. For example, a person who abuses credit cards and charges large amounts that he will be unable to pay will not be protected simply because of bad judgment. Adults are presumed to have the legal capacity to contract, and those seeking to be excused from contractual obligations on this ground would be required to prove that they lacked legal capacity. It is incumbent on those contracting to determine the legal capacity of the other party.[10]

Mutual assent. Cases less frequently turn on the question of whether there are two parties to the contract or whether the parties had legal capacity than on the issue of mutual assent. The question is whether the two parties have a true "meeting of the minds"; that is, "the parties must reach an agreement on the same bargain on the same terms and at the same time."[11] The mutual agreement is generally measured on an objective standard, and the subjective intent of the parties is usually irrelevant. Courts examine the language of the contract and construe it by the usual meanings of the words. A great jurist, Learned Hand, clearly stated this principle of judicial construction when he wrote, "If, however, it were proved by twenty bishops that either party, when he used the words, intended something else than the usual meaning which the law imposes upon them, he would still be held, unless there was some mutual mistake, or something else of that sort."[12] For this reason, complex contracts often contain sections that clearly define certain terms. It is critical that both parties have the same understanding of the terms. To illustrate, merchants involved in international trading would specify the currency for payment as U.S. dollars rather than merely as dollars, which could drastically affect the amount paid if some other nation's dollars (such as Canadian) were involved. The test used by the courts to measure the party's intention is whether a reasonable person in the position of the other party would also interpret the words and actions in the same light.

The mutual understanding usually follows negotiations in which parties argue back and forth as to the terms of the contract. For example, assume that Joe Starr is a nationally known athlete and winner of his sport's highest honor, and that he wishes to parlay that recognition into a lucrative professional career. Starr and the team owners may enter into extended talks about the terms of his contract. The team owners may offer a $30 million compensation package with a yearly salary of $1 million and the remainder to be paid into a pension plan if Joe plays for the team for a period of five years. Joe may counter with an offer to play for $60 million and a yearly salary of $2 million, with the other terms to remain the same. Such bargaining may continue until a compromise acceptable to both is reached. The final contract could have Joe playing for $40 million with a yearly salary of $5 million, a no-cut provision, and a percentage of the team's profits. When one party (the *offeree*) accepts the terms offered by the other (the *offeror*), the negotiations are completed and the contract may then be drafted in final form.

Surprisingly, most newspaper or catalog advertisements that state that goods will be sold for a certain price do not constitute offers in this sense. Instead, they are technically considered to be an invitation for the consumer to offer to pay this price for the goods. The merchant, although not required to have an unlimited supply of the items, is expected to have enough to meet the demand; if he intentionally lacks the needed number and tries to substitute another, he may run afoul of certain consumer protection laws. The language of some advertisements does constitute an offer. An offer from a corporation facing a hostile takeover to buy its own stock at $30 per share is interpreted as an offer. The issue of whether the specific advertisement or circular constitutes an offer depends on the intent of the parties, the specific language, and the circumstances.[13]

Offers are often accompanied by a restriction that the offer will remain open only for a given number of hours or days. When that time has lapsed, the offer is terminated. If no time limit is provided, a reasonable time, as determined by the judge or the jury, will be imposed. Offers may also be terminated by revocation or retraction of the offer, such as when a property owner removes her home from the market. An offer may be rejected by the offeree, and that rejection must be communicated to the offeror directly.[14]

Like rejection, acceptance of the offer must be manifested directly to the offeror by words—either oral or written—or by action, such as performance of one's part of the contract. If the offer is to paint a house and the painter does, in fact, paint the house, that performance is considered acceptance of the offer. The acceptance must be in the format demanded by the offeror, if any, to be valid.[15] The person accepting the offer must be the one to whom it was directed, but a *third-party beneficiary* may be entitled to enforce the contract even though a stranger to the offer and acceptance.[16] A typical third-party beneficiary contract is one in which parents agree to pay tuition for a student to a university. The student could sue the university for failing to place her name on the roll if the fees have been paid. The student did not participate in the bargaining process, but it was the clear intent of the parties that she was the intended beneficiary of the contract, and the law therefore provides an avenue of redress for her.

Consideration.   Valid contracts are accompanied by *consideration*. Consideration is not limited to money but instead is usually defined in terms of an exchange of benefits or detriments; that is, the parties agree to do something they are not legally obligated to do or refrain from carrying out some activity that they are bound by law to do.[17] This consideration may include the exchange of mutual promises, such as one party's agreeing to perform household tasks this week in exchange for a promise that the other party will do so next week, or the exchange of money or goods, such as trading one car for another. The consideration must be the result of the bargaining, and past consideration is not sufficient. The fact that one party did a favor for another last week is not valid consideration for this week's contract. Generally, even economically inadequate consideration will be sufficient to support the bargain, but the key is that both parties must suffer a detriment. Again, the courts are very hesitant to correct the foolish errors or bad judgment of the parties if there has been no fraud or duress involved in the bargaining.

In determining the formation of a contract, courts look to three factors: the capacity of the parties, the offer and acceptance, and consideration. These factors are measured by an objective-person standard, which often requires the judge or the jury to reconstruct the negotiations. This is often difficult, particularly in the case of oral contracts. Oral contracts are as valid as written contracts, with a few exceptions, as we will discuss later; and simple contracts are as valid as the most laboriously drawn ones.

Parties often enter into contracts without realizing the full ramifications of their actions; therefore, it is imperative that both parties read the entire written contract and carefully consider all aspects of it. To illustrate, suppose that Samantha buys an automobile from a dealer with the understanding that she is to make monthly payments to him. However, a provision may allow *assignment* (a present transfer of a contractual interest to a third party) of the contract to a financial institution or to someone else without the permission of the obligor. Samantha could owe the bank or some other unknown party; this frequently occurs with notes for consumer goods, which may be considered assets of the business and are often sold. Another example would be hiring a particular carpenter and then discovering that he had assigned the contract to someone else. In order to avoid the possibility of assignment, the contract should clearly state that it is not assignable.[18]

BREACH OF CONTRACT

Defenses.   Failure to carry out the terms of one's obligations may result in a lawsuit for a *breach of contract*, defined as any failure to perform a contractual duty. Just as in other areas of law, certain recognized defenses are available that may protect one from liability for breach. Two of these excuses for nonperformance have been previously discussed: that the contract contravenes the Statute of Frauds and that the contract is for illegal purposes. In addition, a party may claim impossibility of performance and repudiation as protection from legal liability. *Repudiation* is when one party withdraws from performing the contract based either on his positive statement to the other party that he is unwilling or unable to perform, or on a voluntary affirmative act that makes his compliance impossible or seemingly impossible. If the act is involuntary and renders contract performance impossible, then the party may be relieved of the contractual obligations without liability. For example, an opera diva who permanently loses her voice due to an accident may repudiate future singing contracts with impunity because the loss of her voice was involuntary rather than voluntary. If the repudiation occurs before the other party has suffered any detriment, there is total protection; however, if the other party has complied or changed positions in reliance on the contract, the court may assess damages. Voluntarily failing to perform under the contract or claiming an impossibility that is the result of one's own acts may result in an award of damages.[19]

Other defenses involve the genuineness of the mutual assent. If there has been an inadvertent, material mistake of fact, the contract may be voided, depending on the stage in the transaction at which the mistake is discovered. Recession of the contract will be denied to one who is negligent if the other party is innocent and changed positions in reliance of the contract. The same policy is applied to those who fail to read contracts and are then bound by their terms.[20] If fraud or duress is involved, however, the courts will nullify the contract, and tort remedies may also be available. Allegations of this nature allow juries to examine the negotiation process despite the fact that courts normally do not go behind the contract itself.[21]

Remedies for breach of contract. The most common remedy for breach of contract is for the court to assess monetary damages against the wrongdoer. Many contracts provide for liquidated damages—that is, a predetermined sum to be paid in the event of nonperformance. Compensatory damages, as discussed in Chapter 4, are designed to place the aggrieved party in the economic position in which he would have been had the contract been performed; they constitute the most frequent type of award. Punitive damages, which are designed to punish intentional or malicious wrongdoers by heaping additional costs upon them, are generally not awarded in traditional contract cases.[22] In contract law, the plaintiff may recover those damages which "may fairly and reasonably be considered . . . arising naturally, i.e., according to the usual course of things, from such breach of contract itself" as well as those damages "such as may reasonably be supposed to have been in the contemplation of both parties, at the time they made the contract, as the probable result of the breach of it."[23]

The result is that damages will be assessed only for the harm that was foreseeable when the contract was made. A corollary legal rule imposes an affirmative duty on the aggrieved party to mitigate damages stemming from the breach and not to sit idly by allowing the damages to mount. Assume that the G. F. Hope Corporation is a wholesale turkey distributor which buys turkeys from locals to sell in New York to a world-renowned restaurant. The restaurant unexpectedly closes and breaches the contract to purchase the turkeys. G. F. Hope must take steps to sell the turkeys elsewhere or to otherwise preserve them rather than intentionally allowing them to sit on the dock and die then claiming the entire loss. The courts do not look kindly upon such procrastination and may reduce the amount of damages awarded; on the other hand, the aggrieved party is required to take only reasonable steps that do not lead to undue expense or humiliation.[24]

Damages are the traditional remedy for contract breaches; however, because damages are not always adequate recompense, equity has stepped in to formulate two additional remedies. The first is *promissory estoppel*, which is applied in cases in which the promisee has substantially changed positions in reliance on a gratuitous promise from the promisor, and the promisor is now claiming inadequate consideration as an excuse for nonperformance. The court will step in to prevent injustice and to force the promisor to comply with the terms of the agreement.[25]

Another remedy for breach of contract is specific performance; that is, the court orders the party breaking the contract to comply with its terms. It is particularly appropriate when an item with unique attributes is involved. To illustrate, suppose that you contract to buy the Hope diamond. Another diamond with the same number of carats and the same cut is not an acceptable substitute. The remedy for breach is for the court to reject the offer of another diamond and to order the seller to deliver the Hope diamond or to void the contract if compliance is not possible. Specific performance is not the proper remedy for breach of employment contracts. A musical group that declines to honor its contract to perform on a certain date in a certain city because of a more lucrative order could not be placed under a court order to perform that evening. Such an order would resemble involuntary servitude or slavery, which is prohibited by the Constitution; the court could enter an injunction prohibiting the group from performing elsewhere, however, as well as awarding damages to the concert backers.[26]

RULES OF CONSTRUCTION

Despite the well-known need for clarity in contract language, the terms of contracts are frequently disputed. Courts and, to some degree, legislatures have devised tools to deal with these controversies. One of the foremost tools is the Statute of Frauds, which requires that certain contracts be in writing in order to be enforceable; this is contrary to the general rule that oral contracts are valid. Depending on state law, a writing is required when the contract involves any of the following: (1) contracts affecting interests in land, such as the sale of real property or the creation of a lien; (2) prenuptial agreements or agreements made in contemplation of marriage; (3) contracts that cannot be performed in one year, such as a construction project that will take three years to complete; (4) agreements involving a surety, such as when the executor of an estate repays the debts of the deceased from her own pocket; and (5) contracts involving the sale of goods valued over a set amount ($500 under the Uniform Commercial Code). If such agreements are not written and signed by the parties, the contract is generally unenforceable, although equity may step in to provide remedies.[27]

If the contract is written, the *parol evidence rule* is a critical rule of construction. It provides that only those terms stated in the contract will be considered, or that the court will look at only what is contained within the four corners of the document. Earlier negotiations or contemporaneous oral agreements are irrelevant. The purpose of the parol evidence rule and the Statute of Frauds is to ensure certainty and stability in contractual relationships.[28]

Courts have developed other rules of construction to help them when the terms of contracts are not clear; an example of such a rule is the requirement that language will be interpreted in its usual meaning or in accordance with previous court decisions if the interpretation cannot be determined from the contract. Courts sometimes strain to interpret conflicting terms as consistent and to give validity to as much of a contract as possible. Courts may even provide missing terms of contracts if they can derive them from the facts of the cases. The policy position is to uphold contracts, and courts are sometimes quite creative in determining the intent of the parties or in dealing with ambiguities in contracts in order to reach that goal.[29]

Unfortunately, breach of contracts, with resulting litigation, is a frequent occurrence. Some of these cases are quite complex, requiring years to complete and involving the expenditure of many thousands, if not millions, of dollars on discovery and attorneys' fees. Other contract suits, such as a creditor suing someone for failure to make a car payment, are relatively easy to resolve. Nevertheless, both types of lawsuits exact a toll on the judicial system in terms of the time both of court personnel and of other litigants, whose cases remain on the docket unheard.

UNIFORM COMMERCIAL CODE

Contracts are the core of most business transactions, and the law governing such agreements is primarily case law, which has developed over hundreds of years. However, various legislative bodies have entered the fray and codified many of these rules. The *Uniform Commercial Code* (UCC) is an example of a set of laws governing commercial transactions that has been enacted by state legislatures. The initial draft was proposed by the National Conference of Commissioners on Uniform State Laws, but each legislature may modify the provisions when adopting the Code. The goals of the Code are "(a) to simplify, clarify, and modernize the law relating to commercial transactions; (b) to permit the continued expansion of commercial practices through custom, usage, and agreement of the parties, and (c) to make uniform the laws among the various jurisdictions."[30] In order to facilitate the uniformity of statutes governing commercial transactions, relatively few changes have been enacted by state legislatures.

The UCC contains ten articles:

Article 1.   General Provisions
Article 2.   Sales
Article 3.   Commercial Paper
Article 4.   Bank Deposits and Collections
Article 5.   Letters of Credit
Article 6.   Bulk Transfers
Article 7.   Warehouse Receipts, Bills of Lading, and Other Documents of Title
Article 8.   Investment Securities
Article 9.   Secured Transactions; Sales of Accounts, Contract Rights, and Chattel Paper
Article 10. Effective Date and Repealer

Most of the latter articles deal only with commercial transactions between merchants, but the first five articles are relevant in varying degrees, to the average consumer. However, a note of warning must be issued at this point. The UCC does not cover all commercial transactions, nor does it render contract law obsolete. The UCC is concerned primarily with the sale of goods and does not cover various service and real estate contracts. Previously developed common-law contract principles are codified and not abolished. In addition, there is ongoing interpretation by the courts of the various provisions. Different courts, in interpreting the provisions and applying them to specific situations, attribute different meanings and constructions to phrases. Thus, while uniformity is a desired goal, it is not automatic.

Many law students spend an entire semester studying the UCC, but our scope here is much more limited. We will briefly examine Article 2 because of its common applications. Article 2 deals with contracts for the sale of goods and applies to sales between consumers and merchants as well as between merchants. Goods are defined in Section 2–105 as all things that are "moveable at the time of identification to the contract for sale other than the money in which the price is to be paid, investment securities and things in action." Contracts for real property and services are not covered by this provision. Article 2 covers such topics as the formation of the contract and discusses the offer and acceptance. The major differences from the common law are the expansion of the form of acceptance to any "reasonable" manner and to allow the existence of new terms in the acceptance, rather than considering it a counteroffer if the sale is between merchants. Again, the policy is to uphold contracts whenever possible.

An important aspect of Article 2 is the warranty provisions it contains. A *warranty* is "an assurance by one party to a contract of the existence of a fact upon which the other party may rely . . . [and] is intended to relieve the other party of any duty to personally ascertain the fact."[31] Under the UCC, the seller automatically warrants the title as being good; that is, he warrants that he owns the property and has the legal right to transfer ownership. It also guarantees that the goods are being transferred free of a lien or other interest in the property by a third party unless the buyer is notified of the existence of such interest.

Warranties may be either express or implied. *Express warranties* are created by statements or promises made by the seller regarding the durability or other characteristics of the goods or by technical descriptions of goods. No specific language is required to create an express warranty, but the statement must have been a part of the bargaining process and must have become a basic assumption for entering the contract.

The UCC also contains two very important implied warranties. The first is the *Implied Warranty of Merchantability*. This implied warranty applies only to sales in which the seller is a merchant and is a rich source for contract actions as well as tort lawsuits. In order to collect, the plaintiff must show the following: (1) that the seller is a merchant; (2) that this merchant sold these goods; (3) that the goods were not merchantable at the time of sale; (4) that the plaintiff or his property were injured; (5) that such injuries were proximately and actually caused by the defective goods; and (6) that notice of the injury was given to the merchant. Merchantable goods are defined as goods which minimally

(a) pass without objection in the trade under the contract description; and
(b) in the case of fungible goods, are of fair average quality within the description; and
(c) are fit for the ordinary purposes for which such goods are used; and
(d) run, within variations permitted by the agreement, of even kind, quality and quantity within each unit and among all units involved; and
(e) are adequately contained, packaged, and labeled as the agreement may require; and
(f) conform to the promises or affirmations of fact made on the container or label if any.[32]

The effect of the inclusion of this provision is to allow the consumer to sue not only the manufacturer but also the middleman or the merchant for injuries sustained because of defective goods. For example, plaintiffs injured because of defective automobiles may sue the car dealer as well as the manufacturer.

The second important implied warranty, the *Implied Warranty of Fitness*, applies to all sellers of goods, be they merchants or not. Here a seller is warranting that the goods are fit for a particular use, which is a narrower warranty than the previous one. In order to collect, the plaintiff here must prove many of the same elements, such as that this seller sold these goods and made certain representations about them, as well as that the injury was the result of the defective goods. In addition, however, the plaintiff must show that, as the buyer, he relied on the seller's skill or judgment in selecting these particular goods to perform these specific tasks. It is relatively easy for a plaintiff to show that he has less knowledge about the goods and their suitability than the seller and to show that he relied on the seller's expertise and superior knowledge; this, however, is an issue for the jury to decide.[33] These warranties may be specifically disclaimed—which is another reason to read all contracts carefully and completely. The UCC provisions regarding warranties and their possible waivers are bolstered by federal legislation.[34]

The UCC provides remedies for the breach of contracts. Generally, although the UCC distinguishes between solvent and insolvent buyers, the seller may withhold the goods, stop delivery, and sue for the price of the goods. The seller may sue for the price of the goods (§ 2–709) and for incidental damages (§ 2–710), for the difference between the contract price and resale price of the goods (§ 2–706), for damages (§ 2–708), and to cancel the contract. The usual formula for computing the seller's damages is the difference between the market price at the time of performance and the contract price, plus the costs incurred in mitigating the damage, minus any expenses saved as a result of the buyer's breach.[35] The buyer's remedies for breach are also provided. If the goods do not conform to the contract, the buyer may reject the goods and advise the seller in a timely fashion.[36] If the buyer keeps the goods, the usual formula is the difference between the value of the goods as they are and the value of the goods had they conformed to the contract. The buyer is also entitled to incidental and consequential costs (§ 2–715) and to the costs of obtaining substitute goods (§ 2–712), or to specific performance if the goods have unique qualities (§ 2–716). The buyer may also deduct damages from the unpaid portion of the price for the goods.[37]

The UCC is another attempt to add stability to commercial transactions. In our mobile society, uniformity of laws among the various jurisdictions greatly facilitates that goal. In addition, the codification of these provisions into one statute, rather than having the principles scattered throughout legislative enactments and court decisions, allows merchants, consumers, and lawyers to more easily identify the rules and obligations governing such transactions.

CONSUMER LAW

Since the 1960s, new laws and court decisions have expanded protections for consumers, although the trend in the 1990s has been to weaken such laws and their enforcement. Consumer law is not actually a separate field; rather, it comprises a conglomeration of elements from torts, contracts, the UCC, usury and bankruptcy, and other areas of law. Heightened awareness on the part of citizens, nurtured by consumer advocates like Ralph Nader, has resulted in major changes in the legal system's approach to the consumer. No longer is the purchaser of goods or services left to fend for himself; instead, because of the inherent imbalance between a single consumer and a large corporation, legislatures and courts have stepped in to enhance the fairness of the marketplace. That benefit is offset by the volume of government regulation to which businesses must adhere, and for many people, the benefits for individuals greatly outweigh the burden of regulation.

The Constitution gives Congress the power to "regulate Commerce" and to "provide for . . . general Welfare." The government has taken seriously that charge to regulate for the safety and well-being of the American people.[38] Scores of Supreme Court cases deal with monopolies, labor and employment laws, and other aspects of commerce. Administrative agencies regulate the sale of securities under the SEC, the safety of the skies under the FAA, and new medications and food items under the Food and Drug Administration (FDA). Corporate America is accustomed to government regulation of entire industries, but the expectation that they will answer directly to individual consumers for problems with contracts and faulty goods really bloomed in the last three decades. The process was furthered by the willingness of the courts to entertain such large class-action suits as the asbestos and silicone breast implants cases. New statutory remedies were fashioned to offer the consumer additional protection against the corporations and merchants of goods.

All agree that some government oversight of commerce is acceptable and necessary but the ongoing question is the extent of that oversight. Both the Clinton administration and the Congress acted to reduce the number of regulations to which businesses are exposed. Nevertheless, businesses of all sizes and types continue to complain about overzealous regulatory agencies and burgeoning court judgments. Some argue that the recent changes come about at the expense of taxpayers, such as the savings and loan debacle, or at the expense of everyday consumers because of the pattern of dilution of consumer protection statutes by forbidding certain causes of action, by changing the rules of vicarious liability, and by limiting recoveries, especially punitive damages. Many view these changes simply as necessary course adjustments to keep the economy healthy and a move to a more balanced equilibrium between business, government, and consumers.

Deceptive-trade-practices statutes that have been enacted on both the state and national levels exemplify legislative reform. Merchants are forbidden to include in advertisements misleading statements about, for example, geographic origin or condition of goods. A grocer cannot advertise Florida oranges when, in fact, they are California oranges. The "bait and switch" tactic of advertising a particular piece of merchandise for a low price in order to draw customers in and then substituting another in its place is barred.[39]

In addition to the implied warranties in the UCC, many deceptive-trade-practices acts require truthfulness in statements about the condition of goods and allow the consumer to recover damages, attorney's fees, and court costs as damages. In order to allow recovery of additional damages, suits under the deceptive-trade-practice acts may be filed in conjunction with other types of suits, such as those for violations of tort law, breach of contract, or violations of the UCC.

A related issue is that of home solicitation sales. Assume, for example, that a salesperson comes to your home uninvited and persuades you to buy something. Once the person leaves, you reconsider and decide that you do not want or need the goods. You have the right to cancel that sale within a specified time period in some jurisdictions, and the salesperson must provide you with the forms and addresses necessary to revoke your acceptance and to notify the company. Many cities have ordinances prohibiting door-to-door solicitation, but these are aimed at controlling the traffic flow and not at guaranteeing the trustworthiness of the solicitors or the value of goods.

UCC § 2–302 also provides that *unconscionable contracts* are unenforceable, although the concept of unconscionability is not limited to cases brought under the UCC. It has generally been invoked in cases in which the seller has taken advantage of the buyer and relates to fairness.

> Does any principle in our law have more universal application than the doctrine that courts will not enforce transactions in which the relative positions of the parties are such that one has unconscionably taken advantage of the necessities of the other?[40]

The party asking for relief must show an absence of meaningful choice on the part of one party or lack of knowledge of the terms of the contract and substantial inequality in bargaining power between the parties.[41] Because courts are so reluctant to overturn contracts, they hesitate to state that a contract is unconscionable, and they infrequently do so when two merchants are involved in the transaction. This clause is used most often to benefit consumers, particularly those who are poor and uneducated. Courts have voided contracts that contained exorbitant prices for consumer goods or clauses waiving all warranties when the implied warranty of fitness existed. As discussed earlier, fraud and duress may cause a court to nullify a contract.

Lending laws have also been revised, and more information is now available to consumers who are borrowing money. The Federal Truth in Lending Act, substantially revised in 1994, and similar pieces of state legislation require that the debtor be advised of all finance charges, figured annually and expressed at the annual percentage rate. The statute is not all-encompassing; it applies only to those transactions in which (1) the debtor is a natural person who is borrowing the money for personal, household, or agricultural expenses and (2) the creditor is in the business of extending credit in connection with sales, loans, or services. Individuals can now examine their own credit records for accuracy and may include letters explaining that a bill has not been paid because of some dispute with the merchant or provider of the service. In addition, lenders are not permitted to discriminate on the basis of age, sex, race, or ethnic origin.[42]

Many of the adopted statutes have been weakened, in part because of the efforts of business-oriented incumbent policymakers who favor few restrictions on the right to contract. Yet, the imbalance between large corporations and consumers is not as lopsided as it once was because many of the revisions and policies remain a vibrant part of consumer law.

BUSINESS RELATIONSHIPS

As most contracts involve transactions with or among business entities, it is appropriate at this point to briefly discuss various types of organizations. The focus is on relationships established to carry out business activities for profit. Nonprofit organizations such as various charities, universities, and social clubs may exhibit the same structural characteristics but are outside the scope of this discussion.

Sole proprietorships. The most basic business structure is the *sole proprietorship*. Sole proprietorships are found in a myriad of forms from the artisan selling her works from her studio to a college student conducting a snow removal business to professionals in solo practice. As the name implies, there is a single owner of the business who alone profits from the business but who suffers any loss alone as well. Liability for all debts or torts is passed directly to the sole proprietor. There is no legal barrier for the sole proprietor from business debts, and her personal assets are subject to all business claims. She would claim all income and all business deductions on her personal income tax form (possibly at a lower rate than the corporate rate).

Partnerships. A *partnership* has many characteristics of the sole proprietorship with one salient difference. There must be two or more people and/or corporations involved to create a partnership. Partnership agreements generally outline the arrangements for managing the business and providing for possible indemnification among the partners as well as providing for the dissolution of the partnership and division of the assets. The common-law rules relating to partnerships have been substantially altered by such statutes as the Uniform Partnership Act and the Uniform Limited Partnership Act; however, one aspect remains unchanged. Partners, like sole proprietors, must report their share of the profits or losses on their personal income tax return (even though the partnership files an informational tax return).

In a general partnership, partners may all participate in business decisions, or they may appoint a managing partner who is responsible for day-to-day operations. Some may be silent partners whose names do not appear on the door and are not otherwise identified as having an ownership interest. Each partner shares individual and joint liability for all debts and torts of the general partnership, and each, when acting with proper authority under the partnership agreement or under statute, may bind the partnership in regard to business transactions or tort liability. In contrast, in a limited partnership the limited partners are responsible only to the extent of their investment, but they are not entitled to participate in the management of the business. In essence, they may be viewed as investors only, and if they opt for an active role in management, they lose their protected status.

Corporations.   *Corporations* are the most complex form of business organization and must be chartered by the state in accordance with statutory provisions. The primary difference between corporations and other types of business organizations is that corporations generally shield owners (the shareholders) from individual liability; that is, the corporation itself and its assets, not those of the individual stockholder, are the source of compensation for debts and torts. Corporations come in all sizes from immense multinational conglomerates to small closely held corporations in which all the stock is held by one individual or by a small group, often family members, who share management responsibilities for the family ranch, for example. This mixture of management and ownership is one of the distinguishing features of a closely held corporation. Another variation is the professional corporation or association, which has gained popularity during the last two decades. The business of these entities is the practice of one of the learned professions such as law or medicine. Profits are shared among the members, while liability is generally limited to one's own malpractice and generally does not extend to the malpractice of the other partners, although it will vary from state to state. Small corporations (fewer than 35 shareholders) may elect under Subchapter S of the Internal Revenue Code to have the profits passed through to its members on a pro rata basis and taxed as ordinary income rather than paying tax twice—once on the corporate income and once on the profits distributed to the individuals. Losses are also passed through to the individual shareholder under a Subchapter S election.

Corporations, other than professional or closely held corporations, offer the benefit to investors of limited liability and limited management responsibility. Another advantage is that the investment may be made in relatively small amounts of money—the cost of the share and brokers' fees, if any—at any one time, and the investment is usually easy to liquidate if the shares are sold over the counter or listed on one of the stock exchanges. The disadvantage is that the shareholder has limited chance for profit as well. Of course, if the stock price skyrockets, the shareholder may profit handsomely by selling the stock; conversely, if the stock drops in price, the person may lose money. While holding the stock, there is also the chance for profits if the company pays a cash dividend or declares a stock split which increases the number of shares held without additional investment. Only the individual shareholder's profit or loss from sale of the stock or income from dividends or stock splits is reported on his or her income tax form. Common shares are the basic type of stock, and owners are entitled to a pro rata portion based on the number of shares held of the profits, rights of management, and assets if the corporation is dissolved. Preferred stock carries certain rights and benefits such as priority over other types of stock in regard to dividends.

As legal entities, corporations are entitled to own property and assets, and it is to those assets which creditors generally must look for compensation rather than to the property of individual shareholders. It is very rare for courts to allow the "piercing of the corporate veil" to go behind the corporation and its assets to the directors or the shareholders, and courts do so only in the most egregious of circumstances. Directors of corporations, a position once regarded as a sinecure, are coming under more frequent legal attacks. The directors are elected by the stockholders, and they are responsible for managing the stockholders' enterprise. Traditionally, many boards met only to ratify management decisions and not to take an active role in guiding the corporation. However, in various lawsuits, directors have had to defend their actions and have actually been held responsible for corporate policies and activities as well as mismanagement. The effect has been a chilling one; people no longer readily accept positions as a director for either profit or nonprofit corporations without a guarantee of indemnity or some type of malpractice insurance.

The selection of the appropriate type of organization to carry out commercial enterprises is a complex one, dependent on a number of variables, because most businesses could be viable as any of the three—sole proprietorships, partnerships, or corporations. The first factor is the number of people who own the business or share in its profits or losses; that is, whether it is a very large retail store owned by one person, whether it is a closely held family farm, or whether it is a multinational corporation with subsidiaries in foreign countries. The second factor is the desire of the owners to limit their risks—both in terms of funds and legal liability. For example, limited partnerships in real estate or mineral exploration allows investors to reap profits without large investments (or large losses) and without the burden of management. The third aspect (and one which is often determinative) is the tax consequences of the selection for the individuals involved as well as the respective tax rates for individuals and corporations. The owners of the business must carefully weigh the various factors in deciding the form of the business.[43]

CONCLUSION

In this chapter we have discussed the formation of contracts, outlining the required elements of multiple parties, mutual assent as evidenced by the offer and acceptance, and consideration. The courts have created certain tools, such as the parol evidence rule and the Statute of Frauds, to help them resolve disputes concerning the creation and interpretation of contracts. Breach, or failure to perform one's obligations under a contract, may result in the aggrieved party's collecting damages or in an order for specific performance issued against the nonperforming party. The UCC codifies many of the provisions of the common law in regard to contracts, but its coverage is limited. Elements of various branches of law, including contract law and tort law, have been combined with the UCC to create new areas of protection for consumers, exemplifying a shift from a policy of unswerving sanctity of contracts to a recognition of individual rights and concerns.

The overall purpose of contract law and its subsidiaries is to ensure stability in commercial and private transactions. As Justice Swayne wrote:

> A compact lies at the foundation of all national life. Contracts mark the progress of communities in civilization and prosperity. They guard, as far as is possible, against the fluctuations of human affairs. They seek to give stability to the present and certainty to the future. They gauge the confidence of man in the truthfulness and integrity of his fellow man. They are the springs of business, trade and commerce. Without them society could not go on.[44]

NOTES

1. Joseph D. Calamari and Joseph M. Perillo, *The Law of Contracts*, 3rd ed. (St. Paul, Minn.: West Publishing Company, 1987), pp. 1–2.

2. Martin Weinstein, *Summary of American Law* (Rochester, N.Y.: The Lawyer's Co-Operative Publishing Co./Bancroft-Whitney Co., 1988), pp. 134–136.

3. *Dartmouth College* v. *Woodward*, 4 Wheat. 518 (1819).

4. *Fletcher* v. *Peck*, 6 Cranch 87 (1810).

5. *Dartmouth College* v. *Woodward*, 4 Wheat. 518 (1819).

6. *Davis* v. *Concordia*, 9 How. 280 (1850).

7. *Tucker and Thompson* v. *Moreland*, 10 Pet. 58 (1836).

8. Calamari and Perillo, pp. 306–316.

9. *Board of Regents of Univ. of Tex.* v. *Yarbrough*, 470 S.W.2d 86 (Tex. App.—Waco, 1971).

10. *Nguyn Ngoc Giao* v. *Smith & Lamm, P.C.*, 714 S.W.2d 144 (Tex. App.—Houston [1st Dist.], 1986).

11. David Eliot Brody, *The American Legal System: Concepts and Principles* (Lexington, Mass.: Heath, 1978), p. 126.

12. *Hotchkiss* v. *National City Bank of New York*, 200 F. 287 (S.D.N.Y. 1911) at 293.

13. Calamari and Perillo, pp. 36–38.

14. Arthur Linton Corbin, *Corbin on Contracts* (St. Paul, Minn.: West Publishing Company, 1952), pp. 141–142.

15. Calamari and Perillo, pp. 73–91.

16. *German Alliance Insurance Co.* v. *Home Water Supply Co.*, 226 U.S. 220 (1912).

17. *Gary Safe Co.* v. *A. C. Andrews Co.*, 568 S.W.2d 166 (Tex. App.—Dallas, 1978).

18. Calamari and Perillo, pp. 724–725.

19. Ibid., pp. 514–529.

20. Corbin, pp. 534–537.

21. Calamari and Perillo, pp. 336–378.

22. Ibid., pp. 588–593.

23. Corbin, p. 607.

24. *Nguyn Ngoc Giao* v. *Smith & Lamm, P.C.*, 714 S.W.2d 144 (Tex. App.—Houston [1st Dist.], 1986).

25. Calamari and Perillo, pp. 271–274.

26. *Hadley* v. *Baxendale*, 156 Eng. Rep. 145 (1854).

27. Calamari and Perillo, pp. 773–816.

28. Corbin, pp. 534–537.

29. Calamari and Perillo, pp. 165–182.

30. UCC § 1–102.

31. Brody, p. 188.

32. UCC § 2–314.

33. UCC § 2–315.

34. 15 U.S.C. §§ 2301–2302.

35. UCC § 2–709.

36. UCC §§ 2–601–2–603.

37. UCC § 2–717.

38. U.S. Constitution, Art. I, § 8.

39. 16 CFR §§ 228.114(a), 238.

40. *United States* v. *Bethlehem Steel Corp.*, 315 U.S. 289 (1942), at 326.

41. Martin A. Frey and Terry H. Bitting, *Introduction to Contracts and Restitution for Paralegals* (St. Paul, Minn.: West Publishing Company, 1988), pp. 206–207.

42. 15 U.S.C. §§ 1601–1691.

43. John E. Moye, *Law of Business Organizations*, 3rd ed. (St. Paul, Minn.: West Publishing Company, 1989), pp. 1–102.

44. *Farrington* v. *Tennessee*, 5 Otto 679 (1878).

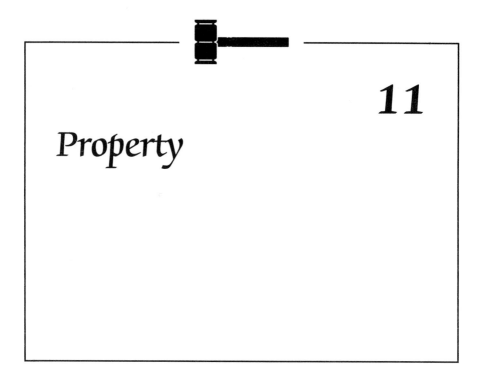

11

Property

Of all legal subfields, property law is perhaps the area in which the principles and terminology of the past are most dominant. The concepts and language used today to create and describe property interests originated during the feudal era of England and have remained virtually unchanged.

> The imprint of the past is still discernible in the present. In this branch of the law more than any other we can time and time again invoke the often quoted statement of Mr. Justice Holmes: Upon this point a page of history is worth a volume of logic."[1]

One of the most basic principles of our system of government is private ownership of assets, and its preservation is secured by constitutional provisions: "No person shall . . . be deprived of life, liberty, or *property*, [emphasis added] without due process of law."[2] We must not overlook the fact that there is public ownership of certain government assets, such as battleships and parks, which theoretically belong to all of us; however, most of the means of production and capital in the United States are held by private investors.

If you were asked whether you own property, what would be your response? Perhaps you would say no, based on the fact that you do not own land. That answer is likely to be incorrect. You own clothes or school supplies; you probably have money in your pocket or bank account. These items are your possessions, and title to them has legally vested in you. Technically, the word *property* means "an aggregate of rights" or "that dominion or indefinite right of use or disposition which one may lawfully exercise over particular things or subjects."[3] Thus, the legal definition of property is one of dominion and control over certain items, whether tangible or intangible. In common parlance, property usually means a thing that is owned or possessed, and judges and lawyers also use the word in that sense.

Two dominant methods are used to classify property. The first is to distinguish between real property and personal property. Real property, or *realty*, is legally interpreted as the land itself and the appurtenances thereto, such as structures constructed on the tract or timber growing on it. In addition, items of personal property that have been securely affixed to the structures or to the land are also considered real property. For example, huge pieces of machinery that are permanently installed in factories lose their character as personal property and assume that of realty. Personal property, or *personalty*, is everything other than realty and includes those items of real property that can be severed without injury to the realty, such as minerals. It includes such diverse items as cash, model airplanes, personal computers, and stocks and bonds.[4]

The second method of classification is to designate property as being tangible or intangible. *Tangible property* includes land and other material items that can be touched, such as paintings and automobiles. Items of *intangible property* are those things that cannot be perceived by touch. For example, debts are intangible even though the promissory note which is the legal acknowledgment of such debt is tangible. A patent or copyright is another illustration of intangible property, although, again, inventors may be given written documentation of their claims.

ESTATES

The Anglo-American notion of estates is based on the concept of ownership measured in terms of time. The duration of ownership determines both the legal rights of the owner and the manner in which he may dispose of the item. A *fee-simple estate* is the maximum estate; it potentially may last through infinity because one is permitted to pass it to one's heirs. The owner of a fee simple may divide it into smaller estates and into nonfreehold estates. The concepts and terms of property ownership are mired in the traditions of the past, particularly the feudal era.

Feudalism. The word *feudalism* is used by historians to describe the social characteristics of Western Europe from the eighth to the fourteenth centuries. It describes a complicated social hierarchy of reciprocal obligations. For example, a tenant might have owed certain military services to his lord in exchange for the lord's protection against attack. Feudalism developed partly because of the dissolution of the Roman Empire caused by the barbarian invaders. Chaos replaced the order and rule of law imposed by the Romans. It became necessary for private individuals to obtain higher levels of protection than they could provide by themselves. They were willing to give up some degree of personal independence and private ownership of land in order to secure the protection offered by the great lords. The effect was to convert Europe from a place where individuals owned land absolutely in prefeudal days to a place where individual and communal ownership of land was destroyed.

Feudalism existed in England before the Norman Conquest, but it was the doctrines and rules of William the Conqueror and his followers that came to dominate English land law. In 1066, William defeated the Saxon King Harold at the Battle of Hastings, and confirmed his somewhat shaky claim to succession from Edward the Confessor by his victory on the battlefield. William's attitude was that because the English landowners had disputed his claim to the throne and required him to assert it by force and because he was justly affirmed as monarch, the Saxon landowners who opposed him should forfeit their land. The king himself became the true owner of every acre of land by right of conquest. As a reward for loyalty and as a tool for maintaining order, William granted dominion over certain manors and castles to his followers with the reservation of ultimate ownership in himself. In exchange for being granted these properties and their revenues, the holders agreed to provide certain services or funds to the king.

A complex structure of reciprocal obligations eventually developed to deal with various social needs. A lord might hold several manors in widely separated areas of the country, and he would have tenants who owed him services for use and occupancy of an estate. This system of holding land in subordination to some superior was known as the *tenure* system; the king was considered to hold the dominion of the soil, while the tenant held the possessory title and the right to the use and profits of the soil, *seisin*. Thus, C might hold of B, who held of A, who held of the king. As more tenancies were created, it eventually became quite bewildering, and in 1290 the *Statute Quai Emptores* was passed. This statute recognized the right of freemen to dispose of their land, but the new holder was obligated to the same person for the same services as the prior holder. In other words, it substituted the new owner for the old in terms of services rather than creating a new level of services. The services due from tenants varied considerably in nature, importance, and duration depending on one's social status.

The tenure system of holding land continued in England until this century, although it was substantially altered by the Statute of Tenures in 1660, which converted most obligations into a simple rent payment. Major land reform legislation was enacted by Parliament in the first quarter of this century, and while land is still theoretically held in tenure and not owned absolutely, it is essentially an empty concept.[5] In the American colonies, land was initially held in tenure. William Penn, for example, was obligated to render two beaver skins annually for his grant.[6] Although lands in the United States were originally held under the feudal concepts of tenure, it is, as a practical matter, not pertinent to land ownership today. Despite the fact that tenure itself is no longer important, the theories that it generated are the basis of modern property law.

Freehold estates. There are three types of freehold estates: estates in fee simple, estates in fee tail, and life estates. Each has its own unique characteristics. An estate in fee simple is the most durable of all estates and connotes the maximum of legal ownership. The holder has the right to possession of the property and the right to dispose of it at will. The title remains fixed in the owner until some affirmative divestment occurs, and title can be passed to heirs. This power of the holder to alienate or transfer the land evolved slowly from the feudal system, in which the lord controlled any changes. By the thirteenth century, however, it was established that the holder could transfer the interest, and that if the holder had conveyed the title with a warranty for both himself and his heirs, then the heirs could not overturn the transfer.[7] Today land conveyances often include the same language, to the effect that the *grantor* and his or her heirs give up all claims of ownership and warrant good title to the purchaser; in addition, land transferred as a fee-simple estate is frequently given "to the purchaser and his or her heirs" although this does not give the heirs a present interest in the property.[8]

Another vestige of feudal law is the *estate in fee tail.* The purpose of the fee tail is to preserve large estates and to keep the property within the family. A fee tail conveys property to a person and the *heirs of his or her body*—that is, descendants of the *grantee.* The effect is to prevent transfer of the property by sale or inheritance outside the family. Like all property transfers, the fee tail may be created by a conveyance of property or by a will. The fee tail, coupled with the system of *primogeniture,* kept many of the major landholdings in England intact and safe from the ravages of dissolute heirs. The grantor could convey the property to a person and the heirs of the body by a particular spouse or limit the lineal descent either through the female line (*fee tail female*) or the male line (*fee tail male*). Such an arrangement may pose difficulties for families if there are adopted children or if the family wishes to sell the property. Fee tails are disfavored by the law, and many courts will dissolve the fee tail so that land can be transferred and then create an equitable trust from the proceeds from the sale. In our egalitarian society, fee tails are relatively rare.[9]

The *life estate* is of limited duration, during the life of the holder or some other person. If the estate is for the duration of the life of a third party, it is known as an *estate pur autre vie.* A daughter's will might read "to

Mother during her life and then to my children." The purpose here is to provide for the mother's welfare during her lifetime and to ensure that the property will ultimately pass to the grandchildren. Life tenants have the right to possession of the property and the right to receive any income and profits from it. They are under an affirmative duty to refrain from any act that would diminish the value of the property and are required to perform ordinary maintenance and repairs. Although a life interest may be transferred, there often is not a market for such limited estates.[10]

Modern conveyances of property employ the same terminology as ancient land deeds in identifying the type of estate created in the grantee. It is ultimately the grantee's responsibility to ensure that the grantor has good title to the property that he is conveying, although the grantor usually warrants that the title is clear. Most buyers delegate the duty of checking the title to trained professionals, such as title companies or attorneys, who examine the courthouse records to determine whether there is any cloud on the title. Many purchases of land involve real estate agents, and their responsibilities and charges should be clarified early in the relationship. Realtors traditionally represent the seller's interest, and today real estate agents are frequently required to provide written disclosure of that fact to both potential buyers and sellers. Many states now allow that pattern to be altered and the realtor to act on behalf of the buyer alone or of both parties with full written disclosure and after obtaining full consent of all parties to the transaction.[11] Ethical realtors will be completely open and honest about all fees, closing costs, and real estate prospects in an area. Lending institutions are frequently involved in real estate transactions; in exchange for lending the money to purchase the property, the institution takes a mortgage or puts a lien on the property. If that loan is not repaid in a timely fashion, the institution may force the sale of the asset. The financial institution from which a loan is taken should be selected carefully. All documents involved in the transaction should be studied and questions should be asked without hesitation because these are important commitments.

Nonfreehold estates.   Nonfreehold estates are leasehold estates that frequently involve periodic payments from a tenant to a landlord; that is, the owner of the fee-simple estate carves out a smaller and temporary estate and keeps the reversion interest in herself. There are three types of leasehold estates: an estate for years, a periodic estate, and an estate at will. The estate for years, which is expressed in terms of a multiple or fraction of a year, has a definite termination date and ends with the expiration of that time or by surrender. The periodic estate resembles the estate for years in that it endures for a year or a fraction thereof and for successive periods of that length until terminated by proper notice by either party. The estate at will has no specified period of termination. It continues at the will of the *lessor* and the *lessee.*

The basis of these arrangements is the *lease,* which is "neither fish nor fowl"; that is, it is neither wholly a contract nor is it wholly a property conveyance. It is based on a series of covenants or promises made by the parties to the lease and is tailored to suit the particular transaction. Typically, the lessor promises the tenant the right of "quiet enjoyment" of the premises; in addition, the landlord may agree to furnish certain services or to maintain the premises in reasonably good repair. In exchange, the lessee agrees to pay rent; to use the premises in the specified manner, such as for residential and not business purposes; to refrain from subleasing or assigning the lease without the landlord's permission; and to refrain from causing any damage beyond the normal wear and tear on the premises.[12]

Leases may be either oral or written. Leases for residential property are often standard forms and are frequently much less complicated than are commercial leases. The lessor, as the person with the largest estate, was favored by the common law if a dispute arose, but statutory enactments now offer the residential tenant much more protection than was previously available. State laws and municipal ordinances vary regarding the landlord's responsibilities, but typically the lessor must maintain the premises in a safe and habitable condition. Failure of either party to comply with the terms of the lease may result in litigation. If a tenant causes excessive deterioration to the property or fails to make timely rent payments, the landlord may evict the tenant under the state's statutory scheme, which may include court action. On the other hand, if lessors do not live up to their part of the bargain, tenants may also sue and punitive damages may be involved. Those who rent property should become familiar with their state and city laws regarding the landlord–tenant relationship. In addition, before a lease is signed, it should be *read*. For the tenant's protection, any preexisting damage, such as stains on the rug, should be listed on the lease itself, and the landlord or its agent should initial it. In addition, any and all provisions relating to the rental of the property should be included in the written lease, and there should be no oral modifications as to the tenant's obligations.

Concurrent ownership. There are a number of schemes for owning property in common with other people. One of the most frequent is the marital estate. As discussed in Chapter 12, marital property comes in two varieties: the *community-property* system and the so-called common-law system. In community-property states, the husband and wife each own an undivided half of the marital estate. Property that was owned by either of them before marriage or that is received as a gift or by inheritance is considered to be separate property.[13] In the common-law states, each spouse has an individual estate; the wife's salary belongs to her and to her alone, although the couple may create cotenancies by mutually contributing money to buy an asset, such as a home. These tenancies are usually treated as tenancies in common.

Tenancies in common are interests in property that are concurrently held by two or more parties. Each has the right to use and enjoy the property; that is, each has a possessory interest. The separate and distinct ownership interests may be created at different times in different instruments, and the rights thereunder pass to the owner's heirs. In contrast, joint tenancies carry a right of survivorship, which means that the co-owner will inherit the interest. *Joint tenancies* are created by one instrument at the same time, and all the owners have the right to possess and enjoy the property.[14] Joint tenancies terminate with the death of one owner, with divorce if it is a marital estate, or by a *suit to partition,* which is a lawsuit requesting the court to divide the property into separate and distinct segments and to assign it to the owners individually.[15]

Limitations on ownership interests. The traditional rule is that the holder of the fee-simple estate owns not only the surface of the land but also the area below it to the center of the earth and the area above it into the skies. Today, however, the perceptions of ownership are more limited.[16] One such restriction is an *easement,* which is a right to use some or all of the property of another and may be created by custom, agreement, statute, or court order. Typical easements include a right-of-way to reach one's land which is surrounded by another's property and easements to prevent the blocking of light, air, and the flow of water.[17] A second development is recognition of limit on the owner's authority over air space above the land; a landowner cannot, for instance, prevent a satellite from being stationed in outer space above his land.

A third limitation is the effect of formally separating the property into surface and subsurface estates. The usual reason for severing the two is to allow for the exploration and production of minerals, often oil and gas. Once severance has taken place, the mineral interest is the dominant one, and its owner has the right to develop that interest even if the surface is damaged. The surface owner may not collect for damage done to his or her interest which is "reasonable" in light of the current industry practices; in other words, the type of injury sustained would have to be unusual or malicious in order for the surface owner to receive compensation.[18]

A fourth limitation is the power of the government over private owners of land. Government has the power of *eminent domain,* or "the power to take private property for public use."[19] This allows government to seize land to construct new housing projects, sports arenas, highways, or other public facilities even over the owner's objections; however, the Fifth Amendment guarantees that "private property [shall not] be taken for public use, without just compensation." Those owners who are dissatisfied with the price offered by the government may file suit and ask for a jury determination as to the fair value of the property.

In addition, local governments frequently restrict the use and occupation of property through zoning ordinances. Zoning determines the type of activity that may be conducted on the property. Typical of such schemes would be delineated areas that are designated for single residences, multi-party residences, commercial purposes, or heavy industry, and landowners would be required to match the use of the land to the appropriate zone and would be barred, for example, from placing a large factory with the resulting traffic in the middle of a residential district and across the street from a school. The owner's freedom to use the land as he sees fit may also be hampered for environmental reasons, for historical preservation, or for aesthetic purposes, such as landscape ordinances. The justification for all of these land controls is in the government's power to protect the general welfare.[20]

INCEPTION OF TITLE AND LIENS

Title to property may be acquired in variety of ways—by property division upon divorce, by award of damages in litigation, by foreclosure for nonpayment of debt, by adverse possession, by inheritance or gift, or by deed. We have previously discussed substantive areas of the law, torts and contracts, which involve transfer of property (usually money) from the wrongdoer to the victim when damages are awarded as compensation. Inheritance and gifts will be covered later in this chapter, and the property aspects of divorce are included in the next chapter, which allows us to focus here on other methods for obtaining title and on liens.

Adverse possession. *Adverse possession* is "a method of acquisition of title by possession for a statutory period under certain conditions."[21] Under this legal doctrine, a person (natural or artificial) who openly uses another's property may wrest the title from the original landowner and cause it to vest in himself. Assume, for example, that Jennifer wishes to add a swimming pool to enhance the value of her home, so she fences the backyard and constructs the pool. Several years later, when a survey is done of the property pending sale, she is told that one-half of her pool is sitting on the property of her neighbor, Jessica. Through her open and continuous use of Jessica's property, Jennifer may have converted the property to her own depending on the length of the adverse possession and the state's statutory time requirements.

Some jurisdictions require that the adverse possession must occur under "color of title." That is, Jennifer would be required to show that her deed to the property indicated that she owned the area of the swimming pool before she could prevail and the mere use of the land would not suffice to change the title. Other states permit the transformation with or without "color of title" but require those who are not acting under color of title to use the land for a longer period of time. The key to adverse possession is always the open, notorious, and continuous use of the land. Paying taxes on the property in question may be a very helpful piece of evidence in such law-suits, and it is through litigation that such issues are generally resolved.[22]

Deeds.   The most common method of conveying property interests is by deed for real property and by various documents of title—bills of sale, certificates of title, receipts, or registration for personal property. There are three common types of deeds: (1) *warranty deeds;* (2) *special warranty deeds;* and (3) *quitclaim deeds.* Deeds contain certain essential information about the transaction—the legal description of the property, the grantor and the extent of his or her interest, the grantee, and the consideration for the transfer, which need not be money ("for the love and affection which I bear my daughter, Mary Sue," for example). Warranty deeds are those in which the grantor of the land guarantees or warrants that he will defend the grantee and his heirs and assigns against title claims and will compensate them for any loss arising from such claims. Such deeds usually encompass a warranty on the part of the grantor that the title is unblemished and that there are no unrevealed encumbrances on the property. The grantor who gives a special warranty deed is stating only that she did not cloud the title herself but is making no guarantees about the state of the title before her ownership and that she will not defend the grantee's title from prior claims. A quitclaim deed contains no warranties about the title at all and effectively puts the grantee on notice that some flaw may exist in the chain of title. Quitclaim deeds should be avoided because they convey only the grantor's interest in the property and not the property itself, and purchasers should be particularly wary if the seller offers a quitclaim deed during the transaction or if a quitclaim deed pops up during the title examination.[23]

As you know from our prior discussions, the Statute of Frauds mandates that contracts for sale of land must be in writing to be effective. Deeds too must be in writing and signed by the grantor. Many states require that the signatures on the deeds be acknowledged before a notary public. It is imperative that the instruments be recorded, because in effect, title does not pass until the deed which gives public notice of the transaction is registered at the courthouse. Not registering the deed does not affect the interests between the parties, but it does affect the rights of third parties such as subsequent purchasers. Missing deeds in the chain of title may cause the transaction to fail.

Purchasers of real property are concerned that they receive marketable title. A marketable title is one that is free from encumbrances or liens and free from doubts as to its validity or concerns about flaws.[24] It is the role of the title examiner or title insurance company to examine the title and determine its validity. The examiner will look at the documents on file to see if there are any unexplained gaps in the chain of title or if any of the deeds hint at some cloud on the title (a quitclaim deed, for example) and if there are any recorded easements or encumbrances.

Liens. Much of the property in this country, both personal and real, is held subject to a *lien,* which indicates that a creditor has a protected interest in the property. The liens on real property may result from a variety of transactions—a mortgage for the purchase money, a contractor's lien for home improvements, a judgment lien for failure to pay a court-ordered judgment, or a tax lien for failure to pay taxes. Liens on personal property are generally covered by Chapter Nine of the Uniform Commercial Code, which covers both tangible and intangible property. Liens on both personal and real property have the same effects and requirements. The creditor who has accepted a security interest in the collateral (be it home, merchandise, or equipment) may act to foreclose and assume ownership of the property if the debtor defaults on loan payments. Indication of the debt must be in writing and, in order for the creditor to assume priority over other creditors, the instrument must be properly recorded.[25]

Real estate ownership, both commercial and residential, is often contingent upon payments to a financial institution that loaned money for the purchase. Most homeowners cannot afford to purchase a home outright, or they may choose not to do so because of the tax advantage in being able to deduct mortgage payments on one's income tax return (as long as Congress allows that exemption). Also, there is a certain advantage to using someone else's money rather than one's own, particularly in commercial ventures. Assume that Creighton and Marion choose to buy a home, but they only have the money for a downpayment and must borrow the rest from a financial institution although various government programs may guarantee the loan or insure a lower interest rate There are typically three instruments involved in such a transaction. One, Creighton and Marion, as purchasers of the home, will receive a warranty deed from the seller transferring ownership to them. Two, as debtors, they will execute a promissory note to the lender for the amount of the loan, using the home as collateral. Third, the lending institution will record an instrument indicating its security interest in the public records as notice to other creditors of its preferred status as a creditor.

Property ownership, whether of a fee simple estate or a leasehold, vests certain rights of use, enjoyment, and transferability of interests in the owner. Ownership may be acquired through diverse methods such as by adverse possession, by deed, by virtue of court order, or by foreclosure for nonpayment of debt. Recording the indicia of title or security interest in public records is critical for protection of one's property rights.

PROBATE AND SUCCESSION

The old adage "You can't take it with you" succinctly frames the legal problem of what happens to a person's property after death. The law, like nature, abhors a vacuum, and a vast and complicated system of laws has evolved to deal with the troublesome issue. Many of the terms and concepts regarding inheritances are borrowed from property law. For instance, statutes provide for different distributions of the descendent's property depending on whether it is realty or personalty. A person who is foresighted enough to prepare a *will* in accordance with the legal requisites is described as dying *testate,* whereas a person who dies without a will is considered to have died *intestate.* In the latter instance, the state will allocate the property in compliance with the intestacy statute. The *testator,* or person making the will, can control "from beyond the grave" who gets the property; otherwise, the state will make that decision.

Provisions relating to succession were a natural outgrowth of individual property ownership. Intestate succession, based on familial or clan relationships, probably preceded testamentary provisions, but the Egyptians were designating their beneficiaries in writing as early as 2548 B.C. The Book of Genesis contains references to testamentary distributions, and the rules governing succession were included in the codes of both Jewish and Islamic religions. The Greeks, during the height of their civilization, had limited testamentary powers, but it was the Romans who fully developed the concept. The Roman traditions were incorporated into English law through the ecclesiastical courts, which retained dominion over matters of inheritance until the mid-nineteenth century. As discussed in the previous section, laws such as the estate-in-fee tail and primogeniture were designed to ensure succession within families and therefore to preserve the family's base of power. Although American laws regarding succession to property are founded in English principles, there are numerous differences. One of the most obvious is the failure to adopt the system of primogeniture and instead to adhere to the Roman principle that the children inherit equally from a parent.[26]

Intestate succession.   The laws of descent and distribution determine the manner in which a decedent's property will be distributed if he dies without making a will, if the will is invalid, or if it does not cover the entire estate. In effect, the law makes wills for those who do not make their own. The statutes disburse the property by fixed formulations based on consanguinity and affinity rather than dependency, age, household connections, need, or other factors. The two key elements in most of the intestacy statutes are the structure of the decedent's family and the categorization of property as realty or personalty. Such laws are blind to the individual needs or equities in a particular family because they are drafted to provide certainty and stability in a wide variety of situations. For instance, if you were deciding how your assets would be allocated after your death, you might want to provide for an aged parent or a handicapped sibling; however, the statute might assign all of your property to your minor children with a reservation of a life estate in your spouse.

The rules governing descent and distribution vary from state to state, but there are patterns in the various schemes. First, descendants receive favored treatment over all other blood relatives. The decedent's children, natural and adopted, inherit the property subject to the interest, if any, of the decedent's spouse. The children are given equal shares without regard to age or sex, and the children of any of the decedent's predeceased children receive the share that their parent would have received if still living. If the decedent leaves no surviving spouse or descendants, the property often goes to the parents, to the siblings, to the children of the siblings, and then to the descendants of the decedent's grandparents, in successive steps. The presence of heirs at any of those levels would stop the process. If there are no *heirs*, then the property will escheat to the state.[27]

Second, every state has some protection for surviving spouses. In community-property states, the spouse already owns half of the marital estate, and the succession laws may omit the spouse entirely in favor of those related by consanguinity.[28] A surviving husband may wind up owning his undivided half of the marital home, with the other half being owned by the children of his wife's first marriage (which can be a most uncomfortable situation). Another favorite statutory provision is to allow the surviving spouse to take one-half, one-third, or some other fractional share of the estate if the decedent left children; if there are no issue, then the spouse may inherit the entire estate.[29]

To iterate, each sovereign state has a different statutory scheme regarding intestacy and the guardianship of minor children. Disposition of the children can be predetermined by a testator, but without testamentary provisions, the state will decide the guardianship of the children. Many of the problems common to intestate succession rear their heads here. You might wish your best friends to have custody of your children instead of your aged parents or your disreputable sibling, but the law gives preference to relatives. The court will base its decision on the objective standard of the best interest of the children in a contested case, but blood relatives are often the preferred choices.

Testate succession.   A person who drafts a will determines the fate of his or her family and disposes of any assets rather than leaving such important issues to the sometimes cold and unfeeling state. No one has a better understanding of a person's wishes in this regard than the person herself, and despite what clairvoyants and mediums proclaim, the law is skeptical of communications "from beyond the grave" and will not give effect to any postdeath property dispositions. Drafting a will is really quite simple, but the process does demand that the testator carefully assess the situation and his own emotions and then make preparations based on that assessment.

Most of us think of a written instrument that has been executed with certain formalities when we hear the term *will*. However, there are other types of wills—holographic and nuncupative—which may be recognized by the law. A *holographic will* is one written entirely in the testator's handwriting and signed by him or her.[30] A *nuncupative will* is an oral will. Oral wills are not favored by the law because of the inherent difficulties in a will contest of determining the exact intent of the testator and the disposition of the property due to the fleeting nature of the will. Typically, statutes governing nuncupative wills set out stringent requirements for validity and may include such provisions as the following: (1) that the testator was aware of impending death; (2) that the witnesses cannot claim under the will; and (3) that only personalty, and not realty, may be affected.[31] Not all states accept holographic and nuncupative wills, and, as previously noted, the validity of the will is determined by the laws of the domicile of the testator. Louisiana, in particular, has unique provisions relating to succession, both testate and intestate, because of its civil-law heritage.

A testator executing a will—of whatever kind—must have *testamentary capacity,* which is defined as being of "sound mind" or understanding "the nature and extent of his property, the persons who are the natural objects of his bounty, and the disposition he is making of his property," and the nexus between all of these.[32] The moment at which the will is executed is the pivotal time, and the fact that one's mental capabilities fade in and out is not determinative of one's capacity. The testamentary capacity needed to make a will is not tantamount to the legal ability to contract. A somewhat related issue is the question of voluntariness. The will is void if the testator was acting involuntarily or under duress, or if there was fraud or undue influence involved. However, disinheriting one's family members, supposedly the natural objects of one's bounty, in favor of someone else does not automatically cast doubt on the validity of one's capacity.[33]

Other formalities must be observed in executing a written will. It is patent that the testator must sign the will for it to be effective. It must be signed in front of competent witnesses whose number and competency, usually age, are determined by state law, and it is axiomatic that someone taking under the will must not sign as a witness. The witnesses must be advised as to the nature of the ceremony they are observing, although they do not read the will and often do not know the testamentary provisions (unless the witness is the attorney who drafted the will or the secretary who typed it). The witnesses sign the will after the testator but in his presence. The will should be stored in a safe place until it is needed.[34]

Wills must be updated periodically as life circumstances alter. People marry, divorce, have children, and see those children become independent while once-independent parents become dependent. One method of changing one's will is to add a *codicil,* which is a formal modification or addition to the existing instrument. A second method is to execute a new will, in which case the old one should be revoked through language in the new document or, even better, by destruction of the original, or both.[35]

It is relatively inexpensive to have a simple will prepared by an attorney, although it is not absolutely necessary to do so. We heartily recommend the avoidance of self-help methods or popular "how-to" books. It is true that one might follow these guides with no particular problems, but on the other hand, disaster can strike if one fails to understand all the ramifications. Remember, too, that each state has a different testamentary scheme and requirements for validity. A corollary issue is that of the "living will," which allows you and your family freedom of choice in regard to medical treatment for the terminally ill. Some states mandate a particular format and language in order for the will to be effective; therefore, if you are interested in executing such a document, be sure that you are aware of the law in your state, and do not assume that a standard form will suffice.

Probate. The purpose of probate proceedings is to ensure that the heirs and beneficiaries receive good title to the property they receive. Probate is conducted in accordance with the laws of the domicile of the decedent or with the laws of the state where realty is located.[36] Probate is generally much simpler (and often cheaper) if there is a will appointing an executor or administrator of the estate; otherwise, the court will appoint someone to carry out these responsibilities. It is this person's duty to gather the assets, prepare the inventory for the court's approval, pay the debts, prepare the estate tax return, if any, and disburse the assets to the beneficiaries or heirs.[37] Creditors of the decedent have priority over the heirs or beneficiaries, although state laws provide some protection for the surviving spouse and minor children. Again, this is not the ideal time to employ self-help methods or to ignore probate if one wishes to have legal title to any property one inherits.

Although dying testate is obviously meritorious, it is no guarantee that everything will be copacetic following a demise. Those who are omitted may be disgruntled, and the dispositions can generate enmity among relatives. Nevertheless, a prudent and considerate person protects those he cares for by preparing a will and engaging in estate planning. This includes maintaining an up-to-date list of all assets and debts, of the location of important documents, and of current advisors such as accountants, insurance agents, stockbrokers, and attorneys. The existence of this list and its whereabouts should be made known to family members. While many of us think of only the elderly as needing wills, it is perhaps more critical for younger people with dependent children to have a will in order to specify the guardianship of those children if something happened to the parent.

TRUSTS AND GIFTS

The laws relating to succession are designed to ensure the preservation of property. Another way to do so is through a *trust*, which is a transfer of property from the *trustor* or settlor to the *trustee* as trustee to manage the property for the benefit of the settlor or a third party, known as the beneficiary.[38] Trusts may either be created in a will—a testamentary trust—or during the lifetime of the settlor—an *inter vivos* trust.[39] Trusts are created for a variety of reasons. There may be certain tax advantages to this type of property transfer. The trustor may wish to transfer the problems of managing the trust assets to a financial institution while reserving the right to withdraw any or all of the money whenever it is needed. Perhaps the most common reason for creating a trust is to place the management of assets in the hands of an impartial party as a form of protection for children or grandchildren. Such appointment may be desirable because the person is a spendthrift and the assets can be protected from creditors, or because the trustor wishes to guarantee the beneficiary an income long after the trustor is gone.[40]

The provisions of the trust can be tailored to suit the trustor's wishes, and while it does allow for extended control "from beyond the grave," all trusts must eventually terminate, and none can last more than 21 years past the lives of the persons living and specified at the time of creating the trust. This is known as the *rule against perpetuities*.[41] A frequent testamentary arrangement is for the surviving spouse to receive the income from the trust, and after the spouse's death, the children or grandchildren would receive the *corpus*, or the principal. This provides the spouse with an income, and at the same time prevents him from wasting the children's inheritance or conveying it to a second spouse. Trustors have been quite creative in the restrictions and control they have exerted.

The trustee has the responsibility to manage the trust assets, protect the corpus, and comply with the directions of the trust instrument. The trustee may be either a natural person or a corporation such as a bank or trust company. Many settlors opt to have a financial institution serve as trustee because a natural person might not survive as long as the trust, while the corporation does not have such a limited lifespan and because of the expertise of the institutions in managing money (although the recent history of the banking and savings and loan industries may cast doubt on both premises). Another factor that settlors must consider in deciding on who is to be named trustee is the size of the management fee that the trustee would receive. Also, many financial institutions will not accept small trusts, as, for example, those with assets below $100,000.

The obligations of the trustee are mandated by the trust instrument, by statute such as a Trust Code, and by the common law. The trustee is legally required to manage the assets with the same skill and diligence as a reasonably prudent person would, and any breach of that fiduciary relationship may lead to both civil and criminal liability on the part of the trustee. The trustee has the duty to invest and manage the property in a productive manner and not to waste the assets by not properly caring for the property or by investing in extraordinarily risky business ventures. The extent of the trustee's powers will be determined by reference to the instrument or to the state's trust laws. Trustees may be removed by court order or by meeting provisions of the trust agreement which allow substitution of trustees.[42]

In contrast, gifts come with "no strings attached." *Gifts* are voluntary transfers of property to the recipient. The *donee* receives full legal title to the property and has full management of it. These are gratuitous transfers; that is, there is no exchange of consideration.[43] An estate planner may recommend a plan of annual gifts to reduce a person's estate below the state or federal inheritance tax levels. Gifts are taxfree to the donee. In other words, substantial gifts to individuals and to charities not only warm the *donors'* hearts but may also provide tax advantages to them, although the tax advantages of charitable contributions are now more limited under the 1986 tax-reform measures.

INTELLECTUAL PROPERTY

Intellectual-property law is really an amalgamation of traditional property, tort, and contract-law principles. Its roots are based in antiquity, and it is enshrined in this country's Constitution among the enumerated powers of Congress "to promote the progress of science and useful arts, by securing for limited times to authors and inventors the exclusive right to their respective writings and discoveries."[44] The second Congress passed the first patent statute in 1790, barely a year after the Constitution was adopted.[45] However, in today's environment of personal computers and digitized information, which is readily available through global communications, some are questioning the basic concept of exclusive ownership of ideas and the products they generate.[46] They are essentially arguing a return to ancient law, which did not recognize a "property" right in intellectual property but instead conceived the matters of plagiarism and intellectual theft as matters of honor, credit, or fame.

Before the concept of intellectual property could develop,

> two prerequisites were necessary. The first was a clear understanding that invention or ideas could indeed be the product of human intellect rather than the random gift of the gods, or in the Judeo-Christian Era, of God. The second which depended from the first was a recognition that the product of the intellect in its intangible form could also have commercial value.[47]

The Greeks and Romans readily accepted the first but not the second. The seeds of intellectual property are often attributed to the guilds of the Middle Ages and their proprietary attitudes toward craft knowledge. Particularly noteworthy in this respect were the Renaissance glassmakers of Venice who recognized that the craft knowledge of the guild and the particular families within the guild had intrinsic commercial worth, separate and apart from the actual glass, and sought to limit the spread of the information in order to achieve control over the industry and to preserve the value of their knowledge.

Then, as today, governments were encouraging economic development by providing financial incentives, granting favorable tax treatment, and awarding exclusive privileges to individuals as well as groups to introduce and develop new industries and crafts.[48] This practice of granting these monopolies originated in Italy, probably in Venice but perhaps in Florence, early in the fifteenth century, and by 1474, the practice was so ingrained that Venice enacted the first patent statute. It provided for protection of newly invented works as well as processes and products not previously known within the realm; however, the work or device had to be sufficiently developed so as to actually be used and operated. There was a temporal limitation on exclusivity for ten years during which time anyone violating the monopoly would be fined, although the patentee could license the work to someone else. The statute is the earliest known version of patent by registration, that is, conforming to set administrative regulations to protect one's property interests.[49] Other nations quickly followed to adopt similar provisions, and patent laws were adopted in France, England, Germany, and the Netherlands, especially Holland, where the most advanced and prolific patent custom developed. There the applicant had the burden of clearly delineating the subject matter of the patent, usually accompanied by a drawing or model in case of later litigation. The review was by committee with the relevant technical knowledge to determine if the invention was indeed so novel as to merit patent protection. In France, for example, this task was assigned in 1699 to the Royal Academy of Science.[50]

The development and practices of patent law in England closely followed the pattern established on the continent—the growth of guilds and the increasing role of the government in encouraging financial development through grants of patents and monopolies. In fact, the practice became so prevalent under Elizabeth I that it was the battleground for an epic constitutional issue—the power of the monarch versus that of Parliament. Patents and monopolies were issued at the discretion of the monarch as a matter of royal grace. Elizabeth I granted so many monopolies and patents to various courtiers that it has been described as a "system of plunder"[51] with the net effects of "hindrance to trade and manufacture, high prices, inferior goods, and unemployment."[52] In November 1601, Parliament debated the subject of royal powers and prerogatives in the guise of "An Act for the Explanation of the Common Law in Certain Cases of Letters Patents." There were actually two facets to the argument: the power of the monarch and the right of Englishmen to freely engage in trade and industry. Elizabeth I won by admitting that there might have been errors in granting some patents and that future disputes would be submitted to the common-law courts if the bill were dropped. She temporarily avoided a parliamentary discussion of her powers by compromising, but the problem remained for her successors.[53] In 1602, monopolies were declared to be against the common law in the famous case of *Darcy* v. *Allin*, also known as *The Case on Monopolies*,[54] which concerned the monopoly on the manufacture, importation, and sale of playing cards. That principle was iterated in the 1623 Statute of Monopolies but there was a key exception—for letters patent issued to the "first and true" inventors for a period of 14 years or less.[55] This law was the sole statute governing patents in England for more than 200 years, and it was still a matter of "privilege" rather than a "property" right.[56]

The basic theoretical conflict—monopoly versus property right—was transported to the United States, and the owners of patents more frequently than not were the losers in the U.S. courts. Those seeking to limit competition in business whether by trademark protection, copyright, or patents are subjected to close scrutiny as the open market is strongly favored as policy and by law.[57] In *Jungerson* v. *Ostby & Barton Co.*, Justice Robert H. Jackson, in his dissent, noted that seemingly the only valid patent was one that had not come before the Court.[58] However, as stated earlier, one of the first major pieces of legislation passed by Congress dealt with the issues of intellectual property despite this hostility. The legal framework basically incorporates three general substantive areas—*patents, copyrights,* and **trademarks**—to protect the originality of works and to prevent unfair competition.[59]

Patents may be one of three different types—utility, design, and plant patents. Utility patents are those covering machines, industrial processes, compositions of matter, and articles of manufacture; the type of items that we normally think of as subject to patent.[60] The length of protection changed in June 1995 from a period of 17 years to 20 years from the time the application is filed with some limited exceptions.[61] Design patents are those protecting ornamental features rather than function. Plant patents are those dealing with the breeding of new plants or discovery of previously unknown plants.[62]

Applications for patents are made to the Patent and Trademark Office, and the processing of such patents is often arduous, time-consuming, and expensive. The application must contain the short title of the invention, identify the inventors, and contain the specifications and/or drawings for the process or item.[63] Once filed, a patent office examiner reviews the patent to determine if the subject matter is both "objectively novel and unobvious to those familiar with relevant technology."[64] Patents allow the inventor to prevent someone from making or copying the subject but not from seeking to improve or change the process. The right to a patent may be assigned or licensed and have the attributes of personal property. If infringement does occur and other methods of resolution fail, litigation must be filed in federal court.[65] Appeal is to the Court of Appeals for the Federal Circuit, established in 1982, subject to infrequent review by the Supreme Court. Decisions of this court indicate a much greater willingness to support the validity of patents against infringement. From 1935 to 1982, the number of patent cases affirmed on appeal was about 32 percent, while between 1982 to 1988, 81 percent of the cases were affirmed.[66]

Copyrights protect original works of authorship in such diverse items as literary works, musical works, dramatic works, pantomimes and choreographic works, pieces of visual art (sculpture, pictures, graphics), audiovisual works such as movies, sound recordings, architectural works, and semiconductor chips.[67] It does not cover such items as various forms, calendars, schedules for sporting events, or timetables for airlines, for example.

One issue within copyright law is whether the work is done by a fulltime employee; if so, it is done "for hire" and the employer owns both the work and the copyright. On the other hand, if it is completed before being sold, the author owns the copyright unless it is separately conveyed. The issue can become quite sticky as, for example, university professors who produce literary or artistic works. For example, consider the graphics art professor who invents the "better mousetrap" or writes the great American novel, both of which are clearly outside the scope of his teaching responsibilities, and the same professor who produces the piece which is heralded as the greatest graphics masterpiece of this century but which was produced on his own time in his own studio. Generally, the courts have adopted a narrow policy that most works are not "for hire" and then only if specified in writing.[68] The distinction is also important in the duration of the copyright. Most copyrights last for the lifetime of the authors plus 50 years, but those for works for hire or anonymous works last for a flat period of 75 years from date of publication.[69]

Protection under the copyright laws is no longer dependent upon "notice," although registration is required before initiating an action for infringement; that is, the famous © is not required in order to trigger the protection. Registration of copyrights, as contrasted with patents, is very routine and inexpensive and is done by depositing copies with the Copyright Office. Infringement of copyright is punishable in federal courts as both a civil and criminal matter. The chief defense is "fair use" in which the purpose and amount of copying pose little chance of injury and are justified on policy grounds. This includes, for example, xeroxing articles for use in your research for a class paper; however, reproducing a thousand copies for sale clearly goes beyond fair use.[70]

Another work product that inventors and corporations may wish to protect is trade secrets. This protection originated under the common law and is governed primarily by state law although federal copyright law may also be involved. This area is particularly ambiguous as to the type and nature of violations, especially in light of the maxim, "information leaks." Information obtained by tortious or criminal methods is clearly excluded from protection. The criminal law may provide the only protections offered by some states. Information submitted by outsiders seems to be governed by contract law with dependence upon the trade custom and the professional status of the person submitting the innovation. Trade secrets are of potentially limited duration because secrecy is undercut by both the practical limitations of keeping information secret and by what constitutes misappropriation.[71]

Intellectual property also encompasses the notion of "unfair competition" under both the common law and the Lanham Act, 15 U.S.C.A. §§ 1051–1127. Included in the Lanham Act are prohibitions against a number of unfair trade practices including provisions relating to source misrepresentation and protections of trademarks. The chief issue about trademarks is what devices or symbols are so distinctive or so well-recognized that they deserve protection. "The courts and the Patent and Trademark Office have authorized for use as a mark a particular shape (of a Coca-Cola bottle), a particular sound (of NBC's three chimes), and even a particular scent (of plumeria blossoms on sewing thread)" and even extends to colors.[72] Public personaes may also be protected by either state or federal law. For example, the blocks of stamps honoring Marilyn Monroe in the Legends of Hollywood stamp series bore the notation "All rights reserved. Signature of Marilyn Monroe™, MARILYN™, NORMA JEANE™, and the name, image, voice, and likeness of Marilyn Monroe are properties of the estate of Marilyn Monroe. © 1995 U.S. Postal Service." This right of publicity obviously survives the death of the individual while the tort right to privacy does not.

Common names of products, trademarks already used by others, or functional aspects (car freshener, for example) do not qualify for trademark protection. The trademark must identify and distinguish the goods from those produced by others and must identify the source of the goods. "It can act as a symbol."[73] It does not prevent the use of words or symbols in the customary way. Registration of the term "Apple" as a brand of computers cannot prevent fruit growers from advertising their product as apples. Trademarks may be registered under both federal and state laws. Trademarks have no value without the underlying business, although they can be assigned and licensed. The holder of the trademark has the burden to prosecute any infringement and may obtain injunctive relief as well as damages.[74]

Despite the longstanding legal framework for protection of intellectual property, today it faces renewed challenges. The first comes as the United States becomes more entangled with the global economy with new treaty provisions which sometimes override long-term policy and law within this nation. Title V of the Uruguay Round Agreements Act (commonly known as GATT) deals with the reciprocal rights of intellectual property holders in the signatory nations.[75] Under the North American Free Trade Agreement (NAFTA),[76] Mexico managed to restore copyrights to old movies which had previously become part of the public domain, a feat one lawyer likened to Lazarus rising from the dead.[77]

The second challenge is to the notion of knowledge as "property." It is based on the premise that knowledge is more accessible than it is has ever been due to technology and that it is increasingly more difficult to hoard. Harland Cleveland employs the analogy of the "futile struggle of the boy with his finger in the dike" to describe the issue.

> Five kinds of waves are rolling in. Dynamic information technologies keep producing new *kinds of works* (computer software); new *means of delivery* (compact disks, microfiche, videocassettes, computerized teletext, facsimile); new *ways to assemble* complex facts and ideas in more readily accessible form (computerized databases, electronic inventory controls, energy-use data, online reservation systems); new *ways to simulate futures* through the use of supercomputers; and better *techniques of piracy* (wiretapping, parabolic listening devices, videotape recorders, backyard dishes, satellite images, computer hacking, and above all, the great pirate ship of xerography).[78]

Laws and theories written to protect books, broadcasts, and phonograph records are outmoded, insufficient, and likely to stay behind the technological advances. Society should recognize that "most of humankind's heritage is in some sense a 'commons'" and Cleveland argues that perhaps we are applying the "wrong verb" to the "wrong noun" in the "protecting" of "intellectual property."[79] With the onslaught of new advances, the underlying philosophy of intellectual property is indeed open for debate and perhaps a return to the ancient doctrines of no legal protection will occur.

CONCLUSION

The maintenance of a system of private property has been of paramount importance in this country from its earliest days. It is entrenched social policy to preserve wealth in the hands of individuals, and the laws reflect that commitment. Americans look askance at those who attempt to limit the use of their property, especially land, and some only grudgingly comply with various zoning and building codes and with corporate regulation. They view these as interference with their God-given right to own and control their property as they see fit.

This chapter conforms to the traditional approach to property law. It discusses the creation of property rights, the traditional classifications, the means of preserving such interests, and the methods of transferring the property from one person through another. The nature of this work precludes an in-depth discussion of the complexity of landlord–tenant relations, financing land purchases, or tax issues related to property. The cursory treatment is not intended to minimize the importance of any of these issues, however.

Although we opted for the traditional approach, you should be aware of emerging trends in property law. Real property is no longer the dominant form of wealth in the United States; instead, billions of dollars are invested in pension and profit-sharing plans, mutual funds, stock markets, and government-backed securities. The result is that more attention by the government and courts is being directed toward these forms of wealth and toward civil and individual rights than was the case in the past. This focus is producing two shifts in American law. First, the courts are employing a balancing test of the owner's right to unfettered use of his land versus the interests of the other party.[80] In First Amendment and other cases, there is no longer an automatic reaction to rule in favor of the landowner, and the proprietor's use and enjoyment of the land are being circumscribed. Second, the concept of property is being expanded. Courts have held that one's means of livelihood, income, or career are defined as property for due-process purposes, which means that certain procedural requirements must be met before a person is deprived of his property interest.[81] Thus, as society evolves, the law of property is changing.

NOTES

1. Cornelius J. Moynihan, *Introduction to the Law of Real Property*, 2nd ed. (St. Paul, Minn.: West Publishing Company, 1988), p. 1.

2. U.S. Constitution, Amend. V; see also Amend. XIV.

3. Henry C. Black, *Black's Law Dictionary*, 4th ed. (St. Paul, Minn.: West Publishing Company, 1968), p. 1382.

4. Harold F. Lusk, *Law of Real Estate Business* (Homewood, Ill.: Richard D. Irwin, 1965), pp. 48–49.

5. G. C. Cheshire, *The Modern Law of Real Property* as cited in John E. Cribbet, William F. Fritz, and Corwin W. Johnson, *Cases and Materials on Property*, 3rd ed. (Mineola, N.Y.: Foundation Press, 1972), pp. 1377–1385.

6. Moynihan, p. 23.

7. Ibid., pp. 25–32.

8. John E. Cribbet, William F. Fritz, and Corwin W. Johnson, *Cases and Materials on Property*, 3rd ed. (Mineola, N.Y.: Foundation Press, 1972), p. 29.

9. Ibid., pp. 52–53.

10. Moynihan, pp. 43–55.

11. Interview with Richard A. Jackson, real estate broker. See, for example, Texas Real Estate Commission Agency Disclosure Form.

12. John W. Wyatt and Madie B. Wyatt, *Business Law*, 3rd ed. (New York: McGraw-Hill, 1966), pp. 716–722.

13. Robert Kratovil, *Real Estate Law*, 6th ed. (Englewood Cliffs, N.J.: Prentice-Hall, 1974), pp. 212–213.

14. Ibid., p. 190.

15. Ibid.

16. Kratovil, pp. 5–10.

17. Ibid., pp. 18–42.

18. David Eliot Brody, *The American Legal System: Concepts and Principles* (Lexington, Mass.: Heath, 1978), p. 202.

19. Black, p. 616.

20. *Village of Euclid* v. *Ambler Realty Co.,* 272 U.S. 365 (1926).

21. Black, p. 73.

22. Martin Weinstein, *Summary of American Law* (Rochester, N.Y.: The Lawyer's Co-Operative Publishing Co./Bancroft-Whitney, 1989), pp. 463–464.

23. Am. Jur. 2d *Deeds* § 261; 20 Am. Jur. 2d *Covenants* §§ 50–53.

24. Weinstein, p. 442.

25. UCC, Chapter 9.

26. Thomas E. Atkinson, *Handbook of the Law of Wills,* 2nd ed. (St. Paul, Minn.: West Publishing Company, 1953), pp. 7–30.

27. Eugene M. Wypyski, *The Law of Inheritance in All Fifty States* (Dobbs Ferry, N.Y.: Oceana Publications, Inc., 1976), pp. 5–7.

28. Ibid., p. 17.

29. Ibid., pp. 10–11.

30. Gilbert Thomas Stephenson and Norman Adrian Wiggins, *Estates and Trusts* (Englewood Cliffs, N.J.: Prentice-Hall, 1973), p. 41.

31. Albert M. Lehrman, *Complete Book of Wills and Trusts* (Englewood Cliffs, N.J.: Institute for Business Planning, Inc. 1978), pp. 35, 480–484.

32. Atkinson, p. 232.

33. Ibid., pp. 255–270.

34. Ibid., pp. 291–354.

35. Lehrman, pp. 48–55.

36. *In re Barrie's Estate,* 240 Iowa 431, 35 N.W.2d 658 (1949).

37. Stephenson, p. 219.

38. George G. Bogert and George T. Bogert, *Handbook on the Law of Trusts,* 5th ed. (St. Paul, Minn.: West Publishing Company, 1973), p. 1.

39. Stephenson, p. 95.

40. Ibid., pp. 98–103.

41. Bogert, p. 183.

42. Dennis R. Hower, *Wills, Trusts, and Estate Administration for the Paralegal,* 2nd ed. (St. Paul, Minn.: West Publishing Company, 1985), pp. 228–244.

43. Black, p. 817.

44. U.S. Constitution, Article I, § 8.

45. Edward C. Walterscheid, "The Early Evolution of the United States Patent Law: Antecedents (Part I)," *Journal of the Patent and Trademark Office Society,* 76 (September 1994), 697–715.

46. Harlan Cleveland, "How Can 'Intellectual Property' Be 'Protected'?" *Change* (May/June 1989), pp. 10–11.

47. Walterscheid, "Early Evolution (Part I), pp. 702–703.

48. Ibid., pp. 706–708.

49. Ibid., pp. 708–710.

50. Ibid., pp. 712–714.

51. W. Hyde Price, *The English Patents of Monopoly* as cited in Edward C. Walterscheid, "Early Evolution of the United States Patent Law (Part 2)," *Journal of the Patent and Trademark Office Society,* Vol. 76 (November 1994), p. 864.

52. Edward C. Walterscheid, "The Early Evolution of the United States Patent Law

(Part 2)," *Journal of the Patent and Trademark Office Society*, Vol. 76 (November 1994), p. 864.

53. Ibid., pp. 855–872.

54. *Darcy* v. *Allin*, 72 Eng.Rep. 830 (Moore 671), 74 Eng.Rep. 1131 (Noy 173), 11 Coke Rep. 86 (King's Bench 1602).

55. 21 James I § 6, VII Statutes at Large 255, § 6.

56. Walterscheid, "Early Evolution (Part 2)," p. 875.

57. Thomas G. Field, Jr., "Intellectual Property Some Practical and Legal Fundamentals," *Idea: The Journal of Law and Technology*, Vol. 35 (1994), 79.

58. *Jungerson* v. *Ostby & Barton Co.*, 335 U.S. 560, (1949) (dissenting) at 572.

59. Field, pp. 79–128.

60. 35 U.S.C.A. § 101.

61. 35 U.S.C.A. § 154 (a)(2).

62. 35 U.S.C.A. §§ 161–164, 171–173.

63. Field, pp. 86–96.

64. Ibid., p. 81.

65. Ibid., pp. 88–89, 96–97.

66. "Corporate Counsel Roundtable: Intellectual Property," *Texas Lawyer*, Vol. 8, no. 39 (December 14, 1992), pp. 12–14.

67. 17 U.S.C.A. §§ 102 (a), 901–914.

68. Field, pp. 102–103.

69. 17 U.S.C.A. § 302.

70. Field, pp. 97–106.

71. Ibid., p. 111.

72. *Qualitex Co.* v. *Jacobson Products Co.*, 63 U.S.L.W. 4227, (1995) at 4228.

73. Ibid., at 4229.

74. Field, pp. 116–126.

75. Uruguay Round Agreements Act, P.L. No. 103-465, 108 Stat. 4810 (1994).

76. North American Free Trade Agreement, P.L. No. 103-182, 107 Stat. 2057 (1993).

77. Edwin Komen, "United States Copyright Restoration Under GATT: The Return of the Vampire Copyrights," *Copyright Today*, Vol. 47 (February 1995), pp. 22–30.

78. Cleveland, pp. 10–11.

79. Ibid., p. 11.

80. *Amalgamated Food Employees Union Local 530* v. *Logan Valley Plaza Inc.*, 391 U.S. 308 (1968).

81. *Goldberg* v. *Kelly*, 397 U.S. 254 (1970); *Board of Regents of State Colleges* v. *Roth*, 408 U.S. 564 (1972).

Family Law

12

Families in this country generate a great deal of litigation. Few lawsuits match the magnitude of the impact on the individuals involved, with the exception of more serious felony cases. These suits impinge upon the most sensitive and personal of relationships; these are the cases that dissolve marriages and determine the custody of children. Many are decided without blazing courtroom battles (the arguments have usually gone on earlier, behind closed doors). Many family-law cases are settled by agreement between the parties, and the courtroom proceedings may seem routine and bland to the detached observer, but the emotional impact on the parties is immeasurable.

Laws that affect familial relationships span many fields, including property law, wills and estates, contracts, torts, and criminal law. This chapter focuses on the creation of the family relationship by marriage, by paternity suits, and by adoption; on the legal principles governing such relations; and on the dissolution of the spousal and parent–child relationship through various types of court action. State legislatures and courts bear the primary onus of dealing with the sometimes complex, often time-consuming issues of family law. It is rare for the U.S. Supreme Court to consider a case involving these matters, although a few involving constitutional questions, such as equal protection, have reached the Court. It is state courts, often specially created domestic-relations courts, which try and then decide the overwhelming majority of such cases.

ROLE OF THE STATE IN FAMILY RELATIONSHIPS

The role of the state in regulating family relationships is so firmly entrenched in jurisprudence that it is virtually unchallenged by today's litigants. It began in Rome during the Republic where the law allowed two alternatives—a ceremony symbolizing the purchase of a bride or a religious ceremony—for the creation of the monogamous marital relationship. The wife and her property were fully under the husband's control, and only he could obtain a divorce. The formal requirements for the creation of a marriage were eventually relaxed, and marriage required only the reciprocal consent of the couple, a precursor of today's informal marriages. During this time, the parties were essentially equal; the husband controlled neither the wife nor her property, although he was obligated to maintain her financially, and either party could end the marriage.[1]

The first formal requirements for obtaining a divorce occurred during the reign of Augustus Caesar in A.D. 40. There were two grounds for divorce: mutual divorce or "no fault," in which the spouses agreed to everything and divorce "for cause," such as adultery. If fault was involved, then the innocent party was favored in the property settlement, and the case was heard by one of the praetors. In the mutual divorce, no judge was involved and the couple settled the matter between themselves.

For a time, there was complete freedom in matters of marriage and divorce, and they were not justiciable matters unless there was controversy over the property settlement. The precepts of Christianity contravened such attitudes, particularly regarding divorce, because marriage was considered to be permanent and to remain indissoluable until death The Emperor Justinian, a Christian who codified the Roman laws in the sixth century, confronted these countervailing views and chose the moderate path of compromise. The Codes contained limited grounds for divorce—mutual agreement, amicably without cause imputed to either party, and for cause—but the major change was that an agreement between the parties would no longer suffice for a divorce. That was revoked by Justinian's son who, like most of his subjects, shared neither his father's Christian beliefs nor his concern about divorce. However, Justinian's Code served as the basis for the legal systems of most European countries and for canon, or church, law, and his position that divorce by agreement should be barred has prevailed in the western world.[2]

Initially, Christianity had little effect on marriage under Roman law. The major change was in limiting freedom to marry by imposing additional barriers such as age requirements (14 for males and 12 for females) and by forbidding marriages within certain degrees of *consanguinity* (related by blood) or of *affinity* (by marriage). Eventually, however, the domination by the Catholic Church in the Middle Ages led to the replacement by canon law of many of the previous legal traditions, but it certainly did not obliterate them, and many remnants linger today. As early as the seventh century, marital laws in England included many of the Church's precepts. Among these was the principle that marriage was of divine origin and the attendant corollary that ecclesiastical courts should have exclusive jurisdiction over marriage, a situation that lasted until the mid-nineteenth century and the passage by Parliament of the Matrimonial Causes Act of 1857. The wife was essentially a chattel, and her property rights were not protected until the equity courts interceded beginning in the seventeenth century.

Divorce was also regulated by canon law, which offered few opportunities to escape from an unhappy marriage. One alternative was to have the marriage dissolved because the husband and wife were related within forbidden degrees of consanguinity. Henry VIII used this strategy to end his marriage to Catherine of Aragon in order to marry Anne Boleyn. The other alternative, available after 1660, was divorce by special parliamentary act on the grounds of adultery. Both alternatives were possible only for the rich and the powerful.

The colonists transported English legal traditions along with their worldly goods to the New World. The rules governing the creation of marital relationships, such as the form of the ceremony and age requirements, remained virtually unchanged. However, the colonies, populated primarily by Protestants following the teachings of Martin Luther and John Calvin, regarded divorce as a legal rather than religious matter, and most adopted general divorce statutes. As new areas opened up and the population migrated westward, the domestic relations laws in the western states and territories became more liberal, to the point of allowing, for a short time, the practice of polygamy, or having a plurality of spouses at the same time.[3]

Some states deliberately enhanced their liberal divorce laws and became havens for those seeking simple and speedy divorces from states with stringent requirements. Those states, like New York, that retained arcane and harsh divorce laws often turned a blind eye to the perjury and exaggerated claims that were prevalent in divorce suits.[4] This atmosphere of chicanery and the recognition of class discrimination against the poor, who could afford neither a trip to Nevada nor the purchase of witnesses to perjure themselves, eventually led to the enactment of no-fault divorce statutes by 49 states.[5]

The role of the state in regulating family relationships has strong historical roots, and it is therefore virtually uncontroverted today. The rationale for such involvement is succinctly explained in the following excerpt:

> Marriage is more than a personal relation between a man and a woman. It is a status founded on contract and established by law. It constitutes an institution involving the highest interests of society. It is regulated and controlled by law based on principles of public policy affecting the welfare of the people of the state.[6]

Families are perceived not only as social but also as legal entities, and government therefore issues rules governing the creation and dissolution of those relationships. Politicians of all ilks, sociologists, and others continually claim that today's families are under attack and frequently blame all of society's ills on the breakdown of the family. Part of the difficulty is in defining "family" in a society marked by diversity in interpersonal relationships. Do people who live together, commingle their assets, and care for each other constitute a family? Are widowed sisters who move in together following the deaths of their respective spouses a family? What about single adult children who live separate and apart from their parents but provide the emotional and physical support for the parent; are they still a family? Do a divorced great-grandmother, her widowed son, his never-married eighteen-year-old son, and the son's eighteen-month-old daughter qualify as a family unit for purposes of insurance, protection under the Family Leave Act, and benefits under the tax laws as would the traditional model of father, mother, and children? What about if there are no blood ties in the relationship but all other indicia of a family are there? Should the definition of family encompass emotional, psychological, and financial ties rather than blood relationships? Merely defining "family" and what is the ideal family is a major policy decision with extensive implications for the legal system.

Some argue that government is too intrusive into family life in such things as providing sex education classes in school while also maintaining that government does not go far enough in such matters as imposing a total bar on abortion. This ambivalence has prevented the United States from creating a consistent framework of policy and laws dealing with the family. However, the traditions and laws are so strong and society's interest so important that withdrawal of all government involvement is most unlikely.

MARRIAGE

Marriage is a legal status founded on contract law in American jurisprudence. As such, states have created certain rules and regulations to govern the creation of such status, just as the law establishes certain requirements for the existence of contracts. In both instances, for example, parties must have the legal capacity to enter into the bargain, and there must be a mutual assent in order to establish each. There are two methods for creating a valid marriage relationship: informal, or the so-called common-law marriage, and formal, whereby the couple is married by someone authorized to do so by law. In determining the validity of the marriage, it is critical to examine the local laws of the jurisdiction in which the marriage occurred. If the creation of the marital relationship satisfied the local requirements, then it is valid everywhere in the United States.[7]

Each state has control over those who marry within its boundaries; regulating marriage is essentially outside the sphere of Congress.[8]

> Marriage, as creating the most important relation in life, as having more to do with the morals and civilization of a people than any other institution, has always been subject to the control of the legislature. That body prescribes the age at which parties may contract to marry, the procedure or form essential to constitute marriage, the duties and obligations it creates, its effects upon the property of both, present and prospective, and the acts which may constitute grounds for its dissolution.[9]

The minimum age requirement for marriage has several bases: biology, as the age is generally related to the time of puberty; tradition, such as the age requirements set by canon law; and contract law, which provides that those entering into a contract must be able to comprehend the event. The ages of 18 for men and 16 for women were common requirements, although many states have revised the law so that the same age requirement is applicable to men and women.[10] Beyond the age of majority (which often does not match the age requirements for marriage), couples may freely enter into the relationship; however, for those who are unemancipated minors, permission to marry is required from parents or the courts. In the same vein, those who are mentally incompetent lack the legal capacity to contract, and they are barred from marrying.

An additional restriction that states place on the freedom to marry is the requirement of monogamy, or having only one spouse at any given time; this requirement is a remnant of Roman and canon law.[11] In other cultures, such as in some African and Islamic countries, polygamy is legal. Obviously, each jurisdiction has wide authority in governing the marriages within its boundaries. The major exception is that states cannot prohibit interracial marriages. In 1967, the miscegenation statutes, which forbade marriage between blacks and whites in 16 states, were struck down by the landmark case of *Loving v. Virginia*.[12]

Laws also prohibit marriage between those who are related within certain degrees of consanguinity and of affinity. That is, one is barred from marrying one's parents, brothers and sisters (both full- and half-blood), children and other descendants, and direct ancestors, such as grandparents or great-grandparents. Individual jurisdictions may add to the list of those who cannot marry because they are related.[13]

By the middle of the 1990s, one of the seemingly basic premises regarding marriage was being legally challenged. In May 1993, the Supreme Court of Hawaii handed down the case of *Baehr v. Lewin*.[14] The suit was brought by three same-sex couples challenging the denial of marriage licenses to each couple by the State of Hawaii on the grounds that such action violated the couples' right to privacy, equal protection, and due process under the *Hawai-*

ian Constitution. The lower court issued judgment for the defendant on the pleadings.

The Hawaiian Supreme Court chose first to examine the question of whether same-sex marriage is a fundamental right by employing the standard tests of identifying such:

> a right . . . so rooted in the traditions and collective conscience of our people that failure to recognize it would violate the fundamental principles of liberty and justice that lie at the base of all our civil and political institutions [or so] implicit in the concept of ordered liberty, such that neither liberty nor justice would exist if it were sacrificed.[15]

The court held that same-sex marriage was not a fundamental right included in the state right to privacy. However, the court did find the Hawaii Marriage Law created a sex-based classification in violation of the state constitution and that the proper standard for testing the constitutionality of such a statute was the strict-scrutiny test. The court remanded the case to the lower court to consider that equal protection argument under the guidelines enunciated by the higher tribunal.

The Hawaiian legislature intervened by enacting a law providing that marriage licensing laws within the state were to apply only to male and female couples and that any change in this aspect of the marriage laws should come about only through legislative or constitutional amendment and not through the courts.[16] That Hawaiian courts gave any credence to the idea of same-sex marriage fueled the national debate.[17] By mid-1995 no state had officially recognized same-sex marriage. However, in 1989 homosexual couples in Denmark were given almost equal legal rights with heterosexual married couples with two exceptions—adoption of children and the right to marry in the Danish Lutheran Church. Couples are required to register the relationship with the government, and dissolution of the relationship is by means of divorce. Sweden and Norway have similar laws, although Sweden's statute places the couple in the same status as unmarried heterosexual couples in terms of inheritance, pension, social security, property, tax, and other laws.[18]

In this country, domestic partnership ordinances provide the "only government-sanctioned method of solemnizing committed relationships."[19] These ordinances, often applicable to both same-sex couples and heterosexual couples, generally require that the parties are at least 18 years of age, are residing together, are competent to contract, and are not violating any state laws against incest before the relationship may be officially registered. In addition, the couples typically must affirm that they are responsible for the welfare of each other and that they are the sole domestic partner of the other. Official termination of the relationship follows only after proper notice. The ordinances vary widely in the amount of legal protection and benefits that they provide to the partners but they do provide the psychological benefit of recognition of the relationship.[20]

For many legal scholars, the question is when, not if, a state will officially recognize same-sex marriage. The legal issue is then whether other states will accept the validity of such marriages. This strikes at the heart of federalism. Marriages created in one state are usually recognized in other jurisdictions on the basis of comity,[21] that is, as a matter of deference and respect, although some states have enacted marriage validation statutes or adopted the Uniform Marriage and Divorce Act, which includes a validation provision.[22] If a status such as marriage violates a strong public policy, a state is free to ignore the relationship under comity.[23]

While marriage is a status normally created by the states and not subject to the type of enforcement that traditional legal judgments (including divorce) receive automatically under the Full Faith and Credit Clause of the U.S. Constitution, it is axiomatic that all judgments affect the status of two or more persons within society. Some states may not wish to create or to recognize the status of same-sex marriage. What policy arguments would they be likely to advance against recognition? First, the state's interest in promoting procreation is likely to be advanced. However, heterosexual couples are not required to produce children and are not officially punished for failure to do so. Human survival would not be threatened by recognition of these relationships, which numerically would be proportionally low among the population. Also this argument overlooks the fact that many gay men and lesbians do have children, and recognition of the relationship with the accompanying health care benefits might actually encourage more couples to have children.

Second, an alternative argument is that same-sex households are not desirable environments for raising children because it places the children at risk of being sexually abused or of becoming gay themselves. The bulk of empirical data, criminal justice statistics, and studies indicates that children are more likely to be at risk of sexual abuse from heterosexuals than homosexuals in their own households and that it is not the parents' sexuality which determines that of their children.

Third is the argument involving the basic governmental structure of the nation itself. The imposition of one state's values and culture upon other states would be a violation of the principle of federalism that allows each state to set its own policies. However, this may be true of other types of unpopular judgments that are routinely enforced—suits to enforce gambling debts, to collect a judgment for a corporation whose environmental policies are abhorrent to the state, or to recover damages for a person who won a whistleblower suit against a neighboring state.

Many states mask their views that same-sex marriage is immoral or fundamentally wrong with other arguments. Proponents of same-sex marriage argue "just as the policy of antimiscegenation was premised on racial prejudice, the ban on same-sex marriages rests fundamentally on antihomosexual prejudice," and government should not enforce private bigotry.[24] Whatever one's personal view of the morality of homosexuality or same-sex marriage, the issues are unlikely to disappear, and the legal system will continue to grapple with all the attendant constitutional questions—the scope of the Full Faith and Credit Clause, the right to interstate travel, the state's interest in marital relationships, the right to privacy, and the extent to which government should intervene in the private lives of its citizens. It is also probable that

> our nation will fail to face this challenge squarely. Rather than compel interstate recognition of marriage under the Full Faith and Credit Clause, the courts will most likely consign the question to the 'dismal swamp' of conflicts of law. In all likelihood, the battle for recognition of same-sex marriages will be fought state by state; we are unlikely to see sudden or sweeping change . . . These battles will provide a fascinating exchange of competing views of family, law, community, and the individual.[25]

Assuming that the parties have the capacity to marry and are not barred from doing so by statutory provisions, there are two methods of creating a legally binding marriage in the United States. All states have standards for formal marriages, while only a few make provisions for informal marriages, but the validity of a marriage is determined by the local law. *Informal marriages* are sometimes called "common-law marriages," a term that may refer to their nonstatutory origin. The basis of an informal marriage is the *present* consent or agreement between the parties that they are married. An agreement to marry in the future is not sufficient. Most statutes additionally require cohabitation and a public declaration of marriage.[26] This declaration may consist of sharing a joint bank account, introducing the other party as the spouse, or some other indication that the couple considers themselves married. The fact that the woman keeps her own name is not a determining factor if the elements are otherwise met.

An informal marriage is a valid marriage, requiring divorce for dissolution. A spouse who enters into an informal marriage and later formally marries without first obtaining a divorce may be subject to bigamy charges. Proving the existence of an informal marriage is sometimes difficult, however; it is particularly difficult to prove the element of intent. Spouses may try to disclaim intent in a divorce suit in order to avoid a property settlement, but the requisite intent may be shown indirectly by other evidence. Informal marriages are disfavored in part because there is seldom a record of such relationships, which complicates such legal matters as receipt of insurance or social security benefits if one spouse dies; nevertheless, they are valid marital relationships if all other prerequisites are met.[27]

The vast majority of couples are joined through ceremonial marriages. Typically, they begin the process by paying a fee and obtaining a license from a public official, often the county clerk. Both parties generally must appear to apply for the license and are required to provide certain basic information, including full names, birthdates, and present marital status. Many states impose a short waiting period, and the licenses generally expire within a given time period. Physical examinations, particularly blood tests for venereal disease, AIDS, and rubella, may be required. In addition to requiring marriage licenses, statutes specify those with authority to perform marriage ceremonies, including ministers, rabbis, priests, or others authorized by religious organizations, as well as certain public officials such as justices of the peace and judges. Once the couple is married, the marriage license must be returned to the proper official, whereupon it becomes a matter of public record.[28]

DISSOLUTION OF MARRIAGE

States regulate not only the creation of the marital relationship but also its dissolution. *Divorce* by consent alone is not allowed in the United States, and some type of judicial action is necessary to dissolve marriages. The adoption of *no-fault* grounds both facilitates obtaining a divorce and reduces the involvement of the judicial system to a minimum. For example, California statutes provide that couples who have been married less than five years, have no minor children, and have less than $10,000 worth of community property may avoid court entirely and may merely advise the proper authorities of their divorce.[29] In many other instances, judicial approval is purely *pro forma*, an acceptance of the parties' agreements in regard to custody of minor children, if any, and to the property division. Couples are often urged to enter into such agreements because, like a plea bargain in criminal law, it removes the issues from the vagaries of a judge or jury and provides for certainty. Courts favor these agreements for two reasons: (1) More cases can be processed through the system in a shorter period of time than would be the case if the judge had to consider the evidence and merits of each situation; and (2) courts avoid having to decide complex issues such as child custody, as well as the tiresome minutiae of which spouse gets the towels and pots and pans.

Annulments. Marriages may be dissolved either by divorce or by *annulment*. Divorces are much more common than annulments because of the extremely limited grounds for annulments. An annulment differs from a divorce in that the legal basis of an annulment is that the marriage was invalid from its inception, whereas a divorce acknowledges the initial validity of the marital relationship. The goal in both cases is to dissolve the legal ties between the spouses.[30] Some statutes distinguish between *void* and *voidable* marriages. Voidable marriages are those which do not meet the requirements for a valid marriage and which can be dissolved on that basis. For example, Jane and Peter were both underage when they wed. If this is considered a voidable marriage, either could file for annulment based on that ground, or they could continue their marriage as if they had met the prerequisites. On the other hand, if Peter were married to Sally at the time that he married Jane, the second marriage would be void, or totally invalid.

The grounds for annulment are rather limited and vary from jurisdiction to jurisdiction. They are generally directed to the capacity or the intent to marry. Those who are underage or mentally incompetent may lack the necessary understanding to enter into a marriage relationship, much as they lack the capability to enter into a binding contract. Mental incompetency may be an issue for the trier of fact. Those who have been treated for mental illness and those who are slightly mentally retarded may have the requisite competency. Those who marry during an involuntary state of intoxication such as persons who have been drugged against their wills generally have grounds for annulment; the key here is that the intoxication is not voluntary. (Those who wish to disclaim their marriage vows because of a nip or two before their wedding are out of luck in qualifying for an annulment.)

Couples related to each other within prohibited degrees of consanguinity or affinity may file for annulments; some of these marriages are void while others are voidable according to state law. In addition, some of the relationships will also fall afoul of such criminal laws as incest statutes. Fraud and duress are other grounds for annulment. *Fraud* involves knowingly making false statements about a material and essential fact in order to induce someone into marriage, such as denying that one is currently married. *Duress* results from employing coercion or force in persuading someone to marry.[31] A facetious example is the reluctant groom who is marrying with the bride's father's loaded shotgun pointed squarely at his back.

Logically, declaring a marriage void from its inception leads to extremely harsh results. Any children born of the marriage are bastardized, and the economic results could be devastating. The effects have been mitigated by laws that legitimize the children and provide for equitable property division; these issues are decided in accordance with the rules that apply in divorce actions.[32] It is important to recognize that annulments are rather rare because most couples do not meet the statutory grounds for filing such a suit.

Divorce. The prevalent method for terminating a marital relationship is divorce. Three issues are generally involved in such suits: (1) the procedural aspects, such as residency and the technical grounds for divorce; (2) the property settlement; and (3) the custody of the children, if any. The result of a divorce suit is to dissolve the legal ties between the couple. As a practical matter, parties often remain connected to each other because of the children or mutual property interests, including debts, which frequently cause them to reappear in court as litigants against each other. Some divorce-related issues may drag on for many years; the failure to pay alimony or child support in accordance with the court order is a common example. Divorce rarely resolves all the issues or complaints that couples have against each other, which is somewhat deceptive to many people who anticipate otherwise.

Procedural aspects of divorce. A court must have jurisdiction to grant a divorce, to enter a property settlement, and to decide custody of the couple's children. This jurisdiction stems from state constitutional and legislative provisions. A typical requirement is that one or both parties must meet residency requirements. Nevada is famed for its short residency period of 6 weeks, while Texas requires 6 months in the state and 90 days in the county preceding the filing of a divorce suit. Venue is generally in the county of residence of the parties.[33]

Divorce petitions must allege the grounds for the action. Most proceed on no-fault grounds, which merely allege incompatibility, marriage breakdown, or similar circumstances that indicate that the parties are no longer getting along and wish to end the marriage. This greatly simplifies the proof required to obtain a divorce; a simple statement to that effect by one of the parties while on the witness stand usually suffices to prove the grounds for divorce.[34]

The practice of claiming fault as a ground for divorce has fallen into disfavor because of the problems of proof. The party who alleges adultery must introduce evidence and persuade the trier of fact that such activity did occur. This is often an expensive (and somewhat embarrassing) procedure. Typical grounds of fault are adultery, desertion, and cruelty. One reason to allege fault in a divorce petition is to affect the property division against the wrongdoer. In contested cases, the allegations will generally be brought out in testimony and may be considered by the judge in allocating the marital resources. In uncontested cases, they may be used in negotiations as a bargaining chip. The fact that many couples do not wish their private lives to be revealed to public scrutiny, coupled with the difficulty of proof in fault cases, results in most divorces proceeding under the no-fault provisions of the statute.[35]

Property division. During the existence of the marital relationship, the parties are required to financially support each other. When they decide to divorce, a grant of temporary alimony or maintenance for a spouse who needs it during the pendency of the divorce is usually authorized by state legislatures. Such maintenance orders are entered by the court after adequate notice and the opportunity for a hearing on the matter. Of course, that may be circumvented by agreement between the parties.[36]

At the time of the divorce hearing, the property and the debts are divided between the spouses. This aspect of divorce is often the one that causes the most bitterness and ill will. Spouses may control the property division by entering into a prearranged property settlement which is generally ratified by the court, but few agreements satisfy both parties. Some couples anticipate the possibility of divorce and enter into a *prenuptial agreement* outlining the property division even before they marry. According to the Statute of Frauds, such contracts must be in writing.[37] Prenuptial agreements are frequently employed by wealthy individuals who are concerned about preserving their assets. The courts scrutinize such arrangements carefully to ensure that no overreaching or coercion was involved. Others who are likely to use prenuptial agreements are older couples who are marrying for the second time and who want their children from their first marriage, rather than their second spouse's children, to inherit their property. In either event, the goal of the prenuptial agreement is to predetermine the disposition of assets at the time of divorce or death.

Marital property is generally defined as all property acquired by either spouse during the marriage relationship, except for gifts or inheritances. In the eight community-property states (Arizona, California, Idaho, Louisiana, Nevada, New Mexico, Texas, and Washington), community property belongs equally to both spouses, regardless of whose efforts garnered the property. Each has an undivided interest in the property; the husband's or wife's salary belongs equally to both, and the issue of who holds the title to the property is irrelevant if it is community property. In contrast, property owned before marriage or property one inherited or was given during marriage belongs only to that spouse. In the so-called common-law states, the early rule was that the wife had no property rights and that her estate was under the control of her husband. The husband's control was abolished in many states by statutes usually known as the Married Women's Act, which often gave married women the right to own property and often to enter into contracts on their own behalf.[38] In these states, ownership of the property still vests in one of the parties unless specifically created in both; for instance, the wage earner has sole ownership of wages. In other words, "under the common-law system, a housewife who does not also work outside the home has no legal right to any marital asset, unless her husband puts it in her name or adds her to the title as a tenant in common or joint tenant."[39]

In both the community-property and common-law states, the same factors are typically considered in the property settlement. These factors include age, health, occupation, other assets, and the earning capacity of the respective parties. For example, Barbara completed one year of college before marrying James, after which she dropped out of school and worked as a bank teller to pay for his undergraduate and dental training. During the 25 years that their children attended public schools, Barbara did not work outside the home. Now Barbara and James, both age 50, are divorcing. He has an annual income of $60,000, while she has no income and no assets other than the marital property. Her age and lack of recent work experience will hinder her efforts to obtain employment, and any job she finds will probably not pay well.

On the other hand, James enjoys a relatively secure income which is likely to continue for some time. The court may consider these factors in dividing the property and in setting *alimony* if permitted by state law.

Most statutes provide that the property be divided in a fair and equitable or reasonable manner. This is not tantamount to requiring that property be divided equally between the spouses. In addition to the aforementioned factors, courts may also consider other items, such as the allocation of debts and custody of minor children, in determining the final property division.[40]

Few topics stir up as much calumny as the subject of alimony. "No one likes alimony. Not the men who pay it, nor the women who receive it. But men are louder in their complaints. . . . There are some women . . . who believe . . . it stifles women, both socially and professionally."[41] Charles V. Metz, in his polemic *Divorce and Custody for Men*, writes:

> Of all the sadistic shackles that the modern, freed, and equalized woman has placed upon men, alimony is the worst. Because alimony can never pay for services rendered, and because alimony inevitably results in mutual hatred, it should be abolished altogether. . . . We can presently only hope that the courts which wantonly place men in bondage have their hell-fires stoked by the victims.[42]

Such rhetoric obscures the ultimate question about the justice and fairness of alimony.

Technically, there are differences between orders relating to the division of property and alimony. Property orders relate to marital property already in existence. Alimony, on the other hand, is a payment for support and maintenance usually payable from future income, although the court may approve a lump-sum payment; further, alimony may be founded on the couple's present standard of living as well as on the factors previously discussed in connection with the property settlement. In some instances, installment payments of the property settlement are permitted, but these must be distinguished from alimony. To illustrate, George and Lucy worked together to build a chain of stores now valued at $350,000. The court, having considered all of the factors and all of the couple's assets, orders Lucy to pay George $250,000 for his share of the business. Withdrawing that amount of the money from the business at one time might well destroy it; therefore, Lucy may be permitted to pay George $25,000 plus interest for each of the next ten years. This is not alimony, but instead represents a division of existing assets. In addition to saving her source of income, such installment payments offer certain tax benefits as well.

Differentiating alimony from property settlements is important for several reasons. Court decrees dividing the property generally cannot be modified at a later date, whereas alimony orders can be changed upon proof of a change in the circumstances of the payor or recipient. Alimony payments automatically terminate upon remarriage in many states, but the obligation to make the installment payments for the property continues. The IRS treats the two differently for tax purposes. Property orders typically cannot be enforced by civil contempt, whereas alimony orders can be. Any court order involving both alimony and property division should clearly distinguish one from the other.[43]

Custody and support of the children.   Deciding the custody of children is often a difficult decision for a judge or jury, who are well aware that however tormenting the decision is for them, it is much worse for the parties, especially the youngsters. Children, even those who have been mistreated, usually feel loyalty and affection toward their parents, and custody battles exact more from them than from anyone else. Custody arguments generally arise through two types of litigation: (1) cases in which the state is alleging that the children should be separated from their parents and (2) divorce actions. For a fact-finder, it is relatively easy to decide the issue if one spouse is a model parent and the other is not, but that is rarely true in contested cases.

The current standard used in awarding custody—that of the ***best interest of the child,*** rather than the old standard of proving the parent unfit for custody—shifts the emphasis from the parent to the child's overall well-being.[44] This intentionally vague standard of best interest allows a number of factors to be considered: (1) the parenting skills of the person seeking custody, (2) the physical safety of the child, (3) the stability of the home and parent, (4) the present and future emotional and physical needs of the child, (5) present and future plans for the child, (6) acts or omissions of the parent that would affect parenting performance, and (7) the child's preference, which is not binding on the court. The items on this list indicate that the parent with the highest earning potential or the most assets does not automatically receive custody, although the ability of each contestant to support the child is considered.

The last two decades have seen major revisions in custody laws, and a large number of them have come about through the feminist movement. One of these changes is the general abolishment of a sex preference in granting custody. The old common-law rule that the father's claim to custody should be paramount was supplanted by a preference for giving custody to the mother, particularly when the case involved girls or children under the age of 6, whereas fathers were generally awarded custody of older sons. Today most statutes are neutral, and juries are instructed that the sex of the parent is not to be a determinative consideration. More fathers are seeking and obtaining custody today, either by agreement with their spouses or by court order in contested cases.[45] This is partly due to recognition of three factors: (1) that fathers often have parenting skills equal to or better than those of mothers; (2) that couples share household tasks, including the rearing of children, more equally than in the past; and (3) that both parents are employed in many American families, and no longer do mothers automatically stay at home with the children. Economic reality usually dictates that most single mothers must work outside the home, and there is essentially no difference in the amount of time that a working parent, male or female, could spend with the children. Thus, women's search for legal equality and fair treatment under the law has reaped an important benefit for men as well.

Custody orders are not immutable; they can be modified. The typical requirement is that there must have been a substantial and material change in the circumstances of either the parent or the child before the court will modify the original order.[46] The requirement is intended to discourage frequent relitigation of custody orders in order to promote stability in the children's lives. One unfortunate trend that has been somewhat checked is for noncustodial parents to snatch the children, move them to another state, and litigate in a more favorable forum, with the frequently fulfilled hope that the new court will change custody. It is axiomatic that in order to consider the matter, the court had to have jurisdiction; jurisdiction in child custody cases, as frequently defined by statute, vests not only in the court where the order was originally entered, but also in states where the child is presently located or where the most recent and best evidence of the child's care is located. Thus, parents who snatch their children and remain undetected for a substantial period of time can invoke the new state's jurisdiction. The enactment by the states of uniform child custody laws that acknowledge the validity of sister states' original orders and promote compliance with those orders, along with the adoption of the Parental Kidnapping Prevention Act (28 U.S.C. §1738A), has strengthened the enforcement of original orders and curbed the tendency to modify orders or issue new ones.

When parents live apart and a court order is entered regarding custody, one parent is granted possession of the child and the right to determine the child's domicile, while the other is granted visitation rights. Typically, visitation is specified for certain weekends, for longer periods during summer school vacation, and for holidays. Visitation rights may be withheld or circumscribed at the court's discretion. An abusive parent or one who has previously snatched the child may be limited to visits with the child in a grandparent's home or in the offices of the state social service agency. There is a growing trend toward providing visitation rights for the grandparents as well. Custody and visitation rights may be tailored to fit the needs of the children and can be rather creative; an example is a decree that allows the children to remain in the family home while the parents move in and out rather than moving the children.

Parents are legally obligated to support their unemancipated children, and while courts generally do not intervene to enforce this provision if the parents and children are living together, they frequently do so in suits affecting the parent–child relationship, including paternity suits and divorces. The parties may set the amount of child support by agreement, subject to ratification by the court, or the court will assess the amount after considering the relevant evidence. The following factors are often considered in such decisions: actual and potential earnings and other assets of the parents, especially the obligor; division of property and debts; life-styles of the parties and the children; the children's age(s); health of both the parents and children; and the cost of living.[47]

Child-support orders, like custody orders, may be modified if there are substantial and material changes in the circumstances of the children or the parents. A well-paid executive who has lost her position because of economic depression in a particular industry may seek to decrease her child support; or, the custodial parent of a child who develops severe medical problems may seek to increase the support. These are extreme examples, but modification of child-support orders may be triggered by increases in the cost of living or by increased demands as children become older.

Determining the initial amount of support or modifying it are seldom as difficult a legal problem as enforcing the court order. Both visitation orders and child support are enforceable primarily through contempt proceedings and are a fertile source of litigation. Visitation and child support are parallel rights and are not tied to each other. Failure to pay child support on a timely basis does not authorize the custodial parent to withhold visitation as punishment; self-help methods are not favored by the courts in this regard. Both parties in such a situation could be held in contempt of court, which is punishable by fines or by jail sentences, or both, after a hearing that involves adequate notice and the opportunity to present any defense. True inability to pay child support is a valid defense, but courts carefully scrutinize such claims. A parent who claims that he is unable to pay because he lost his job, but who is not looking for work, is unlikely to find favor with the courts; nor is the parent who supports his new wife's children. However, parents who are unable to work because of injury or who are actively seeking work may win a reprieve and time to catch up on the payments at a later date.

Other remedies for nonpayment of support include reducing the amount to judgment and putting a lien on the obligor's property, garnishment of wages, and criminal nonsupport charges. To facilitate collection of child support when the obligor has moved outside the state, states have enacted the Uniform Reciprocal Enforcement of Support Act or its revised form; in addition, treaties provide for collection across international borders. The lawsuits are initiated in the children's home state in the required format and mailed to the site of the parent's new home. Authorities there file the papers, give legal notice and an opportunity to be heard to the parent, collect the support payments, and remit them to the children, all without forcing any of the parties to incur travel expenses.

Intense concern about the spiraling costs of welfare, along with increasing awareness that nonpayment of child support was reaching epidemic proportions, led Congress to enact P.L. 93–647, the Social Security

Amendments of 1974 (42 U.S.C. §§651–666). The statute encourages the states to create child-support programs by threatening to withhold federal AFDC funds if such a program is not created. The scheme is primarily directed toward the absent parents of children collecting AFDC; if the monthly amount of child support collected equals the amount of the monthly AFDC grant, AFDC is denied. These child-support programs also assist nonwelfare parents in establishing and enforcing child-support obligations. These state agencies also have access both to the parent-locator service, which uses Social Security numbers to locate absent parents, and to additional methods, such as intercepting tax returns and applying them to unpaid child support.[48]

The dissolution of a marriage is an emotion-laden, if not traumatic, event for most people. Many initiate the process hoping that it will be a cathartic experience, and are therefore disappointed in the detached and apparently insensitive attitudes of judges and attorneys. The parties often want the courts to allocate blame and to punish the other person for perceived injustices and grievances, but that rarely happens. The courts are there only to resolve the legal issues of dissolution, property, custody, and support in accordance with the statutes and legal precepts.

THE PARENT–CHILD RELATIONSHIP

The relationship between parents and children is both biological and legal. The two may not be identical, however. The potential difference arises because of legitimacy statutes, adoption, and, oddly enough, modern medical technology, which allows artificial insemination. Legally, the parent–child relationship may be created by operation of law; by contract, as in the case of surrogate parents; and by court order. As used here, the term *parent* refers to the legal, rather than biological, parent. Parents owe certain duties and responsibilities to their minor children, including the duty of care, support, and supervision. Whereas the biological relationship lasts as long as the parties live, legal parent–child relationships end. Children who reach the age of majority are no longer legally under the control of their parents. This is true of the mentally handicapped as well; most jurisdictions require the appointment of a guardian, who essentially carries out the parental responsibilities and, in fact, often is the parent. In addition, the relationship can be terminated by court order.

Establishment of the parent–child relationship.   Traditionally, illegitimacy, or birth out-of-wedlock, has been both a social and legal handicap. For many years, bastards (in the legal sense only) could not claim support or inherit from their natural fathers. Today illegitimacy no longer makes one a social pariah, nor is it an absolute bar to enforcing legal rights. Children whose biological parents are married to each other at the time of conception or at the child's birth are legitimate. Over the years, laws have evolved that grant that status to children whose natural parents subsequently marry.[49] Children who are conceived by artificial insemination and born of married women are considered the legitimate children of her husband; in some states, the written prior consent of the husband is required before the procedure is performed. Legitimate children are allowed by the law to claim support from both parents as well as to inherit from them.

Relationship of child to mother. In the past, the biological mother was considered the parent without further action and the child was considered as her legitimate offspring until the relationship was terminated by court order.[50] However, this situation has been altered by the use of artificial insemination to impregnate so-called surrogate mothers who contract with infertile couples on the basis that the child will be turned over to the couple to raise. In exchange, the couples generally agree to pay the woman a set fee, pay her medical bills, and perhaps pay her living expenses. There have been several instances in which the natural mother has refused to turn over the child after the birth. There has been no definitive court decision on the respective rights of the parties, but the emerging pattern is to uphold the contract. These arrangements apparently establish parenthood by contract.[51]

Relationship of child to father. Establishing the parent–child relationship between a child and the natural father may be more difficult. Many states provide a mechanism by which the father may voluntarily acknowledge the relationship. In addition, there are paternity statutes—the bases for judicial determination as to the existence of the relationship. Texas was the last jurisdiction in the United States to incorporate a paternity statute in its laws; wags in the state always claimed that it was to prevent the legislators from being sued, and, in fact, the legislature enacted the law only after the U.S. Supreme Court decided in *Gomez* v. *Perez*, 409 U.S. 535 (1973) that denial of paternal support to illegitimate children was a violation of the equal protection clause and therefore unconstitutional.[52]

Paternity suits, as do all other suits, require that the putative father be given adequate notice and an opportunity to present a defense. Typical defenses include denying sexual intercourse with the mother at the pertinent time or alleging that she was also having intercourse with other men during that time period. A crucial factor in many paternity suits is the results of tests run on blood drawn from the alleged father, the mother, and the child.[53] These sophisticated blood tests can exclude over 98 percent of the male population from being the natural parent—a remarkable feat. They cannot prove that a particular individual is the father, however. Taken together, the facts that the man had access to the mother at the relevant times and that he falls within the 2 percent who could be the father is amazingly persuasive for most fact-finders. Many cases settle out of court once the blood tests are returned. Establishment of paternity invokes rights to visitation or custody and the obligations attached to such relationships, including financial support for the child.[54] Results of genetic fingerprinting and DNA testing are also being routinely admitted in paternity cases.

Adoption.   Another method of establishing the parent–child relationship is by adoption. *Adoption* is defined in *Black's Law Dictionary* as "the act of one who takes another's child into his own family, treating him as his own, and giving him all the rights and duties of his own child" and as "a juridicial act creating between two persons certain relations, purely civil, of paternity and filiation."[55] As used here, the term refers to formal adoptions (which are court-approved, as opposed to merely taking a child into one's home for succor) and to adoptions of children rather than adults. The process legally substitutes one set of parents, the adoptive set, for another, the biological ones. The chief limitation on the right to adopt is the child's status in regard to his biological parents; that is, the child's relationship to his biological parents must have been terminated by court order before adoption may occur.

The criterion used by the court to judge whether to grant an adoption petition is whether the adoption will be in the child's best interest. As previously discussed, the best interest of the child is a nebulous standard which allows judges to exercise a great deal of discretion. The focus in applying the standard is the *fitness* of the proposed parent or parents, another rather vague term. Statutes and case law provide some guidelines, and judges frequently call upon neutral social service agencies to investigate the parents and the home environment and to file a report with the court or even to testify. It is firmly established that, if other prerequisites are met, an adoption cannot be denied solely on the basis of different religious backgrounds or even on the basis of the parents' lack of belief in a Supreme Being.[56] An absolute bar on interracial adoptions is also unconstitutional. In addition, many states now allow single persons to adopt, reflecting the legislatures' awareness that many families in the United States are headed by single parents. Another recent modification is the relaxation of the rule that the adoptive parents must meet certain physical specifications; those who have been deemed unfit by adoption agencies merely because of physical handicaps or obesity have successfully challenged those rejections in court.[57]

Thus, there are two traditional methods of legally establishing the parent–child relationship: by being the biological parent and having legitimate offspring or by obtaining a court order through paternity suits or adoption. We may be seeing the emergence of a third method: by contract, in situations of artificial insemination or with surrogate mothers. Accompanying the initiation of such relationships are certain duties and responsibilities.

Parental rights and obligations.   The obligations and responsibilities of parents, or of those having custody of children, are many and varied. The primary right is to have physical possession of the child and to establish its legal domicile without interference by third parties. The state may intercede to assume physical possession if child abuse is suspected or proven, or under other circumstances ordered by the court. Parents also have the power to make legal decisions for the child and to sue and be sued on the child's behalf. They have authority to consent to medical, surgical, and psychiatric treatment for a child and to approve of marriage or military enlistment for minor children.

The primary parental responsibilities toward children are twofold: (1) to provide the basic necessities of food, shelter, and clothing and (2) to provide care, control, supervision, education, and reasonable discipline. Violation of either of these obligations by the parents may result in the state's intervening in the situation. The parent–child relationship is a privileged one in the eyes of the law, and legislatures and courts hesitate to intervene, as indicated by the following quote from the U.S. Supreme Court.

> It is cardinal with us that the custody, care, and nurture of the child reside first in the parents . . . And it is in recognition of this that these decisions have respected the private realm of family life which the state cannot enter . . . But the family itself is not beyond regulation in the public interest.[58]

The law imposes a duty on parents to supervise children and allows a corollary right of discipline. Failure to adequately supervise children may lead to either civil or criminal liability on the parents' part as well as removal of the children from the home by the state. The duty to control one's offspring is offset by restrictions limiting the punishment a parent may dole out to children. Statutes generally employ such language as "reasonable" discipline. Locking children in closets for days, withholding food or water, and burning them with cigarettes do not fall within this category. Corporal punishment is permitted, but it must not be excessive, an issue which sometimes becomes a fact question at child-abuse trials.

Parents are also obligated to financially support their children and to provide the basics of life, including food, shelter, and clothing.[59] Generally, the standard of living within each home is outside the state's sphere, but if there is a complaint that children are being neglected, the family will be investigated by representatives of the state social service agency. A destitute family may be offered emergency or long-term assistance from private or public sources. If the neglect is intentional, however, a suit may be filed to remove the children from the home and to place them under the care of the state, either temporarily or permanently.

The societal goal is the protection and best interest of the children, but balancing that against the parents' interest is often difficult, even when there is common agreement on what constitutes the best interest of the children. Those instances in which a parent severely injures a child demand that the child be protected. Where is the line to be drawn, though, between spanking a child for disciplinary purposes and physically abusing the child? Parents are given the primary responsibility for the moral and religious instruction of children, but there is a public interest in seeing that children are educated.[60] A growing number of parents are teaching their children at home because of dissatisfaction with public schools or for religious reasons. If the parents are prosecuted for violation of school attendance laws, then the court must attempt to balance the competing interests. Such complex and weighty matters are politically sensitive issues for legislators and judges.

Termination of parental rights.   The parent–child relationship may be ended by the child's being emancipated or by court order. Parents may accede to the termination of parental rights or it may be involuntary. As previously discussed, a child cannot be adopted until the rights of the biological parents have been terminated. Voluntary relinquishment is common among unwed and often young parents in order that the child may be placed for adoption. Generally, the written assent of both natural parents is required even if paternity has not been legally established, and a "cooling off" period is imposed, often 30 days, during which the parents may revoke their consent. That the parent who is relinquishing the child is a minor does not invalidate the consent.[61] Voluntary termination also frequently occurs when the noncustodial parent agrees to adoption by the custodial parent's new spouse.

Suits to involuntarily terminate a parent's rights are usually generated by the state. These stem from abuse of the child—physically, mentally, or sexually—from neglect of the child, or from failure to properly supervise the child.[62] Permanently removing the child from the home by the state on these grounds requires a court order, but legislation provides for immediate removal without court approval if there is a serious or life-threatening emergency; in such a case, judicial review must take place as quickly as possible, often within 24 hours. Again, it is necessary to square the rights of the children with those of the parents and also to protect against hasty, ill-considered state action or excesses on the part of overzealous social service agency representatives, many of whom are under a statutory charge to assist in keeping families together. Involuntary termination may be, but much less frequently is, initiated by a custodial parent against a divorced spouse. The basis of the suit is often an alleged failure to financially support the child or an allegation that the parent ignored the child and has failed to visit or establish contact. The impetus behind such suits often is to facilitate adoption by the petitioner's new spouse.

The effect of terminating the parent–child relationship is to sever all connections between parent and child. It relieves parents of all duties and obligations toward their children, but it also means that the parents are to have no contact at all with their offspring. It voids the original legal relationship, and in adoption cases, the court records are sealed and new birth certificates may be issued.

CONCLUSION

Domestic-relations law touches every American because it deals with family issues. It is an area in which the state is reluctant to intrude; yet, for many people, the minimal intrusions are accepted and seldom controverted. Most citizens accept the necessity of meeting certain statutory requirements, such as those of obtaining a marriage license and attending school. They applaud the intervention of the state to protect abused children and battered spouses. They recognize the rationale for accurate government records regarding marriages, births, and dissolutions of marriage. The need for a neutral third party to referee domestic disputes and to render impartial decisions is apparent.

The topics discussed in this chapter, including marriage and the parent–child relationship, are only a sampling of the issues involved in family law. For example, juvenile laws are often contained in family codes or are routinely decided by family-law judges. Family litigation often seems interminable because of various modification and enforcement orders. It is the area of law in which many have their only contact as parties with the legal system. Decisions made in these lawsuits have immeasurable and permanent effects on the lives of the spouses and their children. Family law is intensely personal in many ways, while in others it is the most public area of law. National debate centers around the family, its configuration, and its role in society as a whole. It is a most troublesome area for policymakers who have thus far failed to set coherent family policies because of the diverse nature of these relationships and the deeply rooted social and religious attitudes of the American people about the sanctity of family and government involvement therein.

NOTES

1. Homer H. Clark, Jr., *Cases and Problems on Domestic Relations,* 2nd ed. (St. Paul, Minn.: West Publishing Company, 1974), pp. 2–3.

2. Peter J. Riga, "Are We Copying Ancient Rome on Divorce?" *Texas Lawyer,* December 18, 1985, p. 13.

3. *Reynolds* v. *United States,* 98 U.S. 145 (1878).

4. Clark, pp. 3–11.

5. Riga, p. 13.

6. *Fearon* v. *Treanor,* 272 N.Y. 268 (1936), at 272; 5 N.E.2d 815 (1936), at 816.

7. *Patterson* v. *Gaines,* 6 How. 550 (1848).

8. *Simms* v. *Simms,* 175 U.S. 162 (1899).

9. *Maynard* v. *Hill,* 125 U.S. 190 (1888), at 205.

10. Clark, pp. 102–104.

11. *Reynolds* v. *United States,* 98 U.S. 145 (1878).

12. *Loving* v. *Virginia*, 388 U.S. 1 (1967).

13. Clark, pp. 102–104.

14. *Baehr* v. *Lewin*, 852 P.2d 44 (Haw. 1993).

15. Ibid., p. 57.

16. Noel Myricks and Roger H. Rubin, "Legalizing Gay and Lesbian Marriages: Trends and Implications," *American Journal of Family Law*, Vol. 9 (Spring 1995), pp. 35–44.

17. Jeffrey J. Swart, "The Wedding Luau: Who Is Invited?: Hawaii, Same-Sex Marriage, and Emerging Realities," *Emory Law Journal*, Vol. 43 (Fall 1994), pp. 1577–1616.

18. Myricks and Rubin, p. 41.

19. Swart, p. 1599.

20. Ibid., pp. 1598–1600.

21. Habib A. Balian, "'Till Death Do Us Part: Granting Full Faith and Credit to Marital Status," *Southern California Law Review*, Vol. 68 (January 1995), pp. 397–426.

22. Thomas M. Keane, "Aloha, Marriage? Constitutional and Choice of Law Arguments for Recognition of Same-Sex Marriages," *Stanford Law Review*, Vol. 47 (February 1995), pp. 499–532.

23. Balian, pp. 398–399.

24. Keane, pp. 517–522.

25. Ibid., p. 531.

26. *In re Estate of Fisher*, 176 N.W.2d 801 (Iowa, 1970).

27. Clark, p. 82.

28. Ibid., pp. 58–60.

29. Cal. Civil Code, Chap. 5, § 4550.

30. *Perlstein* v. *Perlstein*, 152 Conn. 152, 204 A.2d 909 (1964).

31. Clark, pp. 170–171.

32. *Sefton* v. *Sefton*, 45 Cal.2d 272, 291 P.2d 439 (1955).

33. Clark, pp. 577–578.

34. Riane Tennenhaus Eisler, *Dissolution* (New York: McGraw-Hill, 1977), pp. 12–13.

35. Michael Wheeler, *No-Fault Divorce* (Boston: Beacon Hill Press, 1974), pp. 1–18.

36. Clark, pp. 730–732.

37. John D. Calamari and Joseph M. Perillo, *The Law of Contracts*, 3rd ed. (St. Paul, Minn.: West Publishing Company, 1987), pp. 793–794.

38. Eisler, pp. 32–34.

39. Ibid., p. 33.

40. Ibid., pp. 34–40.

41. Wheeler, p. 50.

42. Charles V. Metz, *Divorce and Custody for Men* (Garden City, N.Y.: Doubleday, 1968), p. 67.

43. Clark, pp. 752–753.

44. Eisler, p. 56.

45. Ibid., pp. 55–56.

46. Clark, pp. 900–902.

47. Robin Green, *Divorce without Defeat* (Amarillo, Tex.: Cimarron Press, 1982), p. 152.

48. Susan Coleman and Franci Smith, *Child Support Enforcement in Texas* (Austin: League of Women Voters of Texas, 1982).

49. Eisler, p. 122.

50. *Barnardo* v. *McHugh,* as cited in Sophonisba P. Breckinridge, *The Family and the State* (Chicago: University of Chicago Press, 1934), pp. 444–446.

51. *Matter of Baby M,* 109 N.J. 396, 537 A.2d 1227 (1988).

52. John J. Sampson, "Texas Family Code Symposium, Chapter 13, Determination of Paternity," *Texas Tech Law Review,* Vol. 13 (1982), p. 898.

53. Eisler, pp. 122–123.

54. *Stanley* v. *Illinois,* 405 U.S. 645 (1972).

55. Henry C. Black, *Black's Law Dictionary,* 4th ed. (St. Paul, Minn.: West Publishing Company, 1968), p. 70.

56. *In re Adoption of "E,"* 59 N.J. 36, 279 A.2d 785 (1971).

57. Clark, pp. 328, 339.

58. *Prince* v. *Massachusetts,* 321 U.S. 158 (1944), at 171.

59. *Hunt* v. *Thompson,* as cited in Sophonisba P. Breckinridge, *The Family and the State* (Chicago: University of Chicago Press, 1934), p. 242.

60. *Wisconsin* v. *Yoder,* 406 U.S. 205 (1972).

61. *Johnson* v. *Cupp,* 274 N.E.2d 411 (Ind. App. 1971).

62. Eisler, pp. 59–60; Clark, pp. 290–296.

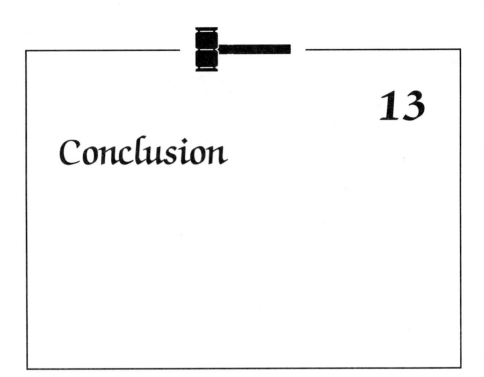

Conclusion

13

We began this book by observing that one who wishes to understand the American legal system must first understand the meaning of law. We noted that law can be defined in terms of the functions that it performs in a society, the sources of law, and the different kinds of law. This book has attempted to acquaint the reader with the many facets of law in our society. Viewing law can be compared to the pleasant pastime of cloud gazing. Most of us at one time or another have looked up at the sky and described what we thought we saw in the various cloud formations above—a kind of heavenly Rorschach test. If accompanied by others, we soon discover that there are differences of opinion about the pictures formed by the various combinations of clouds. We also discover that, unless it is an unusually calm day, the cloud formations begin to change, drawing new pictures across the sky. An image we once thought to be clear and distinct is soon misshapen. What is formed by the clouds is a function of time, space, and the perceptions of the viewer.

In a sense, looking at the law is like looking at cloud formations. Law has the same elusive qualities as a cloud. Like a cloud, the law has a real presence, and yet our understanding of it may evaporate in an instant. Like a cloud, the law is constantly changing, but often at a rate so slow that it is almost imperceptible. Like a cloud, the law may appear to be different to different people at various points in time. In this chapter, we will try to bring together some of the facets of the law that have been described either explicitly or implicitly in previous chapters. We will try to pull together the loose ends we have left untied. In so doing, however, we will remind the reader that others have spent a lifetime trying to define and explain the concept of law. The reader may conclude, as we have after years of studying it, that law, like beauty, is in the eye of the beholder.

LAW AS PROTECTOR AND OPPRESSOR

Abraham Lincoln once used the example of the shepherd, the wolf, and the sheep to illustrate the potential variety of perceptions of government. The sheep looks to the shepherd for protection from those who would prey upon him and even kill him. The wolf, on the other hand, sees the shepherd as an oppressor. After all, a wolf, like all living things, needs food to survive, and it is hardly his fault that nature made him carnivorous. To the wolf, the shepherd is an enemy who keeps him from the food he so desperately needs for survival. Lincoln's point was that government, like the shepherd, represents different things to different people. To some, government is the guardian of liberty and the protector of the weak from the strong. To others, government is a source of oppression that interferes with their "pursuit of happiness." To some extent, neither view is entirely incorrect. Government is indeed capable of being both protector and oppressor, as history certainly confirms.

Like the shepherd and government, the law can be viewed as a source of both protection and oppression. For example, consider how the divorced parents of a minor child might view child-support laws. To the custodial mother, the state's child-support laws may seem like the protector of the child's rights. Most children need the financial support of both parents. The law provides the custodial mother with the means (albeit often inadequate) to force her recalcitrant husband to pay his fair share of the financial burden of child rearing. On the other hand, the noncustodial father may see the state's child-support laws as a burden, particularly if there is a controversy about how the funds are spent. Forced to maintain a separate household, the father has living expenses that may make child-support payments an onerous burden. If he remarries, the father often finds himself drained by the job of trying to support two families emotionally and financially. Although he clearly has a legal and moral obligation to provide financial support for his child, he cannot help but feel that the law has placed an intolerable burden on his shoulders.

One more example should help clarify the view of law as protector and oppressor. In Chapter 10 we discussed contract law. A common form of contract is a rental agreement or lease. To the landlord, such agreements are designed to protect the rights of the property owner against abuses by renters. That is, the law serves as the protector of property rights. To the renter, the typical lease gives the landlord unfair advantages, especially if the renter is desperate to find a place to live. Although the law assumes that the two parties entered into the rental contract as equals, the renter often feels that he has no choice but to accept the terms set out in the lease. That the lease permits the landlord to profit from his advantage seems to the renter patently unfair. In the eyes of the law, however, the renter was not forced to sign the lease and consents to the terms of his free will.

More examples could be cited, and the reader can doubtless think of others. It is not our place to say who is right or wrong on these issues. Like most questions of law, there are two sides to every story. We will allow readers to decide for themselves which party is the wolf and which is the sheep in the examples we have cited. Suffice it to say that there will always be those who will use the law to their advantage or to exploit others. As we noted in Chapter 1, law is a function of the society that creates it. Consequently, law is only as good or as bad as the people who make it.

LAW AND POLITICS

It is almost impossible to escape the conclusion that law and politics are inseparable. The legal profession has a vastly disproportionate amount of influence on both our legal and our political institutions. A few examples will illustrate this point. Under normal circumstances, about half the members of Congress are lawyers. Compared to their percentage of the American population as a whole, lawyers are vastly overrepresented. Although there may be good reasons for this overrepresentation, the fact remains that lawyers have disproportionate influence over the making of national laws. The same is true, but to a lesser extent, at the state level. One authority on state government has noted that "Lawyers, farmers, and business owners are heavily represented in state legislatures."[1] Similarly, lawyers almost completely dominate the judicial branch of government. Although there is no constitutional requirement that a president's choice for the Supreme Court be a lawyer, the likelihood of a nonlawyer being approved by the lawyer-dominated Senate Judiciary Committee is remote. At the state level, the possession of a law license is a requirement for appointment or election to most judicial offices. Also, as noted in Chapter 3, the selection of judges at the state and federal levels is a highly politicized process. It makes little difference whether judges are elected, appointed, or chosen by merit; politics will always play a role. Different selection methods do nothing more than change the level of politics involved. As long as judges make political decisions, politics will enter into the selection process. It appears that the close relationship between law and politics will continue. Political science majors still constitute the largest single group of students taking the Law School Admission Test (LSAT).

The dominance of the legal profession in our political institutions is not the only way that law and politics interact. Courtrooms are increasingly becoming the battlegrounds for causes won or lost in the political arena. Americans have a tendency to turn to courts to resolve the most controversial issues of our society. As noted in Chapter 8, the issues of abortion, discrimination, school prayer, and capital punishment are perennial issues before the courts of the nation. We can anticipate that controversies surrounding issues such as Acquired Immune Deficiency Syndrome (AIDS) and the right to die will require additional judicial resolution in the future. Civil rights, environmental, women's, and other special-interest groups often turn to courts to win the results they have failed to achieve in other political arenas. A loss today is a mere temporary setback for most groups because they know that in time the makeup of the courts could change in their favor. Today's loss is tomorrow's victory. They know that, with perseverance, they can eventually achieve the desired results. Law, then, becomes a never-ending battle between the status quo and the forces of change.

LAW AND SOCIETY

We noted in Chapter 1 that law is a function of the society that creates it, and we have already observed in this chapter that law is only as good or bad as those who make it. Law reflects the values of the lawmaker and the dominant political and economic forces in a society. In Chapter 7 we discussed this relationship in the area of criminal law. Just what kind of behavior society deems unacceptable is manifested by the acts it prohibits by its criminal law. Just how serious society deems that behavior to be is reflected in the vigor with which the law is enforced and the severity with which it is punished. Let's take littering as an example. While it is true that most American cities have ordinances prohibiting littering, it is equally true that these ordinances are infrequently enforced and that the punishment is a relatively small fine. What this seems to indicate is that while littering may be universally condemned and prohibited, it is generally not viewed as a serious offense in our society.

Other, more serious, examples could be cited to reflect upon the relationship of law to society. Only fairly recently have states begun to get really tough with drunk drivers. Although few, if any, rational persons would seriously defend drunk driving, it is not uncommon for drunk drivers to have been arrested several times for the offense before they are severely punished. Often this is because those in our judicial system have empathy for the drunk driver, especially the first offender. Few, if any, persons who drink have not at one time or another driven while legally under the influence of alcohol. Jurors are inclined to think, "There but for the grace of God go I." That is, any one of us could easily picture ourselves in a predicament similar to that of the defendant. Prosecutors and judges, knowing how difficult it is to convict first offenders, will allow the drunk driver to plead guilty to some other offense. When the repeat offender finally kills or injures someone, citizens ask in disbelief how a repeat offender could be allowed to drive at all. Fortunately, through the efforts of groups like Mothers Against Drunk Driving (MADD), states have cracked down on driving under the influence. But as long as alcohol use and abuse remain a part of our culture, drunk driving will remain a legal and social problem. Similarly, until such time as problems like abuse of children, spouses, and the elderly are viewed as serious by our society, the law will continue to treat them as relatively minor offenses.

We also noted in Chapter 7 that law reflects a society's attitude toward the lawbreaker. Critics of American criminal justice argue that our legal system is overly concerned with the rights of those accused of crime and almost totally unconcerned about the rights of the victims of crime. Our purpose here is not to reopen that debate. Suffice it to say that our Founding Fathers, themselves branded as "outlaws" by the British government, were sensitive to the ability of government to use its coercive power against the individual. Whether they "overreacted" by placing so many safeguards into the Constitution is also open to debate. The point is that we, as a society, are divided over the proper balance between the rights of the accused and the rights of society. Consequently, there is a constant struggle among law enforcers, civil libertarians, and the public at large over what is the proper balance. The likelihood of reaching a consensus on this issue seems remote.

Finally, we would like to reiterate the evolutionary nature of the law. Law, like the clouds we discussed earlier, changes over time as our society changes. Our ideas and ideals about decency, justice, and due process evolve over time. As noted in Chapter 7, we have narrowed the range of offenses for which a person can be put to death. Crimes that once resulted in hanging, such as horse stealing and bank robbery, are today treated like any other theft of property. It is true that there are still those in our society who would like to see harsher penalties imposed. Generally, however, we have reached a consensus on those offenses that merit the ultimate punishment. Perhaps someday we will reach a similar consensus on the decriminalization of a range of other activities, including gambling and marijuana use.

LAW AND ECONOMICS

One frequently overlooked facet of law is the relationship between law and economics. As previously noted, landlords have historically used the law of contracts to their economic advantage. In addition, landlords have used local city ordinances or state laws to evict tenants who failed to pay their rent on time. Disputes typically arose over the failure of the landlord to effect some needed repairs, and the tenant withheld the rent only to discover that the law favored the landlord. Fortunately, that situation is a thing of the past in most jurisdictions. Laws have been changed to guarantee the tenant the right to live in a habitable dwelling, and informal as well as formal methods have been devised to mediate landlord–tenant disputes.

The use of eviction laws was just one way in which an economic group used the law to gain an advantage over another. During the early struggle between labor unions and management, the latter would use court injunctions as a weapon against striking workers. If an owner were able to convince a judge that a labor strike caused him "irreparable damage," the judge would issue an injunction ordering an end to the strike. Stripped of their principal weapon, the workers were fired and replaced by other workers desperately in need of employment. In this manner, employers were permitted to keep wages low, hours long, working conditions unsafe, and workers insecure. The use of the injunction as a strike breaker also illustrates the importance placed upon property rights in our legal system. Judges, often sympathetic to the views of the owners, placed property rights above the workers' rights to decent wages and working conditions. It is fascinating to read accounts of state and national efforts to enact laws to protect the rights of workers only to have those laws ruled unconstitutional by the courts.[2] In a sense, the law was a battleground in an economic class war.

The modern era can provide similar examples of the influence of economics on the law. Tax law is frequently cited as an example of how laws are written to benefit a particular economic class. Laws that provide tax breaks and tax incentives for wealthy investors in municipal bonds and other tax shelters are widely known. A common complaint of the average American is that the tax code gives unfair advantages to those in our society who are already wealthy. Whether this accusation is actually true or not is seldom questioned. The fact is that most Americans believe it to be true. Another example of the relationship of economics and law is in the area of criminal law. Until the 1963 *Gideon* v. *Wainwright*[3] decision, indigent persons accused of noncapital offenses were forced in most states either to defend themselves at trial or to plead guilty. Until the *Gideon* decision ruled that states must provide counsel for indigent defendants, those who were economically disadvantaged were also legally disadvantaged.

One final example of the relationship of law and economics is in order. In recent years the medical profession has been plagued by an increase in both the number of malpractice suits and the amount of damages awarded to successful plaintiffs. The response to the crisis has been twofold. First, the cost of medical malpractice insurance premiums has skyrocketed to the point that the costs are nearly prohibitive for many physicians. Second, pressure has increased from both the medical profession and the insurance industry to put a ceiling on the amount of damages that can be awarded in a malpractice suit. In fact, many states have enacted such limits. These two groups have sought legislation in various states under the general label of "tort reform." Physicians and insurance companies have been opposed in their efforts to win tort reform by segments of the legal profession. Lawyers, especially those who represent plaintiffs, argue that the problem has been grossly exaggerated. Physicians argue that lawyers may not be totally neutral parties since they are often working on a contingency-fee basis. Consequently, physicians argue that lawyers have a financial interest in maintaining a system that encourages large awards. Lawyers counter that large awards are given only in cases of extreme or gross negligence, that they are usually justified, and that the jury system serves as a check on any abuses. Although strong arguments can be made on both sides, our point is that physicians, lawyers, plaintiffs, and insurance companies all seek to use the law to promote some economic self-interest. Despite disclaimers to the contrary, economics is central to this controversy.

We are not prepared to say, as perhaps an economic determinist would, that economics is the only or even the major force behind the enactment of every law. We are, however, prepared to say that the economic impact of the law is a powerful influence on the way that law in our society is shaped.

FINAL REFLECTIONS

We will conclude with a few final reflections on law in American society. As we noted at the beginning of this chapter, law is perceived differently by different people. In a sense, then, our perceptions about the nature and meaning of law have colored the contents of this book. What we have chosen to emphasize or to ignore is a function of our own individual biases. The fact that hundreds of books have been written on law is a testimony both to its complexity and to the fascination with which law is viewed.

What is this fascination with the law? Part of it is due to the need for humans to have an ultimate answer. There is a finality in law that is comforting to most people. Even those who have lost a lawsuit are sometimes comforted by the fact that they did everything possible to prevail. Even in defeat, they know that they will never have to wonder what would have happened if they had not pursued their case to the fullest extent of the law. A losing litigant may analyze what went wrong and what might have been done differently, but in the final analysis there is the realization that the issue has at least been resolved.

Another reason for our fascination with the law is the feeling of righteousness that often accompanies our involvement with it. One usually hears the relative of a murder victim express satisfaction that "justice was finally done" upon learning of the killer's conviction. Despite the efforts of religion and philosophy to persuade us to rise above our human failings, the fact remains that the need for retribution is powerful in most humans. The old saying "Don't get mad—get even" appeals to many. Law provides us with a civilized way to exact revenge, because even if the individual victim is forgiving, society, in its role as avenger, is not. The same is true for litigants in civil cases. Although we would not entirely rule out avarice as a motivator, litigants in civil suits frequently disavow the desire for money as their reason for suing. Instead, they cite "the principle involved." Given the expense in time and money and the uncertainty of success, principle probably does play a major role in most lawsuits. Law, then, helps fulfill the basic human need for justice.

Finally, law is a source of comfort to most of us. In a world described by Thomas Hobbes as "solitary, poor, nasty, brutish, and short,"[4] it is comforting to realize that we have risen above the law of the jungle, where the strong prey upon the weak. As previously noted, the law really does serve as the sheep's protector. People want a hero who will protect them from the injustices of life and the wrath of their enemies. To many, the law is such a hero— a great equalizer ready to come to our assistance if needed.

We hope this book has made its readers think about the law. Regardless of whether the reader accepts or rejects the ideas presented herein, we will have succeeded if each reader has reflected upon the nature and purpose of the law and perhaps has even grown to understand the law a little better.

NOTES

1. Murray S. Stedman, Jr., *State and Local Governments* (Boston: Little, Brown, 1982), p. 118.

2. See, for example, *Lochner* v. *New York*, 198 U.S. 45 (1905); *Hammer* v. *Dagenhart*, 247 U.S. 251 (1918); *Bailey* v. *Drexel Furniture Co.*, 259 U.S. 20 (1922); and *Adkins* v. *Children's Hospital*, 261 U.S. 525 (1923).

3. *Gideon* v. *Wainwright*, 372 U.S. 335 (1963).

4. Quoted in Kenneth Janda, Jeffrey M. Berry, and Jerry Goldman, *The Challenge of Democracy: Government in America* (Boston: Houghton Mifflin Company, 1987), pp. 8–9.

Appendix

Legal Research

"It is a matter of deep study to be exact in the law."[1] Fortunately, those who seek to be "exact in the law" have available to them a highly organized and widely indexed knowledge base because "that which is law to-day is none to-morrow."[2] Law evolves and changes with each legislative enactment and court decision. The legal researcher must be aware of what the law was yesterday (*stare decisis*), what it is today, and often what it will be tomorrow. The chief tools available for such research include both the traditional configuration of books and case reports and the new mode of computers and networks of sophisticated databases in law, business, and social science literature.

Because this country follows common-law principles, the chief law-givers are the legislative bodies and courts at all levels. The primary sources in legal research include the national and state constitutions, legislative enactments (or those adopted by the people through initiative), the written decisions of the courts, administrative regulations, rules of procedures, and any constitutional or statutory provisions accepting or receiving the common law of England. All jurisdictions except Louisiana, which utilizes the civil or code law, have adopted English common law as the basis of its jurisprudence. The effects of these statutory or constitutional provisions adopting English common law have been diluted by the development of uniquely American jurisprudence since the establishment of the colonies nearly 400 years ago. Today's legal precepts, while founded on English common-law principles, are more the product of American jurisprudence than English. One factor contributing to the lessened dependence on English law is our federal system, which permits each state to incorporate its own values and mores into law which weakens uniformity.[3]

The secondary sources in legal research include various legal encyclopedias, learned treatises, legal periodicals, and computer research bases such as WESTLAW and LEXIS-NEXIS as well as literature in fields other than law. Judges do not limit themselves only to law in arriving at their conclusions but draw on information from a variety of other fields including medicine, engineering, and social science studies. The openness of courts to information from a variety of sources mandates that researchers must also be flexible.

For example, judges often integrate history into their opinions. Two very different cases by the same justice in the 1971 and 1972 terms of the U.S. Supreme Court illustrate that point. In *Flood* v. *Kuhn* (a case dealing with whether antitrust laws applied to baseball as they do to other professional sports), Justice Blackmun, in writing for the majority, began the opinion by tracing the history of professional baseball from its beginnings over a century earlier.[4] For *Roe* v. *Wade,* Justice Blackmun was described as having "immersed himself in research at the huge Mayo Clinic medical library," while other justices also pursued their own independent research into the medical and philosophical issues surrounding abortion.[5] The result is that *Roe* v. *Wade* contains not only a lengthy discussion of attitudes toward abortion from ancient times to the present but also a discussion of medical procedures and philosophy.[6]

Extensive use of statistics and materials from the social sciences has been debated by those on the bench and by legal scholars; nevertheless, such studies are rather routinely accepted in various cases alleging discrimination. In *Craig* v. *Boren,*[7] the Court mentioned several statistical surveys about youthful drivers and alcohol while considering Oklahoma's discriminatory gender-based traffic safety laws. In *McCleskey* v. *Kemp,* Warren McCleskey, a black, employed as his primary defense a sophisticated statistical study which revealed significant disparities in sentencing of blacks and whites to the death penalty in Georgia. The Court, with some discussion, accepted the statistics but eventually decided that McCleskey had not shown that discrimination actually existed in his case.[8] Just as judges themselves go outside the narrow confines of "legal" materials, the legal researcher, particularly those drafting appellate briefs, may find himself or herself doing research in areas other than law.

THE STAGES OF RESEARCH

The basis of any scholarly inquiry is a clear understanding of the goal of research—drafting a document, preparing for trial, writing an appellate brief or a legal memoranda for a supervising attorney, or counseling a client on her legal business—before one begins. The initial step is assembling the facts, evaluating their relevancy to the legal issue, and determining the legal problems to be researched. The factors to be considered in that determination include some of the following: (1) relevant characteristics of the parties such as age in contract cases or level of expertise in malpractice suits; (2) the events (a car accident) or the subject matter (a professional athlete's employment contract); (3) cause of action (a child custody suit) or ground of defense (consent in a sexual assault case); and (4) the remedy sought such as injunction or monetary damages.[9]

The next step is to plan the research and choose the logical starting point. If the researcher is unfamiliar with the issue, he or she might begin with one of the general legal encyclopedias which are arranged (like other encyclopedias) by topics. Searches involving statutory interpretation might start with an annotated code which would identify related cases and where to locate the legislative history, that is, the committee reports and debates which accompanied the enactment of the statute. A researcher with a case name in hand might begin with the digests, which are listings of cases arranged by subject matter or with an index. The type of problem and type of research lead will determine where the researcher begins.

The third step is to actually conduct the research. Legal research is rarely done only in one type or set of books. An annotated code of statutes would steer one to case reporters, to legal periodicals on the topic, to legislative histories, and to sources which indicate whether the case was appealed and what happened during the appeal. Since law does change and evolve, it is necessary for the researcher to always be aware of the most current developments in the law. Obviously reference may be made to nonlegal news periodicals such as *Time* or *Newsweek* or daily newspapers which cover important cases, but there are also various loose-leaf services which are updated very frequently—sometimes weekly—to assist the researcher in this task. Bound volumes of statutes and the legal encyclopedias often are updated through means of "pocket parts" inserted at the back. It is incumbent on the investigator to check these when doing research. The fourth step is to actually compile the research and present it in the appropriate form— as argument at trial, as communications to courts or attorneys, or as documents for clients.[10] Obviously, legal research has become much more complex than in the days when the relatively few copies of Blackstone's *Commentaries* circulating in the colonies was the chief source of the law, but those undertaking legal research today are very fortunate that basic legal materials are, for the most part, readily available and even more fortunate that the law is highly organized and easily cross-referenced whether the researcher is using a computer or doing things the old-fashioned way, looking things up in books.

TOOLS OF RESEARCH

Mandatory and persuasive authority. The foundation of a common-law system is the decisions of judges on both the trial and appellate level. This is because of the doctrine of *stare decisis*, which dictates that courts follow precedent; however, you will remember from our discussions in Chapter 5 that judges are bound only by decisions of superior courts in their jurisdiction, that is, judges in Michigan are bound by Michigan appellate decisions and not by Utah law. The same is true on the national level; federal trial courts in the Eleventh Circuit are obligated to follow decisions of that Court of Appeals and not those of the First Circuit. In certain instances, such as interpretation of the U.S. Constitution, federally enacted law is also binding on state courts, but not all federal statutes are binding on state courts. Similarly, federal courts must apply the state law of the state where they are situated in certain types of cases.

Authority which must be followed is termed *mandatory authority* and may come from constitutions, cases, or statutory enactments. Mandatory authorities are primary sources, and such things as law review articles, decisions from other states, and learned treatises are nonbinding in nature and are deemed to be *persuasive authority.* For a case to be mandatory authority or to be binding precedent, it must be "on point," which means that there must be sufficient similarity between the key facts in the two cases and between the rule of law which was interpreted in the first case and the rule of law to be applied in this case. When these similarities do not exist, the case is not mandatory authority.[11]

In addition, lower courts are not bound by plurality opinions that are of "limited" precedential value. A majority opinion is one in which a majority (five of nine, for example) of the judges agree on both the holding and the reasoning of the opinion. In contrast, a plurality opinion is one that receives "more votes than any other opinion supporting the outcome on which a majority of the judges have agreed."[12] As Chief Justice William Rehnquist has stated, discussion in a plurality opinion is the "considered" opinion of several of the judges and provides guidance for later cases but it is not "binding precedent."[13]

Similarly, *obiter dictum* must be distinguished from the *ratio decidendi* of the case. *Ratio decidendi* is the ground for a decision, while *dicta* are gratuitous comments by a judge about a solution to a question that is not necessarily involved in the case at hand or essential to its determination.[14] *Dicta* are not binding as precedent.

Case law.   Collections of court opinions are gathered and published in sets of volumes called reporters or reports. Originally these reports were prepared and published by individuals, and private publication is still the general rule although official reports are published by various governments. Cases are cited in a fairly uniform manner which facilitates locating the case. The standard reference work for citing legal materials is *A Uniform System of Citation* published by Harvard Law Review Association, but there is some slight degree of variance because of state court preferences; these can be determined by examining the reported cases, court rules, and state bar journals. Examples of the meaning of the citations are given below.

Hornbuckle v. *McCarty,*	243	S.W.	327	(Mo.	1922)
Appellant Appellee	vol.	reporter	page	Ct.	year
	no.	abbrev.	no.	i.d.	
Sostre v. *McGinnis,*	442	F.2d	178	(2d Cir.	1971)

It is important for the researcher to know if the case has been appealed, and if so, what happened on appeal—whether the case was upheld or reversed. The subsequent history of the case should also be included in the citation. For example, someone seeing a citation to *Telex Corp.* v. *International Business Machines Corp.*, 367 F. Supp. 258 (N.D. Okla. 1975), 510 F.2d 894 (10th Cir. 1975), *cert. denied*, 423 U.S. 802 (1975) can track the history of case and determine its status. It began in a federal district court in the Northern District of Oklahoma, was appealed to the Tenth Circuit, and then to the United States Supreme Court although the Supreme Court declined to accept the case. To determine the fate of the case and to locate any other cases which refer to it, one goes to *Shepard's Case Citations. Shepard's Case Citations* are published for both state and federal levels and include not only cases but also statutes, constitutions, and administrative regulations.

At the state level, decisions of trial courts are rarely published, whereas appellate court decisions are generally collected and published either in an official reporter by the state or, more commonly, the National Reporter System, which is published by West Publishing Co. West Publishing compiles the court cases and prints them in various regional reporters. The state and level of court is included in the citation since several states are included in the regional reporters as are at least two levels of courts in each state. For instance, seeing only this information, *Bristol Telephone Co.* v. *Weaver*, 243 S.W. 299 (1921) and *Oder* v. *Commonwealth*, 243 S.W. 877 (1922), the reader would not know that the former was decided by the Tennessee Supreme Court while the latter was a product of the Court of Appeals of Kentucky. It is therefore very important to include all the information in the case citations.

At the national level, the cases are reported by the level or type of court as, for example, district court cases or tax court cases. Supreme Court cases are officially published by the government in the United States Supreme Court Reporter (U.S.), by West Publishing in the Supreme Court Reporter (S.Ct.), and by Lawyer's Co-operative Publishing in the United States Supreme Court Reports, Lawyer's Edition (L.Ed.). Publication by the three companies leads to the triple citation format often used for Supreme Court cases—*Reynolds* v. *Sims,* 377 U.S. 533, 84 S.Ct. 1362, 12 L.Ed.2d 506 (1964)—which allows the researcher to readily access whichever set is available. At the intermediate appellate level, the cases are published in the set known as the Federal Reporter, and the case citations must indicate which circuit actually issued the opinion—*Knafel* v. *Pepsi-Cola Bottlers of Akron, Inc.*, 899 F.2d 1473 (6th Cir. 1990)—allowing the researcher to determine at a glance whether it is mandatory or persuasive authority. Federal district court cases are generally self-reported and, when published, are found in the Federal Supplement Reporter. The district, if there is more than one in a state, is indicated in the citation. An example is *Banks* v. *Havener*, 234 F. Supp. 27 (E.D. Va. 1964).

Recent decisions are published in the form of advance sheets or slip opinions, which are paperback collections of newer decisions or individual case opinions. In addition, private companies also publish various loose-leaf services which are updated monthly or even weekly. For example, current U.S. Supreme Court decisions may be found in either *United States Law Week* (U.S.L.W.), published by the Bureau of National Affairs, or in the *United States Supreme Court Bulletin* (S.Ct.Bull. CCH), published by Commerce Clearing House. Reporters on specialized subjects (e.g., Media Law Reporter or Education Law Reporter) are also available. Court opinions are almost instantaneously available through fax and online services today.

A secondary source that can be used to assist with locating relevant cases is the Digest. The American Digest System, published by West, is a subject classification system which brings together cases on a similar point of law. In addition to the General Digest, West also prints the *Federal Practice Digest, 4th* and *U.S. Supreme Court Digest* on the federal level, state and regional digests, and some subject digests such as those on bankruptcy and military justice. Under each subject heading is included a very abbreviated summary of each case on the point of law. The topics are subdivided, and points of law are assigned unique key numbers. These key numbers facilitate movement among the digests, cases, statutes, and other West publications, which include the key numbers. There are other helpful features of the Digests including the Descriptive Word Index and Table of Cases. Like *Shepard's Case Citations,* the Digests are indexes—research tools only—and should never be cited as a source.[15]

Constitutions, statutes, and administrative regulations. Constitutions, statutes, ordinances (passed by local governmental units), and administrative regulations are also published both by the government and by private companies in annotated form. The annotations often include summaries of cases interpreting the provision, citations to legislative histories, mentions of pertinent articles in legal periodicals, and references for accessing the computer databases. If the research problem involves a statute, an annotated code can be an extremely useful research tool.

Neither state legislatures nor Congress pass laws in any sort of organized manner, that is, one law may deal with financing the space program while the next may deal with the type of nets required for commercial fishing. Each law as it is passed is published in the form of a slip law—an individual printing of each bill. These are then collected and published in chronological order of passage without reference to subject matter nor any effort to correlate amendments with the original legislation. On the national level, the collection is known as the *Statutes at Large,* whereas state collections are generally referred to as session laws. These are helpful if one knows the session and year of passage, but since the volumes are organized chronologically and not topically and are published yearly or after each session, they are not overly helpful for tracing the development of a point of law or ensuring that one has the most current information.

That need has been met through codification on both the state and national levels. Codes are arranged topically, which simplifies the task of working with statutes. They also are updated and contain amendments to the statute. It is very important to check the pocket part of these volumes to have more recent information. The official edition of the national laws is the *United States Code* (U.S.C.) which is published by the national government, and there are annotated versions such as the *United States Code Annotated* (U.S.C.A.) and the *United States Code Service* (U.S.C.S.), which are published by private companies. A national statute which has not yet been codified would be cited to the *Statutes at Large*, or if it has been, to U.S.C. or one of the annotated versions. On the state level, the same holds true. A state statute would be cited to the session laws—Laws of Wisconsin—or to a state code, if one exists—Wisconsin Administrative Code. Most sets of codes also contain conversion tables in order that one may move from the session laws to the codes as well as a Popular Names Table. The latter identifies cases by the popular name such as the Selective Service Act and provides the citation for it.

Locating the legislative history or what is said during various committee hearings and floor debates may be critical when dealing with statutory ambiguity. While legislative history is not actually law and therefore is persuasive authority only, it is valuable because it provides information about the intent of the legislators. In cases involving statutory interpretation, courts frequently rely on this type of information to divine the actual intent of those writing the law. Legislative history may be found in transcripts of committee hearings, committee reports, and reports of debates on both the state and national level.

Administrative regulations are promulgated by governmental agencies under their rule-making authority. The public is often invited to comment on proposed regulations, and these (if federal in nature), along with adopted regulations and other matters such as executive orders, are printed in the *Federal Register,* a daily publication. The *Code of Federal Regulations* (C.F.R.) is the compilation of the administrative regulations by subject matter and, through a rotation basis, is entirely revised each year.[16] Generally, agencies with decision-making authority, such as the Internal Revenue Service or the National Labor Relations Board, must make their decisions available to the public. This is done either through official or private publication, often in the form of loose-leaf services, which are easily updated. On the state level, similar publications exist along with publication of the state Attorney General's Opinions which indicate his or her opinion of the legality of the state officials' activities or interpretations of state law.

Legal encyclopedias, annotations, and treatises. When the researcher needs to begin with a general overview of the topic and legal principles, the best source is one of the legal encyclopedias. Two extensive and widely accepted legal encyclopedias are *American Jurisprudence 2d* (Am. Jur.

2d) and *Corpus Juris Secundum* (C.J.S.). Both are topically arranged and present succinct, but thorough, narrative discussions of general legal rules with extensive cross-references to other types of materials such as cases, statutes, and law review articles, and C.J.S., a West publication, also utilizes the key number system. Courts often cite both works in their opinions, although local practice will dictate whether Am. Jur. 2d or C.J.S., rather than cases, is acceptable for trial or appellate arguments, especially formal appellate briefs.

Local reference encyclopedias are available for some states such as *California Jurisprudence 2d* or *Pennsylvania Law Encyclopedia*. In addition, single-focus encyclopedias are also published. Examples of these are *Corbin on Contracts* or *Wigmore on Evidence*. These encyclopedias are distinguishable from learned treatises in that the encyclopedias merely summarize the law, whereas treatises also interpret and evaluate the law. Some treatises are multivolume sets, while others resemble other library books.[17]

The topical organization of legal encyclopedias is similar to that employed in the American Law Report (A.L.R.) series. The editors at Lawyer's Co-operative/Bancroft-Whitney choose appellate court decisions and supplement them with extensive, thorough annotations on selected points of law. It is the annotation, and not the case itself, to which one refers when using this source. These annotations include historical analysis of the legal doctrine, current law in those jurisdictions which have considered the matter, and probable future developments. Like Am. Jur. 2d and C.J.S., A.L.R. is frequently cited by judges in their opinions, but practitioners should use caution in relying on it in court since it is secondary authority and therefore not binding.

Legal dictionaries. One of the most basic of all research aids, irrespective of the type of research, is the dictionary. Specialized law dictionaries are available which contain definitions of legal terms drawn from cases and which assist with pronunciation of the words. Three of the most commonly used and more traditional dictionaries are *Black's Law Dictionary*, *Ballentine's Law Dictionary*, and *Bouvier's Law Dictionary*. Legal thesauri and glossaries are available as well.

Legal periodicals. Legal periodicals, also persuasive authority, contain commentaries and analysis of the law and include not only law reviews, but other law-related journals as well. Law reviews are journals published by law schools with scholarly articles on legal issues by law professors, outstanding students, attorneys, and judges. Most law reviews contain articles on a potpourri of subjects, although some symposium issues in which all articles relate to a single topic (e.g., Fifth Circuit Symposium issue of Texas Tech Law Review) are published and some are focused in scope (e.g., *Harvard Women's Law Journal*). Law review articles are particularly helpful in critical analysis of court decisions and in identifying trends in the law; they frequently contain extensive case and statutory citations which can assist the researcher.

The *Index to Legal Periodicals* indexes legal materials from selected journals and other sources. It closely resembles other periodical indexes in that it cross-lists articles by author and subject matter. Other indexes such as the *Public Affairs Information Service* and various social science and business indexes may also be helpful to the researcher.

Computer-assisted research. Law with its entrenched reliance on history and precedent is not always forward looking, and its practitioners are sometimes recalcitrant and somewhat leery of changing established patterns of behavior and operation. However, the legal profession has joined the computer age, albeit with varying degrees reluctance. Computers are ubiquitous—in lawyers' offices, on the floors of various legislative bodies, in judges' chambers, and in courtrooms as well (as even the most casual observer of *California* v. *Simpson* must have noted). Lawyers today communicate with their clients via e-mail or establish a home page on the World Wide Web to advise other firms and clients of their specializations. Online seminars with the nation's leading experts are available through commercial services on the Internet. Legal encyclopedias and the various reporters are being linked on CD-ROMs. Software packages designed especially for attorneys allow them to internally administer the firm's business, including billing and tracking clients' cases, to draft and modify various legal instruments quickly, to manage complex cases that involve literally thousands of exhibits, and to access pleadings, briefs, and court opinions for research.

Today there are many commercial legal databases but in the beginning there were two—LEXIS (now LEXIS-NEXIS, a division of Reed Elsevier) and WESTLAW (a division of West Publishing Co.). Initially these interactive networks, available only on a contract basis with time-related and/or transaction-related fees, were relatively expensive. However, like so many other computer-related products and services, they have declined in price and broadened the richness of their coverage as others have joined the field. Whether dealing with the specialized legal databases or other research services, it behooves the researcher to carefully hone the research problem, or he or she will be inundated with irrelevant material. Identifying the problem and the descriptive words is a critical part of formulating the research plan when using computer-assisted research. The databases are somewhat checkered in that older cases, especially state court decisions, and other materials are not always available. Even given the limitations and the expense of computer-based research, many law firms and researchers feel that the advantages of speed, thoroughness, scope, and flexibility are worth the investment.

Technology is affecting not only the retrieval of information but also its storage. Justice Joseph Story bemoaned, "The mass of law is, to be sure, accumulating with an almost incredible rapidity . . . It is impossible not to look without some discouragement upon the ponderous volumes, which the next half century will add to the groaning shelves of our jurists." The date of his complaint, 1821.[18] Professor Thomas Baker points out that the growth rate has been accelerating. Using the *Federal Reporter, Second Series* as an example, he noted that the total volumes reached: "100 in 1939 (14 years); 200 in 1953 (14 years); 300 in 1962 (9 years); 400 in 1969 (7 years); 500 in 1975 (6 years); 600 in 1979 (4 years); 700 in 1983 (4 years); 800 in 1987 (4 years); 900 in 1990 (3 years); and 999 in 1993 (3 years)."[19] The proliferation of volumes poses problems of storage for all libraries with limited shelf space. Technology has relieved the acuity of the problem. Many government records—statutes, administrative rulings, court opinions, and others—are being placed on microfilm and microfiche that require very little storage space. Perhaps even more important, this information is available from both government and private companies on CD-ROMs that researchers may use on their personal computers—both those on the office desk and the smaller notebooks that travel with the attorney to court, to depositions, and elsewhere. This effectively provides the attorney with a portable library that is instantaneously available, possibly the advantage needed to win the case.

CONCLUSION

A legal system that is founded on precedent requires that practitioners be able to locate that precedent in order to sway judges and juries at trial and to adequately perform their responsibilities to clients. The findings of the research form the basis for advising the client and acting as advocate. Because the task is so important, researchers are blessed in that the rich body of knowledge encompassed in the law is very organized, widely indexed, and widely circulated.

Also, researchers are favored in that there is no single correct approach to initiating or designing the research. There are a variety of research media available whether the researcher has only the sketchiest of information or is an expert in the field. Cases and statutory materials are the primary sources of the law and may be found in case reporters, session laws, or annotated codes. Other secondary sources—for example, legal periodicals and encyclopedias—are also readily obtainable and provide theories, philosophies, and summaries which are persuasive to judges and helpful in ascertaining the status of the law in order that one "may be exact in the law."

NOTES

1. Gilbert Burnet, *History of His Own Times,* as cited in Simon James and Chantal Stebbings, comps., *A Dictionary of Legal Quotations* (New York: Macmillan Publishing Co., 1987), p. 88.

2. Robert Burton, *The Anatomy of Melancholy*, as cited in James and Stebbings, p. 88.

3. Martin Weinstein, *Summary of American Law* (Rochester, N.Y.: Lawyers Co-operative Publishing Co., 1988), pp. 100–101.

4. *Flood* v. *Kuhn*, 407 U.S. 258 (1972).

5. Bob Woodward and Scott Armstrong, *The Brethren* (New York: Simon and Schuster, 1979), p. 229.

6. *Roe* v. *Wade*, 410 U.S. 113 (1973).

7. *Craig* v. *Boren*, 429 U.S. 190 (1976).

8. *McCleskey* v. *Kemp*, 481 U.S. 279 (1987).

9. Steven J. Barkan, "The Legal Research Process," in J. Myron Jacobstein and Roy M. Mersky, *Fundamentals of Legal Research*, 5th ed. (Westbury, N.Y.: The Foundation Press, 1990), pp. 15–20.

10. Larry L. Tepley, *Legal Research and Citation*, 3rd ed. (St. Paul, Minn.: West Publishing Company, 1989), p. 33.

11. William P. Statsky and R. John Wernet, Jr., *Case Analysis and Fundamentals of Legal Writing*, 3rd ed. (St. Paul, Minn.: West Publishing Company, 1989), pp. 203–206.

12. George E. Dix, "A Plea for Clarity," *Texas Lawyer*, October 12, 1992, p. 10.

13. *Texas* v. *Brown*, 460 U.S. 730 (1983).

14. Henry C. Black, *Black's Law Dictionary*, 4th ed. (St. Paul, Minn.: West Publishing Company, 1968), pp. 541, 1429.

15. J. Myron Jacobstein and Roy M. Mersky, *Fundamentals of Legal Research*, 5th ed. (Westbury, N.Y.: The Foundation Press, 1990), pp. 74–109; Teply, pp. 293–300.

16. Tepley, pp. 71–73.

17. Thomas E. Eimermann, *Fundamentals of Paralegalism*, 2nd ed. (Boston: Little, Brown and Co., 1987), pp. 301–304.

18. Justice Joseph Story as quoted in Thomas E. Baker, "The Third Millennium of Federal Reporter," *Texas Lawyer*, January 17, 1994, p. 18.

19. Baker, p. 18.

Glossary

Acceptance   In contract law, the compliance by the offeree with the terms of an offer and the manifestation of such compliance.

Accessory   A person who contributes to or aids in the commission of a crime.

Accessory after the fact   A person who receives, relieves, comforts, or assists another knowing that he has committed a felony.

Actus reus   The "guilty act"; the forbidden act or omission which is an element of a crime.

Adjudication   The resolution or settlement of a dispute between two parties by a third party.

Administrative law   Law that governs the actions of administrative agencies.

Adoption   The act of voluntarily assuming the rights and obligations of a parent over a child.

Adverse possession   A method of acquiring title to land by possession.

Adverse witness   Also called a hostile witness, an adverse witness is one who provides prejudicial information against the party conducting the examination.

Affinity   Related by marriage, such as a mother-in-law and son-in-law or stepchildren or stepbrothers.

Age of majority   The age set by statute at which one loses the disabilities of minority and becomes able to enter legally binding contracts.

Alimony   Court-ordered support payments from one spouse to the other following the dissolution of a marriage.

Annulment   Dissolution through judicial action of a marriage which was invalid from its inception.

Answer   The defendant's response to allegations made by the plaintiff in the latter's complaint.

Appellant   The party, usually the losing one, that seeks to overturn the decision of a trial court by appealing to a higher court.

Appellate court   A court that hears appeals on points of law from trial courts.

Appellee   The party, usually the winning one, against whom a case is appealed.

Arbitration   The submission of an argument to a neutral party for resolution under an agreement by the parties to be bound by the decision or under a court order.

Arraignment   The stage of the criminal justice process in which the defendant is formally informed of the charges and allowed to enter a plea.

Arrest warrant   A court order that allows the police to take a person accused of a crime into custody.

Artificial persons   Corporations that are given certain human attributes by legal fiction in order that they may sue and be sued.

Assault   The apprehension of an offensive or unwanted contact from another person.

Assignment   Transfer of a present contractual interest to a third party.

Battery   Harmful or offensive contact with another person.

Bench trial   A trial conducted without a jury in which the judge serves as the trier of fact.

Best interest of the child   An objective standard used by the courts in determining custody of a child in contested cases.

Bilateral contract   A contract in which the parties exchange promises to do some future act.

Bond   Something of value, either money or property, posted by a criminal defendant to ensure the defendant's appearance in court.

Bound over   If, at the preliminary hearing, the judge believes that sufficient probable cause exists to hold a criminal defendant, the accused is said to be bound over for trial.

Breach of contract   Failure to perform any aspect of a contract.

Brief   A legal document in which an attorney outlines the facts, alleged errors, and precedents in a case appealed to a higher court.

Canon law   A system of church law.

Capacity   The ability of an individual who is not under some legal disqualification, such as infancy or insanity, to enter into legally binding agreements.

Case law   Law that develops through the interpretation of statutes, constitutions, treaties, and other forms of written law.

Caveat emptor   Literally, "let the buyer beware." At common law the doctrine that purchasers of goods must inspect them to avoid being cheated by merchants.

Certification   One method of appealing to the U.S. Supreme Court by which the lower court formally identifies questions of law for decision.

Challenge for cause   Method for striking a potential juror because of specified reasons such as bias or prejudgment.

Charge to the jury   The instructions given to the jury by the judge in which the judge outlines what the jury must find in order to rule for the plaintiff and what they must find to rule for the defendant.

Chattel   An item of tangible property other than realty.

Choice-of-law questions   In conflict of laws, determining which state law will be applied when some or all of the operative elements occurred in a jurisdiction other than the forum state.

Circumstantial evidence   An indirect method of proving the material facts of the case. Testimony that is not based on the witness's personal observation of the material events.

Civil action   A civil lawsuit brought by one person or corporation against another.

Civil disobedience   The theory that a person may disobey human laws that conflict with natural law or God's law.

Civil law   A system of laws in which the legislature is the ultimate lawmaker and which relies on codes rather than court precedent as the basis of decisions; the dominant system in Europe and South America.

Closing statement   Address made by an attorney at the end of the presentation of evidence in which the attorney summarizes the case for the jury.

Codicil   A formal modification of the terms of a will.

Comity   In conflict of laws, a willingness to accept judgments of foreign courts as a matter of courtesy or respect.

Common law   Law developed, mainly in England, by judges who made legal decisions in the absence of written law. Such decisions served as precedents and became "common" to all of England.

Community property   Property gained during marriage that belongs to each spouse equally unless it is a gift or inheritance as defined by the marital property laws in community property states.

Comparative negligence   A theory that allocates negligence between the plaintiff and the defendant and that allows the plaintiff to recover even if he or she contributed to his or her own injury.

Complaining witness   In criminal law, the person, often the victim, who swears out a complaint against another leading to an arrest warrant being issued against the latter.

Complaint   In civil law, a legal document in which the plaintiff makes certain allegations of injury and liability against the defendant. In criminal law, it is the written accusation of a criminal act against a criminal defendant.

Concurring opinion   An opinion by an appellate court judge in which the judge agrees with the decision of the majority but not for the same reasons given in the majority opinion.

Consanguinity   Related by blood such as parents and children, siblings, or cousins.

Consideration   The inducement to contract, which may include money, mutual exchange of promises, or the agreement of parties to do or refrain from doing some act which they are not obligated to do.

Constitutional courts   Federal courts created by Congress under its power under Article III of the Constitution to create courts inferior to the Supreme Court.

Constitutional law   Law that consists of court decisions that interpret and expand the meaning of a written constitution.

Contingency fee   The normal fee arrangement in a civil suit in which the attorney receives a percentage of any award won by the plaintiff.

Contributory negligence   A legal theory that totally bars the plaintiff who contributed, even slightly, to his own injury from recovering damages.

Conversion   The deprivation of an owner of possession of tangible property.

Copyright   Exclusive legal right to sell, reproduce, or publish a literary, artistic, or musical work.

Corporation   A business organization in which the owners are the stockholders who have limited liability and management responsibilities based on the *pro rata* share of ownership.

Corpus   The principal of a trust as opposed to the interest or income.

Court of last resort   At the state level, the highest court with jurisdiction over a particular case. At the national level, the U.S. Supreme Court.

Court of record   A court in which a record of the proceedings are kept, usually in the form of a transcript made by a court reporter.

Courts of general jurisdiction   The trial courts responsible for major criminal and civil cases.

Courts of limited jurisdiction   Lower-level state courts, such as a justice of the peace court, whose jurisdiction is limited to minor civil disputes or misdemeanors.

Criminal law   Laws passed by government that define and prohibit antisocial behavior.

Cross-examination   At trial, the questions of one attorney put to a witness called by the opposing attorney.

Culpability   In law, a person who is blameworthy or responsible in whole or in part for the commission of a crime.

Damages   Pecuniary or monetary compensation paid by the wrongdoer in a civil case.

Defamation   The injury to one's reputation in the community by defamatory comments.

Default judgment   A judgment awarded to the plaintiff because the defendant has failed to answer the complaint.

Defendant   The person against whom a lawsuit is brought.

Delegation theory   In administrative law, the theory that allows a legislative body to delegate its lawmaking power to administrative agencies.

Delegatus non protest delegare   Literally, "a delegate cannot delegate." A person who has been empowered by another to do something may not redelegate that power to another.

Demurrer   A motion by the defendant asking for dismissal of a case on the grounds that the plaintiff has insufficient grounds to proceed.

Deposition   A form of discovery that involves taking the sworn testimony of a witness outside of open court.

Determinate sentencing   A sentencing structure in which a flat or straight sentence is imposed, generally without possibility of parole.

Direct causation   The causing or bringing about of an effect without the interference of an intervening variable or factor.

Direct evidence   Evidence derived from one or more of the five senses.

Direct examination   At trial, the questions asked of a witness by the attorney who called the witness to the stand.

Directed verdict   An order from a judge to the jury ordering the latter to decide the case in favor of one of the parties for failure of the other party to prove its case.

Discovery   A pretrial procedure in which parties to a lawsuit ask for and receive information such as testimony, records, or other evidence from each other.

Dissenting opinion   A written opinion of an appellate court judge in which the judge states the reasons for his or her disagreement with the decision of the majority.

Diversity of citizenship suit   A specific type of federal lawsuit between citizens of two different states in which the amount in controversy exceeds $50,000.

Divine right of kings   The medieval theory that kings were chosen by God to rule, thereby establishing the king's legitimacy.

Divorce   Dissolution of the marital relationship through judicial action.

Domicile   A person's legal home.

Donee   One who receives a gift.

Donor   One who gives a gift.

Due process of law   Term appearing in the Fifth and Fourteenth Amendments which refers to the process that is due before government may deprive a person of life, liberty, or property.

Easement   The right to use someone else's property.

Emancipation   The removal of one's legal disability of being a minor either by reaching the age of majority or by other statutory reasons such as marriage or court order.

Eminent domain   The power of the government to take private property for public use.

En banc   A situation in which all of the members of an appellate court participate in the disposition of a case.

Equity   A branch of law which provides for remedies other than damages and is therefore more flexible than common law.

Estate in fee tail   A freehold estate which limits the succession to the "heirs of the body" or descendants of the donee or devisee.

Estate pur autre vie   An estate which is held during the lifetime of another.

Exclusionary rule   A judicially created rule that holds that evidence obtained through violations of the constitutional rights of the criminal defendant must be excluded from the trial.

Executed contract   A contract in which all the terms have been met or all action completed.

Executive privilege   The doctrine that permits the president to withhold information sought by Congress or the courts.

Executory contract   A contract in which some or all of the terms remain to be completed.

Exhaustion of administrative remedies doctrine   In administrative law, the doctrine that requires persons aggrieved to avail themselves of all administrative remedies before seeking judicial relief.

Express contract   An oral or written contract that explicitly states the contract terms.

Express warranty   An explicit statement or promise that a certain fact in relation to the subject of the contract is true or accurate.

Federalism   A political system in which governmental powers are divided between a central government and regional and/or state governments.

Fee-simple estate   An absolute interest in property; the fullest amount of control over property possible.

Fee tail female   An estate in fee tail that may only pass through the female line.

Fee tail male   An estate in fee tail that may only pass through the male line.

Feudalism   The social system of the Middle Ages which involved a series of reciprocal responsibilities from the king through the lords to the serfs.

Forum non conveniens   A legal doctrine that allows a court to refuse to accept jurisdiction over a case.

Foundation   Also known as "laying a predicate." Preliminary questions that establish the relevancy and admissibility of evidence.

Garnishment   Process whereby money owed to one person as a result of a court judgment may be withheld from the wages of another person known as the garnishee.

General damages   Damages, such as payment of medical bills, awarded to the plaintiff to restore him to the condition he was in before he was injured by the defendant.

General intent   In criminal law, a general showing that the prohibited act was performed voluntarily, whether or not the person meant to do it.

General verdict   A verdict in which the jury finds the defendant liable and awards the plaintiff the monetary damages he sought, less than what he sought, or more than what he sought.

Gift   A voluntary transfer of property without consideration.

Grand jury   A group of citizens who decide if persons accused of crimes should be indicted (true billed) or not (no billed).

Grantee   The person to whom property is being conveyed.

Grantor   The person who is conveying property.

Habeas corpus   Literally, "you have the body." In criminal law, a judicial writ ordering a law enforcement official to bring a person before the court and show cause as to why the person is being detained.

Harmless error   An error made during a trial which an appellate court feels is insufficient grounds for reversing a judgment.

Hearsay   An out-of-court assertion or statement, made by someone other than the testifying witness, which is being offered to prove the truth of the matter stated. Hearsay evidence is excluded from trials unless it falls within one of the recognized exceptions.

Heir   Generally, one who inherits property under a will or by intestate succession; technically, a person who receives a property interest through intestate succession.

Holographic will   A will that is written entirely in the handwriting of the testator.

Hung jury   A jury that is unable to reach a verdict. Especially significant in criminal trials if a unanimous verdict is required.

Impanelled   After jurors are sworn in, the jury is said to be impanelled and the defendant is placed in "jeopardy."

Implied contract   A contract that is inferred from the conduct of the parties.

Implied warranty of merchantibility   The warranty imposed on merchants that the goods are merchantible as defined in the UCC; the warranty is imposed even though the merchants do not actually make such claims.

Incorporation theory   The theory that the Bill of Rights has been incorporated or absorbed into the due process clause of the Fourteenth Amendment, thereby making it applicable to the states.

Indictment   A formal accusation of a criminal offense made against a person handed down by a grand jury.

In forma pauperis   Literally, "in the manner of a pauper." Permission of the court for a poor person to seek judicial relief without having to pay the usual court fees.

Informal marriage   A type of legally recognized marriage created by informal means; also known as common-law marriage.

Information   A formal accusation charging someone with the commission of a crime, signed by a prosecuting attorney, which has the effect of bringing the person to trial.

Initial appearance   During the initial appearance, the accused is informed of the charges against him, given his constitutional rights, informed of the amount of his bail, and given a date for a preliminary hearing.

Injunction   A court order directing a person to refrain from doing certain acts or carrying out certain activities.

In personum **jurisdiction**   Judicial jurisdiction of a court to enter a personal judgment or decree against the person.

In rem **jurisdiction**   Judicial jurisdiction of a court to enter a decree affecting property interests.

Intangible property   Those items of property that are not capable of being touched such as debts owed to someone.

Interpretivism   The doctrine that judges should decide new constitutional issues in light of the underlying constitutional principles, as well as the literal meaning of the written provisions.

Interrogatory   A form of discovery in which written questions about a lawsuit are submitted to one party by the other party.

Inter vivos   During life.

Intestate   To die without a will.

Invitee   In tort law, a business visitor on one's premises.

Jeopardy   The point in the criminal justice process where the accused is in danger of criminal liability. Once in jeopardy, the accused must either be acquitted or convicted and may not be placed again in jeopardy.

Joint tenancies   Concurrent ownership of property where the survivor inherits the entire property.

Judicial conduct board   An official body whose function is to investigate allegations of misconduct made against judges.

Judicial gatekeeping   Term used to describe how judges control access to the judicial system by either opening or closing the judicial "gates" to certain kinds of controversies.

Judicial notice   A method of providing trial evidence which allows the court to accept facts that are commonly known or verifiable without formal proof.

Judicial review   The power of a court to declare acts of governmental bodies contrary to the Constitution null and void.

Jurisdiction   The power and authority of courts to render a binding decision in a case.

Laying a predicate   Also known as laying a foundation. Preliminary questions that establish the relevancy and admissibility of evidence.

Leading question   A question by which an attorney attempts to put words into the mouth of a witness, that is, a question that states the information the attorney wishes the witness to testify to.

Lease   An agreement, oral or written, that governs the rental of property.

Legatee   A person who inherits personal property under the will.

Legislative address   A method of judicial removal used in some states which allows the state legislature to remove a state judge, usually by a two-thirds vote.

Legislative courts   Federal courts created by Congress under one of its legislative powers, for example, military and territorial courts.

Legislative veto   An action by one or both houses of Congress which nullifies an executive proposal.

Lessee   Also known as the tenant; the person who is in possession of the property under a lease.

Lessor   Also known as the landlord; the person who owns the fee simple estate and carves out a small estate for a tenant.

Libel   Defamation that is preserved in some permanent form.

Licensee   In tort law, a social guest on one's property.

Lien   An encumbrance on property that is the result of a security interest held by the creditor.

Life estate   An estate in land that is held only during one's lifetime or during the life of another.

Long-arm statute   A legislative enactment that extends a court's jurisdiction to non-resident parties as long as there are "minimum contracts" between the litigant and the state, which is a requirement of due process.

Majority opinion   The opinion of a majority of appellate court judges in which the decision of the court and its reasons for that decision are given.

Malum in se   Literally, "wrong in itself." In criminal law something that is made illegal because it is inherently or morally wrong.

Malum prohibitum   In criminal law something made illegal because government has deemed it undesirable, thereby prohibiting it, e.g., gambling.

Mandatory authority   Prior court cases, constitutional provisions, legislative enactments, court rules, or administrative regulations which are binding upon courts in rendering decisions.

Mandatory release   Punishment for a crime, which involves automatic release from prison when the calendar time and good time served equal the maximum time for which the inmate was sentenced.

Marriage   A legally recognized special relationship between a man and a woman that is founded in contract.

Mediation   The process whereby a neutral third person intervenes in a controversy to assist the parties in achieving a resolution.

Mens rea   Literally, "the guilty mind." The wrongful purpose, which is an element of a crime.

Missouri Plan   The name given to a method of judicial selection which combines merit selection and popular control in retention elections.

Mootness   Term used to describe a case that has become a dead issue because the controversy that gave rise to the case was resolved before a final judicial decision could be made.

Motion *in limine*   A motion which bars prejudicial questions and statements on specified topics.

Natural law   The theory that human law must conform to the laws of God and nature, just as the physical world must conform to the laws of physics.

Negligence   A theory of tort recovery involving a legal duty, a breach of duty, proximate cause, and injury.

Negligence per se   A method of establishing the defendant's negligence by proving a violation of a safety statute or regulation.

No bill   Term used to describe the decision of a grand jury not to indict a person for a crime.

No-fault divorce   A divorce in which neither party must allege or prove fault (adultery, cruelty, etc.) in order to dissolve the marriage; the grounds are generally incompatibility or failure of the marriage.

Nolo contendere   Literally, "I will not contest it." A plea, tantamount to a guilty plea, in which the accused refuses to admit culpability but accepts the punishment of the court.

Noninterpretivism   The doctrine that the Constitution should be interpreted according to evolving standards of decency and justice and not frozen in time or meaning.

Nuisance   The use of the defendant's land in such a way that it interferes with the plaintiff's use or enjoyment of plaintiff's land.

Nuncupative will   An oral will.

Obiter dictum   Also known as *dicta;* statements in a judicial opinion which were not essential to the resolution of the case and are not binding precedent.

Offer   A proposal to enter into a contract.

Offeree   The person to whom an offer is made.

Offeror   The person making an offer.

Opening statement   Address made by attorneys for both parties at the beginning of a trial in which they outline for the jury what they intend to prove in their case.

Oral argument   The part of the appellate court decision-making process in which lawyers for both parties plead their cases in person before the court.

Oral testimony   A form of evidence that is given by the witness on the stand in open court or in a deposition under oath.

Ordinance power   The power of cities and other local government units to enact regulations binding on citizens within their jurisdiction.

Original intention   The doctrine that holds that judges should interpret the Constitution in accordance with the intent of the Framers.

Panel   A group of appellate judges, less than the full membership of the court, assigned to review a case on appeal.

Parol evidence rule   A rule of contract construction that prevents modification of written contracts by any oral statements.

Parole   Punishment for a crime which involves release from incarceration on the condition of good behavior.

Partnership   A business organization in which ownership is shared by two or more people and/or legal entities.

Party   One of the principals, either the plaintiff or the defendant, in a lawsuit.

Patent   Exclusive legal monopoly granted by the government to sell, use, or assign the right to use or sell a product or process that one has invented, created, or discovered.

Per curiam **decision**   Literally, "for the court." An unsigned Supreme Court decision, usually very short, in which the Court's judgment is announced.

Percmptory challenge   A method used to strike a potential juror from the jury without specifying the reason for doing so.

Personal service   A notice to a party of pending litigation or providing a copy of a subpoena to a witness which is personally delivered.

Personalty   All property except realty or those items that cannot be severed from the realty without damage to it.

Persuasive authority   Secondary sources or materials from other jurisdictions by which courts are not bound but upon which they may rely in deciding cases.

Plaintiff   The person or party who initiates a lawsuit.

Plea bargain   An arrangement whereby the accused agrees to exchange a plea of guilty for a lesser sentence, a reduction of charges, or some other consideration by the court.

Plurality opinion   Any written opinion that reflects the views of less than a majority of the justices who heard the case.

Political question   The doctrine that courts will not decide cases that involve issues for which a final decision is clearly left to one of the political branches of government by the Constitution.

Positive law   The theory that law is merely a reflection of the will of the strongest in a society.

Precedent   A case previously decided that serves as a legal guide for the resolution of subsequent cases.

Preliminary hearing   Either a pretrial hearing at which motions are considered or, in criminal law, a pretrial hearing to determine if there is probable cause to hold the accused for an indictment.

Prenuptial agreements   Also known as antenuptial agreements; these are contracts entered into before marriage by the spouses which outline certain conditions such as the division of the property in case of divorce.

Preponderance of the evidence   In civil law, the standard of proof required to prevail at trial. For a plaintiff to win, he must show that the greater weight, or preponderance of the evidence, supports his version of the facts.

Pretrial publicity   Prejudicial information, often inadmissible at trial, which is circulated by the news media before a trial and which reduces the accused's chances of a trial before an impartial jury.

Prima facie **case**   The plaintiff's version of the facts, which if taken at first glance or "first face" seem to substantiate the plaintiff's allegations against the defendant.

Primary jurisdiction doctrine   In administrative law, the doctrine that requires litigants to take a dispute to the administrative agency with primary responsibility for handling the dispute before seeking judicial relief.

Primogeniture   A legal doctrine whereby the oldest son alone inherits the property of his ancestors.

Principal   In criminal law, a chief actor who participates in the crime or who recruits an innocent agent to participate.

Principal brief   Brief filed by appellant that includes the issues and legal arguments to be appealed.

Privilege   In evidence, a recognized right to keep certain communications confidential or private.

Probable cause   Standard used to determine if a crime has been committed and if there is sufficient evidence to believe a specific individual committed it.

Probation   Punishment for a crime that allows the offender to remain in the community without incarceration but subject to certain court-established conditions.

Procedural due process of law   A theory of due process that stresses "by the book" adherence to predetermined rules of behavior that government must observe.

Procedural law   Law that outlines the legal procedures or process which government is obliged to follow.

Product liability   A theory of tort recovery that imposes liability on the manufacturer, seller, or distributor of dangerous products for injuries sustained by consumers and bystanders who use the product.

Promissory estoppel   A contract remedy that is employed where one party has changed positions in reliance of the other party's gratitous promise.

Property   The legal right to use or dispose of particular things or subjects.

Proximate cause   The theory that the injury sustained by the plaintiff and the defendant's action were so closely connected that the defendant's act caused the injury and there were no intervening causes.

Punitive damages   Money beyond actual damages awarded against a defendant whose conduct was so wanton, reckless, or reprehensible as to justify additional punishment.

Quasi-in-rem **jurisdiction** The power and authority of courts to enter a judgment affecting property interests to satisfy the owner's personal obligations even though the owner is not otherwise subject to the court's jurisdiction.

Quitclaim deed A written instrument conveying the grantor's interest in property, not the title to the property itself.

Ratio decidendi Those statements in a judicial opinion that are essential to the resolution of the case and are binding precedent.

Realty Also known as real property; land and the appurtenances thereto.

Reasonably prudent person A mythical person created by the courts that is used as the objective standard by which the party's conduct is measured.

Recall A method used in some states to remove judges from office. Recall elections allow the voters directly to remove judges from the bench.

Recognizance Term used to describe the releasing of an accused person from custody without requiring a property or money bond.

Recross-examination Questions asked of a witness after direct examination, cross-examination, and direct examination. Essentially a second series of questions asked of a witness called by the opposing attorney.

Redirect examination Follow-up questions asked of his or her own witness by the attorney who originally called the witness to the stand.

Regulatory law Rules and regulations promulgated by administrative agencies which are just as binding as statutes passed by legislatures.

Remittitur The process by which a jury verdict of money damages is reduced because the amount is excessive.

Renvoi A legal theory applicable where there is a choice-of-law question and the forum state adopts the entire law of the sister state.

Reply brief Brief filed by appellee which attempts to rebut appellant's grounds for the appeal.

Repudiation The contract remedy excusing one party from performance of the contract terms based on the other party's statements of prospective nonperformance.

Res ipsa loquitur A method of showing the defendant's tort liability by proving that all the instrumentalities were under its control and that the accident is of a kind that would not have occurred without negligence.

Respondeat superior A theory of vicarious liability in which the employer or master is financially responsible for the torts of employees or servants.

Reversible error An error made at trial serious enough to warrant a new trial.

Ripeness The doctrine that an appellate court will not review the decision of a lower court until all remedies have been exhausted. Courts will not decide an issue before the need to do so.

Roman law A system of laws created by the Romans and codified in the Code of Justinian.

Rule against perpetuities The rule that interests in property must vest not later than 21 years after the lives of the persons specified at the time that the interests were created.

Rule enforcement The power of an administrative agency to enforce rules promulgated by the agency under its rule-making authority.

Rule-making The power of an administrative agency to promulgate rules and regulations concerning matters that fall within its jurisdiction. Rules promulgated by administrative agencies have the force of law.

Rule of four   The requirement that four Supreme Court justices must agree to hear a case before the Court will grant a writ of *certiorari.*

Scienter   An element of a crime that requires knowledge or awareness that a particular act is illegal.

Seisin   Possession of land under a claim of a freehold estate; very akin to absolute ownership of land.

Selective incorporation   As opposed to total incorporation, the doctrine that only those parts of the Bill of Rights deemed "fundamental" are incorporated into the Due Process Clause of the Fourteenth Amendment.

Senatorial courtesy   The custom in the United States Senate that requires the president to clear judicial appointments with the senators of the state wherein the appointment occurs when the senators are of the president's party.

Separation of powers   The constitutional arrangement whereby legislative, executive, and judicial powers are exercised by three separate and distinct branches of government.

Sequestered   A jury is sequestered when its members are isolated from the community until it has reached a final verdict.

Service   The process of formally delivering the complaint or a subpoena to the defendant or a witness in a lawsuit.

Shield law   A law which allows a newspaper or other reporter to refuse to disclose the source of his or her information in a criminal case. Shield laws are a type of privilege.

Slander   Defamation that is spoken or not preserved in permanent form.

Small-claims court   A lower-level state court whose jurisdiction is limited to a specified dollar amount, e.g., damages may not exceed $1,500.

Sociological theory of law   The theory that law is a function of the society that makes it and that law changes as society changes.

Sole proprietorship   A business organization in which ownership is vested in a single individual who receives all profits but who also bears all liability.

Special-issues verdict   A verdict in which the jury answers a series of questions rather than merely entering a general finding.

Special warranty deed   A written deed conveying all property interests held by, through, or under the grantor.

Specific intent   The requisite intent that must be proved as an element of some crimes such as killing another "with malice aforethought."

Specific relief   Equitable remedies which are directed to the defendant personally and obligate him to do or refrain from doing some activity.

Spoils system   Term used to describe the awarding of public jobs to political supporters by victorious politicians since "to the victor go the spoils."

Standing   The doctrine requiring that a party bringing suit before a court must have a legal right to do so.

Stare decisis   The policy of courts to follow the rules laid down in previous cases and not to disturb settled points of law.

Statutes of limitations   Statutes that prescribe the time periods in which lawsuits must be filed.

Statutory law   Laws, called statutes, passed by legislative bodies that bestow benefits, impose obligations, or prohibit antisocial behavior.

Subpoena   An order from a court directing a person to appear before the court and to give testimony about a cause of action pending before it.

Subpoena duces tecum   An order from a court directing a person to appear before the court with specified documents that the court deems relevant in a matter pending before it.

Substantial evidence rule   Rule that says a finding of fact by an administrative agency is to be final if there is substantial evidence to support the agency's conclusion.

Substantive due process of law   A theory of due process that emphasizes judging the content of a law by a subjective standard of fundamental fairness.

Substantive law   Law that deals with the content or substance of the law, for example, the legal grounds for divorce.

Substituted service   A notice of pending litigation or other legal matters that is not personally delivered to the person; an example would be publication of such notice in the newspaper.

Substitutionary relief   The award of money damages as compensation for legally recognized losses.

Suit to partition land   A lawsuit dividing land held by co-owners or joint tenants into separate and distinct parts.

Summary judgment   Decision by a judge to rule in favor of one party because the opposing party failed to meet a standard of proof. For example, if a plaintiff fails to present a *prima facie* case, the judge may enter a summary judgment in favor of the defendant.

Summons   A court order directing the defendant to appear in court at a specified time and place, either in person or by filing a written answer to the plaintiff's complaint.

Suspect classification   Classification of persons, such as by race, to which the Supreme Court applies strict judicial scrutiny and for which government must offer compelling reasons to justify its use.

Suspended sentence   Punishment for a crime in which either the determination of guilt or the sentence is held in abeyance for good behavior and probable completion of certain court-imposed obligations.

Tangible evidence   Any evidence that the trier of fact may touch or observe in the courtroom.

Tangible property   Land and other material items that can be touched.

Taxpayer's suit   A suit brought by a person who claims standing on the basis of his or her status as a taxpayer.

Tenancies in common   Current ownership of property that does carry a right of survivorship.

Tenure   The system of landholding in the feudal era wherein land was held in subordination to a superior.

Testamentary capacity   The mental ability of an individual to understand the legal consequences of the act of making a will.

Testate   To die with a will.

Testator   The person making a will.

Third-party beneficiary contracts   Contracts intended to benefit a third party, that is, one who is not a party to the contract.

Tort   A private or civil wrong in which the defendant's actions cause injury to the plaintiff or to property, and the usual remedy is money damages.

Tortfeasor   The wrongful actor in a tort suit.

Trademark   Distinctive sound, symbol, color, device, or word that is associated with a product or service that identifies its origin and is legally reserved for that product or service.

Trespass to chattel   The damage to another's item of tangible, personal property.

Trespass to land   The injury to another's real property by an unlawful entry.

Trial *de novo*   Literally, a trial "from the beginning." Cases appealed from courts that have no transcript are reheard in their entirety "from the beginning."

Trier of fact   The trier of fact is responsible for hearing and viewing the evidence at trial and evaluating the veracity of it. The trier of fact may either be the judge or a jury.

True bill   A bill of indictment by a grand jury.

Trust   A right or property held by one person for the benefit of another.

Trustee   The person or institution that is vested, under an express or implied agreement, with property to be used for the benefit of another; also known as a fiduciary.

Trustor   The person creating a trust.

Ultra vires   Literally, "beyond the powers of." In administrative law, the doctrine that an administrative agency has exercised powers beyond those delegated to it by a legislative body.

Unconscionable contract   A contract in which one party imposed an unreasonably favorable contract on the other, who lacked a meaningful choice as to the contract terms.

Unenforceable contract   Contracts that cannot be legally enforced because of some missing legal element such as being notarized or witnessed.

Uniform Commercial Code (UCC)   A set of uniform statutes governing commercial transactions which have been enacted by state legislatures with some modifications.

Unilateral contract   A contract in which one of the parties acts immediately in response to an offer.

Venire   A group of citizens from which members of the jury are chosen.

Venireman   A person called for jury duty.

Venue   The geographic location of a trial, which is determined by constitutional or statutory provisions.

Vicarious liability   The shifting of liability from the tortfeasor to another party, usually an employer.

Void   Null, ineffective, not able to support the purpose for which it was intended.

Voidable   Something such as a contract or marriage that is not void in and of itself but can be voided at the option of the parties.

Voidable contract   A contract that one party may safely disaffirm under certain conditions while the other party is bound by its terms.

Void contract   A contract that is void from its inception.

Voir dire   Literally, "to speak truth." The process by which prospective jurors are questioned by attorneys to ascertain if there is cause to strike them from jury.

Voluntary assumption of risk   A defense used in tort law that the plaintiff was cognizant of the danger and voluntarily chose to encounter the danger.

Warranty   A covenant or promise that a statement or fact is true.

Warranty deed   A written deed conveying property in which the grantor guarantees title and warrants that he or she will compensate the grantee for any failure of the title.

Will   The legal expression of one's wishes regarding the disposition of one's property, which is to be effective after death.

Witness   A person called to the stand to give testimony in a trial.

Writ of certiorari   An order from a higher court to a lower court in which the former orders the latter to send up the record of case for review by the higher court.

Writ of execution   A court order allowing a law enforcement official to seize the property or assets of a defendant against whom a civil judgment has been rendered.

Table of Cases

Index